Dead Seas

Taras Grescoe is a prize-winning journalist and the author of three highly acclaimed non-fiction books. His work has appeared in major publications in the United States, the United Kingdom and Canada, including the *New York Times*, *National Geographic Traveler*, *Gourmet*, *Condé Nast Traveller*, the *Guardian*, *The Times* and the *Independent*. Taras lives in Montreal, Canada. *Dead Seas* is his fourth book.

* * *

'A stunning exposé of human folly with fishing around the globe' *Guardian*

'Grescoe charts [the state of our oceans] with muscular prose and a well-stamped passport. One moment we're in Marseille, worrying about whether rascasse, the toxic scorpion fish that's key to bouillabaisse, is going to run out (it isn't, yet); next we're in Bangladesh, counting the flavour enhancers, pesticides and antibiotics that go into tiger prawn feed . . . Finger-wagging literature like this needs to be fun and Grescoe's book succeeds in this respect. I enjoyed his table-thumping, which is fired by a foodie's passion for the animals whose disappearance he mourns.' *Observer*

'Every page of this book had me reaching for pen and paper to record yet another horrifying statistic about the way humanity is plundering the seas. This is not merely an entertaining treatment of a vital issue, it is an important book that anyone who thinks they care about the environment must read.' *Guardian*

Also by Taras Grescoe

Sacré Blues: An Unsentimental Journey Through Quebec

The End of Elsewhere: Travels Among the Tourists

The Devil's Picnic: A Tour of Everything the Governments of the World Don't Want You to Try

Dead Seas

*How the Fish on Our Plates
is Killing Our Planet*

TARAS GRESCOE

PAN BOOKS

First published as *Bottomfeeder* 2008 by Macmillan

First published in paperback 2009 by Pan Books
an imprint of Pan Macmillan Ltd
Pan Macmillan, 20 New Wharf Road, London N1 9RR
Basingstoke and Oxford
Associated companies throughout the world
www.panmacmillan.com

ISBN 978 0 330 44591 7

1 3 5 7 9 8 6 4 2

A CIP catalogue record for this book is available
from the British Library.

Printed and bound in the UK by
CPI Mackays, Chatham ME5 8TD

Visit **www.panmacmillan.com** to read more about all our books
and to buy them. You will also find features, author interviews and
news of any author events, and you can sign up for e-newsletters
so that you're always first to hear about our new releases.

To Erin

CONTENTS

Introduction   1

1 New York City – Pan-Roasted Monkfish   19
The Rise of the Goblin

2 Chesapeake Bay and Brittany – Oysters   54
In the Kingdom of the Oysters

3 England – Fish and Chips   89
Panic at the Chippy

4 Marseilles – Bouillabaisse   122
Small Pond

5 Portugal and France – Sardines   156
'Fish She is Very Small'

6 India – Shrimp Curry   187
Wave of Mutilation

7 China – Shark Fin Soup   223
Buddha Jump over the Wall

8 Japan – Bluefin Tuna Sashimi   243
Sorry, Charlie

9 British Columbia – Grilled Salmon   281
An Economy of Scales

10 Nova Scotia – Fish Sticks 323
Fast Fish, Slow Fish

Conclusion 348

Appendix: Advice on Choosing Seafood 358

Sources 372

Further Reading 388

Acknowledgements 389

INTRODUCTION

For those who like to believe some things will never change, it must be good to know that places like Hubbards still exist.

On the road west from Halifax, you know you are getting close when you see the sign for the Shore Club, 'Nova Scotia's Last Great Dance Hall', which has been serving lobster and fresh berry shortcake since the end of the Second World War. Along the side of the road, fishermen sell discount scallops and solomon gundy, the local version of pickled herring, from the back of beat-up vans. Between the seaside rocks and the tiers of pine trees, black-roofed bungalows face the waves, many of them lobstermen's homes now turned into summer cottages for city dwellers.

St Margarets Bay, on which Hubbards sits, is a notch cut into the granite barrens of Nova Scotia's south shore, filled to the rim twice daily with a generous cupful of Atlantic. This morning, the bay is socked in with fog, but the sun is already punching holes through the scrim of grey, making the plastic buoys and wooden dories on the water appear to glow from within. Standing on the deck of the *Vicki & Laura*, Lorne Harnish turns the wheel of his thirty-two-foot lobster boat, circling hard towards a wooden buoy attached by rope to a trap at the bottom of the bay.

Cutting the motor, Harnish grabs a long gaffing pole, hooks the rope out of the water with a quick twist of his wrists, and threads it over a hubcap-sized pulley; a hydraulic winch rapidly pulls the forty-kilogram trap to the surface. A semicylinder of bent oak roofed with maple slats and walled by netting, the trap looks like a miniature Quonset hut. Inside, four brownish-green lobsters cling to its seaweed-covered mesh. Harnish detaches one with difficulty – it raises its claws in challenge, like a boxer facing a foe. After using a metal gauge to measure its carapace, he throws it into a plastic tub. The rest are shorts, too small to keep, and get tossed back into the water.

Though lobster is coming up undersized this late in the season, all in all it has been a good year for the local industry. Back in December, Harnish was catching half a tonne a day and selling them locally for $7 (£3.40) a pound. At the Halifax airport duty-free, a good-sized lobster, conveniently boxed for carry-on, sells for $27.98 (£13.70).

By now the fog has burned away and St Margarets, in all her ill-punctuated beauty, has revealed herself, the deep blue of the surface pixelated with thousands of fluorescent-hued buoys, each corresponding to a sunken lobster trap. All told, ten boats profitably work this tiny bay. For the last decade, from the Irish Sea to the Scotian Shelf, the lobstermen of the North Atlantic have been experiencing boom times. In the Gulf of Maine alone, southwest of Nova Scotia, there are thought to be three million traps in the water. When Lorne Harnish started fishing in the early 1970s, there was barely enough lobster in the bay to keep him going for a week. Now he can haul up over three tonnes in a season that lasts a full five months. Harnish, who has just turned fifty-seven, says he has no plans of retiring.

Harnish figures the lobster boom has something to do with 'whore's eggs', local slang for sea urchins. Thirty-five years ago the bay was full of them. In the Gulf of Maine the urchins disappeared when they were harvested for their roe for the Japanese market; here, Harnish believes, they simply gnawed through the kelp, eating themselves out of house and home. Once the sea urchins were gone, the kelp returned, providing shelter and hunting grounds for lobster which flourished in turn.

Ecologists have another explanation for the boom. The shallow waters off Nova Scotia used to be full of swordfish and bluefin tuna, as well as untold numbers of hake, halibut and haddock. Cod in particular were the apex predators in these parts. They prowled the gullies offshore in dense shoals, using their powerful mouths to suck up free-swimming lobster larvae, sea urchins and even full-grown crustaceans. But cod was fished to collapse in the early 1990s. With cod gone, stocks of lobster and other low-in-the-food-chain species exploded. It is a story that has been repeated throughout the Atlantic: with top predators fished to a fraction of their former abundance, it has become an ocean increasingly populated by shrimp, lobster, crab, and other resilient, fast-growing crustaceans. An ocean, in other words, of bottom-feeders.

Harnish's day continues: he gaffs a rope, hauls up and empties the trap, fills the wire bait box with rotten mackerel, drops the trap, then moves on to the next buoy, until all 130 traps have been cleared out and rebaited. For the cottagers relaxing on lawn chairs on the shore – perhaps looking up from a headline about another ice shelf collapsing in the Antarctic – the sight of the *Vicki & Laura* finishing her rounds must seem soothing. St Margarets Bay looks timeless and unchangeable, and the fishing boats seem busier than ever.

They are wrong. The Atlantic is an impoverished ocean, and Harnish is actually working a monoculture, one whose single crop is American lobster. Around the world, more unappetizing creatures are proliferating in the absence of big fish. Carpets of primitive sea squirts now cover continental shelves, preventing other forms of life from growing. Flotillas of jellyfish, some ten square miles in area, are stinging farmed salmon in floating sea cages to death. The filter-feeding fish that once cleaned the oceans are being caught and ground into fertilizer, causing giant blooms of toxic plankton which poison long stretches of coast-line. The lobster boom of the Atlantic, in other words, may just be a tiny blip on a slippery slope to oceans filled with jellyfish, bacteria and slime.

If these are salad days for bottom-feeders, it is only because human beings are doing something unprecedented, and perhaps irrevocable, to the seas of the world. With great application – and faster than anybody thought possible – we are eating our way to the end of the food chain. Unless we change our attitude to seafood, the future of the oceans may look a lot like the present of St Margarets Bay: a once varied ecosystem, being reduced by human activity to a few weedlike, and increasingly inedible, species.

The Case *for* Seafood

I love seafood. And by seafood, I mean fresh-caught sardines as well as raw salmon tartare; piles of just-peeled coldwater shrimp and trays of raw flat-shelled oysters; sesame-oil-drenched jelly-fish salad and deep-fried haddock; in fact just about any squirmy, wriggly, fishy, edible thing that comes out of the ocean. I have some almost every day.

Let me explain. Ten years ago I cut meat and poultry out of my diet and limited my flesh-eating to fish. I had read too many news items about growth hormones, factory farms and anti-biotics to feel good about a regular diet of steaks, burgers and chicken; the alternative, organic meat, was expensive and at the time hard to find. (In the years that followed, as the mad cow scandal broke and it became advisable to treat salmonellosis laden raw chicken in your kitchen as if it were a biotoxin, it was a decision I had no cause to regret.) Seafood was a logical choice: fish not only had half the fat of beef but also seemed to be in endless supply. The oceans were immense and apparently inexhaustible. True, the cod fishery off Newfoundland had recently collapsed, but that, I figured, was a fluke that could be blamed on bad science, greed and inept bureaucrats. The supermarket shelves were still piled high with canned tuna, the fast-food joints were selling bargain all-you-can-eat shrimp, and a fillet of Atlantic salmon was cheaper than it had ever been. There were lots more fish in the sea. There would *always* be lots more fish in the sea.

I quickly began to discover the advantages of being a piscivore, a fish eater. A seafood meal, after all, is one of life's great simple pleasures. Find a pier, a creek or a fishing hole, dangle a hooked line into the water, and with a bit of luck (as well as a fire, some foil and a wedge of lemon), you've got dinner. Centuries after agricultural societies replaced game and fowl with domesticated livestock, and venison and partridge became rarities reserved for the tables of the rich, there are still hunter-gatherers going to sea – fishermen* – who bring back a form of game that people of all classes can afford to eat. In most supermarkets, fish is the only real wild food – a product not created by industrial agriculture – that you are likely to find.

And human beings will eat just about any kind of seafood, no matter how daunting. South Americans enjoy *picoroco*, a huge edible barnacle with a Krakatoa-shaped shell that conceals a golf-ball-sized sphere of glistening white flesh, as sweet as crabmeat. The French have figured out a way to make the

---

* Around the world, fishing and fish trading are overwhelmingly masculine trades. In contrast, fish processors, from sardine canners in Brittany to prawn peelers in Kerala, tend to be women. The term 'fisherpeople' is used to refer to members of fishing communities in the developing world. On the issue of gender, I defer to Linda Greenlaw, former swordboat captain, who wrote in *The Hungry Ocean*: 'Fisherwoman isn't even a word. It's not in the dictionary. A fisherman is defined as "one whose employment is to catch fish". That describes me to a tee.' Fisherman it is.

reproductive organs of cuttlefish, *la pousse de la seiche*, into a delicacy, and the Japanese long ago mastered the art of making poisonous pufferfish into sashimi. More astonishing to me is the fact that anybody eats hagfish, a lampreylike bottom-dweller that haunts abysses two miles beneath the surface. Lacking a spine, a gas bladder, or even a jaw, it employs a rasping tongue to burrow into its prey. Marine biologists who find whale corpses on the ocean bottom often observe that the flesh of the dead giants is actually crawling – a grisly submarine puppet show courtesy of the thousands of hagfish writhing through the rotten meat. Threatened by a shark, the hagfish will excrete mucins from dozens of pores, choking its attacker's gills with gallons of rapidly expanding slime. (It then sloughs off the mucus by tying itself into a bow and squirming the knot down its body.) The hagfish gets my vote as the most repellent fish in the sea. Yet Koreans consider it a delicacy: they import four million kilograms a year and savour it as an appetizer after broiling it in sesame oil.

Entire cultures have built elaborate identities around the cooking and consumption of seafood. In a world of homogenized fast food and microwavable frozen dinners, seafood cultures serve as bastions of local tradition. To be Venetian is to have grown up with the taste of *spaghetti alle vongole veraci* (though the Lagoon's native bivalves have succumbed to pollution and must now be replaced with Manila clams). To be Japanese is to know the rituals of the sushi bar, the taste of seaweed-wrapped salmon roe, and the fact that the finest cut of the finest tuna you can order is called *o-toro* (though bluefin is now in such short supply that Tokyo's sushi bar owners are substituting other red-fleshed meat, such as smoked venison and horse). And to have lived on the shores of Chesapeake Bay is to fetishize deep-fried clam strips, the taste of breaded and battered oysters and all the pleasures of a shoreline-kitsch-drenched seafood shack (even if the crabmeat in the cakes you are eating happens to come from Asian swimming crabs, flash-frozen in Indonesia and air-freighted to Washington, DC).

Fish have shaped human history. From medieval times the vast shoals of herring that annually poured down from Scandinavia forged Dutch and English seapower and created the wealth of the Hanseatic League and thus the balance of power that drew the map of Europe. Fish are responsible for humanity's spread across the globe: the technology for curing cod allowed men to undertake long sea voyages, permitted the Vikings to raid England and France and colonize Iceland, and brought the Basque whalers to the Grand Banks.

And there is increasing evidence that, were it not for seafood, we would not be human at all. Life began in the sea, about four billion years ago, and the ancestors of all mammals were fish that crawled out of the oceans and colonized the land 360 million years ago. Because the remains of the earliest humans were found in what is now African savannah, anthropologists have long believed that man's ancestors left the forests for the open plains, in the process evolving the upright gait that led to bipedal humans. But recent research on pollen records has shown that four million years ago such regions were not Serengeti-like plains at all but heavily wooded shorefront environment. Protohumans such as Lucy, like most of her kin, evolved close to the water.

These seaside roots may explain why our brains weigh twice as much as those of our closest early human relative, *Homo habilis*. Around two million years ago the hominid cranium started to expand, with an exponential growth spurt occurring about one hundred thousand years ago. Evidence from shell middens around early human settlements shows that this is exactly the time people started eating seafood in great quantities. Brain size is limited by the availability of docosahexaenoic acid (DHA, one of the fatty acids found in omega-3 supplements), without which it is impossible for the body to build

7

brain cell membranes. The only place this acid is abundant in the food chain is in fish from the world's oceans, lakes and rivers. It is likely our seafood-rich diet provided the nutrients that make us the world's brainiest primate. Without fish, we might still be microcephalic apes, swinging through the trees.

For generations, mothers have known that fish is brain food. It turns out that forcing children to choke down cod liver oil – or its modern equivalent, a capsule of omega-3 fatty acids – is a very good idea indeed. The human brain is 60 per cent fat, and the kind of fats you eat determines what your brain cells are made of. At the beginning of the twentieth century, much of the protein in the Western diet came from nest-laid eggs, beef and milk from grass-fed cows, and other free-range animals, all of which have higher levels of omega-3s than their industrially farmed counterparts. Starting about 1960 an unplanned study in brain chemistry has been taking place, one whose subject is the entire population of North America and much of Europe. Around that time corn and soybean oils and grain-fed livestock, all of which are relatively low in omega-3s but high in the structurally similar omega-6s, became the dominant sources of fat in our diets. Both forms of omega fatty acids are essential for making cell membranes more liquid, but people who have high levels of omega-3s – sometimes called the happy acids – are less prone to depression, dementia and Alzheimer's disease. Thanks to half a century of consuming cheap vegetable oils, the cell membrane of the average American is now only 20 per cent omega-3-based fats. In cultures where fish is still a staple, such as Japan, the average cell membrane is 40 per cent omega-3-based.

The results of this experiment may already be in. In 1998 a paper in the British medical journal *The Lancet* showed that major depression spiked in New Zealand, Germany, the United States and other countries with lower rates of fish consumption, but declined in such seafood-loving cultures as Japan, Taiwan and Korea. In Europe suicide is highest in such landlocked countries as Austria and Hungary (where per capita consumption of fish is, respectively, 11 kilograms and 4.5 kilograms a year) and lowest among seafood-eating Portuguese (57 kilograms) and Norwegians (52 kilograms). A researcher with the American National Institutes of Health has shown that a mother's consumption of omega-3s during pregnancy can predict her child's intelligence and fine motor skills. The children of women who had consumed the smallest amount of omega-3s, the study found, had verbal IQs six points lower than the average. Telltale signs of a lack of omega-3s include dry skin and dandruff, lifeless hair, brittle nails and raised bumps on the skin. Perhaps most surprisingly, a lack of omega-3s seems to predict antisocial behaviour: a daily dose of fish oils given to inmates in a UK young offenders' prison reduced recidivism by 30 per cent.

Nature's richest source of omega-3 fatty acids, which are ultimately derived from oceanic plankton, is wild-caught seafood. River fish such as trout have much lower levels, as do farmed fish, which are now often plumped up with vegetable oils. Though flaxseed oil is also a source of omega-3s, the human body is inefficient at converting it into DHA and eicosapentaenoic acid (EPA), the latter of which is essential for cardiovascular health. Most national public health authorities now recommend having at least two meals of fish, especially such fatty species as mackerel and sardines, a week.

'There are no limits to Jeeves's brain power,' Bertie Wooster once marvelled about his fictional gentleman's gentleman. Author P. G. Wodehouse repeatedly had the clueless Wooster attributing his manservant's intelligence to his seafood-heavy diet: 'He virtually lives on fish. If I had even half his brains, I would take a shot at being prime minister.'

The evidence may be circumstantial, but I concur: if getting more omega-3s in my diet means lowering my risks of major depression, dementia, Alzheimer's, suicide and ending up in prison, then eating fish is a no-brainer.

The Case *against* Seafood

Just as it is becoming clear that opting for fish may be the smartest dietary choice you could ever make, newspapers seem to be full of stories about how seafood can be very bad for you indeed.

The flesh of some common fish, we now know, can be extremely toxic. In 2004 the influential journal *Science* reported that salmon contains dangerously high levels of carcinogenic dioxins and polychlorinated biphenyls, and it recommended eating no more than six meals of farmed salmon a year. Mercury, a heavy metal that can interfere with brain development – and, in cases of severe poisoning, cause tremors, dementia, hallucination and death – was found to be so prevalent in fish that in 2007 the Royal Swedish Academy of Sciences recommended that a worldwide health advisory be issued. And a *National Geographic* exposé showed that two meals of large, long-lived fish such as swordfish, halibut, shark and tuna in less than twenty-four hours could more than double the amount of mercury in an adult's blood.

In spite of these risks, fish and seafood are inspected much less rigorously than even the cheapest sides of beef. There is no Food and Drug Administration, British Food Standards Agency, or Canadian Food Inspection Agency seal of approval for salmon, tuna or any other form of seafood; in most jurisdictions, processing plants are inspected only once a year, and from day to day they rely on a self-regulating system developed by the American food company Pillsbury in the 1950s – essentially an industry honour system. Since it is highly perishable, imported fresh fish is almost never inspected. What's more, consumer fraud is endemic in the seafood trade. Retailers routinely pass off farmed salmon as wild-caught, and imported farmed fish are sold as more expensive fillets of grouper and red snapper. The kind of cheap farmed shrimp found on fast-food menus is often treated with carcinogenic antibiotics, and scallops are soaked in a neurotoxicant used in paint strippers and carpet cleaners. Hole-punches are used on the flesh of skates to create instant ersatz scallops. And processors in countries like India and Thailand use caustic soda and borax to artificially colour the shrimp they export to Europe and North America.

It is enough to put you off your dinner.

The Sea, Changed

There is another argument against eating seafood. The indiscriminate catching of fish may be contributing to global environmental collapse.

Over the last decade the evidence has been coming in thick and fast. Rather quickly, the oceans are becoming environments unlike any we have ever known. To make such an observation these days, you don't need to be an oceanographer – just an attentive reader of the news.

Dateline, the Pacific Ocean, east of Hawaii: A permanent feature of the world's largest ocean is now a swirling sargasso of floating debris. This gyre of detritus includes Nike basketball shoes spilled from a container ship, Lego blocks, highlighter pens, yellow rubber ducks, six-pack rings, hockey gloves, cans of paint and disintegrating plastic bottles. Floating amidst the trash are quadrillions of tiny plastic pellets called nurdles that soak up pesticides and deadly chemicals, and enter the food chain as toxic pills when they are swallowed by jellies and salps, the zooplankton that are the oceans' most efficient filter feeders. Floating just beneath the surface are ghost nets, lost or abandoned tangles of translucent mesh that fatally entangle sea turtles, albatrosses, seals and dolphins. The Great Pacific Garbage Patch, as it is known, is now almost the size of Africa.

The Caribbean Sea, off the shores of Puerto Rico: Thanks to unusually high water temperatures, coral reefs in shallow tropical waters are dying en masse. Biologists explain that when the temperature of the surrounding water reaches 32 degrees Celsius, coral polyps start to expel the symbiotic algae that nourish them. In a phenomenon known as bleaching, the dying reefs then turn a blinding white. Others have been blanketed in sediment or covered by seaweed. Thanks to sewage, dynamite fishing, bottom-trawling and increasing water temperatures, it is estimated that half the coral reefs in the Caribbean and a quarter of the reefs around the world are already dead. Meanwhile carbon dioxide emitted by the burning of fossil fuels is dissolving into the seas and changing their chemistry, a process known as ocean acidification. As ocean pH levels plunge, carbonate and calcium levels diminish in the water: without these building blocks, coral reefs simply stop growing. Computer models predict that, at current rates of greenhouse gas emission, all of the world's coral reefs will be dead by the year 2075.

The South Atlantic, off the shores of Namibia: A stinking, oxygen-free 'dead zone', where nothing but jellyfish can live, has been getting larger from year to year off the coast of Africa. It is caused by an increase in the amount of algae, tiny floating marine creatures that normally form the bottom of the food chain. The algae were once consumed by sardines, but over the last decade European and Asian seiners have removed 10 million tonnes of the tiny fish, so the algae bloom now grows unchecked. When it sinks to the bottom of the ocean, the decaying algae rots and releases deadly hydrogen sulphide, a toxic gas that kills off hake, a major food fish for Namibians. Scientists say 150 such dead zones, oxygen-free patches of ocean where no life can exist, regularly crop up from the South China Sea to the Oregon coast. Some of them are now as large as Ireland.

In the first decade of the twenty-first century, it is becoming clear that the world's oceans are being transformed, and not for the better. A paper in the esteemed journal *Nature* reports that 90 per cent of the population of top-level predators – among them tuna, marlin, and swordfish – have already been caught. A team of ecologists makes headlines worldwide by predicting that all major fish stocks, at their current rate of exploitation, will collapse within our lifetimes; the world, in other words, will run out of wild seafood by the year 2048.

For anybody who lives within a hundred miles of a body of water, the fact that the planet's rivers, lakes and oceans could soon become tepid and acidic wastes, barren of anything but bacteria, jellyfish and toxic algae, should be disquieting news. For any of us who have spent an afternoon cracking lobster in a Maine seafood shack, joining a queue on a London backstreet for a battered cod fillet, or feeling that perfect chunk of raw fatty tuna deliquesce over the tongue in a Tokyo sushi bar, this will sound like a portrait of a poorer world. And for the billion or so of us – I include myself in the head count – who derive most of our protein from seafood, it will sound like a dystopia: a world, in fact, hardly worth living in.

Scientists now know that it is the eating habits of a single species, *Homo sapiens sapiens*, that is driving these changes. Every one of us participates by adding our tons of carbon dioxide to the atmosphere; simply by flushing our toilets or fertilizing our lawns we contribute nitrogen and phosphates that can lead to harmful algae blooms and coral reef death. But the single worst thing we are doing to the oceans is devastating the food chain through overfishing. By knocking out the chain's upper levels, which include big predatory fish like tuna, swordfish and shark, and skimming off the middle and bottom levels for industrial use, we are changing, perhaps permanently, the structure of an environment that nourishes us.

Already, bottom-of-the-food-chain sea life that was once considered fit only for bait – jellyfish, squid, cuttlefish – is being marketed as a delicacy. In other words, as the last of the wild tuna and salmon are put into cans, we are in the process of eating our way to the bottom of the food chain. Our future, as one fisheries expert has memorably put it, may be a diet of peanut butter and jellyfish sandwiches.

Like it or not, if we don't start seriously questioning the way we are eating today, we are all going to have to get used to the idea of becoming bottomfeeders.

Bottomfeeding

Seafood is big business, and as awareness of the health benefits of fish-eating spreads, so do total sales: worldwide, this £35-billion-a-year industry employs 200 million people and provides 2.6 billion people with at least 20 per cent of their protein. In 2006 Americans bought more than 2 billion cans of tuna and tucked away 2 kilograms of shrimp per person; by volume, the United States is consuming 70 per cent more seafood than it did a generation ago. In 2005 seafood for the first time surpassed poultry in total sales in the United Kingdom. Globally, fish consumption has doubled in the last thirty years. Given our eating habits, it is no wonder the oceans are in trouble.

I began writing this book knowing that our generation might be among the last generations in history able to enjoy the down-to-earth luxury of freshly caught wild fish. If that was the case, there were a few seafood experiences I wanted to have before I died. My life would not be complete until I had eaten a bowl of rockfish soup – within view of the Mediterranean – made according to the official rules laid out in the Marseilles Bouilla-baisse Charter. I was dying to try *fugu*, the poisonous pufferfish beloved by the Japanese which, if improperly prepared, can cause a terrifying death by paralysis and asphyxiation. I was curious to confront a plate of *zhui xia* – drunken shrimp, a Chinese dish in which the still-living crustaceans are brought to the table half-drowned in rice wine, their swimmerets still twitching. And I had yet to experience the simple pleasure of fresh grilled sardines eaten in a beachfront restaurant on the Atlantic shore of Portugal or the taste of a half-dozen fat Chesa-peake Bay oysters fried up and served on a soft roll.

When I started planning my voyage, a decade of fish-eating had left me half-educated about some of the crucial issues sur-rounding seafood. I already knew it was better to steer away from such traditionally fetishized predators as tuna, salmon and swordfish, whose position at the top of the food chain meant they were likely to accumulate toxins in their flesh. I knew that some popular species, like Chilean sea bass and swordfish, were overfished, and certain stocks, most notoriously the northern cod of the Grand Banks, had collapsed. And I knew it was healthier, for both myself and the oceans, to favour seafood near the middle and bottom of the food chain – mackerel and sar-dines, tilapia and carp, oysters and jellyfish. I strongly suspected that the best policy of all would be to become a bottomfeeder – by which I mean somebody who routinely eats fish from closer to the bottom than the top of the oceanic food chain. (Not to be confused with hyphenated bottom-feeders, such as monkfish and lobster, organisms that actually live and feed on the ocean floor.) Though I had stuffed my wallet with the cards issued by the Monterey Bay Aquarium and other seafood-choice organi-zations, I was vague about the details of nourishing myself according to these principles. I had heard all the talk about sustainable seafood, but I still was not sure how to walk the walk.

A few words about myself. I may be a fish lover, but I am no fish hugger: I have no ethical qualms about killing fish – humanely – to nourish myself, and while I have never butchered a pig or cow, I have caught, killed, gutted and cooked fish, and will continue to do so. I draw the line, however, where the pursuit or cultivation of my dinner obviously damages the environment, where cruelty is involved, or where pollution or adulterants make it unsafe to eat. I would get no pleasure from knowingly eating a nearly extinct songbird, wine made from tiger bones, or the last few grams of beluga caviar from the Caspian. For me, a pleasure that diminishes the experience of everybody else on earth is no pleasure at all. And saying that fish feel no pain is just a convenient fiction for sport fishermen and Cantonese chefs: too many studies have shown fish have pain receptors identical to other animals, and that they clearly demonstrate stereotypical stress motions when injured. There is never any excuse for treating them cruelly. But I also believe that our evolutionary past as omnivorous primates not only justifies fish-eating but in a sense demands it: without the fatty acids present in seafood, our brains simply do not develop and function as they should.

I began to plan my journey. It was going to be an international one as, thanks to airfreight and shipping technology, seafood has become one of the most globalized industries there is. Before I was through, it would see me grilling leading New York seafood chefs on their menu choices, snorkelling in a Mediterranean marine reserve, touring great fish markets from London to Tokyo, sneaking marine ecologists into supermarkets, and talking my way into salmon farms and on to fishing boats. Eventually, my journey would take me around the world, from the shores of the North Atlantic to shrimp farms on the Indian Ocean and the polluted waters off China's Pacific coast.

As I set out, the list of seafoods that I enjoyed eating was long. I knew it was going to get shorter, but I figured the process would be worth it. I was going to acquire a simple but crucial skill: how to eat nutritious food ethically.

A word of warning for the squeamish: I am an adventurous eater. If it is in the name of research, I will try just about anything once. In my travels, I have picked up the habit of eating what the locals eat – whether it is bull's testicles in Spain, fermented candlefish grease in First Nations communities, or llama steak in Bolivia. This book is the education of a fish eater, and getting educated sometimes involves doing things you later regret. But stick with me to the end, and you will pick up a set of principles that will ensure you can shop for, order and enjoy seafood, without significantly diminishing the planet's resources or poisoning yourself in the process.

The good news is that there is a way to reconcile conservation, flavour and health – even when it comes to the complex, multispecies cuisine that is seafood. And it can be done without leaving the oceans, or our plates, empty.

1

NEW YORK CITY -
PAN-ROASTED MONKFISH

The Rise of the Goblin

Q: Why are fish so thin?
A: Because they eat fish.
– *Jerry Seinfeld*

The most hideous denizen of the deeps you are ever likely to eat is the monkfish, also known as the goosefish, allmouth, bellyfish, molligut and frogfish. A cross between a goblin and a tadpole, the monkfish has a broad shovel-shaped head that appears to taper into its tail without bothering to pass through the intermediary of a body. With its beady eyes, warty skin and scowling froglike mouth filled with needle-sharp teeth, the monkfish resembles the flattened Halloween mask of some Texas chainsaw psycho. Scottish fishermen call it Molly Gowan. In parts of New England it is known as a lawyerfish, which gives you an idea.

The monkfish's physiology is beautifully adapted for ambush. It scuttles along the sea bottom using fleshy, handlike ventral fins. Its tiny eyes look like limpets, its fins could be mistaken for clams, and its skin is mottled to resemble stones and gravel. Marvelling at this design, the Eighth Duke of Argyll wrote: 'The whole margins of the fish, and the very edge of the lips and jaws, have loose tags and fringes which wave and sway about amid the currents of water so as to look exactly like the smaller algae which move around them.' Virtually invisible, the monkfish entices its prey with a modified spine that juts out of its forehead, trailing a little flag of tissue on the end that acts as a lure. When a shrimp or sand-eel tries to take the bait, the monkfish springs upward with a flick of its powerful tail while simultaneously opening its mouth, creating a suction that vacuums up its prey. When pickings get slim below, a hungry monkfish will even rise to the surface: fishermen in Massachusetts have hauled up specimens from depths of three hundred metres with half-digested seagulls in their guts.

This Quasimodo of the Atlantic is not only hideous to look at, but as a bottom-dweller, it is also particularly prone to parasites. I have talked to fishmongers who shudder at the memory of uncooked monkfish flesh – especially the liver, which can be virtually ambulant with marine worms – and privately say they would never eat it themselves. The biggest monkfish grow to five feet in length. If you caught one on a line, you would probably happily throw away your rod and reel just to be rid of the thing.

One weeknight evening in late spring, Eric Ripert, the executive chef at Manhattan's, if not America's, most famous seafood restaurant, has prepared his monkfish tail pan-roasted, in a fanciful tribute to Antonio Gaudí, the eccentric Catalan architect. The sauce is an emulsion of chorizo and white albariño grapes, spiked with spicy sausage that gives the tiniest bite to the quite rubbery, slightly sweet squares of flesh, which are served with crispy *patatas bravas* drizzled in alternating white and red bands of mayonnaise and paprika sauce. At Le Bernardin the ocean's finest fruits are slowly braised, barely cooked, thinly pounded, soothingly presented and easily digested.

Gaudí, a reclusive vegetarian who deplored excess, would have felt out of place here: Le Bernardin is at the top of all kinds of food chains. Ever since the first Michelin guide to New York consecrated Le Bernardin with three stars – its top rating – a table has to be booked weeks, if not months, in advance. In this blue silk and teak temple of seafood, a block away from Rockefeller Center, the money is old, the atmosphere reverential.

'This is the best restaurant in New York, you know,' a snowyhaired alpha male in a gold-buttoned blazer proclaims to his guests (before inviting them to come elk-shooting at his estate). Anticipating the entrance of a matron in head-to-toe Chanel, a hostess gives the revolving door a nudge. Self-effacing young men in black shirts and black ties wage war on tablecloth crumbs with metal scrapers, materializing at one's elbow like stagehands in a kabuki drama. With the wine pairing and Ripert's signature dessert – a whole brown egg, hollowed out and filled with milk chocolate, caramel foam and maple syrup – the bill for the tasting menu is $295 (£145). For your money, you get some of the world's great delicacies: quail eggs and osetra caviar imported from Iran, foie gras, and wild salmon flown in from Alaska.

For a bottom-feeding monkfish from the shores of Maine, it is all pretty heady company. A decent-sized monkfish used to earn fishermen 30 cents (15 pence) a pound. If, that is, they bothered to land them at all; trawler captains tended to throw them back as unsaleable trash fish. But thirty years ago monkfish experienced an apotheosis: the finger of culinary fashion descended, and this repulsive sea creature was elevated from mere bycatch to ubiquitous entrée, its price increasing tenfold in the process.

Fish à la Mode

'There is a new fish just beginning to appear in the markets around where I live,' wrote Julia Child in the May 1979 issue of *McCall's* magazine. She had first seen it at a fishmonger's in New England. 'That is to say, it's not a new fish at all, but one that's been nosing about in Atlantic waters from New Foundland [*sic*] to North Carolina ever since fish began. However, we had not paid it any mind until the price of our usual fish became so astronomical that our fishery people began looking more carefully at their catch . . . Monkfish is what I saw the other day at my fish market – as soon as word gets around there will be demands for it, and it will be shipped all over the country.'

Child herself made sure of that. The cookbook author who introduced French cuisine to the American mainstream memorably wrestled with an eleven-kilogram monkfish on *Julia Child and Company*, showing a national audience how to decapitate the monster and poach its tail. George Berkowitz, founder of the Legal Sea Foods chain, would later marvel, 'By mentioning monkfish on her show, she introduced it to America . . . she could take an underused item and after one show, monkfish takes off and it's still popular twenty years later.'

Culinary trends can be deadly for fish, driving obscure species that happen to become fashionable to collapse. Particularly in North America, a market of 334 million curious consumers. In the 1980s New Orleans chef Paul Prudhomme, one of the instigators of the Cajun trend, put blackened redfish – a species more commonly known as red drum – on everybody's lips: by 1986, fishermen were taking 6.6 million kilograms a year from the Gulf of Mexico to keep up with demand. Eighteen years later the catch was down to a mere

33,000 kilograms, and wholesalers had taken to importing farmed drum from Taiwan and Ecuador.

Pity the fish that catches the wrong eye at the wrong time. If its flesh happens to be tasty enough, its fate is sealed, and ships with the latest satellite technology will chase it to Antarctic seas and oceanic abysses to keep plates in London, Tokyo and New York filled. Analysing the decline of predator fish in the Atlantic, ecologists Boris Worm and the late Ransom Myers concluded in a paper published in *Nature* in 2003 that it took only fifteen years for an industrialized fishery* to reduce the biomass (the combined weight of all the organisms in a population) of a targeted species by 80 per cent.

In 1978 Massachusetts' fishermen were getting 35 cents (16 pence) a pound for monkfish. Three years later, thanks to Child's advocacy, the price had almost doubled, and an obscure bottom-feeder was on its way to being declared overfished.

For the monkfish, things have never been the same.

The Goblin at the Market

These days, a trip to the New Fulton Fish Market is a sobering experience. It used to be a drunken one: in the nineteenth century, slumming citizens would stop for soft-boiled eggs and a dozen bluepoints at its many oyster stands. Late into the twentieth century, it was a place where guys with Runyonesque names like Johnny Dirtyface could disinfect a knife wound with half a bottle of whisky, drink the rest and still set a record for filleting shad.

At four o'clock in the morning, the South Bronx is a lonely

* 'Fishery' refers to all the activity, from netting to selling, centred on the catching or harvesting of a single species of fish, which in this context can include oysters, abalone and other sea creatures.

place. I walked through the New Fulton Fish Market's security gate, where drivers must now pay six dollars just to enter the floodlit parking lot, and entered the market by a side door. Inside, the building was a horizontal bunker the size of an upended Empire State Building, lit with all the charm of a bus station. I had come looking for trouble: a face-to-face encounter with a freshly caught monkfish.

I have a theory about the great fish markets of the world. When a metropolis loses its central market, it also loses its belly, and with it, its soul. (Though, in New York's case, perhaps id is the apposite term.) Paris, I knew, had given up its lumpen-*âme* in 1969 when the city centre food market Les Halles, that haven for the inebriated in search of late-night onion soup, moved to suburban Rungis. The relocation of the Fulton Fish Market to Hunts Point in the Bronx in 2005 was the culmination of years of gentrification and confirmed something old-time New Yorkers have long known: whatever is left of the class-mixed, gritty Manhattan of legend moved to the boroughs a long time ago.

On either side of the New Fulton's central corridor, there were signs over crates and sinks every dozen yards or so announcing the leading purveyors to New York's restaurateurs: Slavin, Blue Ribbon, Gloucester Fish Company, Smitty's Fillet House. Fulton's new location has not stopped the chefs and retailers from coming, and for the thirty-seven wholesalers who survived the move, business has apparently improved. In 2006 the market sold 115 million kilograms of fish, putting it second only to Tokyo's Tsukiji in terms of volume.

An employee at Frank W. Wilkisson, Inc., seemed happy to take a break from unloading boxes of fish from a hi-lo, one of the miniforklifts that crisscross the market floor. Casually dangling a steel gaffing hook from the shoulder of his white smock, Nick Dantuono talked of all the changes he had seen in his thirty-three years at the market.

'Cod used to be really big, like so,' said Dantuono, placing his right palm a foot past the tail of a slimy specimen sitting on a bed of ice. 'We'd get the market cod – the smaller cod with its head still on – and steak cod, which came with the head already off. We used to see a lot more Atlantic pollock and haddock, too, but suddenly that stuff dropped off. All the cod gets snapped up by the processors to make fish fingers now; it never even gets here.

'With air freight, the whole world opened up to us about ten years ago. Now they can catch swordfish in Australia, bluefin tuna in the Mediterranean – any place on earth, really – and they'll put it in a Styrofoam box and within twenty-four hours, bang, it's here.' He explained that his company was now making most of its money from a fish called whiting. For every red snapper from the Gulf of Mexico, he said, they sold a hundred pounds of whiting from Nova Scotia. A foot-long Atlantic forage fish with bland, pale flesh, whiting was actually the market's most popular fish. Dantuono figured they sold fifty tonnes a week, mostly to fry shops in African-American neighbourhoods.

Looking around, Dantuono said he had to admit the new market was a lot cleaner than the old. There were stainless steel tables everywhere, floor drains and sinks, and you no longer had to wear a hat to keep the pigeon shit off your head. Most important, the boxes of fish no longer sat under a section of motorway flyover for hours in forty-degree heat. The entire building was chilled to a fish-friendly four degrees Celsius.

'The thing is, there's no atmosphere here,' said Dantuono. 'In Manhattan you had the pier, you were on the street, you felt like you were part of the city. Here it's more like being in a box. You don't get the people coming off the street. It was nice. We liked that.'

Inspecting the wares of other vendors, I saw that exotic fish, once a rarity, were now a market staple. In fact, parts of Fulton looked like a casting call for *Finding Nemo*. I recognized parrotfish from Antigua and a berry-eating fish called tambaqui from South America; there were butterfish, grouper, sea robins and an iridescent and exophthalmic deep-sea species called orange roughy. It was a sign of the times. Rather than North Atlantic staples like cod, haddock and tuna, New Yorkers were eating aquarium fish, taken from distant, already-picked-over seamounts and coral reefs.

I continued my quest for the hobgoblin of the deep. It was not difficult to find: every dealer seemed to sell monkfish, from Montauk Seafood (which displayed them pre-decapitated) to South Street Seafood (where they were sold already filleted). The tails went for $3.25 (£1.60) a pound – meaning the retail mark-up is severe: Manhattan restaurants charge as much as $25 (£12.25) for a single serving. When an employee at Blue Ribbon Fish, supplier to some of the city's finest restaurants, noticed me eyeing his wares, he asked: 'Can I show you a real interesting fish?'

Plunging his gaffing hook into a Styrofoam box, he pulled up a kind of drooping, slimy jabberwock with a bulldog's grin. The monkfish, it seemed, had found me: I was looking at a perfect eleven-kilogram specimen, landed in Cape May, New Jersey, the day before. It was even more hideous than I had thought it would be, its brown skin glistening toadlike in the fluorescent light.

'It hides in the sand,' the Blue Ribbon man explained, 'and uses this little pole to fish.' He tugged at the filament projecting out of the monkfish's forehead. 'This little black membrane kinda looks like a worm to any fish passing by. He just wiggles it around like that, and then – *whooooa!*' With a yank on the gaff hooked beneath the monkfish's upper jaw, he made the monkfish leap upwards. Right towards my nose. Twin lines of pointed teeth loomed as a maw the size of a dinner plate opened. When I involuntarily leaped back, the vendor laughed. 'Gets 'em every time!' he roared, as his buddies chuckled. (Fishmonger humour, I would learn, is an acquired taste.)

Maybe I had gotten off easy with a monkfish to the face. People who got out of line in the old Fulton, after all, used to end up swimming with the fishes. In its South Street location the market had been a notorious haven for organized crime, and syndicates skimmed huge sums from the tills of fish dealers over the years. The Genovese family was accused of using bogus unloading and security companies to turn Fulton into a private laundrette for ill-gotten cash.

It all meant you had to be careful what you bought in Fulton. One dealer was arrested for selling wild striped bass from the lower Hudson River, illegal because it is so full of pollutants. It turned out he had been peddling his stock to other Fulton wholesalers; eventually thousands of kilograms of fish tainted with polychlorinated biphenyls, highly toxic industrial chemicals, made it to the plates of some of Manhattan's finest restaurants. In 1995 then-Mayor Rudolph Giuliani started an aggressive campaign of licensing and background checks. Any fish dealer who had the slightest criminal record was fired. Within a few months thirty companies were ejected. The clean-up turned out to be a good thing for the city's fish lovers: prices fell, and trading volumes at Fulton jumped by 50 per cent.

Not that seafood fraud has stopped altogether. Far from it. There is a good reason that monkfish is called the 'poor man's lobster'.

Bait and Switch

Seafood fraud is not that hard to pull off: when it comes to passing off one species for another, fish dealers have proven all too willing to take advantage of the fish-eating public's lack of taxonomic rigour.

Take the words 'sea bass'. They appear in the names of one hundred different species, only a few of them related to one another, from chain-gang sea bass to Chilean sea bass to striped sea bass. Meanwhile, in Italy, a single species of fish, the common grey mullet, is known as *cefalo*, *muletto*, *muzao* and thirty-seven other names. Nothing would kill sales of overfished species faster than forcing restaurants to use their real names. The orange roughy, for example, is known in New Zealand as slimehead. Mahi-mahi was originally called dolphin fish – and nobody wants to be accused of eating dolphin. And in the UK, fish-and-chip shops should certainly be forced to sell rock salmon by its real name: spiny dogfish. Unlike beef, pork and chicken, 'fish' is a generic term for a wide range of animals: all told, 350 species of seafood can be found in markets in the United States. It is not difficult to pass off one species as another, and even easier to label farmed fish wild-caught. Depending on where you live, if you eat seafood in restaurants a couple of times a week, you will almost certainly be the victim of fraud at least once, and maybe twice, a month.

Every part of the world has its endemic form of fish fraud. In the American Midwest walleye often turns out to be zander, a cheap white-fleshed fish imported from Europe. In Australia barramundi is replaced with the cheaper Nile perch, imported from Africa. In Canada the cod on diners' plates often turns out to be haddock. In South America sharks are filleted, relabelled and sold as tuna.

In the United Kingdom, skate sold in many chippies is actually thornback ray, a species that is severely overfished. In 2007, the Food Standards Agency conducted a spot check of British supermarkets, buying 128 samples of fish labelled wild-caught. Twenty-six of the samples turned out to be farmed fish – including salmon purchased at Harrods, and Alaskan salmon bought at Sainsbury's and labelled Marine Stewardship Council-approved. (Harrods blamed human error: a clerk at the fish counter, a representative explained, had accidentally switched labels.) Overall, the FSA estimated that 15 per cent of the fish sold in Britain as wild-caught is actually farmed.

Fraud is not necessarily on the rise among fishmongers. It is just that new technology has been catching up with old practices. Accurate DNA tests are now relatively cheap, and a New York-state lab has devised a way to test fish samples even after they have been cooked. The *Chicago Sun-Times* in 2007 found that out of fourteen local Japanese restaurants offering red snapper, four were in fact serving red sea bream, and the remainder were using tilapia, a bland farmed fish. All told, three-quarters of the snapper sold in eight states turned out to be some other species.

In the United States, the most common scam of all centres on grouper. This bulbous, Jagger-lipped reef fish is a southern state favourite: grouper sandwiches are as much a trademark of coastal Florida as key lime pie and roadside panhandlers. Three quarters of the US catch comes from the Gulf of Mexico, but the fishery went into decline in the 1980s, and when the National Marine Fisheries Service (NMFS) introduced two-month closures, importers took advantage of the gap in supply. Ordering grouper in south Florida, local television stations found, might get you hake, emperor fish, green weakfish or even painted sweetlips – a whole *Underwater World* of species, none of them grouper. The most frequently substituted species were such farmed Asian catfish as basa, ponga and swai, which were often treated with dangerous antibiotics and fungicides. Even major restaurant chains were found to be serving catfish rather than grouper. Some restaurants may have been genuinely unaware of the substitutions: investigators found that the shipping boxes were usually labelled grouper (though many kitchens had conveniently lost their invoices). It is difficult to believe, however, that everybody was fooled. Real grouper wholesales for $10 (£4.90) a pound, but some Florida restaurants were offering all-you-can-eat specials for $7.99 (£3.90). In 2006 a Florida importer ended up taking the fall for the grouper scam; he was sentenced to an astonishing fifty-one months in prison.

Monkfish, it turns out, is one of the most popular fraud species. With this particular fish, however, it is the restaurateurs, not the wholesalers, who tend to cheat.

Here is a recipe for making a dish of pasta with lobster sauce last in your trattoria for a week – all for less than a hundred and fifty bucks. Buy two whole lobsters and twenty kilograms of cheaper monkfish tail. Combine the cooked meat from the two species, sauté in butter, add heavy cream, some brandy and some parsley, and cover your linguini with the sauce. There is no need to mention the monkfish on the menu: after all, you are simply making your lobster linguini in cream sauce stretch a little.

And that is why it is accurate to call monkfish 'poor man's lobster'. Too bad the poor man is usually the last to know.

The Goblin's Apotheosis

Having gained Julia Child's imprimatur, the once-scorned monkfish became a sought-after table fish.

Traders soon discovered that the monkfish was the possessor of an organ that, like the gonads of sea urchins, already had a cult following abroad. While sea urchin roe distils the essence of the tideline of some unpolluted Pacific beach, the liver of the monkfish captures the quintessence of a more corrupt body of water. At first bite the foamy loaf tastes like a mouthful of Sargasso, of rotting kelp and whale parts, before swerving towards the creamiest of foie gras. Fetching up to $19 (£9.30) a pound at market, the livers are shipped via Boston's Logan Airport to the sashimi emporia of Japan and such Parisian seafood temples as La Coupole. Monkfish liver never really caught on in the United States; even in such sophisticated markets as New York, tastes that flirt with putrescence can be a hard sell. Or maybe the problem lies in the name: after all, the French *foie de lotte* and the Japanese *ankimo* sound a lot better than plain old monkfish liver.

As the monkfish's popularity grew, catches started to decline. In the 1990s, in spite of a series of ultimatums from the federal government, the New England Fishery Management Council, one of eight regional bodies in the United States responsible for setting fishing quotas, refused to establish a management plan for monkfish. Catches peaked at 28,000 tonnes, but the nets were coming up filled with small and juvenile fish, and federal officials estimated that by the mid-1990s the population was at its lowest levels since trawl surveys had started thirty years before. In 1999, twenty years after it came to Julia Child's notice, the monkfish was officially declared overfished, and quotas were finally set.

By then, it was probably too late. Monkfish has become big business, and fishermen have proved all too willing to risk penalties to cash in. According to the trade journal *SeaFood Business*, monkfish now earns fishermen $50 million (£25 million) a year, making it the single most valuable species caught off the east coast, beating out cod and flounder. After temporarily classifying monkish stocks as 'rebuilding', the NMFS declared monkfish overfished in 2006. In spite of all the evidence of declining biomass, the fishing continues.

As I strolled through Manhattan reading menus, every seafood restaurant, and some others besides, seemed to be featuring monkfish. Picholine on West Sixty-fourth was doing it osso bucco style, with a rich Spanish romesco sauce. Nobu on

Hudson Street was offering a cold pâté of monkfish served with caviar. At Vong on East Fifty-fourth, the Alsatian master Jean-Georges Vongerichten was serving it baked with special spices. At Midtown's Russian Tea Room it was being served ukha style – as a fish soup – with Dungeness crab broth. Even the down-to-earth, always-packed Mary's Fish Camp in the West Village was serving it pan-roasted. It was not cheap: as an entrée, an order of monkfish tail averaged $22.50 (£11).

Though monkfish is far from endangered, it is definitely overfished: on the Monterey Bay Aquarium's Seafood Watch wallet card, it is red listed in the 'avoid' column. Even if it were as abundant as lobster, though, monkfish would still be a fish to avoid for one reason: the way it is caught.

The Trouble with Monkfish

The monkfish's bottom-dwelling ways were once its best defence against fishermen. Long ago, however, technology caught up with it.

Lophius americanus, the species served in American restaurants, can be found from the Gulf of St Lawrence to northern Florida, lurking on coastal shelves at depths of up to half a mile. (On the European side of the Atlantic, the closely related monkfish species *Lophius piscatorius* has recovered since severe restrictions on the Scottish fleet allowed declining populations to rebound. In 2007, the Asda supermarket chain announced that it would sell monkfish again, after temporarily having removed the fish from its counters. The Marine Conservation Society's Good Fish Guide now lists monkfish as a 'fish to avoid' only if it comes from certain overfished stocks; Scottish monkfish is listed as a 'fish to eat'.) Monkfish prefer habitats like the Hudson Canyon, a submerged cleft scoured into the continental slope by the meltwater from retreating glaciers, extending from New York's harbour almost five hundred miles into the Atlantic. Rich ecosystems for lobster, shark and yellowfin tuna, such canyons are within striking distance of Gloucester, New Bedford and other New England ports. In US waters most monkfish are caught with bottom-trawls, cone-shaped nets that rake the sea bottom at speeds of two to six knots. Even the smallest trawlers now rely on precision satellite navigation and computer imaging for tracking fish. In areas that once provided safe havens for bottom-feeders, canyon-busters, tickler chains and rockhoppers (heavy steel and rubber wheels that can jump huge boulders) scour every cranny in the sea floor.

Against such technology, even the best-camouflaged monkfish does not stand a chance. A trawl's bottom edge dislodges the fish from their lairs and knocks them into the net, raising choking sand clouds as it carves gouges into the seabed. The nets are not selective; about 22 per cent of the monkfish catch consists of other species, especially the overfished skate. Too many of these unwanted fish, known in the industry as bycatch, are thrown back into the water, dead or dying.

'Don't demonize one type of fishing gear,' implored a spokesperson for the National Fisheries Institute, a trade organization that defends the interests of American fishermen and processors, when conservationists started campaigning against bottom-trawls. Yet when biologists, fisheries managers and fishermen themselves were asked to rate types of fishing gear on a scale of 1 to 100 – with 100 being the most destructive – they overwhelmingly ranked bottom-trawls as the worst. Purse seines, nets that can be selectively cinched around schools of sardines or tuna, received the lowest rating, 4, and lobster-style traps scored an acceptable 38. With a rating of 91, bottom-trawls were found to be by far the most destructive – in terms of habitat impact and bycatch – of the ten fishing methods surveyed. Bottom-trawls, fishermen and scientists alike agreed, should also be the most stringently regulated.

If the floor of the ocean were a featureless plain populated only by economically useful groundfish, then the bottom-trawl, now one of the most commonly used methods of catching fish, might be a relatively benign technology. In reality, many parts of the sea floor are complex three-dimensional habitats, about which we still know far too little. Eighty per cent of the ocean is more than a mile deep, and these deep-sea areas are continuous, so that the basins of the Atlantic, Pacific and Southern oceans actually connect. Though vast stretches of the sea bottom are muddy plains crossed only by large species like tuna and whale, even these underwater deserts contain crucial oases of life. In the last decade alone explorers have charted submerged hydrothermal vents three thousand metres beneath the surface, crowded with life-forms that evolved without sunlight. Since the first of these vents, nicknamed black smokers, was discovered in 1977, a new vent-dependent species has been identified on average every ten days. Among them are blind shrimp, lobsters, anemones and giant 250-year-old tube worms that feed on bacteria capable of metabolizing the hydrogen sulphide spewed from the earth's crust. Some speculate that life on earth may have begun around such vents and could well develop on distant planets in a similar fashion.

The oceans also hide at least fourteen thousand major seamounts, submerged peaks where uprushing currents deposit nutrients, creating areas akin to watering holes in the African savannah. Small in total area, seamounts are important refuges for the oldest and largest fish – which also tend to be the most fecund. Like tropical reefs, they are home to deepwater corals that can be four thousand years old, and provide habitat for the hairy seadevil, the umbrella-mouth gulper, the roughhead grenadier and other little-studied deep-water species. (The grenadier has special rods for night vision that allow it to see two hundred times better than humans, and has a special gland that, when squeezed, causes luminescent bacteria to light up, providing the fish with its own deep-sea torch.) When scientists recently reached one of these seamounts off a remote part of Australia, however, they found it had been scraped clean by bottom-trawls.

'Imagine using a bulldozer to catch songbirds for food – that's what it's like,' says Sylvia Earle, an American biologist who has led more than sixty deep-sea expeditions, describing the devastation of bottom-trawling. 'Before trawling, you see eyes that look out from all the little crevices, crannies, burrows and little hills . . . After a trawler has gone by, it looks like a super-highway, it's just flat. Nobody's home. A few fish may swim in and out, but the residents, those that occupy the substrate, they're just smothered, they're crushed. It's like paving them over.'

Not much can stand in the way of supertrawler nets, whose mouths, held open by doors that can weigh six thousand kilo-grams each, are big enough to swallow whole cathedrals. The steel rollers that keep the net off the sea bottom plough through corals, sea fans, sponge gardens, gorgonians and other fragile, centuries-old structures like street ploughs going through snow forts. In the Gulf of Maine, repeated trawling with heavy gear has flattened species-rich underwater hills into mere bumps on the sea floor. Biologists believe that, thanks to bottom-trawls, species after species is becoming extinct before science even has had a chance to describe them. We are, in effect, clear-cutting the oceans: sea bottom scars two and a half miles wide have been found off Norway, where 40 per cent of cold-water reefs have already been damaged by trawls. Off the coast of Florida bottom-trawling has ground 90 per cent of the state's fragile Oculina coral reefs into rubble.

Amazingly, some trawls can go down 7,500 feet – almost one and a half miles – putting a quarter of all known seamounts within reach of the world's fishing industry. Moreover, half of them are within international waters, beyond two-hundred-mile national limits. For the world's trawlermen, these 75 million square miles of unregulated ocean represent the last frontier, where they can fish without worrying about red tape or environmentalists. Although there are fewer than two hundred of these vessels on the high seas, they are amazingly efficient: every year they manage to scour an area of sea bottom twice the size of the continental United States. Obscenely, the world's governments subsidize the industry with £74 million in taxpayers' money every year. Without this public money, the world's high-seas fleets would operate at a loss.

When the proposal for a moratorium on high-seas fishing came up before the United Nations in 2006, a thousand scientists worldwide signed a petition asking for a total ban, a measure supported by Great Britain, Australia and the United States. A few key fishing nations opposed the petition; it was tiny Iceland that finally blocked the moratorium. A watered-down agreement was eventually signed, allowing some of the most rapacious nations, like Russia and China, to police their own vessels. Russia, which gives £15 million a year to its deepwater trawl fleet, has since announced plans to *increase* its fishing activity on the high seas.

Canada also opposed the moratorium, even though none of its own trawlers worked outside its two-hundred-mile limit. What was the motivation? The federal government wanted to protect Canada's inshore bottom-trawling sector, an industry worth half a billion dollars a year to the economy of Nova Scotia alone.

Worried that a high-seas ban would affect the lucrative fisheries for shrimp, plaice and scallops, the biggest players in the Canadian industry fought back with shamelessly misinformed assertions: 'There is zero scientific evidence, not one shred of scientific evidence, that these [bottom-trawling] fisheries do any damage to the bottom environment whatsoever,' John Risley, the president of Clearwater Seafoods, insisted to a room full of reporters in 2006. (The exact opposite is true: there are volumes worth of scientific papers showing that fragile coral reefs have been decimated by Canadian trawlers, some of them right off Nova Scotia's coast.) Asked point-blank by a reporter if Canada's refusal to support the moratorium was driven by a desire to protect big fishing companies like Clearwater, Canada's federal fisheries minister replied: 'Certainly it is part of the decision.' He went on to explain: 'If we banned bottom-trawling across the board, we would wipe out many of the coastal communities in Canada.' In truth, fishing communities have more to fear from the long-term effects of high-seas bottom-trawling, the most definitive destroyer of ocean habitat yet invented, than from any moratorium.

And that is the *real* trouble with monkfish: not only are they caught with bottom-trawls that tear up fragile nearshore sea floor canyons, but protecting this fishery, and fisheries like it, has provided justification for the destruction of fragile seamounts. When you add up the costs, the bill for poor man's lobster, that staple on the white tablecloths of North America, is simply far too high.

I had seen worse things in New York's markets and on its menus than monkfish: for example, orange roughy, an endearing, bug-eyed deep-sea fish that grazes on seamounts, can live to be 150 years old, and does not start reproducing until the age of forty. Much of the pillaging of the deep seas has been done in pursuit of this single species; the Australian government officially listed orange roughy as threatened in 2006.

It is impossible to overstate what a bad idea fishing for such deepwater species is. The fact that we are dragging nets one and a half miles below the surface should suggest how difficult it has become for humanity to find wild-caught protein. It is as if, after shooting most of the birds in Europe and North America, we have resorted to burning down the Amazon so we can catch the fleeing parrots and macaws in butterfly nets. And then eat them.

Wandering through the Village one afternoon, I paused on Thompson Street, between Third and Bleecker, and idly read the menu in the window of a Thai restaurant. The day's special was seared orange roughy from New Zealand, probably one of the last of its kind, served with a red pepper purée. At $14.50 (£7.10) it was a real steal.

It is true what they say about New York. You can find anything in this town.

Blacklisting the White Tablecloths

While culinary trendsetters have the power to drive fish to commercial extinction, a person who convinces the public to rethink its eating habits can actually save a species. In 1987 a biologist named Sam LaBudde got a job as a chef on a Panamanian tuna-fishing boat. Using a Sony Camcorder, he videotaped dolphins being drowned in purse seine nets as the boat hunted yellowfin tuna in tropical waters. Aired on CNN, ABC and *Today*, the shocking footage, which showed dolphins shrieking as the nylon nets tore away their fins, instantly changed people's eating habits; tuna sales immediately plummeted. By 1990, when polls revealed that 60 per cent of the American public was aware that the canned tuna industry was responsible for killing hundreds of thousands of dolphins, several major canners announced that they would purchase only tuna taken using nets with panels that prevented dolphins from becoming fatally entangled.

Buying 'dolphin-friendly' tuna was probably the first conscious ethical seafood-purchasing choice North American consumers ever made. In 1998 two conservation organizations, SeaWeb and the Natural Resources Defense Council, teamed up to launch the 'Give Swordfish a Break' campaign. Fishermen and fishmongers had been noticing a disturbing change in the size of this spectacular trophy fish for years: swordfish weights dropped from an average of 118 kilograms in the 1960s to forty-five kilograms twenty years later, and 'puppies' under twenty-five kilograms were routinely being sold at Fulton and other fish markets. As prices skyrocketed, swordfish became a culinary cliché in restaurants across Europe and the United States, favoured by chefs for its firm, beefsteak-like flesh. Fishermen started using longlines, up to fifteen thousand baited hooks on lines that were so long – twelve miles or more – they could take an entire day to haul in, killing sea turtles and dozens of other species that also took the bait. Eventually seven hundred chefs and three cruise lines signed a pledge not to serve swordfish.

The next species selected for boycott was a deep-sea monster known to biologists as the Patagonian toothfish. Brought to American tables for the first time by a Los Angeles importer in 1977, it was redubbed Chilean sea bass; by 1990 it was being served at the Four Seasons in New York, and in 2001 *Bon Appétit* magazine named it their 'Dish of the Year'. A year later, with stocks near collapse, it was the subject of a boycott. The 'Take a Pass on Sea Bass' campaign, launched by the National Environmental Trust, was successful in calling attention to overfishing. To this day, many high-profile restaurants refuse to serve Chilean sea bass.

At best, however, such boycotts are blunt instruments. Even the most focused of them can unfairly penalize fishermen who fish sustainably. In her memoir *The Hungry Ocean*, swordboat captain Linda Greenlaw expressed her frustration with the impact the swordfish boycott was having on her livelihood: 'I wonder how these chefs keep themselves abreast of the state of the fishery and how they can be so conceited to presume they might know better than the fishermen and scientists who have been working together for years to keep the stocks healthy. In my opinion, little Chef Fancy Pants should work at perfecting his creme brulee and leave fisheries management to those who know more about swordfish than how best to prepare it.' Many swordfish in the Pacific are taken by harpoons or handlines, which are singularly sustainable methods of fishing. Thanks to the campaign, however, in the public mind all swordfish has become *verboten*. (Greenlaw, incidentally, now fishes for lobster.)

Yet there is no denying that a well-run public awareness campaign can save certain fish populations from commercial extinction. Some Atlantic swordfish stocks, for example, are now on their way to recovery. The impact of the 'Take a Pass on Sea Bass' campaign is less clear. Populations have recovered since the campaign started, and a single fishery has been certified as sustainable – which is why you can now find the once-forbidden fish at Whole Foods and Wal-Mart. Yet 40 per cent of Chilean sea bass on the market is still caught illegally, which means that a consumer who finds the fish on the menu of a cruise ship or a midmarket seafood restaurant has no way of knowing if it was caught by a pirate ship. Critics argue that the existence of a single certified fishery can put the stamp of sustainability on a species that may still be in serious trouble.

To highlight their distance from questionable sources, many leading chefs have started peppering their menus with qualifiers, emphasizing that their tuna is 'hook-and-line' (suggesting there is little bycatch), their cod is 'dayboat-caught' (by small, inshore boats), their scallops are 'diver-harvested' (by hand), or their grouper is 'wreck-caught' (from around sunken ships). Taking their cue from Alice Waters of Berkeley's Chez Panisse, whose menus specify the valleys and counties from which her peaches and goat cheeses come, some seafood chefs even indicate the fishing port or state their fish comes from. And thanks to vigorous promotion, Copper River and Yukon king salmon are becoming familiar brands of sustainably caught Pacific salmon in North America.

Yet in their cookbooks and showcase restaurants, America's star chefs seem to have a blind spot when it comes to serving overfished seafood. *Charlie Trotter's Seafood*, by the renowned Chicago chef, features recipes for raw red snapper, steamed cod and baby monkfish tail. Manhattan's BLT Fish, run by star chef Laurent Tourondel, makes a pious nod towards ecological correctness, noting on its menu: 'Most of our fish are line caught, our scallops are harvested by divers and the lobsters are flown in from Maine.' When I visited his restaurant, however, Tourondel was still serving such severely overfished species as red snapper, skate, halibut, monkfish and bluefin tuna.

Nobu Matsuhisa, whose empire of thirteen restaurants was founded with the financial help of Robert De Niro, has written the most stunningly profligate cookbook of them all. In *Nobu: The Cookbook*, amid recipes for Chilean sea bass, abalone, grouper and red snapper, Nobu devotes an entire section to *toro*, the fatty belly meat of the critically endangered bluefin tuna. 'Many Japanese, including myself,' Nobu wrote, 'would naturally have some resistance to "wasting" a fillet of *toro* by not serving it raw. Fortunately, however, my American customers are free from such prejudices and are able to enjoy *toro* steak on its own terms.' This is a fish that has lately become so rare in Japan that sushi chefs have been forced to replace it with horse and whale meat. Yet Nobu is hardly alone: virtually every Japanese restaurant in Manhattan serves this most pre-eminent of predators.

I even discovered a Japanese restaurant in New York's Chelsea district that boasted a bluefin tuna pizza, spiked with anchovy aïoli.

The Raw, the Cooked and the Extinct

By value, 68 per cent of the seafood eaten in North America is ordered in restaurants. From a Friday-night duty for Catholics, fish has become the prestige protein at the centre of the American plate. In New York, where diners can choose from 26,000 restaurants, one in every five dining dollars is now spent on fish.

Esca, leading critics agree, is the most original seafood restaurant to open in New York in years. (*Esca* is the Italian word both for bait and for the little membrane the monkfish uses as a lure.) Its success was heralded by a glowing 7,500-word feature in the *New Yorker*, in which the writer observed that Esca was the only place in town that offered 'year-round wild game that has been personally bagged by the chef'.

The dinner atmosphere at Esca on a Thursday night was remarkably relaxed: it was part French bistro, where diners crowded elbow to elbow seemed naturally to fall into conversation with one another, and part Mediterranean-themed trattoria, where the trim, relaxed waiters joked with ease, while never crossing invisible lines of decorum.

I had come for the *crudo* tasting menu and was not disappointed. Presented on glass plates, the raw and barely cooked seafood seemed to float beneath me like Platonic ideals of themselves. There was a single plump wild Belon oyster from Maine, its flat shell nestled in a bed of ice. I savoured an uncooked rectangle of weakfish, studded with irregular pieces of crushed almond. Finally and most exquisitely, there was a single razor clam, whose flesh had been removed, mixed with red chillis, spring onions and mint, and then stuffed back into the shell, so it looked like a canoe full of Christmas presents. The *crudo* flights, sampling freely from many levels of the food chain, were a model of their kind. The rest of the menu, however, was a problem.

I pointedly refrained from asking the waiter whether the seafood was fresh. At a joint like Esca, such a gaffe would display as much expertise as kicking tyres in a used car lot.

In the seafood industry freshness is a loaded term. In most sushi bars, for example, the fish arrives in frozen bricks that are cut into pieces with wood-cutting saws; the Food and Drug Administration insists that fish that are to be served raw first be frozen to kill parasites. (Tuna is the exception: as fast swimmers, they tend to be naturally parasite-free.) The vast majority of midmarket and chain seafood restaurants work with frozen fish, and consumers are probably better off this way. While well-iced warm-water fish, especially catfish, snapper and other lean species, can stay edible for up to three weeks, salmon, mackerel and other fatty coldwater species remain fresh only for about a week. By the time that 'fresh' cod gets to your table, it may have been sitting on ice on a fishing vessel for ten days. Before that, it may have been violently tumbled and crushed, often for hours, at the rear end (known as the cod end) of a trawler's net. A frozen-at-sea fish, in contrast, chilled to −57 degrees Celsius minutes after it is caught, can stay cryogenically preserved in perfect condition for up to two years, to be thawed just a few hours before the chef cooks it. Modern liquid-nitrogen 'snap freezers' work so quickly that the moisture does not have time to crystallize, preventing a mushy thaw.

Contrary to popular belief, fish should not be served *too* fresh. The muscle fibres of a just-killed fish temporarily lock into rigor mortis, making its flesh as tough as shoe leather and just about as easy to cut. Like beef, fish needs to be aged: it takes between eight hours and a day for rigor to end and enzymes to start breaking down proteins, softening the flesh and releasing the amino acids that are essential components of flavour. (The enzyme-filled flesh of crustaceans starts auto-digesting into pablum at the moment of death – which explains why good restaurants keep their lobsters alive in tanks up until the last minute.) If you are not in a three-star restaurant, and the seashore is nowhere in sight, the apposite question is not *Is your fish fresh?* but *How long ago was your fish thawed?*

At Esca and Manhattan's other leading seafood restaurants – which offer some of the world's costliest culinary experiences – you can be sure of getting really fresh seafood, which also explains the high prices: you are paying the chef's courier bill. A twenty-five kilogram box of salmon shipped overnight from Alaska to Manhattan immediately adds $100 (£50) to the invoice, and those shipping costs are passed on to the consumer. Turbot from France and langoustines from Scotland are actually packaged live – and thanks to temperature-controlled boxes, that is how they arrive. Masayoshi Takayama, owner of the Manhattan sushi bar Masa, has a buyer in Tokyo who selects fish at Tsukiji Market, then rushes them to Narita Airport, where they are shipped overnight to New York on Japan Air Lines flight 006. This is one reason Masa is Manhattan's most expensive restaurant – with a set dinner that will set you back $350 (£172) (wine and sake not included).

Chef David Pasternack of Esca knew that if he was going to serve raw fish that had never been frozen, he had to be pretty sure of his suppliers. After a field trip to Italy with celebrity chef Mario Batali, Pasternack – a Jewish kid who grew up surrounded by Italians in Long Island – decided to offer seafood served the Italian way, *crudo*, still raw or barely cooked: pink snapper with sea salt, tuna carpaccio, and sardines and anchovies in home made marinades.

There was much to love, I thought, in Pasternack's approach to fish. He regularly went out on friends' boats, from Montauk Point to the Rockaways, and was known to bring plastic trash bags full of the previous day's catch to Manhattan on the Long Island Rail Road. Most seafood restaurants rely on less than a half-dozen purveyors, but Pasternack had established relationships with at least a hundred over his career. Every day, Alaskan troller captains shipped him their prime King salmon, Canadian farmers sent him their best oysters, and purse-seine captains dispatched sardines from California – with FedEx ensuring it all arrived fresh. (At a seafood emporium of Esca's calibre, the received wisdom that fish should not be ordered on Mondays simply does not apply. At Esca, *every* night is Friday night.) None of Pasternack's big-ticket fish are farmed, and his selection of seafood from low on the food chain includes house-marinated sardines and anchovies, local squid and 'steamers' (clams from Long Island's Great South Bay).

Yet Pasternack seemed to have no qualms about serving some of the most overfished species in the Atlantic. On the day I visited, Esca was featuring a *fritto misto* of crispy skate, Atlantic halibut and cod from Casco Bay, American red snapper and swordfish, and the most troubling choice of all, bluefin tuna, done several ways: *bottarga*-style, air-dried like a *bresaola*, and even in the form of meatballs on rigatoni. A quick tally showed that his menu included one-third of the species listed in the 'avoid' column of the Monterey Bay Aquarium's Seafood Watch card, including Manhattan's seafood of choice: monkfish, served roasted with a three bean salad and red-leafed Bordeaux spinach.

On a weekday afternoon Pasternack, a stocky man in his early forties, was seated at Esca's small bar, multitasking. A waiter brought the day's menu for his perusal; he scrawled 'Montauk' next to the monkfish, fielded questions from a wine dealer and stole bites from a grilled processed-cheese sandwich. When I mentioned some of the problems associated with the species on his menu, he replied with the chopped diction of somebody who would have been completely at home in the Old Fulton.

'Cod is God,' he said. 'My grandmother is from England, so I grew up eating cod. I use salt cod, I use fresh cod. Funny thing, the cod kind of disappeared from the south shore of Long Island. The water temperature changed, and the cod don't seem to make it around Montauk any more. Recently, I went to fish with some buddies about sixty miles out in the ocean to a spot that was always very lucrative for us. We only caught one cod. And I threw it back because it was too small. These days I get most of my cod from the auction in Portland, Maine.

'Bluefin tuna's got a lot of issues right now. It's kind of sad, because it's a great fish. The conservation thing is a tricky issue. I've tried some of the farmed stuff from Japan, and it can be spectacular, but they're having trouble getting any consistent product.' Pasternack said he preferred his bluefin wild-caught from the Atlantic.

'The way I look at it, you follow the rules that the government sets forth. When you see that the sea bass season is open, you buy sea bass; when bluefin is open, you buy bluefin. It's true there will always be fishermen who decide the rewards are worth the fines they might get. When you're getting thirty grand for one fish, the risk can definitely be worth it.

'There's a fine line with the whole morality of the thing,' Pasternack concluded. 'Trust me, I get e-mails from these environmental groups every day about all these issues. I've never served Chilean sea bass, and I never will. I won't serve farmed salmon – it smells rancid to me and tastes like soybeans. I don't serve caviar – mostly because it's too expensive. And I only use local swordfish, stuff caught from the Carolinas down to the Gulf. If American fishermen don't catch them, somebody in Costa Rica will reap the benefits, so why put our guys out of business?'

For Pasternack, it seemed, a policy of favouring small producers excused all. He served what the authorities let him, and avoided the big companies he saw as really responsible for overfishing.

'The government doesn't regulate smartly. They should be

helping the moms-and-pops, the fourth-generation fishermen that I buy from, but everything they do helps these big commercial guys, with boats that have fucking nets that go down two miles and destroy the coral reefs. The government needs to get smart; we're ten years behind the program now.'

Pasternack did not seem to be aware of any of the issues surrounding monkfish.

'Monkfish – I don't really know,' he said. 'There seems to be a lot of that around.'

What, I asked, about the way it is caught?

'It's true that we're doing a lot of damage to the ocean with bottom-trawls,' he replied. 'But I'm not too worried about the oceans. I was out fishing the other day, and there were lots of cormorants and terns and loons around, and when there's food for them to eat, that's always a sign the water is clean.'

Before leaving Esca, I bought a copy of Pasternack's cookbook, *The Young Man & the Sea*, whose cover shows him holding up a striped bass on the deck of a friend's boat. Beautifully illustrated, with an introduction by Mario Batali, it is an interesting volume – one you can imagine as an artefact in some future museum display explaining what happened to the world's wildlife.

Its tough-talking tone hearkens back to the days of Ernest Hemingway, when the seas were still full of huge game fish. 'Catching a tuna,' Pasternack writes, 'is like trying to stop a VW bug going 60 miles an hour with a piece of string. I've fought tunas at 40 pounds and almost broke my back.' In Hemingway's day, of course, the tuna tended to weigh hundreds, not scores, of pounds.

Reading *The Young Man & the Sea* – as well as other leading chefs' menus and cookbooks filled with red-listed species – you could easily forget that the Atlantic has been stripped of all but 10 per cent of its big predator fish. Monkfish, its author writes, 'has a lobsterlike texture with a mild flavor that's perfect for those more assertive ingredients, plus it's usually a bargain'; the book gives three separate recipes for the fish. And Pasternack seems to have an original explanation for the North Atlantic cod collapse: 'In the last couple of years, the cod stopped coming to my 'hood: they stopped making that right turn at Montauk. Maybe they're afraid of me because I catch so many. But it doesn't really matter – there are enough cod in the sea.'

Pasternack's *crudo* menu is excellent. He plays the role of the tough-talking bag-'em-and-serve-'em chef to the letter. But I am not sure what planet he is living on. If it is indeed earth, it must be the globe circa 1950, when Hemingway was still in his prime and a young man really could catch all the fish he wanted.

The French Invasion

Vernacular seafood cooking in North America has traditionally involved a lot of frying, breading and seasoning – techniques that cover up the flavour of fish, turning it too often into indistinguishable lumps of chewy protein. At regular intervals, chefs from Europe, and in particular France, with its long tradition of seafood cookery, have taken the raw ingredients available to North Americans and transformed them into haute cuisine.

In nineteenth-century New York, a city of dance halls and oyster cellars, a Swiss-born wine merchant opened the first fine-dining restaurant, Delmonico's, at 23 William Street. For almost thirty years, starting in 1862, Delmonico's chef, the Alsatian Charles Ranhofer, embellished such local ingredients as trout and duck with rich sauces, and elevated the harbour's bivalves into 'oysters in béchamel sauce with truffles'. In the twentieth century the French pavilion at the 1939 World's Fair in New York reintroduced French cuisine to Americans, but for too long, *sole meunière* and *salmon verte* were the alpha and omega of seafood gastronomy in North America.

The real revolution came in 1979, when a chef named Jean-Louis Palladin opened a forty-seat restaurant in the basement of Washington DC's Watergate Hotel. In France, Michelin had bestowed a second star upon Palladin when he was only twenty-eight years old, making him the youngest chef so honoured. Palladin transformed American seafood cooking by transforming his suppliers. His most lasting contribution was arguably the education of Rod Mitchell, a marine biologist and scuba diver who had left academia to open a small wine and gourmet food business in Camden, Maine. When Palladin waxed nostalgic about lampreys stewed in their own blood with red wine, the enterprising Mitchell put on rubber boots and found the eel-like parasites nesting in an unused dam in the backwaters of Maine, and delivered them to Palladin still squirming. The delighted chef killed them moments before serving his signature *lamproie à la bordelaise*. With Palladin's support, Mitchell mastered the caviar trade, and his Browne Trading Company became one of the finest purveyors in the business. Mitchell encouraged local fishermen to gear their methods to the white-tablecloth trade, thus boosting profits: dayboat captains began to gut their fish on deck and pack them immediately in salt-flake ice to prevent spoilage. As 'fish purveyor to the stars', Mitchell's client list eventually included such celebrity chefs as Wolfgang Puck, Emeril Lagasse and Charlie Trotter. Diver-caught scallops, baby glass eels and peekytoe crabs were all among Rod Mitchell's gifts to the menus of America.

But it was a brother-and-sister team from Brittany that really transformed the fish business in New York. Maguy and Gilbert Le Coze founded Le Bernardin in 1986, introducing fish carpaccios and tartares to the United States; their menu was also the first to apply such terms as 'seared' and 'medium rare' to seafood. Gilbert Le Coze was responsible for the apprenticeship of another supplier, David Samuels of the Blue Ribbon Fish Company at Fulton. Samuels was a third-generation wholesaler; his grandfather, who came from central Europe in 1914, used to drive his horse and wagon over the Brooklyn Bridge to buy fish. Samuels had never seen such care lavished on seafood; to demonstrate his idea of freshness, Le Coze one day whipped up an exquisite sea urchin soup speckled with roe. Talking to a *New York Times* reporter, Samuels recalled that Le Coze never asked about prices but always insisted on freshness: 'He took the whole industry to a new level. He took *us* to a new level.'

Other French chefs started coming to the market, including Alsatian Jean-Georges Vongerichten of the Restaurant Lafayette, who would show up at four A.M. to pick out his own skate wings, pompano and tuna. By reacting with justifiable horror to fish bruised and pierced with gaff marks – a Fulton signature – these young chefs taught purveyors exactly what selling high-quality fish meant. By the time the next generation of seafood chefs hit the market, Samuels could afford to be picky. Rick Moonen, now of RM Seafood in Las Vegas, recalled Blue Ribbon's boss refusing to serve him until he could prove he was serious about his fish.

Jean-Louis Palladin continued to facilitate the fin-de-siècle French invasion: he got Daniel Boulud his first job in New York and hired Eric Ripert to work at his Washington DC restaurant. The young chef, who grew up in Andorra, had already served in the kitchen of Paris's La Tour d'Argent, but working for Palladin in Washington was his trial by fire. Ripert recalled throwing down his apron and being on the verge of walking out on the senior chef, returning only when Palladin questioned his manhood (and threatened not to give him a reference). Ripert finally attained the level of sous-chef, and Palladin made sure his protégé got a job at Le Bernardin. When Gilbert Le Coze died in 1994, Ripert took over as executive chef. Under his direction, Le Bernardin has maintained and consolidated its reputation, earning three Michelin stars in 2005, one of only fifty-six such restaurants in the world.

I had been looking forward to meeting Ripert. He had a reputation for being a thoughtful man, a star chef who eschewed the trappings of Food Network-style celebrity. Waiting for him in a windowless office buried in the bowels of a Midtown tower block, I glanced at shelves lined with seafood cookbooks (including two authored by Ripert) but also with serious tomes about the decline of the fisheries. Ripert is a member of Seafood Choices Alliance, a national organization that works with chefs to increase awareness of sustainable seafood; he was also one of the first chefs in the country to take swordfish and Chilean sea bass off his menu. A handsome man with full lips and square-cut features, he came to the conference table dressed in full chef's whites.

'When I started in this business twenty years ago,' he began, in a voice nicely balanced between staccato New York and mellifluous French, 'I was very ignorant about what was going on in the oceans, especially overfishing. I didn't even know about organic vegetables and fruits. But since then, I have travelled, and I've been to the Caribbean and seen how the coral is being bleached, things like this. I have much more knowledge than when I started. And I'm aware of the power chefs like myself have in influencing people.'

Ripert estimated 40 per cent of his fish came from Rod Mitchell's Browne Trading in Maine, another 40 per cent from purveyors at Fulton – he was an early adopter of David Samuels's Blue Ribbon – and the rest from connections in Japan. He prided himself on serving mostly wild-caught fish. Only his sea urchin and hamachi, a form of yellowtail imported from Japan, were farmed. Yet Le Bernardin's menu featured several overfished species. I ran through his menu, listing some of them: halibut, skate, cod, red snapper and of course monkfish.

'It's true, every day we seem to see a new fish on the red list.

I'm bombarded with information about this. We don't serve bluefin or black grouper. I've started serving farmed Iranian caviar, rather than caviar from the wild sturgeons, which are totally disappearing. We still serve some fish that are on the list, but these ones we get from dayboats. It is difficult to know where your fish is coming from, of course, if you are not catching it yourself. But I have confidence in my purveyors. Rod Mitchell buys line-caught fish, fish from dayboats. I think there's a big difference between a cod, for example, that is caught in one of those giant boats in the middle of the ocean, and one that has been caught by a local fisherman in a little boat. I've been to Maine and seen the dayboats coming in; I've been to the auction in Portland. I can really identify where they're coming from.' He had also had to deal with the wrath of fishermen, among them Linda Greenlaw, who accused him of wrecking livelihoods by joining the swordfish boycott. 'It is true that as a chef you are influential – you can be putting fishermen and their families out of work. So you really have to think about what you're doing.'

Like Pasternack, though, Ripert seemed sanguine about the future of the oceans. 'Despite the fact we've seen a very fast deterioration of the environment, through a combination of pollution and overfishing, I'm not pessimistic. We are waking up. Governments are setting more quotas for fish like halibut and snapper. We maybe have to be smarter and more aggressive, but I don't see it as the end of the world. And it's much more positive than it was thirty years ago, when nobody gave a fuck.' With that, he headed upstairs for a last inspection of the restaurant before the dinner crowds arrived.

Ripert had clearly given the issues some thought. He was hardly obliged to: culinary convention allows chefs to fall back on the art-for-art's-sake argument, the conceit that, in the pursuit of exquisite sensations and rarefied textures, only an inferior artist allows his palate to be limited by such temporal concerns as the relative scarcity of raw materials. I had eaten at Le Bernardin and knew that Ripert was no amoral practitioner, catering to the jaded palates of Manhattan's *feinschmeckers*: he genuinely endeavoured to source from ethical purveyors. As I left Le Bernardin, however, I suspected that I had been charmed by a smooth and diplomatic practitioner. I looked at his latest menu: sure enough, he was serving monkfish in a red wine and brandy sauce, served with string vegetables.

Wandering the streets of the theatre district, idly reading menus filled with Chilean sea bass, cod, orange roughy and other red-listed seafood, I realized what was bothering me. Though the chefs I had met were buying from small businessmen who worked sustainably, their menus were still filled with overfished species. I passed yet another sushi bar serving bluefin tuna, and an Italian trattoria with swordfish steak and monkfish on the menu. For every Bernardin and Esca, there are thousands of restaurants across the continent serving red-listed seafood. Their menus may have been influenced by the reviews their chefs had read of New York's greatest restaurants; or their clients may have asked for the fish they had enjoyed on a visit to Manhattan. Though Ripert and his peers can afford to buy the scallops Rod Mitchell has personally harvested, or the monkfish from the dayboat whose captain they have met, the chef at a bistro in Milwaukee, or a salmon house in Calgary, almost certainly does not have that kind of access. Yet thoughtlessly sourced monkfish, scallops, and other species end up on menus across the continent – more often than not from the industrial-scale fisheries that are wrecking the oceans. The prestige of the world's leading chefs legitimizes the ongoing pillage.

It is not necessarily the fault of New York's star seafood chefs. It is, however, their doing.

2

CHESAPEAKE BAY
and BRITTANY –
OYSTERS

In the Kingdom of the Oysters

This is a tale of two oysters.

It begins with *Crassostrea virginica*, the deep-shelled American oyster of the East Coast of the United States, sold under the aliases Chincoteague, Wellfleet, bluepoint – too many names, in fact, to list here – and concludes with *Ostrea edulis*, the flat-shelled, grey-fleshed oyster eaten at least since Roman times in Europe and variously known as Colchester, Belon and Ostende. At the same time, it is the story of biological invaders, pillaging by moonlight, man-made disease, low-tech solutions, ever-spreading dead zones and terminal short-sightedness.

More important, it is the tale of two attitudes towards the world and of two very different philosophies of nature. The first of these, as ancient as humanity itself, sees the world as a vast wilderness of endless abundance, a kind of supermarket whose aisles are constantly being replenished by a higher power. It is the philosophy of the hunter, and it evolved in the time of expanding frontiers, when resources were seemingly endless and competition limited. The second, the philosophy of the farmer, sees nature as something to be cultivated and enriched in the present so it can be harvested in the future. Surprisingly, the clash of these prehistoric worldviews is still being played out in the twenty-first century, on the shores of our planet's great bodies of water. The way this conflict is resolved will determine not only the fate of the oceans but also all the life that depends on them.

Starting with, but certainly not limited to, the oyster.

Troubled Waters

The Pilgrims, requesting permission from King James to charter a colony in the New World, airily informed him they would make a living by fishing. ("Tis an honest Trade,' the king replied. "Twas the Apostles owne calling.') However, even though the *Mayflower* was surrounded by whales when it arrived in Cape Cod, the Puritans had neglected to bring fishing tackle with them and had no idea how to profit from the sea's abundance or even how to survive through the winter. A Wampanoag Indian nicknamed Squanto showed them how easy it was to dig for eels and gather shellfish – though the squeamish newcomers drew the line at eating mussels and quahogs.

If you knew what to look for, though, the new land was one big seafood buffet. Early accounts described an ecosystem of ten-kilogram lobsters, two-metre-wide halibut and salmon as long as a man was tall. Up and down the East Coast, there was no greater source of readily available food than Chesapeake Bay. Penetrating almost two hundred miles inland, with an average width of fifteen miles, it is the continent's largest estuary, formed by the outflow of 150 creeks, streams and rivers, the largest of which is the Susquehanna. In the Chesapeake, the meeting of the salty Atlantic Ocean and the meltwater from the Appalachian mountains creates a multitude of microhabitats, and rich blooms of plankton provide the nutrients that feed 2,700 species of plants and animals. The colonists of Jamestown, which was founded in 1607, reported seeing killer whales and porpoises, giant sturgeon and manatees, alligators and dia-mondback terrapins. The water teemed with croakers, striped bass and a little fish called the menhaden, 'so thick', wrote a nineteenth-century traveller, 'that for 25 miles along the shore there was a solid flip-flap of the northward-swimming fish.' Hundreds of thousands of acres of the bay were covered by more than thirty distinct species of aquatic grasses – immense fields of underwater vegetation. The Chesapeake's rich natural biodiversity would soon be rivalled by its diversity of human cultures. There were the picaroons, or local pirates, who harassed the British schooners; the Methodist skipjack captains of teetotalling Tangier Island; the ubiquitous Chesapeake water-men, tonging for oysters from draketail workboats; and the African-American families who picked crabs in Crisfield, a town whose streets were literally paved with shells. The people of the Chesapeake lived on the water but also made their living *from* the water, on a bay that, up until a generation ago, produced more seafood per acre than any other body of water on earth.

A vast sheltered estuary with waters of varying salinity, the Chesapeake should be an uncommonly good place for oysters to grow. Once upon a time, it was. *Chesepioc* is said to mean 'great shellfish bay' in Algonquian, and natural oyster bars – great ver-tical structures that have been compared to the coral reefs of the Caribbean – were once widespread enough to make navigation treacherous. At the bottom of middens, the shorefront shell piles of native Americans, archaeologists have found the remains of oysters nearly a foot long. Later, Chesapeake Bay oysters were shipped to the capitals of Europe, and for much of the early twentieth century thirteen oyster-filled railway wagons would leave Baltimore for the raw bars of America every day. Yet a little over a century after intensive harvesting began, less than 1 per cent of the original oyster population remains. Today, if you stop for a meal in a bayside seafood shack in the lean summer months, the oysters you are served may have been trucked from Louisiana, and the crabs flown all the way from Venezuela.

From a plane, it is immediately apparent how great the challenges facing the Chesapeake are. Civilization lies all around. To the north, the rich farmland of Pennsylvania is a crazy quilt of irregularly shaped fields. On the eastern shore of Maryland, vast poultry and pig farms discharge their effluent right into the water. The vibrant green lawns and preternaturally turquoise swimming pools of the region's suburbs glint in the sunlight, even as they suck up ground water, increasing salinity levels. The bay, which before the 1830s was circled by dense forest, is now completely surrounded by highways and bridges; the twin-spanned marvel of the Chesapeake Bay Bridge Tunnel cinches the Eastern Shore to Norfolk, and every tailpipe on those roads leaks greenhouse gases. The sewage from four major urban centres – including Baltimore and the nation's capital – ends up in the bay at the rate of 1.5 billion gallons a day. All told, sixteen million people live in the Chesapeake's watershed, which covers sixty-four thousand square miles and six states. Yet the average depth of the Chesapeake is only twenty-one feet, meaning that a six-foot-tall man could wade through seven hundred thousand acres of its waters without ever being fully submerged. If a replica of the bay the size of a football field were built, the layer of water representing its average depth would be no thicker than a penny.

It all adds up to a lot of golf courses, suburban lawns and pastures draining into one very shallow bay. In fact, the land-to-water ratio for the Chesapeake is higher than for any other major body of water on the planet. Even far from shore the waters look turbid and murky, shading from opaque muddy green to unhealthy-looking bluish-browns near the main stem of the bay.

More than ever, the Chesapeake needs its oysters. Automobile exhaust, fertilizer-rich run-off and the pollution from the coal-fired power plants of the Midwest are filling the bay with more nitrogen than it can handle – 130 million kilograms a year, seven times more than when humans first came to the shores of the Chesapeake. And nitrogen, along with another plant nutrient, phosphorus, is exactly what feeds algae and allows it to thrive. Oysters in turn feed by filtering algae through their gills – a fully grown oyster can suck up fifty gallons of water a day – but in their absence the algae remains in the bay, causing vast blooms of the floating plant material to spread as the water warms.

'Mahogany tides' have lately turned entire rivers reddish-brown, making what little shellfish remained inedible. In 1997 fifty thousand fish died in the mouth of the Pocomoke River, and biologists discovered a sinister micro-organism called *Pfiesteria piscicida* was eating their flesh, revealing their guts. After exposure to the 'cell from hell', as *Pfiesteria* was dubbed, dozens of watermen complained of confusion, short-term memory loss and other mental problems.

Such fish kills begin when algae blooms cover the bay, choking out other life, a process known as eutrophication. Huge carpets of dead algae, no longer removed from the water by oysters and other filter feeders, start to sink to the bottom, and in decomposing rob the bottom layer of the bay of all its oxygen. During the summer, when there is little vertical mixing of water, the bay bottom becomes a sealed coffin devoid of oxygen, a condition known as anoxia. This bottom layer of stinking mud in turn starts to emit toxic hydrogen sulphide, which kills off animal life. In 2005, 41 per cent of the main stem of the bay was so anoxic that even crabs, known for their ability to tolerate extreme conditions, could no longer survive. Watermen reported phalanxes of Chesapeake's famous blue crabs fleeing the water for land, an event locally known as a 'jubilee'.

'The bottom line,' wrote Tom Horton, in his book *Turning the Tide: Saving the Chesapeake Bay*, 'is that massive regions of the Bay may become as devoid of oxygen as the surface of the moon . . . and may in fact be as hostile to fish and crabs as a sandy desert.'

Ecologists believe that much of this is a consequence of the removal of that keystone species *Crassostrea virginica*, the American oyster. At the peak of their abundance, the oysters of the Chesapeake filtered much of the bay's eighteen trillion gallons of water through their gills and were capable of cleaning the bay of algae in less than five days. They cleaned the water with the help of the menhaden, an oily, bony fish, also a filter feeder of algae, that forms schools in the millions. These days, the Chesapeake menhaden stock is fished by a single company that grinds them up to make fertilizer. (The scarcity of menhaden has put an end to the recovery of stocks of striped bass, a favourite game fish, which now succumb to emaciation and infection because their chief prey has disappeared.) With oysters and menhaden systematically overfished, it is as though the liver of the Chesapeake has been cut out, leaving the worst industrial toxins to circulate through its system unchecked.

Even as the warming that is raising global water levels worldwide affects the Chesapeake at twice the worldwide average rate, the land is subsiding, which means that traditional communities like Smith Island are being swallowed whole, their baseball diamonds and wharves disappearing into the bay. Thanks to changing temperatures and eutrophication, the bay's underwater grasses, which once served as a nursery for juvenile striped bass, crustaceans and molluscs, have died off, and are at one-tenth of their historic highs. Long gone are the vast schools of shad and herring, sturgeon and salmon, and whales that used to nose their way into the bay for a quick feed. The Chesapeake even risks losing its signature species – the blue crab, caught by generations of schoolkids using twine baited with chicken necks – to the southern states.

In this emerging waterscape of sea-nettle jellyfish and toxic algae, the most endangered species of all may well be the Chesapeake waterman.

Lords of the Bay

Captain Wade Murphy steered the *Rebecca T. Ruark* out of Dogwood Harbor, heading away from the setting sun and into the shallow waters where the Choptank River meets the Chesapeake.

I was his mate for a day. With long pulls on a halyard, I hoisted the mainsail up a wooden mast, and soon we were under full sail, leaving behind clouds of the maddening flies known as 'no-see-ums' as we pulled away from tiny Tilghman Island.

Since the nineteenth century, the watermen of Maryland have been fishing for oysters with light, flat-bottomed, manoeuvrable sailboats called skipjacks. Captain Murphy explained that the *Rebecca T. Ruark* was originally built in 1886; though she followed a skipjack's sail plan, her hull was curved, a feature that meant technically she pre-dated the first skipjack. Murphy acquired the vessel in 1984, but he had been a waterman on the Chesapeake since 1957. (The term 'waterman', which simply refers to somebody who makes his living on the water, is thought to go back to Elizabethan England.)

Dressed neatly in a polo shirt and chinos, Murphy squinted from beneath lopsided brows, commanding the wheel with muscled hands mottled and moulded by decades of sun and strain.

'My grandfather came from Ireland,' he said. 'My dad was born in nineteen hundred, and he was thirteen when his father got drownded off an oyster boat. He had to go to work to help his mother with her eight other children. There were no child labour laws back then; you had to do what you had to do. I was sixteen when I started myself.'

Why was a nineteenth-century sailboat still being used to fish in the age of echo sounders and satellite imaging? It was a long story, but one Murphy liked to tell.

People, he explained, had been fishing for oysters in the Chesapeake as far back as anyone could remember. They would go out in log canoes with 'tongs', standing over the oyster beds and scissoring their prey off the rocks with two long wooden shafts tipped with opposable metal baskets. Around the time of the War of 1812 schooners from New England started appearing in the bay, searching for oysters to feed the cellars and bars of New York City. The Yankees brought with them a new instrument, the sailboat-pulled dredge, an all-too-efficient tool that raked the bottom and brought up in a few minutes as many oysters as a waterman could tong in an hour. They had already worked their way south through Cape Cod, Long Island Sound and Staten Island, progressively grinding the oyster reefs bare.

At first the newcomers were satisfied with taking mature oysters from the Chesapeake and 'embedding' them on the shores of New England, a process that imparted the saltier taste favoured in the oyster cellars of New York. Local watermen sold their catch to the new arrivals for 10 cents (5 pence) a bushel (an eight-gallon measure carrying about seventy oysters) but gradually refined their skiffs and log canoes into agile sailing vessels called brogans, bugeyes, bateaux and eventually skipjacks. Soon hard-chimed, single-masted skipjacks – Chesapeake originals – were outsailing, and outfishing, even the fleetest

Cape Cod schooners. They led to the birth of one of the roughest and most rapacious fisheries the world has ever known.

'Dredgers have had a bad name for one hundred and fifty years,' Captain Murphy told me. 'It was written in the books: "an unscrupulous bunch of people that come out and rape the oyster bed with the dredge." They said we worked at night, we stole the oysters, they said there was shooting between the hand-tongers and the dredgers. We've *still* got a bad name. In the lower bay they used to call us the "whores of the Chesapeake".'

The confluence of ice-making machines, an ever-spreading railway system and the invention of steam canning in the 1870s made Chesapeake oysters into a sought-after commodity. It was a gold rush for a species as common as dandelions, and it attracted desperate men, often foreigners who spoke no English. Floating brothels lined the shores, and in the boom years there were four to five murders a week. In the streets of Crisfield a technique called crimping, which involved the swift application of a billy club to the head, was routinely used to assemble crews. If a captain decided he did not want to give a mate his pay, a quick blow from a pivoting boom could be arranged to knock him overboard, unconscious and unpaid. The authorities' Oyster Navy, with its single steam vessel, was hard pressed to patrol the lawless fleet. (Only the coming of Methodism, it was later claimed, truly tamed the watermen.) By 1879 seventeen million bushels of oysters were being extracted from the Chesapeake. To curtail the scramble, legislators proclaimed that dredging would be legal only under sail power. Thanks to the 'Maryland solution', as it became known, sailboats are still being used in a modern fishery, exactly two hundred years after Robert Fulton launched the first commercial steamboat.

Murphy showed me the dredge, a triangular metal frame with a toothed lower edge and rope netting to catch the oysters dislodged from their beds. Swivelling his hips, he tossed the contraption over the side. Normally, he explained, the dredge is bigger – enough to hold five bushels – and an identical dredge is thrown from the other side of the boat to balance the load. As the dredge settled to the bottom and the steel teeth started to rake the bay's bottom, the taut line that attached it to the skip-jack began to thrum. After ten minutes on an even keel, Murphy hauled up the dredge and emptied the catch onto the wooden deck.

'Well, this oyster is undersized,' he said, holding it against a three-inch metal gauge. 'This oyster is dead. This one's alive. This one's dead.' Of the twenty shells and half-shells we had pulled up, ten were empty and got tossed back, to provide cultch – a surface for young oysters to fix on. Only six oysters were alive and large enough to keep. It was a pitiful catch. Were we fishing for jellyfish, however, it would have been considered a success: the rope mesh of the dredge was clogged with translucent gel and dripping with ropy tendrils.

'They call them winter nettles,' said Murphy, grimacing. 'You've got to watch out. They sting.' Every year, he said, he was encountering more and more jellyfish. They were the least of the changes he had seen in the Chesapeake since he started fishing half a century before.

'A disease called MSX hit the oysters in the early fifties,' Murphy said, 'and started working its way up to Maryland. By 1985, it wiped out eighty per cent of the beds in this area. The disease didn't happen here at first, because it needs salty water to survive. You see, the good Lord had a plan. He made the bay perfect, and He made the Susquehanna River to flush it out with fresh water from the mountains. But we started building dams and reservoirs, which held back the fresh water, and made the bay salty enough for MSX to survive.'

Murphy believed the changing climate was having an impact on the oysters as well. 'I remember when the bay would freeze over for seven weeks at a time. But we have made this global warming, and because of it we don't have the ice we used to have. The good Lord made the ice to kill the bacteria, the germs and the diseases.'

Sweeping his arm towards the houses on the shore of Tilghman Island, Murphy said: 'Then there's too much development, too. All these homes on the shore, these people have all come from Pennsylvania, Washington, DC, New Jersey, in the last twenty years. They all have a swimming pool, they all need to fertilize their green lawns, and those chemicals are running off in the bay. When the Indians were here, they didn't do much polluting. This Bay needs to be cleaned up. That's why I don't eat raw oysters. Oysters filter whatever junk there is in the water, and I don't want to eat junk. I will eat them any way cooked, though.'

Murphy asked me to take the wheel, instructing me to head towards the setting sun, which was now touching the horizon behind Dogwood Harbor. He had given up fishing three years before, when he realized he could no longer make a living at it. In that year only 25,000 bushels of oysters were taken in the whole Chesapeake, a little over one-tenth of 1 per cent of what the watermen took in the boom days of the nineteenth century. Lately Murphy had survived by taking sightseers out on sunset cruises. In the whole bay, he figured, only five skipjacks were still oystering. At the height of the fishery, there had been two thousand.

Finding the oysters – hardly the most elusive of prey – had never really been the problem. The invention of the patent tong, whose netted heads were hydraulically operated, made the process even more efficient. Unchecked, scuba divers, who started working in the 1980s, could have stripped the oyster beds in a few months. The real challenge lay not in increasing efficiency but in *slowing down* the fishing process, ensuring that the people who kept Tilghman Island and other watermen's communities alive got their fair share of the stock. The genius of the picturesque Maryland solution, which filled the bay with slashing bowsprits and sun-catching sails, was to put some brakes on the progress of the fishery. The wonder of it was that it worked for as long as it did. But the skipjacks only delayed the inevitable. Saving the oysters would have required a radical change in philosophy – from a culture of hunting and gathering to one of stewardship – a change Captain Murphy and his ilk had always been temperamentally disinclined to make.

Murphy was proud of the fact that he had spent his career fishing from a low-tech skipjack, using only sail power. When other watermen called for the rules to be changed to allow dredging from motorboats, he was always against it. 'I wasn't for power-dredging, because I wanted the oysters to be here for my son, and grandsons, and great-grandsons. I thought dredging with power would lead to overharvesting. But then all of a sudden the oysters started dying from disease.' Even so, Murphy said there was not much he could have done. 'The overharvesting really happened before I was born, in the early days.' Nineteenth-century watermen had permanently torn apart the natural oyster bars. In spite of decades of work, and tens of millions of dollars of public money spent growing oysters from seed in hatcheries, the oysters had not returned.

Jumping ashore, still nimble at the age of sixty-five, Murphy displayed something of the contempt of the fleet-footed hunter for the sedentary farmer. When I suggested that allowing people to farm oysters might be the only way left to improve the quality of the water, he squinted past me and said, with something unmistakably lordly in his voice:

'I am not for oyster farming for the general public. Because then there won't be no more free enterprise.'

The Freedom to Plunder

In his great book *Beautiful Swimmers*, written after a sojourn among the watermen of Maryland in the early 1970s, William

DEAD SEAS

W. Warner cites a telltale utterance overheard at an oystering community on Smith Island, sixty miles from Tilghman Island. A government biologist was interrupted as he vainly tried to convince a group of watermen to adopt conservation measures to spare the Chesapeake's fauna.

"'There is something you don't understand,'" Warner reported a young islander telling the biologist. "'These here communities on the Shore, our little towns here on the island and over to the mainland, was all founded on the right of free plunder. If you follow the water, that's how it was and that's how it's got to be.'"

The key words were 'free plunder'. Like a Shakespearean aside spoken aloud, it was as blunt an expression of the attitude that underlies most fisheries as you are ever likely to hear.

In 1968 ecologist Garrett Hardin published a paper in the journal *Science* that succinctly explained what had happened to the Chesapeake oyster fishery – and to a thousand other fisheries around the world. He asked readers to picture a pasture open to all. For centuries tribal herdsmen have grazed their cattle on the commons, and for centuries internecine wars, poaching and disease have kept the numbers of both the tribespeople and their livestock well below the carrying capacity of the land. But when social stability arrives, a new scenario emerges. Each herdsman seeks to maximize his gain by adding another animal to his herd; however, each animal added to the commons reduces the amount of land available for grazing, depleting the forage available for all. Since the effects of overgrazing are shared equally by all the herdsmen, the impact of introducing another animal to the commons will always be much smaller for the individual herdsman than the positive economic benefit of enlarging his herd.

'Each man,' wrote Hardin, 'is locked into a system that compels him to increase his herd without limit – in a world that is limited. Ruin is the destination towards which all men rush, each pursuing his own best interest in a society that believes in the freedom of the commons. Freedom in a commons,' he concluded, 'brings ruin to all.' Hardin called this the 'tragedy of the commons' – tragic, in the classical sense, because the outcome was at once foreseeable and unavoidable.

If we think of Chesapeake Bay – and indeed the oceans of the world – as a commons, then we see the tragedy writ large. For most of human history we have looked upon the seas as being limitless, intrinsically open to all. The freedom to buy a vessel and go fishing is enshrined in international law, and 'right to fish' legislation, aggressively promoted by recreational anglers, is still being written into local constitutions in the United States. In a world of unlimited resources, such an attitude sounds laudably democratic; as it becomes all too apparent that the oceans are finite, however, the tragedy is revealed. Though individual fishermen have an economic interest in hauling up another bushel of oysters, or another net full of monkfish, in a finite world every member of a species removed from the environment diminishes the resources available to other fishermen and, by extension, to every human being (and exponentially more so if the oyster or monkfish in question happens to be spawning). As fecund as fish can be, producing eggs by the millions, the notion that the overall supply of seafood is infinite is Victorian hyperbole, long superseded by the discoveries of modern ecology. Human beings have proven all too talented at finding the limits of the apparently inexhaustible seas.

Starting in the eighteenth century, nations laid claim to their territorial waters, for a distance of three miles from the coast, which was then about the range that a shore battery could fire. In 1882 the North Sea Fisheries Convention – signed by France, Germany, Holland, Denmark and Britain – enshrined the first three-mile limits in international law. In 1945 President Harry Truman asserted authority over the continental shelf of the United States (mostly as a means of controlling mineral rights).

Latin America followed, and then Iceland paved the way by progressively enlarging its Economic Exclusion Zone (EEZ). Since 1994 a nation's sovereign right to natural resources within two hundred nautical miles of its coastline has been codified in the United Nations' Convention on the Law of the Sea. At three hundred million square miles, the EEZ of the United States is the largest in the world, roughly the size of the lower forty-eight states combined. Fully 90 per cent of the world's fishing grounds are now contained within two-hundred-mile limits.

The establishment of EEZs turned international commons into national commons, with all their potential for tragedy intact. In the commons of the Chesapeake, dividing the bay's waters between Virginia and Maryland, and eventually excluding the dredgers that had come from New England, slowed down the extraction of the oysters; but finally the sail powered skipjacks of local watermen, abetted by disease, proved up to the task of destroying the natural stock.

Around the world the most varied strategies – introducing quotas, limiting the kinds of gear and vessels allowed to fish, permitting only certain members of the community to fish and restricting the days on which they could fish – have been no better than dilatory tactics in the rush towards the collapse of fisheries. We are reaching the 'day of reckoning' predicted by Garrett Hardin in his seminal paper: the carrying capacity of too many ecosystems has been surpassed. We have got too good at catching fish, and tragedy is striking our global commons.

How then can the Chesapeake be saved, its waters restored to their erstwhile clarity by a healthy population of filter feeders? Since at least 1891, when zoologist William K. Brooks wrote a proleptic treatise called *The Oyster*, scientists have been coming to the same conclusion: oysters in the Chesapeake should be raised like crops, not hunted down like wild prey. Brooks recommended that Virginia and Maryland lease out the bay bottom to private entrepreneurs, who could then use the grounds to culture oysters.

The watermen of Maryland in particular were infuriated by the proposal, and their influential lobby group ensured that the north end of the bay has been free of oyster farms – and, tragically, oysters. The God-given right to plunder the commons, after all, was nothing to be trifled with.

Even when there was nothing left to plunder.

The Chesapeake Swamp

'I'll take it one step further,' Mark Luckenbach told me. 'I believe oyster aquaculture is the only game in town.'

We were in a lab on the Eastern Shore, the peninsula shared by Maryland and Virginia, in a tranquil Atlantic-facing village called Wachapreague. Luckenbach, the director of the Virginia Institute of Marine Science's lab, is an oyster specialist, and he has watched, with a somewhat jaundiced eye, public interest in oysters seesaw during his career. When a colleague's back-of-the-envelope calculation showing that a healthy oyster population had the potential to filter the entire bay in less than a week became well known, oyster restoration suddenly became the flavour-of-the-month among populist politicians. The Oyster Recovery Partnership has encouraged the raising of baby oysters in backwater creeks, using thousands of citizen volunteers to dump them overboard on depleted oyster bars.

'It seemed every backyard school group and NGO was growing oysters to clean up the bay,' recalled Luckenbach. 'I think oysters really got oversold that way.' But not a lot of the spat – the larval oysters attached to shells and other cultch – successfully took on the replanted bars, and those that did almost inevitably succumbed to disease in their third year.

Oysters, which have no immune systems, are particularly susceptible to environmental stresses; scientists look upon them as canaries in the oceanic coal mine. Public health officials have used oyster flesh to measure environmental levels of DDT and even radiation. In 1884 a German bacteriologist proved Louis Pasteur's germ theory of disease after demonstrating how an organism called *Vibrio cholerae*, found in the flesh of oysters in sewage-choked waters, could cause cholera in humans. In 1957 the protozoan parasite MSX was discovered in the southern reaches of the Chesapeake. Researchers now believe it arrived clinging to the hull of one of the eight hundred mothballed Second World War navy ships moored in the James River, which were brought out of retirement to ferry troops back and forth to Asia during the Korean War. MSX, though harmless to humans, is deadly to oysters. Absorbed through their gills, the parasite multiplies rapidly in their flesh, killing them before they can reach marketable maturity. A second pathogen, Dermo, probably native to the bay, gradually spread as the Chesapeake's salinity levels rose because of damming and drought. (Both parasites grow best in salty water.) Dermo, like malaria in humans, is a chronic disease: its host is not always killed outright, but progressively weakens and can die prematurely.

Dermo, Luckenbach explained, is now found in all of Virginia's oyster beds, and has started showing up in Maryland. Since all efforts to eradicate the parasite have failed, some scientists and legislators are campaigning to plant the bay with disease-free *Crassostrea ariakensis*, the Asian or Suminoe oyster, a hardy species with a taste similar to its native cousin. Starting anew with a foreign oyster is hardly an unprecedented move: most of the oysters raised in Europe and Washington State are *Crassostrea gigas*, the Pacific oyster, originally native to the coasts of Asia.

In a building overlooking coastal Atlantic marshland, Luckenbach showed me plastic tubs full of Suminoe oysters, quietly filtering plankton out of seawater. Congress, he explained, had mandated a study of the Suminoe oyster, and Luckenbach was charged with gauging its potential impact on the ecosystem.

'Most people are still looking for a simple answer to a complex problem. It does turn out the Suminoe has the same salinity tolerance as our native oyster, and it is highly tolerant of both the diseases we've got here.' The hope is that the Chesapeake's oyster industry, once the biggest in the country, can be revived by the simple expedient of introducing a new, non-native species. Luckenbach, though he was happy to do the research, said he would rather see more effort devoted to expanding and maintaining the bay's remaining bars of healthy native oysters. He explained that large-scale aquaculture has never really been attempted in the bay – for reasons more cultural and historic than ecological.

While the skipjack captains of Maryland were dredging for wild oysters under sail, Virginia developed a kind of feudal system of exploiting its wild stock. The oyster lords came from rich families with shorefront property; the state leased them salty sections of bay bottom, where the transplanted oysters tended to grow more quickly. The serfs were the watermen, who harvested seed oysters from wild bars for as little as $5 (less than £2.50) a bushel and sold them to the oyster lords, who owned shucking houses where mostly African-American women were employed to prepare the oysters for canning. (The legacy of feudalism persists in the Chesapeake to this day: until recently, skipjack captain Wade Murphy sold his catch to Ronnie Bevins, Maryland's main oyster buyer, who he referred to as 'the oyster king'.)

For Luckenbach, this system has never, strictly speaking, been farming: 'Virginia's industry would have liked to call that old fishery aquaculture, but it never increased the overall population of oysters in the bay. It was just a two-staged harvest.'

What's more, transplanting oysters to higher-salinity environments, where Dermo and MSX are most likely to be found, actually hastens the spread of the parasites, leading to the decline of oyster populations.

Luckenbach is proposing something that has never really been tried in the Chesapeake, and something to which its inhabitants, with their predilection for free plunder, are temperamentally opposed. He believes that if people really want to end harmful algae blooms, decrease the ever-spreading dead zones and revive the industry, hatcheries should be allowed to provide private entrepreneurs with oyster spat to encourage large-scale aquaculture.

'I'd like to see a very concerted effort,' Luckenbach told me, 'at restoring wild oyster populations in selected areas where we think we can be most successful. At the same time I'd like to see the expansion of environmentally sound native oyster aquaculture.' Luckenbach says this is already happening on the Atlantic shore of Virginia, where private companies are successfully raising shellfish. 'Thanks to aquaculture, there are more people working on the water, making more money, than there were a quarter of a century ago.' He showed me a photograph of an inlet filled with mesh bags containing cherrystone clams. 'Cherrystone Aquafarms employs three hundred people, and about half of what they do is a co-op, with ex-watermen leasing part of the operation to grow their own clams.'

He admitted that these operations are not without controversy. Shellfish farms mean boundary markers, generators, miles of netting and skiffs on the water. The last thing some city folk who retire to the Chesapeake want to see is an industrial operation wrecking their idyllic view of the water.

'When aquaculture is small,' Luckenbach pointed out, 'everybody likes it. But if it stays mom-and-pop scale, it won't last; to be competitive, it has to be large scale.' That is where the problems arise. In Washington State, for example, there are so many oysters being raised in racks and bags on Willapa Bay that they have added a layer of faeces to the sea floor, which then becomes infested with burrowing shrimp, whose tunnelling in turn stirs up sediment (and eventually causes the oyster racks to collapse into the muck). Yet oyster farming has far less impact than shrimp or salmon aquaculture: there is no need to net millions of tons of other species to grind into feed pellets, as the oysters feed themselves and in so doing clean the environment. The most vocal opposition tends to come from retirees from the city, whose 'not in my backyard' attitude apparently precludes the survival of the centuries-old watermen's communities.

'If we're going to make a decision to farm parts of this very populated bay,' Luckenbach said, 'we need to make that decision based on current demographics and ecology. We need to zone parts of the bay.'

And zoning, which would mean hiving off parts of the bay from popular exploitation, would be anathema to many of the Chesapeake's old-timers, who do not want anything interfering with a bay they see as a vast and enduring commons.

The alternative, sadly, is a bay of jellyfish and toxic algae, already on its way to becoming a swamp.

The Turncoat Waterman

'Look out the window,' Tommy Leggett said. We were sitting in the living room of his ranch-style home, looking towards the shores of Sedgers Creek, a tributary of the York River, which flows into the Virginia side of the Chesapeake. The scene framed by the picture window was lulling, bucolic: at the edge of a lawn a wooden pier zigzags into slowly flowing water edged by cord grass and salt-marsh bushes. I saw a twenty-four-foot skiff called the *Spatboat 1*, but no other signs of industry. 'My oyster nursery,' said Leggett, 'is right out there by my pier.'

Unless you looked hard, you would never guess that Leggett is growing one hundred thousand healthy specimens of *Crassostrea virginica*, the Chesapeake's native oyster, at the end of his dock.

Once upon a time Virginia-born Leggett, a vigorous, well-tanned man in his fifties, was a waterman. Throughout his career he potted for crab and eel, used patent tongs to haul up clams, and set gill nets to trap croakers and rockfish.

'When I was a commercial fisherman,' he explained, 'I kind of caught the tail end of all the fisheries. I've seen the crab fishery plummet, the clam fishery tank, and in the eighties I literally walked into the end of the oyster fishery.' He has seen creeks turn blood-red with algae blooms, and oxygen levels so low that two-thirds of local shellfish had died. He has also watched salinity levels rising, favouring the spread of MSX and Dermo, and the slow increase of water temperatures, which killed off the eelgrass that provided habitat for the very species he was trying to catch.

But Leggett is a new breed of waterman: one with a master's degree in marine science. When his chosen career became impossible to pursue, he was hired to do environmental education for the Chesapeake Bay Foundation, generally considered the most successful regional environmental group in the United States. (Their 'Save the Bay' stickers have adorned local bumpers since 1967.) As much as he values taking groups of school-children out on field trips to islands to show them how pristine the Chesapeake once was, his heart is now in the project he has been developing in his backyard: his oyster farm, six-tenths of an acre leased from the State of Virginia.

'Ever since I was in graduate school,' he said, 'I wanted to be in aquaculture. I wanted to grow things.' Outside we walked over the wooden planks of his pier, and Leggett used a hooked pole to lift a bag rattling with a thousand oysters. Opening the mesh, he pulled out a clump of shells, sending a half-dozen fingernail-size mud crabs and some slippery-sided naked gobies flipping back into the water. Bearded with algae, the oysters were about three inches long, already near market size.

Leggett has the harvesting down to a science: every week he goes down to the end of the dock, picks out about 1,200 of the biggest specimens, and sells them for 35 cents (16 pence) apiece to a buyer. (If he marketed them himself, he figures he could get twice that amount.) They are sold on the half-shell as York River oysters – 'the sweetest-tasting oysters around', according to Leggett – in expensive restaurants in Williamsburg and Richmond. He figures his oyster-farming revenue now equals his income from his full-time job at the Chesapeake Bay Foundation.

Leggett has no time for the old-school attitudes of such skipjack captains as Wade Murphy. As a working waterman, who once eked a living from the commons using the old techniques of the hunter-gatherer, his words have a certain amount of weight.

'In Maryland the watermen say they don't want any part of aquaculture; they want a reproducing population on the bottom to harvest in the old ways.' The state has built a £10 million hatchery to grow seed oysters for the scheme. 'They don't even know if that will work, and if it does, it could take decades.

'We aren't trying to save the bay just to look at it and take pretty pictures of it. We want to use it and enjoy it. A healthy bay is a bay with people swimming and boating, and recreational fishermen fishing, and watermen fishing sustainably. This is as much a national treasure as the Everglades or the Great Lakes, and we need to convince Congress of that. Our administrators need to come to grips with the fact that they have to start pouring money into bay clean-up.' The process, he said, should begin with official support for oyster aquaculture.

Leggett told me he has even become evangelical about the cause, convincing a friend to give oyster farming a try.

'He's a lifelong oysterman, a diehard shaft-tonger. But now we've got him set up with tanks and pumps, and he's expecting his first big batch in a few months. The more he's gotten into it, the more gung-ho he is; it's like he's seen the light. I've just turned him loose, and now he's straight-driving by himself.

'Oysters won't save the bay all by themselves,' Leggett conceded. 'But you're not going to save the bay *without* oysters. They are a keystone species, one of the bay's natural filters. They cleanse the water, and the bars provide habitat for other species. But we also need to see sewage plant upgrades, more shoreline buffer zones, and encourage farmers to farm with less nitrogen and phosphorus run-off.' Development must be limited too; Leggett raged over a recent attempt, narrowly defeated after a grassroots campaign, to build a thousand homes on crucial wetlands close to the resort town of Virginia Beach. 'And you just *know* they are going to try it again.'

Leggett, that hunter turned steward of the commons, carefully lowered the mesh bag back into the water.

'Look at them down there,' he said, giving a last fond glance as he returned his farm-raised American oysters to the creek bottom. 'They're just pumping away, filtering their little hearts out.'

'As Long as It Is Oyster'

M. F. K. Fisher, America's 'poet of the appetites', was hardly a snob when it came to food. In *Consider the Oyster*, her charming tribute to the bivalve, she considers oyster gastronomy from all angles, including recipes for baked oysters, stewed oysters, oysters in gumbo, oyster stuffing for turkey and even one that begins: 'Take 300 clean oysters and throw into a pot filled with nice butter . . .' Yet when it comes to oysters as they are eaten in the Chesapeake, Fisher is scathing. It is unfortunate, she wrote, that so 'many chefs dip their oysters in a thick and often infamous batter, which at once plunged into the equally obscene grease, forms an envelope of such slippery toughness that the oyster within it lies helpless and steaming in a foul blanket, tasteless and yet powerfully indigestible.'

At Harrison's Chesapeake House, battered and fried is the only way they serve their oysters – or, for that matter, their clam strips or soft crabs. The Harrisons still own a shucking house, on the island side of Knapps Narrows, just next to the drawbridge that links Tilghman Island to the mainland. The walls of the sprawling waterfront restaurant are filled with newspaper articles about four generations of Harrisons, celebrity testimonials and the inevitable shot of that enthusiastic eater, Bill Clinton, posing alongside Captain Buddy. My dinner came with buttery mashed potatoes, buttery green beans and sweet stewed tomatoes.

'It's a southern thing,' drawled the waitress, when I asked about the latter. The clam strips arrived lightly battered, like dozens of meandering french fries.

Though I prefer my oysters raw, I am willing to try anything once. In fact, the more I knew about the diseases carried by oysters, the more I agree with Captain Wade Murphy that cooking them may be the best policy. Statistically, you have about a one in one hundred chance of falling ill from a mild enteric virus when eating raw shellfish in the United States. (The worst pathogen is *Vibrio vulnificus*, which alone causes 95 per cent of seafood-related deaths in the United States. In a typical case, a middle-aged accountant ordered a dozen oysters on the half shell for a midsummer lunch at a Dallas seafood restaurant. By midnight, he was throwing up in a hotel toilet, between bouts of fever-induced cold sweats. The next morning, his legs were aching and covered with huge pus-filled blisters. When the bacteria spread to his lungs, liver and brain, he went into septic shock. In spite of massive doses of antibiotics, he died five days later.) Oysters from the cold North Atlantic are clearly a better bet than anything from the Gulf of Mexico, and global warming means the line of danger is creeping ever northwards. For me, Tilghman Island in the month of May, at 38 degrees north of the equator and 24 degrees on the Celsius scale, is right on the borderline of the permissible. I was rather relieved that my oysters arrived the way they did: not on the half shell but as convoluted lumps of protein, dusted with flour and spices – the latter probably a liberal shake of celery salt, mustard, cloves and whatever else can be found in a can of Old Bay Seasoning – and fried, literally, to death.

These Chesapeake oysters were not subtle – no muscadet could have handled the onslaught of salt and fat, so I opted for a Budweiser – but they were delicious in their way, chewy and complex beneath all that coating. They were served on a soft bun, with tartar sauce on the side.

'There are three kinds of oyster-eaters,' wrote M. F. K. Fisher. 'Those who will eat them raw and only raw; and those who with equal severity will eat them cooked and no other way.' I am clearly among those she put in the third group of adventurous, if hardly fastidious, omnivores: 'Those loose-minded sports who will eat anything, hot, cold, thin, thick, dead or alive, as long as it is *oyster*.'

Given the world of good that oysters can do for the oceans of the world, perhaps we should all aspire to membership of that third group. A diet that includes oysters, after all, is a diet that helps rid the world's estuaries of algae blooms and dead zones, while encouraging one of the most sustainable forms of aquaculture around – as well as the continued existence of shoreside communities founded by the watermen of the Chesapeake.

I decided to adopt a new dietary motto. Come to think of it, in the regal, semifeudal world of oyster, it would make a heraldic slogan fit for a shellfish baron's coat of arms.

Quidlibet, dummodo ostrea sit, or 'Anything, as long as it is oyster.'

The Raw Truth

It may be the hoariest cliché in all of gastronomy. 'It is unseasonable and unwholesome,' William Butler, a contemporary of Shakespeare, reminded his readers as far back as 1599, 'in all months that have not R in their name to eat oysters.' The Japanese put it more bluntly: not even dogs, they say, will eat summer clams.

Yet here it was the middle of an R-free July – in the midst of a pan-European heatwave – and I was about to eat my way from Paris to the coast of Brittany, leaving behind a trail of oyster shells.

I first learned to eat oysters when I was living in France in my twenties; a girlfriend's father took me aside in his kitchen one Christmas Eve and, putting a towel in my left palm to prevent hand-gouging, set me to work shucking a gross of them. This was in Brittany, that Gaelic, rather than Gallic, barnacle attached to the west of France – where sailors from Saint-Brieuc used to understand the Welsh spoken by fishermen they met in the Channel – and the Bretons were known for priding themselves on their oyster connoisseurship. Everybody knew the best were the Belons, the flat-shelled beauties you saw piled outside the seafood palaces on Boulevard Montparnasse in Paris. I earned my Breton hosts' respect that year when I shucked my share and then downed two dozen, staining neither kitchen nor bathroom with blood nor vomit. The Belons were like nothing I had ever tasted: a mouthful of salty ocean (literally: oysters are one of the few kinds of food that carry a portion of their original environment with them), followed by a taste sometimes metallic, sometimes nutty. My girlfriend's father insisted the flavour was hazelnut, and since then, hazelnut has been what I taste when I chew a Belon. Eating them was clearly a feat. They made me feel virtuous and lubricious at the same time. Since then the Belon has been the king of oysters for me. Cooking one, *à la* Rockefeller, is inconceivable.

Once upon a time the Belon, or *Ostrea edulis*, was Europe's only oyster. Vast natural banks of them arced from Denmark to Portugal. (Europe's most famous oysters, including English Whitstables, Dutch Zeelands and Belgian Ostends, are regional manifestations of this single species.) The Romans doted on them, consuming vast quantities: Seneca was said to eat one hundred dozen a week, Apicius recommended them with a mayonnaise of fermented fish guts and Nero claimed he could identify the provenance of an oyster from a single slurp. The Romans set up an express relay service that carted the oysters of England and France over the Alps, from ice house to ice house. The habits of antiquity survived through the Middle Ages: Henry IV was said to eat three hundred as an appetizer, Rousseau and Diderot downed them for inspiration and Napoleon swallowed a gross to strengthen his resolve before battle.

In a familiar narrative, a resource thought to be inexhaustible soon reached its limits. As early as 1755 the natural banks off Tréguier on the north coast of Brittany were so overfished that the king banned exploitation for six years. Two years before the French Revolution, a royal edict prohibited oyster fishing in Brittany on state-owned banks during the summer months, when oysters were spawning. (This strategy for sparing the broodstock may be the real origin of the R-month ban, rather than any increased risk of disease.) With the coming of the industrial age, the population truly crashed: UK consumption dropped from 1.5 billion oysters a year to 40 million by 1886, and the Channel Island fleet went from four hundred vessels to a few part-time oystermen. Technology hastened the decline: in France, critics dubbed the newly invented dredge 'the oyster guillotine', and a Prussian savant attributed the decline to the coming of the railway, which facilitated shipment to the bistros and bars of European capitals.

It was a foreign invasion that truly ended the reign of the Belons. In 1868 a ship waylaid by a storm was ordered to dump its entire cargo of stinking Portuguese oysters into the mouth of the Gironde River. Some were evidently still alive, and they quickly spread along the French coast. When disease attacked the native Belons, the Portuguese oysters began to thrive. Starting in the late 1960s, the Portuguese oysters were in turn wiped out by two parasites, bonamiosis and marteilia. They were saved, like phylloxera-afflicted grapes in France, by a transplant from the new world: *Crassostrea gigas*, the same oyster grown in Washington State. Ninety per cent of the oysters now eaten in the world belong to this one species (known as *creuse* in France). The once-ubiquitous Belons are now limited to a few oyster farms in Brittany and the UK. Yet they remain the most prized of all oysters, selling for up to €6 (£4) apiece in Paris's best restaurants.

If I was going to risk my life by eating summer oysters, I definitely needed to consult an expert. For dinner, I went to L'Ecailler du Bistrot, a seafood restaurant in Paris's Bastille neighbourhood, where I could be sure of getting a dozen of France's best Belons.

Gwénaëlle Cadoret, the bistro's co-owner, belongs to a family that has been raising oysters in Brittany since 1864, and she gave me a quick refresher course in raw oyster connoisseurship. The plate arrived: a dozen Belons on the half-shell, nestled in a bed of deep-green seaweed, served with rye bread and a dish of half-salted butter. I had forgotten how elegant they could be:

flat-topped when viewed from the side, almost circular when seen from above, the *plates* were far more streamlined and clam-like than the chunky, misshapen *creuses*.

'We never put our oysters on a bed of ice,' said Cadoret. 'We believe that if they get too cold, you can't taste all the flavours.' When she opened an oyster – with a quick flick of a sharp knife across the adductor muscle – a thin liquid oozed out; Cadoret explained that this 'first water', and sometimes the second, should be tossed aside. She prefers to see her clients eating the oysters with, at most, a squeeze of lemon. (Some consider even this a form of sacrilege, pointing out that the addition of lemon juice is simply the legacy of the oystermonger's technique for showing that oysters, which tend to flinch when molested with citric acid, are still alive.) 'If somebody insists on shallots in a vinaigrette sauce, it is possible that we'll allow it. But it is highly discouraged.'

My French companion, never impressed by protocol, shrugged and shook some black pepper on her oysters. We chewed before swallowing: every French person seems to know that if you do not administer the dental *coup de grâce*, the living oyster will excrete substances that make digestion a struggle. My friend lingered over the chewy adductor, the muscle responsible for keeping the shell closed. 'For me,' she said, 'that's the only part that tastes like hazelnut!' (When we eat scallops, by the way, we are actually eating their overgrown adductor muscles.) Washed down with muscadet, the dozen disappeared too quickly. We ordered another.

When our hostess returned to check on our progress, I asked her whether she served the notorious 'four-season' oysters. (Scientists have lately developed sterile oysters known as triploids, which, because they waste no energy on reproduction, also fail to turn milky and flabby with sperm and eggs in the summer months.) Cadoret visibly cringed. It was as if I had exhaled garlicky pesto on a vampire.

'I will not let a single triploid through the door of my restaurant!' she cried. The French horror of genetic modification apparently extends to oysters.

Having noticed her ample belly, I asked her if she ate oysters in the summer.

'*Monsieur*, I am seven months pregnant, and I still eat them systematically.'

That was all I wanted to hear: if an expectant mother, well into her third trimester, could eat oysters in July, I was going to do the same. The next morning, I was on the *autoroute* in a rented car, heading for Brittany, where I had first learned to love oysters.

The Oyster Mafia

The oyster aquaculture finally being attempted by a few pioneers in the Chesapeake has been practised for at least two millennia in Europe. The Greeks scattered pieces of amphorae in the Aegean, providing breeding surfaces to which the spats could attach themselves; and a first-century BC Roman, Sergius Orata, perfected oyster aquaculture in brackish lakes near Naples. Orata used bundles of twigs to attract the spat; much like the mesh bags I saw Tommy Leggett using in Virginia, the twigs could be lifted from the water to pick out those oysters that were restaurant-ready. (Orata, apparently a bit of a marketing genius, even launched a fad for farmed, oyster-fed sea bream.)

In France the nineteenth-century decline of the wild catch led to a revival of Orata's techniques. Oysters are a bit like wine: just as the same variety of grape can take on different flavours according to the geological and climatic conditions of the patch of land on which it is raised, different stretches of seacoast can impart radically different flavours to the same species of oyster. (Perhaps we should talk of *meroir*, rather than *terroir*.) Marennes, for example, are famous for the greenish hue imbued by the blue navicule, a kind of algae found in the Bay of Arcachon on the French Atlantic coast.

In spite of the decades of disease that wiped out flat oysters elsewhere, the Belon has survived in its birthplace on the south coast of Brittany. At the confluence of the Aven and the Bélon rivers, the Port de Bélon is its own microscopic kingdom. Four oyster cultivators remain, raising *Ostrea edulis* where the rivers and the ocean meet. During an idyllic week of oyster-gobbling and muscadet-sipping, I would get to know all of them. This was the world not of fishing but of farming, where disputes were born of generations of living cheek by jowl, rather than the fishermen's rivalry over which boat was getting the greatest share of the sea's bounty.

I visited the factory run by the Cadoret family; I had already enjoyed their oysters in Paris. White-haired women on an assembly line nimbly sorted Belons, packing them in wooden crates for shipment across Europe. Owner Jacques Cadoret, Gwénaëlle's brother, explained that his oysters are initially raised in another part of Brittany, then allowed to soak in the Bélon, in order to absorb the river's unique flavours. He complained of poachers, particularly active around Christmastime, who made off with truckloads of oysters by moonlight, and how a nearby campground had contaminated his winkle ponds when fuel oil spilled from a cistern. I visited an even bigger oyster farm, Thaëron, which supplies supermarkets across Europe; and the tiny shorefront oyster farm called Anne de Bélon, run by a young blond woman with the bluest of eyes. She pointed to the tourists' pleasure boats next to her racks of oysters, which I could see marinating in the mouth of the Aven. She hinted that the untreated sewage they discharged into the river's waters was harming her oysters.

Among the oyster farmers, accusations flew back and forth. I was told that one of these companies was operating the fraud of the century, bringing in oysters from other countries and shipping them out again before they had spent a single minute in the Bélon River. There was muttering of a shadowy 'oyster mafia', death threats and sabotage. It all sounded twisted, medieval – like a Marcel Pagnol saga of envy and petty feuds among the farmers of Provence.

One afternoon a woman whose children were prising tiny starfish off the rocks at the beach at Port-Manech cautioned me to stay away from the local mussels. The Institut français de recherches pour l'exploitation de la mer (IFREMER), the equivalent of the United Kingdom's Marine and Fisheries Agency, had warned that increased ocean temperatures had led to a bloom of dinophysis, a toxic organism that makes the flesh of shellfish inedible. Local restaurateurs were not advertising the fact, but, because of the bloom, the so-called Belons they were selling actually had to be imported from the north of Brittany. A biologist at IFREMER explained to me the algae bloom only occurs in the summer, and rarely lasts more than a few weeks. Global warming had not spared the Breton coast, she said; they were monitoring the situation to see if rising water temperatures were endangering the harvest. She was more concerned about Arcachon Bay, a sheltered notch in the Atlantic coast south of the Loire. Most French oysters were raised in the Arcachon, and its waters were increasingly polluted. (In fact, after my visit, France's first recorded deaths from oyster consumption happened when two women ate contaminated Arcachon oysters.)

Outside the Château de Bélon one afternoon, I sat at a picnic table overlooking the sailboats in the Bélon River, gobbling yet another dozen oysters. The teenager who opened them for me, laying out a quarter of a lemon and a glass of muscadet, admitted they were not local, but came from the owner's park, near Plougastel, on the western tip of Brittany, sixty miles away.

Just as I finished off the last of them, the owner arrived, a middle-aged man with pale blue eyes and a full head of brown hair. I was in luck. I had chanced upon François de Solminihac, the descendant of the erstwhile lords of Bélon. I had been eating my oysters, he explained, next to the family's manorhouse, which was made with white stone from the Loire; its kitchen dated to the fourteenth century. De Solminihac said he had half an hour to spare for an errant writer. First, however, he had to pay a visit to his oysters.

Following him down to the waterfront, I watched him strip to his trunks, don flippers and a snorkel mask, and swim a few yards out to his racks of oysters, which were completely covered by the high tide. 'The water is seventeen degrees Celsius today!' he burbled from the water. 'And the salinity here is about fifteen milligrams per litre, much less than seawater, which is thirty-five milligrams. It's the salinity that gives the oysters their flavour!' Emerging from the water, he bade me follow him into a stone toolshed, where he responded to all my questions while standing unselfconsciously naked. (He explained that it is healthier to let the breeze dry one off after swimming.) It was one of the stranger interviews I have ever done.

'It was my great-grandfather, Auguste de Solminihac, who created oyster aquaculture in Riec-sur-Bélon,' de Solminihac explained. 'Already, before the Revolution, there was a natural bank of oysters here, and it was a tradition to send them to Paris packed in barrels with straw all around them. Our ancestors even sent oysters to such celebrated gourmets as Talleyrand.

'Our family, which was originally from Bordeaux but had spent time in India, of course lost their title during the Revolution. My great-grandfather became something of a gentleman farmer. Like many noble families at the time, he wanted to create something modern. So he began to work with a researcher from the Collège de France, called Victor Costes.' Costes is celebrated as the father of oyster aquaculture in France; under Napoleon

III he cultured the first oysters in the north of Brittany. 'Costes learned that they used to raise oysters on bundles of twigs in the Bay of Naples. My great-grandfather collaborated with this Monsieur Costes, and after ten or fifteen years of experiments, in 1864 they opened the first real oyster farm. At around the same time the first trains arrived, which contributed to the farm's huge success.'

Finally pulling on loose linen pants, de Solminihac took me on a tour of the property, showing off ancestral fig trees imported from the tropics, ornate hand-painted murals in the hallways of the mansion and a natural spring hidden away at the back of the property. 'The water here is very rich in iron,' he said. 'That's what gives it the taste that is often described as hazelnut. Unlike some of the other establishments here' – he pointedly glared in the direction of a rival oyster farm – 'we do a long-term *affinage* in the river – for at least three fortnightly tidal cycles.' In other words, he let the oysters mature in the river for six weeks. 'Unlike some other places, I tell people right away when there's a problem like dinophysis. Though it is only likely to last for a few weeks.'

De Solminihac spoke darkly about an oceanfront restaurant next to his oyster farm, which he accused of selling so-called Belons that had never actually bathed in the local water. 'We believe that an oyster has the right to be called a Belon only if it has lived in the Bélon River.

'That restaurant has no right to be there,' he boomed, warming to the subject. 'When I opened my rustic oyster-tasting spot' – three tree-shaded plastic tables next to the manor – 'I received constant death threats. It's terrible, they are like the Mafia in Italy.' He sighed. 'But that's the way it is in France.'

As I bade adieu to the lord of the oysters, I had to suppress a chuckle. I did not take de Solminihac's complaints too seriously. Ever since the days of the Roman Sergius Orata, oyster farming has provoked conflict and jealousy. Orata's oyster beds eventually took up so much room in the lakes near Naples that he was sued by wealthy bathers. (They opined that if given the opportunity, Orata would even grow oysters on the tiles of his bath houses.) The bickering in Brittany – the allegations of fraud; the stories of poaching; the turf wars – sounded like an age-old narrative. It came with the territory. Every Belon I tasted was delicious. I was just happy to see the oysters out there in the water, pumping, as Tommy Leggett on the other side of the Atlantic had put it, their little hearts out.

For I had seen what a place *without* oysters looked like, and it was not pretty. Chesapeake Bay, a commons subjected to long-term plunder, is a corrupted ecosystem, and until attitudes there change from free-for-all to forward-looking stewardship, the algae blooms will spread, the dead zones will get bigger and the 'jubilees' of crabs fleeing water that is as dead as the surface of the moon will only get bigger.

It set the spat of an idea growing in my mind, like an oyster maturing in the Bélon River. As we now protect parts of the land in national parks, a solution to the crisis in the oceans might involve protecting them from their long history of free plunder by hunter-gatherers.

3

ENGLAND –

FISH AND CHIPS

Panic at the Chippy

'Spank it a couple of times, luv. You've got to be firm,' the counterman at the Rock & Sole Plaice advised a customer with a wink. The pretty Asian woman in the queue laughed and slapped the bottle again. A thick blob of tartar sauce splattered over her plate of cod and chips.

It was Friday night at the little fish-and-chip shop, located in a side street not far from London's Covent Garden. Outside, customers sat on wooden benches, beneath the branches of a tree hung with potted flowers, using plastic cutlery to disassemble their deep-fried fillets of haddock and lemon sole, wings of skate and battered fillets of rock salmon. Inside, co-owner Ahmet, dressed in a yellow polo shirt, coped with the early summer heatwave by mopping his shaved head and keeping up a steady line of banter.

'Don't be shy,' he told an inquisitive visitor from Canada. 'It's not like I'm giving away any trade secrets. We buy all our cod fresh. It's Icelandic. The Icelanders had the bright idea of giving their stock a rest for a little while, and they say it's coming back.

'These days I pay about three pounds a pound for my cod,' Ahmet continued, dipping a wire basket of chips into a bath of bubbling peanut oil. 'That's twice the wholesale price of prime fillet. But you'll pay fifteen pounds for a steak in a restaurant; we only charge eight for our cod and chips. And some people still think cod is pauper's food!

'We buy fish that weigh about five pounds. The flesh can't be cloudy; when you run your finger along the fillet, it can't break down into segments. The best stuff is opaque and firm. If the quality's not good enough that day, we just won't put it on the menu.' Their fish really did look excellent. Once the thick armour of yellow-gold batter had been pierced, the shockingly white cod fell apart in delicate petals, like salmon steamed in its own vapour in a crust of salt.

Though Ahmet's father, Hassan Ziyaeddin – a Cypriot of Turkish descent – has been running the Rock & Sole Plaice only since 1980, a sign outside claims it is London's oldest fish-and-chip shop; people have apparently been lining up for 'Traditional English Fish & Chips' at this location since 1871. For some, the Ziyaeddins' ownership is symbolic of the times – yet another British business taken over by immigrants in a transformed postcolonial Britain. After all, nothing is more British than fish and chips. Winston Churchill dubbed them 'the good companions', and exempted the dish from rationing during the Second World War. George Orwell considered them first among the post-war comforts that kept the proles in their place. 'It is quite likely,' he wrote in *The Road to Wigan Pier*, 'that fish and chips, art-silk stockings, tinned salmon, cut-price chocolate, . . . the radio, strong tea and the Football Pools have between them averted revolution.' More recently, London critic A. A. Gill has opined in *The Sunday Times* that fish and chips is a 'totem of Englishness, a thing that is more than mere dinner and rather less than actual food'. There is no better gauge of the dish's authenticity, he suggests, than foreigners' distaste for it: 'Battered fish leaves Continentals cod-eyed with repulsion.'

In truth, 'Continentals' invented the dish. In the seventeenth century, Sephardic Jews brought their *pescado frito*, fried fish, to Holland and England carried east by Portuguese missionaries, the same dish would become Japanese tempura. Jewish merchants in Soho were the first to combine chipped potatoes with fried fish, and it is generally agreed that one Joseph Malin opened the prototypical fish-and-chip shop in London's Old Ford Road in the 1860s. Tuscan immigrants brought the first such establishments to Scotland, and a wave of post-war Italian immigration introduced the 'fish supper' to Ireland. Pioneered by East End Jews, developed by Cypriots, South Asians and Chinese, fish and chips is, in its way, as quintessentially British as mulligatawny soup, tandoori pizza and chicken tikka masala.

Given the UK's recent culinary renaissance, which has seen London chefs win the respect of Michelin's most sceptical *inspecteurs*, it is easy to forget that the local 'chippy' is still where most people in the UK get their fish. Throughout the United Kingdom, 11,500 of these establishments sell a quarter of a billion servings of fish and chips every year. Chippies are so ubiquitous, and the regional variations so precise, that a modern-day Henry Higgins could pick out the provenance of a chip-loving Eliza Doolittle by the terminology she used when ordering a meal. In Edinburgh, for example, they favour 'chip-shop sauce', a kind of steak sauce; but fifty miles away in Glasgow they prefer salt and malt vinegar (or, in the cheaper venues, a solution of acetic acid and water with a little caramel to add colour). In Yorkshire, they sell 'scallops' – not the shellfish, but slices of battered and deep-fried potatoes (also known as 'smacks' and 'slaps') – as well as the 'fishcake', a piece of haddock between two potato slices, also battered and fried. The aliases for 'scraps' are infinite, and, to speakers of North

American English, comical: depending on where you are, these leftover bits of batter, usually given away for free, might be called 'scrumps', 'scrobblings', 'crimps' or even 'shoddy'. The Welsh eat 'faggots' (a meatball of pork and liver), and Lancastrians enjoy something called 'rag pudding', which is minced meat wrapped in suet pastry and boiled in a rag. But fish has always enjoyed pride of place at the chippy. Though in Ireland they eat ray wings and rock salmon (a commercial euphemism for the sharklike, and severely overfished, dogfish), and in northern England and Scotland they favour haddock, for the majority of Britons the 'fish' in fish and chips can only be cod.

The Atlantic cod, *Gadus morhua*, is perhaps the archetypal ocean species: smooth-sided and multifinned, it is classically fish-shaped, with plump, fleshy flanks and a Vandyke-like barbel dangling from its lower jaw that adds a touch of distinction. It is known both for its voraciousness – an adult cod will gobble Styrofoam, lead fishing weights and its own babies indiscriminately – and its fecundity: a single thirty-five-pound female was once recorded laying nine million eggs. When John Cabot returned from his 1497 transatlantic expedition, he reported to the merchants of Bristol, who had been hoping to find a short-cut to China, the presence of vast shoals of cod, so abundant they 'sometimes stayed the ships', and could be scooped up with weighted baskets. New expeditions were quickly sent to this 'New Found Land', and the western ports of England built distant-water fleets to bring cod back from the Grand Banks. Thus began the British love affair with the fish that eventually funded the Caribbean slave trade and helped build Boston, Halifax and St. John's.

Cod is the ideal food fish: easy to catch (even six-foot-long specimens put up no fight when hooked), its flesh is only 3 per cent fat, which means it can be split, salted and wind-dried in huge sheets which keep for months. A good piece of salted cod – known in Spanish as *bacalao* – is almost 80 per cent protein.

Even today, cod, a fish whose bland white flesh rarely tastes fishy, is by far Britain's most popular species. Almost a quarter of all the seafood sold in the United Kingdom is cod, and Britons consume one-third of the worldwide catch of 900,000 tonnes. Frozen fish fingers, introduced by Birds Eye in 1955 as 'a new, delicious way to buy fish, which takes the time, trouble and smell out of preparing our favourite foods', are the form most cod ends up in: fully 69 per cent of cod in retail shops is now sold previously breaded.

With that said, compared to North America, Britain is a paradise for any seafood lover committed to eating ethically. In the aisles of such leading supermarkets as Marks & Spencer, Asda and Waitrose, labels indicate a fish's place of origin and whether it was farmed or wild-caught. Organic salmon, typically twice as expensive as regular farmed salmon, is widely available. Such celebrity chefs as Rick Stein actively promote recipes for usually discarded species like gurnard and sculpin. The blue and white logo of the Marine Stewardship Council (MSC), indicating that the monkfish, mackerel or haddock in question came from sustainable stocks, can be found at the wet-fish counters of Asda, Tesco and Waitrose.

Sainsbury's, Britain's biggest fishmonger with three hundred counters, recently announced it was dropping overfished skate and dogfish, and selling line-caught, rather than trawled, haddock. Meanwhile, Marks & Spencer have embarked on a programme called 'Plan A', which will see the chain becoming carbon neutral, sending no waste to landfills, and sourcing all its seafood from MSC-certified stocks by 2012. Even Asda, long ranked the least environmentally responsible chain, in 2006 announced it would follow parent company Wal-Mart in buying only MSC-certified seafood (encouraged, no doubt, by a Greenpeace campaign of Asda-style billboards showing photos of mutilated bycatch). On the television, sophisticated ads feature food journalists decrying the dangers of aquaculture. 'We only use wild Pacific salmon,' boasted the frozen food company Birds Eye in one ad. 'No colourants.'

Yet Atlantic cod seems to be everywhere, sold without excuse or explanation, from the shelves of the greenest grocer in Notting Hill to the menus of the most down-to-earth chippy in Brick Lane. When it comes to its addiction to its favourite fish, Britain is apparently a land in denial.

In Canada, I followed the drama of the northern cod collapse when it unfolded in the early 1990s: government scientists, bowing to social and political pressure, set quotas that allowed the world's greatest food fishery to collapse. Overnight forty thousand fishermen in five provinces were put out of work. The resulting diaspora, a potato famine writ small, gutted the economy of Newfoundland, put working families on the welfare rolls, and eventually sent fourth-generation fishermen to the oil fields of Alberta. All told, the crisis cost the nation the equivalent of £850 million.

It looked to me as though the same storyline was being played out on this side of the Atlantic. The difference was that European scientists knew something was wrong, and had been sounding the alarm for years. This time, it was the politicians and the public who were not paying attention.

From Cod to Plankton

What happened to the cod of Newfoundland, and why aren't they coming back?

As mysteries go, it is a good one. Some people will tell you the plankton upon which the cod ultimately depended drifted away. Others think the hole in the ozone increased the amount of ultraviolet light penetrating the ocean's surface, killing off fragile larvae. Many fishermen believe it was the seals and other marine mammals that took all the cod. (And if not them, the bloody Spaniards.) There seems to be as many explanations for the collapse of the cod, and their failure to return, as there are popular accounts of who built Stonehenge.

The answer turns out to be much simpler.

For most of human history, our relationship with the sea has been predicated on the erroneous belief that, even if we wanted to, we could never make a dent in fish populations. If one species was temporarily overfished, the thinking went, another would take its place: nature, after all, abhorred a vacuum. In 1883 the British scientific philosopher Thomas Huxley, writing in a time of 'cod mountains' and endlessly self-renewing salmon rivers, could confidently claim: 'I still believe the cod fishery . . . and probably all the great fisheries are inexhaustible; that is to say that nothing we do seriously affects the number of fish.' As leader of a commission on the state of the fisheries, he advised Parliament to ban all legislation governing fishermen, thereafter allowing 'unrestricted freedom of fishing'.

It took a little over a century to show how gravely mistaken Huxley was. By the end of the millennium, fully *two-thirds* of major fish stocks in Europe were considered overfished, and some estimates put fish populations at only 5 per cent of their historic levels. In the United States, 56 of 287 economically important fish populations are considered overfished. Some of the world's most reliable sources of protein have undergone catastrophic collapses, among them the California sardine fishery in the 1950s, the Peruvian anchoveta in the 1970s and Newfoundland cod in the 1990s. Though fishing effort has increased, and more gallons of fuel are being used to go farther out to sea, fewer fish than ever are being caught. We now know that worldwide, total catches peaked at 78 million tonnes in 1988, and have been declining by about half a million tonnes a year ever since.

The best fisheries scientists in the world, often in the employ of national governments, presided over this decline using a mathematical tool called maximum sustainable yield (MSY). The theory is that a population is most productive when it is reduced to half its pristine, unfished level. As counterintuitive as it sounds, MSY often worked: when a stock was aggressively fished, newly hatched fish, with fewer brothers and sisters to compete with, tend to grow to maturity more quickly. But the scientists who relied on MSY failed to take into account the complexity of food chains and ecosystems: a decline in the abundance of one species can have a catastrophic impact on the fish that eat them.

Nor did they take into account the increased efficiency of the world's fishing fleets after the Second World War. Fishermen were not, it turned out, strictly limiting themselves to 50 per cent of the stock. In fact, North Atlantic fishermen were taking at least 10, and sometimes 30, per cent too much cod every year. The cod collapse of 1992 may have taken everyone by surprise, but the bankruptcy was inevitable. It was as though fishermen were removing 60–80 per cent of the capital from their savings accounts every year and still hoping to keep a healthy bank balance.

How could a fisherman in Newfoundland, whose grandfather built the family home with cod profits, and who had no reason to believe his own grandson would not inherit his boat and keep up the family trade, hunt the species that provided his livelihood to near extinction? The explanation lies in something called the shifting baselines syndrome. The term refers to the very human tendency to take the ecosystem as one first encounters it as the baseline for a pristine environment. A fisherman who started in the 1970s, for example, may have dismissed his grandfather's tales of man-sized fish as the usual hyperbole of old-timers, and barely noticed the slight decline in cod catches from year to year. Had he come to the Newfoundland coast with John Cabot, though, when huge cod could be pulled from the water with buckets, his baseline definition of pristine would have been quite different. Incrementally, over the course of many lifetimes, the baseline shifts without anybody noticing, and natural abundance is gradually whittled away to zero. Thanks to the shifting baselines syndrome, the utter collapse of a fishery can happen before the eyes of well-meaning fishermen who always intended to leave their children with an ample supply of fish.

In 1968 two thousand boats were catching 810,000 tonnes of cod a year off Newfoundland. It was an 'Olympic' fishery: the boats of a dozen nations gathered off the Grand Banks and competed against one another with ever-improving technology: diesel motors with stern trawls, sophisticated echo-sounders and eventually global positioning systems and satellite imaging. The Canadian Department of Fisheries and Oceans first set quotas in 1974, allowing its own fishermen to take half the stock a year. Two-hundred-mile-limits excluding foreign vessels were instituted around Canada and the United States in 1977, but Spanish and Portuguese boats continued to fish just beyond the line, yearly taking a quarter of the stock. (The Spanish were infamous for their pair-trawling, in which two boats worked together to drag gargantuan, ocean-clearing nets.) When catches began to decline in the late 1980s, the scientists blamed natural cycles of abundance rather than overfishing; the same thing had happened in 1868, after all, and the cod had bounced back. This time it was different. By 1992, the year fisheries minister John Crosbie announced a two-year moratorium, there were a mere 22,000 tonnes of cod left. Scientists now believe that, when John Cabot first came to Canada, there may have been seven *million* tonnes of cod off the Canadian coast.

A decade and a half later, the cod show no signs of returning. Though the new fisheries for snow crab and shrimp are now more lucrative than the cod fishery ever was, they have not benefited Newfoundland's traditional fishing culture; because of consolidation, the quotas are now in the hands of a few big companies, rather than independent fishermen. Many of the island's far-flung outports, which were kept alive only by a guaranteed biomass of bottom-feeder, are now near-ghost towns, sustained by kayaking backpackers and day-tripping tourists.

In spite of the moratorium, pressure from Newfoundland fishermen to keep working has been so intense that the government periodically announces small quotas; the catch is generally so pitiful fishermen never come close to filling them. In 2003, the Canadian government officially declared northern cod an endangered species. It took five hundred years, but the world's greatest fishery has disappeared, probably for ever.

For Daniel Pauly, a fisheries scientist at the University of British Columbia, the cod collapse is no mystery. It was not caused by seals, global warming, or the hole in the ozone. Though overseen by scientists and bureaucrats, the collapse was ultimately caused by fishermen – and mainly Canadian fishermen at that.

Before leaving for Europe, I had met Pauly in his office on the Vancouver campus, where he runs the world-renowned Fisheries Centre. A tall, broad-shouldered man born in Paris to a French mother and an African-American father, Pauly is an impressive presence. A speaker, at various times, of German, Swahili, Indonesian and Spanish, he is famous for his abrupt declarations, delivered in rapid-fire, European-accented English. Working in Southeast Asia, he devised simple methods that allow local scientists to track the decline of tropical fish catches using handheld calculators. He went on to launch FishBase, a huge Internet database that documents thirty thousand different fish species, and the Sea Around Us Project, which provides an ocean-by-ocean picture of the decline of the world's fisheries. He is also the popularizer of the shifting baselines theory, and with colleagues proved that Chinese officials overreported catches throughout the 1990s, leading scientists to believe the oceans were producing more fish than they actually were. His outlook is, in the best sense of the word, global. There is no harsher critic of modern fisheries than Daniel Pauly.

'The official estimate of fishery-induced mortality was too low,' Pauly said, when I asked for his explanation of the cod collapse. Government scientists failed to take into account the practice of high-grading: fishermen regularly tossed back undersized cod dead*, so they could continue landing the biggest fish possible. Pauly believed this practice permanently altered the dynamics of the population.

'Overfishing reduced the proportion of large fish, decreased the length of fish, and decreased the size at which the surviving fish were maturing, resulting in fewer eggs per female cod,' he explained. It left a population too compromised to survive. In cod, as in most big fish, fecundity increases exponentially with size and age; it is the older females that produce the most eggs. It was exactly these big spawners that Newfoundland's fishermen were targeting. The remaining fish, driven to mature ever younger, became weaker and less resistant to disease. Gradually they lost their niche in the food chain to shrimp, lobster and other species. The capelin, a small fish that cod once preyed upon, is now believed to be a predator of larval and juvenile cod.

Understanding Pauly's account of what is really happening to the oceans – and why the concept of bottomfeeding is important – requires a grasp of the concept of trophic levels. Every living thing on earth has a trophic number, ranging from 1 in plants to 5 in such larger predators as lions and sharks. The bottom of the oceanic food chain is formed by plankton (a generic term for microscopic drifting organisms, whether plant or animal). Phytoplankton, which correspond to grass and

---

* The discarding of fish is one of the fishing industry's most shameful practices. Fishing vessels the world over are trailed by miles of floating fish, 'bycatch' tossed overboard, dead, because they happen to be too small or the wrong species. Some scientists believe one-third of the world's catch is discarded this way.

other plant life on land, have a trophic number of 1. Zooplankton, among them krill and copepods, are tiny drifting animals that feed on phytoplankton, giving them a trophic number of 2 (which means they feed at the same level as the much larger cow, also a herbivore). Most of the fish we eat feed at a trophic level of 3 or 4. A seal or a human gobbling up a carnivorous fish like cod, for example, is feeding at the highest trophic level, 5.

Though most animals feed at different trophic levels throughout their lives, they can be assigned an average number; size is often less relevant than eating habits. A city-bus-length basking shark that feeds on plankton has the same trophic number as a sardine, 3.1. A great white shark that eats large carnivorous fish and marine mammals, has an average trophic number of 4.5. American lobsters, which are bottom-feeding scavengers, average 2.6. The omnivorous Atlantic cod, which eats anything from plankton to carnivorous fish only a little smaller than itself, averages 4.3. In general, the closer to the bottom of the trophic scale you feed, the better it is for the environment. To heal the oceans, humans should aspire to feeding at a level of 4 or less – a diet closer to the cod's than to the shark's.

For Pauly, the food chain is better described as a multi-tiered food pyramid: the overall biomass of organisms increasing each level one descends from the apex (sharks and other large predators) to the broad foundation (algae and other phytoplankton). Using vast databases of fisheries statistics, Pauly and his colleagues have found that around the world average trophic levels are declining. Fishermen first targeted big species – cod, tuna, salmon – but as these became more scarce, they were forced to move on to species at lower trophic levels. In ecosystems worldwide, the upper levels of food pyramids have been planed off as the big predator fish are removed. In 1950 the average trophic level for the waters off Newfoundland was 3.8, about the level of a predatory skate; by 1995 it had declined to 2.9 – the same trophic level as an anchovy. The data in FishBase have shown that globally, trophic levels slipped from 3.4 to 3.1 in just a few decades. Pauly, a man who does not shrink from dire pronouncements, blames the decline on one thing:

'It's overfishing,' he told me. 'In fact, it's not even *over*fishing: it's fishing, period. Even a small weight of fishing can lead to habitat destruction.' While acknowledging that global warming, pollution and invasive species have all had an impact, Pauly believes it is the human activity we can most easily control (i.e. fishing) that is most responsible for wiping out ecosystems.

Some of Pauly's critics believe he is overstating the case. After all, the overall amount of life in the oceans never really changes; as long as there are sunlight and minerals, plankton will go on producing new life. But as food pyramids are progressively compromised, the kind of life in the oceans becomes progressively simpler – and less edible. In an era of flattening pyramids, only such low-trophic-level species as starfish, sea squirts, salps and sea urchins have a bright future.

'Our seas,' Pauly predicted, 'will soon be full of jellyfish happily feeding on zooplankton.' There are good times ahead, in other words, for bottom-feeders.

Pauly thinks that the fishermen of the world have been calling the shots for too long. 'You don't negotiate with people that you have to regulate at the same time. I've never been in a situation where I could negotiate with a policeman for going over eighty miles per hour. So whether you're speeding on the highway or taking too many fish in the ocean, it shouldn't be open for negotiation: you need to be stopped. But somehow, because we still view the sea romantically, the fishermen are exempt.'

Strange, then, that in spite of the recent collapse of history's greatest food fishery, European cod fishermen are still spared from effective regulation. I asked Pauly what he thought of the fact that cod was still so widely available in the chippies of Britain.

'In Europe, they are managing the cod stocks close to the edge,' Pauly concluded. 'They have already completely eliminated the stocks of many flat fish. If they make even one little mistake with cod, they are going to be in trouble.'

Among the Fishmongers

Early one weekday morning I paid a visit to Billingsgate Market. Operating as London's main fish market since 1699, Billingsgate has been in its present location, a warehouse on the Isle of Dogs, since 1982. Somehow, with its red-brick roof festooned with sculpted sea monsters, it gives the impression of being much older. Inside, it is a Cessna-scaled warehouse compared to the Boeing 747 hangar that is the New Fulton: lately Billingsgate's forty merchants have been selling about 25,000 tonnes of seafood a year, less than a fifth of the volume moved by the New York market. Inside, the slang is Cockney, and the tone is set by porters employed by the Corporation of London, who are responsible for the transport of fish to and from the market – and utterly oblivious to punters' ankles as they push their fork-lifts through the aisles.

'Perkins is still waiting for his fish!' a moustached trader in a battered straw boater called to a porter. 'He wants four-twos of Milford sprags!' (Meaning four twenty-eight-pound boxes of young cod from the Welsh port of Milford Haven.)

In the murky light, many of the fish on display were familiar Atlantic species: boxes of glistening plaice, crates of still-twitching crabs from Shetland, Styrofoam containers of farmed salmon from Scotland. But more striking were all the exotic fish: I saw flat-flanked pomfret from Goa, bourgeois snappers from the Indian Ocean, beaky parrotfish from Indonesia. An elegant South Asian woman in a *salwar kameez* scooped up fish heads for a weekend curry. A man from Ghana bought a seven-pound box of farmed tilapia from Jamaica that, frozen at home, would last his family a month. All together, there were 140 different species of seafood on display at Billingsgate. The clientele, which was almost completely African and Asian, carried dripping plastic bags of fish to their cars, all smiles.

'When I first started, forty years ago,' said John Bennewith, of Stan-Hope Ltd., a firm that specialises in frozen cod, 'it was the Jewish people who had the fish-and-chip-shops, then the Greeks, Cypriots and Italians. Now you find it's the Indians, the Pakistanis and the Chinese.'

'How's your arm?' he shouted, as an Asian man wearing a sling walked by. Bennewith whispered: 'I forget the geezer's name, but he's got a lovely fish-and-chip shop.' Most chip shop owners, he explained, had contracts with big frozen food suppliers that delivered direct to the shop every week. They only came to Billingsgate when their regular supplier had run out of something.

'The quality of the cod in the fish-and-chip shops is better than it was forty years ago,' Bennewith told me. 'Before, none of it was frozen, which it could be sitting on a trawler's deck for days before it got to them.' Now, he said, the fish were snap-frozen within three hours of being caught. 'I'd say eighty-five per cent of the cod eaten in London is now frozen-at-sea.'

I asked him which sea his fish came from.

'Most of it comes from the Barents,' he replied, showing me a cardboard box labelled 'frozen-at-sea *Gadus morhua*' – Atlantic cod. 'This particular box comes from the Faroe Islands, near Iceland.' The box also showed the day the skin-on fillets were caught, the fact that they were trawled in FAO catching area 27 (an enormous division, taking up the whole North Atlantic) and the name of the vessel (the *Sundaberg*, a factory trawler owned by Kósin Seafood, which runs the largest processing plant on the Faroes).

103

Bennewith admitted that he sometimes worries about the state of cod stocks.

'I really think they have to ban fishing from December to February, during the roe season; the fish are quite spent during that period, and the quality is never as high. Unfortunately, there's a big market for the roe. But ultimately I think the industry is self-governing. If the fishermen aren't catching anything any more, they'll just stop fishing.' (By then, however, it may be too late for the fish. Fisheries scientists have a name for it: commercial extinction, and it is exactly what happened to the cod in Canada.)

Bennewith conceded he had seen a lot of 'black' cod – illegally caught fish – in the market recently. 'Last year the Norwegians seemed to be teaching the Russians how to sell black cod.' He looked at the stacks of boxes from distant oceans. 'Years ago I used to know all the frozen-at-sea boats,' he said, sighing. 'Nowadays, they're from all over the place. It's a world market now.'

Bennewith was right to be a little concerned. A sure sign that something is wrong with a fishery – that a finite supply of fish is nearing its end – is when prices start to rise. At Billingsgate, Atlantic cod, once paupers' food brought to the market from North Sea ports, is now being shipped all the way from the Arctic Circle and sold for an unheard-of £10 a kilogram. (In the year after I visited, prices would rise by a further 15 per cent.)

Yet in spite of its high sales price, and the fact that the Marine Conservatian Society's Good Fish Guide lists all cod in the Northeast Atlantic as overfished and thus a 'fish to avoid', I never had trouble finding cod in Britain. Over the course of two weeks, I ate at twelve chippies, from London to Edinburgh. With one exception, they all served cod, and, when asked, the owners and employees inevitably claimed their fish came from 'sustainable' stocks.

Black Cod

The International Council for the Exploration of the Sea (ICES) was founded in Copenhagen in 1902. Every year this august body gives advice to its twenty member nations about the state of fish stocks in European waters, using the best scientific evidence available to estimate the biomass of important commercial species. European nations, governed by the Common Fisheries Policy since 1983, are supposed to use this information to set quotas for each species in each part of the ocean and for each boat in their fleets. Since 2001 ICES has been calling for severe reductions in – and, in some areas, a total moratorium on – cod catches. In 2006 ICES advised: 'Cod stocks in the North Sea, Irish Sea and west of Scotland remain well below minimum recommended levels and the advice for these stocks is zero catch.' It is hard to be more unequivocal than that. Yet every year politicians ignore the scientists and implement only slight decreases in quotas. The situation has got so bad that in 2007 the World Wide Fund for Nature announced it was taking the Council of the European Union to court over its failure to protect its own cod stocks.

Most chip shop owners told me their cod comes from around the Faroe Islands, Iceland or the Barents Sea. Though nowhere near as overfished as the waters around Britain, none of these fisheries is truly sustainable.

In the Faroe Islands, a Danish possession located northwest of Scotland, most of the cod is line-caught. This makes it sound like a cottage industry, as though fishermen in skiffs are catching fish using hunks of cheese as bait. Actually, the lines in question, towed by industrial vessels, are miles long, and can carry tens of thousands of hooks. With the stock stripped by such longliners, the annual catch in the Faroes has fallen to a third of what it was thirty years ago. Ignoring the advice of outside scientists, every year the Faroese parliament allows its fishermen to take a third of the total biomass, an amount ICES considers unsustainable. Overexploited and fished to the limit, the Faroese cod are probably not long for this world.

Iceland has had more than its share of problems with cod. In order to establish its economic exclusion zone, this tiny nation fought a series of 'cod wars' with the UK, using coast guard vessels to ram UK vessels and cut their trawl cables. It unilaterally extended its three-mile limit first to twelve nautical miles from shore in 1958, then to fifty miles in 1972, and finally to two hundred miles in 1975. Iceland then managed to overfish the world's first two-hundred-mile economic exclusion zone; its cod catch plummeted by half in 1994. Only then did the Icelandic government introduce severe quotas, limiting the well-equipped inshore fleet to a quarter of the biomass of spawning fish a year. In spite of official reports to the contrary, in 2001 the e-newspaper *Intrafish* let it slip that the cod biomass had fallen to an all-time low. In truth, apart from a couple of short-lived rallies, the Icelandic cod catch has been in decline since 1980, and ICES officially considers the stock overexploited. Ironically, after fighting wars to protect its own coastal waters, Iceland has become infamous for its rapacious supertrawlers, which strip seamounts on the high seas well beyond its hard-won two-hundred-mile limit.

If you ordered cod at a chippy in the last decade, odds are even that it was caught in the Barents Sea. Harry Ramsden's, king of the chippies, with over 170 branches in points as distant as Florida and Saudi Arabia, boasts that most of its cod comes from the Barents. Birds Eye, the frozen-fish giant, claims in one of its ads that its fish fingers are sourced from the 'Barents Sea in the north-east Atlantic, using only EU-registered trawlers'. They are not alone; half of the world's cod is now thought to come from the Barents.

Part of the Arctic Ocean north of Russia and Scandinavia, the Barents is a frigid northern sea whose fish stocks are jointly administered by Russia and Norway. Serving cod from its waters is definitely nothing to boast about. At least one in five, and maybe as many as one in three, of Barents cod is 'black': illegally harvested fish taken outside the official quotas, whose capture is hastening the collapse of the fishery.

Black cod ends up at British chippies following a circuitous route. Every year a joint Russian and Norwegian fisheries commission sets the quota for catches in the Barents, inevitably exceeding the much lower quotas advised by ICES, often by as much as 250 per cent. In theory, the Russian and Norwegian trawlers that work the Barents are strictly controlled; through catch diaries and daily radio reports, they are obliged to log their daily take of cod, and stop fishing as soon as they exceed their share of the quota. In practice, many keep a second set of books with the *real* catch figures. Rather than return to port with a hold overflowing with illegal fish, they are met at sea by refrigerated transport ships – reefers – that take the catch to European ports where controls are not as strict.

In August 2006, for example, the Russian reefer *Mumrinskiy* docked at a port in Holland, after collecting unreported catch from at least five trawlers in the Barents. Even though Greenpeace members successfully scaled the ship and painted 'Stop Pirate Fishing' on its side, the *Mumrinskiy* managed to unload several hundred tonnes of cod. The Norwegians believe that at least one hundred such Russian trawlers are illegally taking Barents Sea cod. These are not a few captains who have succumbed to temptation: investigators describe them as violent, Mafia-style gangs. At one point, two Norwegian inspectors boarded a Russian trawler called the *Elektron* to investigate reports of illegal nets. Rather than surrender his haul of illegal cod, the *Elektron*'s captain fled with the inspectors still on board, and, with a Norwegian coast guard vessel carrying elite soldiers in hot pursuit, made for the safe haven of the ship's Russian home port.

According to Dutch Greenpeace members and reporters from the *Guardian*, in 2006 the world's biggest cod trading company was Ocean Trawlers, co-owned by Vitaly Orlov (a Russian) and Magnus Roth (a Swede). Roth and Orlov leased out a fleet of modern Norwegian-built trawlers to Russian fishermen who had an official share of the Barents Sea cod quota. After the cod caught in Arctic seas was sent to China to be filleted, Ocean Seafood Services Ltd – the sales arm of Ocean Trawlers – had the frozen blocks shipped to the UK, where they could end up in any one of fifteen hundred fish-and-chip shops that had a contract with Ocean Trawlers, or even at the Birds Eye fish finger factory in Hull. The revelation that Captain Birds Eye had become a purveyor of black cod was clearly an embarrassment. Not only is Birds Eye the largest supplier of fish in the UK; parent company Unilever is one of the fish business's most vocal advocates of sustainable seafood.

Britain's biggest fish companies have since done their best to distance themselves from black cod. After the story broke, Unilever sold Birds Eye and its European counterpart Iglo to an investment company. Meanwhile Ocean Trawlers, after claiming it had no control over the actions of rogue captains, packed up and moved its headquarters to Hong Kong. In May 2007, eight of Europe's biggest seafood buyers – including McDonald's, Birds Eye and Young's Bluecrest – sent a letter to the Norwegian government saying they would do their best to avoid black cod from the Barents Sea, asking for a list of boats known to be fishing illegally. At best, this was a disingenuous move. In the seafood trade the names of the worst offenders are already widely known. (The greenpeace.org website has an extensive database of the world's pirates, including some nice shots of the *Mumrinskiy* offloading illegal cod at sea.)

The fish traders at Billingsgate Market told me that everybody in the industry knows exactly which cod is black. It is the stuff that comes in unlabelled boxes. It also tends to be 20 per cent cheaper than the regular, traceable cod.

Such pirate fishing is not a case of a few bad apples cheating here and there, but a chronic, systemic problem. As long as Britain's love affair with its fish of choice continues, and stocks keep on declining, some of the cod at the local chippy is guaranteed to be black.

Wondyrechauns and Trophic Cascades

The old reliable British chippy is much more than an amusing footnote to gastronomic history. It is no exaggeration to say that, were it not for the fortuitous meeting of the trawl net and the fish-and-chip shop, the world's oceans would be much healthier places.

When it first appeared in 1366, the trawl net (the term simply refers to a net dragged along the bottom of a body of water) was dubbed the 'wondyrechaun', and was greeted with extreme suspicion by traditional trap-and-line fishermen. A complaint was made to the English king Edward III to ban this 'new craftily contrived kind of instrument' that promised to destroy the 'flower of the sea', that is, the mussels, spats of oysters, plants and living slime 'upon which the great fish are accustomed to live and be nourished'. The new trawl nets took more fish than people could actually eat; the excess catch had to be fed to pigs. Though the crown eventually permitted the new device, it was limited to deeper water. Wherever it appeared, the trawl caused controversy: trawling was banned in Flanders in 1499, and a century later the French made the practice a capital offence.

But the wondyrechaun was too efficient to be suppressed. The British and Flemish pioneered bottom-trawling in the North Sea, the body of water that separates Britain from northern Europe. At first the technique involved horses onshore dragging a wooden beam that dislodged prawns into an attached net; it took the combination of steam power and the trawl net to truly launch an industry. The first steam-powered trawler, the *Zodiac*, was built by a shipyard in Hull in 1881 and worked with startling efficiency off the banks of the North Sea. A decade later the first otter trawl – a cone-shaped, bottom-dragging net held open by panels, the prototype for all modern trawl nets – was tested in Scotland and became the standard rig for the North Sea.

There is no question that it was the chip shop business, officially decreed an 'offensive trade' because of the noxious odours of frying in urban settings, that drove the industrialization of fishing. Far less selective than smaller boats, steam-trawlers would return to port with a mixed bag of cod and such other, lesser-known species as coley, huss and megrim sole. The new fried fish shops were willing to take these 'offal' fish, selling them to urban workers for two shillings. (Children might get a pennyworth.) The newly established railway network, which counted seven thousand miles of track by midcentury, combined with the technology of ice packing, meant fish could get from such ports as Grimsby, Hull and Wick to the most landlocked village in excellent condition. Thanks to increased demand, the British trawling fleet expanded from 130 boats in the 1840s to eight hundred only twenty years later.

'Had it not been for the frying trade,' wrote fish trade journalist John Stephen in 1934, 'steam trawling as we know it to-day would not be.' By the 1860s, when the first chippies appeared, the railways were carrying a hundred thousand tonnes of fish a year. By the end of the nineteenth century steam-trawlers had so overfished most species of flatfish that they were already forced to move to northern waters – eventually all the way to Iceland. On the eve of the Second World War

Britain's chippies alone were going through 150,000 tonnes of fish a year, six times what Billingsgate Market sells today.

When domestic waters were emptied of fish, the distant-water fleets were born. In 1954 the *Fairtry*, a Scottish-built stern trawler that was 280 feet long and weighed 2,600 tonnes, appeared on the Grand Banks – inspiring Newfoundland's fishermen to mutter that the Brits had started fishing with ocean-liners. A decade later a fleet of three hundred Soviet factory ships, manufactured on the British model, began fishing the coast of New England, soon to be joined by vessels from Norway, Japan and Spain; these floating fish plants could spend months away from home, processing and freezing their entire catch at sea. Excluded from foreign shores by the gradual establishment of two-hundred-mile limits, Russian and Japanese trawlers discovered vast aggregations of fish over seamounts in the North Pacific; ever since, they have been quietly stripping bare one of the world's last unexplored frontiers.

Thanks to trawling, an unplanned, century-long experiment has recently been completed. What happens when, to feed the fish-and-chip-shops and the fish finger factories of the world, you remove all the big fish from the oceans? As average trophic levels from the Antarctic to Alaska decline, we are now in a position to draw some conclusions.

I asked Ken Frank, a cod specialist employed by the Canadian government at the Bedford Institute in Dartmouth, Nova Scotia, what the waters off Newfoundland looked like in the absence of their apex predator, the cod.

'The top of the food chain is now dominated by little fish,' Frank told me, 'like herring, sand-eel, capelin and mackerel, which have taken the place of cod. The offspring of the few cod that remain are subjected to severe competition, or even predation, by their former prey. The capelin in particular are eating the cod's food and even their larvae. I call this a "trophic cascade", and it isn't good news: it makes it very difficult for the top predator to recover from being so heavily depleted.' That explained the healthy population of lobsters I had seen Lorne Harnish trapping in St Margarets Bay: they had taken over the former niche of the cod. As an unexpected consequence of the removal of cod from the Gulf of Maine and the Scotian Shelf, sea urchin populations boomed and a fishery exporting their roe to Japan developed. When the urchins, unchecked by cod predation, ate their way through native seaweed forests of kelp and bladderwrack, their populations crashed in turn.

Though the trophic cascade set in motion by overfishing is preventing the northern cod from returning, Frank believed that it was the initial fishing pressure that sealed their fate.

'Fish have a social system,' said Frank. 'If you deplete the population of a fish that's used to living in dense groups, all kinds of bad things happen. A lot of people think that migration patterns are learned, and that larger, older fish actually lead the rest of the fish to the inshore spawning grounds. When you take the bigger fish out of the population, as fishermen tend to do, you're destroying a stock's entire knowledge base.'

And Frank made a point of dismissing the North Atlantic fishermen's favourite scapegoat, the seal. While marine mammals do eat an enormous amount of fish, 'their diets don't support the idea that they eat a lot of groundfish like cod. They prefer very fatty species like mackerel, herring and sand-eel. They *definitely* weren't a factor in the collapse.'

The Europeans, Frank said, were repeating all of the Canadians' mistakes. As the fish trader at Billingsgate observed, trawlers in the Barents Sea are targeting fish during the spawning season and removing mature fish before they can reproduce. Driven to mature younger, spawning fish are less resistant to disease, and less fecund. Europe's cod policies are a recipe for disaster: a multinational fishery, with overquota and illegal fishing and far too many discards, resulting in fewer large, mature cod. It sounds a lot like what happened off the Grand Banks in the 1990s.

For Newfoundland, Frank was pretty sure there would be no recovery; too many other species have taken over the cod's place in the food chain. The only hope, he believed, lay in recolonization. One day, a group of cod might cross from Iceland or west Greenland and eventually reseed the Grand Banks.

It was a long shot, to say the least. And given the way things are going on the European side of the Atlantic, the remaining cod may be long gone before they ever have a chance to resettle a thousand miles away.

Cod Gothic

It is strange, given that no spot in Britain is more than seventy-two miles from the coast, that seafood is not more popular here. Though 6,600 fishing boats work out of 280 British ports, landing 654,000 tonnes of fish a year, Britons consume only twenty kilograms of seafood each a year – less than half of what the average Spaniard eats (though almost three times what an American eats). The biodiversity-rich North Atlantic is one of the world's great sources of marine protein, full of such eminently edible species as megrim, redfish, blue whiting, gurnard and eel-pout, yet very few are found in local markets. Virtually the entire catch of crustaceans is sent to the Continent (Norway lobster can fetch £30 a kilogram in Spain). In fact, almost 60 per cent of all seafood sales in Britain come from three of the ocean's most familiar species: cod, haddock and salmon. Compared to the French and Portuguese, who enthusiastically gnaw on every link of the food chain, the British can seem positively seafood-phobic.

My fish-and-chip tour of England finished in the north, the

spiritual home of the chippy. In Lancaster I visited Hodgson's Chippy, recently voted the best in Britain by Seafish, the government's national seafood-promotion agency. Owner Nigel Hodgson explained that haddock, the fish of choice of northern England and Scotland, was all he sold. Until two months before, his North Sea haddock had been delivered fresh from a merchant in Aberdeen. Recently, though, he had started serving frozen-at-sea haddock from Iceland and the Faroe Islands, purchased from a wholesaler in Manchester.

'The quality's fantastic,' said Hodgson. 'It's frozen within two hours of being caught, they say. We defrost it here, so the customer's getting a piece of fish that is maybe twelve hours old. I am fully convinced by frozen-at-sea; the freshness is far superior.' I asked if he had ever sold other fish. 'One Christmas,' he replied, 'when the supplies were very scarce, we had to switch to cod. The customers didn't like it at all.' In northern England and Scotland cod have the reputation of being dirty beasts, fish best left to Londoners. I was inclined to agree. Cod are, after all, lazy bottom-dwellers, known to feast on parasite-laden seal faeces – which explains why cod livers are sometimes more worms than flesh.

Whatever Hodgson was doing, he was doing it right. Sitting on a stoop on a sloping residential street of tightly serried townhouses (Hodgson's had no stools), I opened the Styrofoam box, and a cloud composed of the essence of tempuralike batter, thick chips cut from Maris Piper potatoes, mushy peas and vaporized malt vinegar rose to fill my pores. The light breading broke apart under a little pressure from a plastic fork, revealing a slender fillet of flaky white meat. The haddock was absolutely perfect: sweet and salty and light and filling all at the same time. It just went to show that fish and chips, done well, can be the best of meals. (It can also, of course, be the worst of meals. At 870 calories for a small portion, more than you would get from two McDonald's Quarter Pounders, a fish-and-chip dinner can sit leaden and undigested in your gut longer than a deep-fried Mars bar.) The northerners have it right: haddock is a great fish. And most of the haddock sold in Britain is sustainably fished: Iceland recently had a bumper crop, its biggest catch in twenty-five years. Most are caught by hook-and-line, rather than trawled. (Waitrose's haddock, for example, is now line-caught from Iceland.) From then on, I knew, haddock was going to be my fish of choice in British chippies.

(If you can afford it, organic farmed cod is currently a good alternative to wild-caught. Johnson Seafarms in Shetland markets 'No Catch' cod, which is raised in sea-cages, fed with the offcuts of herring and mackerel, and stocked at much lower densities than farmed salmon. Norway and Canada are also experimenting with farmed cod. Farmers are already encountering problems with disease, however, and the price – up to £16 a kilogram – means organic cod is unlikely to make its way to local chippies any time soon.)

My last stop was Whitby, a North Yorkshire town on the North Sea famous for the filigreed arches of the ruined hilltop abbey whose skeleton glowers over the fishing port's narrow streets. It is perfectly perched on Whitby headland, a crumbling piece of geography where tombstones from the town's grave-yard regularly tumbled into the leaden North Sea. The setting inspired Bram Stoker's *Dracula*: here the Count's rat-infested schooner arrived during a terrible storm, 'unsteered save by the hand of a dead man!', unleashing a plague of vampires. The book also unleashed a plague of post-punks on Whitby; every October hundreds of pale Goths descend on the local guest-houses, walking the 199 steps to the graveyard in stiletto heels, smudging their black lipstick on the town's excellent fish and chips.

For Whitby is also the home of the Magpie Café, a pilgrim-age site for foodies. 'It's the best fish-and-chip restaurant I've ever been to,' raves Rick Stein, England's best-known seafood chef. 'Ian Robson has a gem of a restaurant here, a shrine to Englishness.'

In front of a multiroomed 1750 house once owned by a whaling family, and just across a harbourfront street from Whitby's fish market, a long queue had formed an hour before lunch. I sneaked a peek at the street-level kitchen, where a melting block of pale beef dripping the size of a human head slumped in the deep fryer, as sous-chefs with tattooed forearms prepared trays of cod and salmon fillets. For an English seafood restaurant, the Magpie's menu is extensive. They serve both cod and haddock, catering to south and north, as well as monkfish, skate, baby turbot, Dover sole, and something called Whitby woof.

'Which is catfish, obviously,' chef Ian Robson explained. 'That's why it's called "woof".'

The Whitby-born restaurateur, who has run the Magpie for the last thirty years, is a big, if none too expansive, man. Seated at a table in the homely, low-ceilinged dining room, he told me that none of his cod or haddock is frozen-at-sea. He buys them from a local wholesaler called Dennis Crooks, who sources his fish fresh from boats in Scotland and the Faroe Islands.

'Most of the fish on our menu are locally caught,' says Robson. 'But there's a lot of restrictions on the fishing industry here, and the fleet's gone down quite a bit, so we have to buy from other areas a lot more than we used to. We've been using the same supplier for twenty years, so if he tells us something, we believe him. But I think there's plenty of cod out there.'

Robson is wrong, especially when it comes to the sea fished by Whitby's trawlers. Before the industrial age the North Sea was estimated to contain 7.7 million tonnes of cod, and their average size was forty inches – over a yard long. The entire cod biomass in the North Sea is now thought to be only 45,100 tonnes. Average lengths have fallen to sixteen inches; the perfect size, as it happened, for a chippy's Styrofoam container, but disastrous for the future of the stock.

By all rights, the shallow, nutrient-rich North Sea should still be a highly productive body of water. During the last glaciation, its northern reaches were covered with ice, and Doggerland, a stretch of tundra, linked what is now England to the Continent. Two thousand years ago, there were vast oyster beds here, natural filterers of the seawater; skates the size of barndoors, and so named, have long since disappeared. As the proving ground for industrial fishing, the North Sea – the floor of which was once carpeted with sponge groves, sea whips and cold-water corals – has long since been ploughed into barren mud flats.

After first ridding the sea of invertebrates, the trawlers then killed off the major fish stocks. The mackerel fishery was wiped out in the 1970s, and, after herring stocks collapsed across Europe, a moratorium had to be placed on the North Sea fishery in 1977. Bluefin tuna has vanished, and once abundant skate is now restricted to a few rocky patches. All told, only 2–3 per cent of the sea's big fish are left. Virtually every square yard of the southern part of the North Sea is now disturbed by trawls at least once a year. The remaining cod simply do not stand a chance.

Ecologists believe that closing the cod fishery for even a couple of years would allow the spawning stock to grow to 440,000 tonnes, enough to allow a viable fishery.

Instead, terrified of an outcry, politicians have kept the fishery open, introducing only fractional decreases in the quota and days allowed at sea. Since 1987 fishermen have not been able to fill even this reduced quota: there simply is not enough cod left. In fact, even if the cod quota were set at zero, fishermen would continue to scoop up thousands of tonnes of cod in their nets. Half of the total cod catch is accidentally netted by trawlers chasing haddock, herring and other species.

'European fisheries ministers,' the vice president of the Royal Society memorably declared in 2006, 'should be clear that they may be presiding over the total collapse of the cod of the Atlantic.'

Just outside Whitby's fish market, a stocky middle-aged man wearing a baseball cap, whose shiny track pants drooped into zip-up leather boots, put forth another explanation for what happened to the cod. His name was Robert Cole, and in Whitby he was fishing aristocracy. I asked whether his father had fished too.

'Oh, aye,' he replied, 'and me grand-dad. *And* me great-great-grand-dad, for that matter.' He reckoned the Coles had been fishing since 1760. His great-grandfather, Thomas Cole, had chased herring in a thirty-foot coble – a flat-bottomed sailing boat – called the *Good Intent*. Cole showed me a photo of his latest boat, a sixty-foot steel-hulled trawler, also called the *Good Intent*. His son was the captain, and in a few weeks he would take her north to trawl for Norway lobster all winter. 'She's a good hard ship,' said Cole, looking at the photo fondly.

Pausing from time to time to curse a passing delivery van ('There's another bloody bastard bringing in cheap frozen fillets, already battered'), Cole gave me a fisherman's account of what has been happening to the North Sea.

'Cod just seems to have disappeared,' he said. 'It isn't really overfished; it can't be; there aren't enough boats left to overfish it! About sixty miles north of here, there used to be a hell of a breeding ground for small codlings. There were thousands of tonnes of them. But nobody goes there any more, so we don't actually know if there are any left. Last trip my son came back with eight times as much whiting as he did cod.

'We used to catch spawning cod among the herring. They may come back, I don't know. Now we've introduced global warming. Is that bloody one degree rise in temperature fucking everything up? We just don't know.'

Cole was quick to accuse every fisherman's favourite villain, the seal.

'Those fucking things!' he ranted. 'Horrible, mucky, horrible, sliming, stinking, eye-watering bloody seals. They've decimated the cod, and they're still decimating the salmon industry in Scotland. And the McCartneys and Greenpeace don't think they should be killed? Those plonkers! Then you get the lunatics at the Royal Society for the Protection of Birds. We were drilling holes in seagull eggs a few years ago to keep the population down, but thanks to the bird people, we can't do it any more. Now look at them!' He pointed to a pair of gulls playing tug-of-war with a discarded chip. 'They live off chips, and now they're attacking the children!

'There is something that's worrying me, though. There's no haddock this year. Your haddock loves sand-eels, and now they've stopped the Danes from taking sand-eels, which means they should be in good shape this year. So where is the bloody haddock?' (I later learned the absence of haddock is hardly a mystery. Though abundant in Icelandic waters, British haddock were a victim of the North Sea fisheries' notoriously high bycatch rates: over the last four decades, an average of 87,000 tonnes of haddock have been discarded every year.)

I recognized Cole's name from a BBC news story. Four years earlier, Whitby's entire trawler fleet had been charged for failing to declare hundreds of tonnes of cod. When I brought up the case, he looked surprised, but continued:

'It was the navy that actually arrested us. They said, "We have kept surveillance on you." According to the government, they looked at our logbooks and said we'd stolen one point two million pounds' worth of European Economic Community fish. The whole fleet was taken to court. We've all been twice to the High Court in London. It's made a bloody fortune for the solicitors.' Cole's share of the fine was £12,000.

Like the rogue Russians in the Barents Sea, Whitby's captains were accused of keeping two sets of books and failing to declare their whole catch to inspectors. (Fisheries officers said they witnessed one captain hurling a logbook overboard.) The fish-ermen's lawyer claimed his clients had been driven to their knees by strict controls. 'It was a temporary thing,' explained one of the accused, 'and we didn't want to do it. But we had to make the vessels pay.'

I asked Cole whether there was anything to the charge. Splut-tering slightly, he replied: 'Well, it did happen in a little bit of a way, but not as much as them plonkers say. A million quid worth of fish is a lot of bloody fish to hide. It's a lot to say we got away with.' The consequences, he admitted, had been harsh. 'You can't sell your boat, you can't do bugger all. I would have liked to move on, maybe bought another boat by now.'

As much as I was charmed by Cole and his blustery defiance, this kind of attitude lies at the heart of the problems facing the oceans. It is the ongoing plunder of the seas – done in the name of keeping a boat afloat for another season, and multiplied a hundred thousand times in all the ports of the world – that is leading to the trophic cascades that are souring future oceans for everyone.

There is no need to feel sorry for the fishermen of the North Sea: they are actually doing quite well. Scottish electric beam trawlers are dragging electrified metal grids over the seabed, which induce prolonged muscle contraction in bottom-dwelling fish, breaking their spines and making them easy to scoop up. The much-hated French are out there too, and are accused of wrecking lobster traps with their trawls. As in Nova Scotia and Newfoundland, the removal of big fish has allowed species at lower trophic levels to thrive: crabs, prawns and lob-sters are especially abundant. A new shellfish holding facility has been built in Whitby to process the catch, and a seventy-foot trawler has recently been added to the port's remaining fleet of twelve. The *Our Lass II* will go all the way to Norway in search of prawns; a fisherman with a prawn licence can apparently earn £25,000 in a single trip.

When I asked whether he was considering retirement, Robert Cole looked at me with real consternation.

'I've been doing this since I left school. I'm sixty-four now. I'm like rust, I never sleep! I've got a next-door neighbour, and he retired early, and he's just gone to seed. I see him getting up in the morning at half past eight, going to get the paper. Doing the crossword is the highlight of his day. What a miserable bloody existence. I wouldn't change my life for the world.'

If this were still the age of inexhaustible cod mountains and endless salmon rivers, such a display of spirit might be admirable. It is the essence of the indomitable, short-sighted, buck-passing Atlantic fisherman: an independent, almost lordly working-class hero, romanticized to death in our culture. As long as there is a single jellyfish left in the ocean, he will be ready to go out and catch it.

And, if the politicians do not find the courage to impose the moratoriums Europe's scientists have long called for, this is exactly what the next generation can look forward to finding at their neighbourhood chippy:

Jellyfish and chips.

4

MARSEILLES –
BOUILLABAISSE

Small Pond

The Mediterranean has never got much respect from ocean-ographers: for them, it is a fish-poor, virtually tideless sea, whose lazy waves slop against a continental shelf too narrow to encourage the development of any significant seafood biomass. As oceans go, it is a kitchen sink with two tiny drains: the Strait of Gibraltar at the west end, not even eight miles across, and the man-made outlet of the Suez Canal to the east, a mere sixty-five yards in width. In the days of Ulysses, when Scylla and Charybdis had the power to scuttle galleys, the Mediterranean may have seemed like the entire world. Now that civilization knows the fury of the North Atlantic and the vastness of the Pacific, the suntan-lotion-slicked Med just barely holds its own as a sea.

One morning in July, in the harbour of the little town of La Ciotat, the mistral – the cold wind that sweeps south over the Alps and the Massif Central, and whose persistence is said to drive men mad – has been blowing hard and steady for hours. It is pushing the unusually warm surface water off the French coast out to sea, causing cold water in submerged canyons just offshore to rise to the surface. This dramatic upwelling has accelerated a southerly current, whirlpooling the water in the harbour of La Ciotat into small eddies and white-capped wavelets.

Sixty feet below the surface, this stretch of shoreline is far from barren: it harbours a variety of life and landscapes to rival a Pacific atoll. At the submarine foot of Le Bec de l'Aigle – a clifftop whose dramatically overhanging peak resembles an eagle's beak in profile – iridescent corbs and fat-lipped groupers dart among yellow and red gorgonians, tiny polyps that form into highly ramified colonies resembling flattened fans. Farther out, beneath 125 feet of water, moray eels and a *cigale de mer* – the 'cricket of the sea', whose blunt-clawed carapace makes it look like a lobster whose shell was molten in an industrial fire – have taken up residence in the upside-down fuselage of a twin-boomed P38 Lightning, shot down by a German fighter in 1944. Sea horses and urchins and sponges live among the detritus of the ages, from wine amphoras fallen from the decks of galleys when La Ciotat was a Greek colony called Citharista, to the near-indestructible plastic bottles tossed into the sea by its modern-day citizens. At regular intervals, twin orbs are set into the sandy patches of the bottom: they are the eyes of what the French call the uranoscope (from the Greek *urano*, 'sky', and *scopus* (look)); the stargazer, a frog-mouthed fish that buries itself in the sand and whose uplooking eyes are more intent on passing mullets than any heavenly bodies.

The night before, a female *rascasse* that had spent the day engaged in her preferred activity – lying motionless under a rock – was driven by hunger to go hunting in a patch of sea-grass. Spotting a likely meal, probably a small squid, she lunged, only to run into an invisible wall; swaying her body to escape, she became even more enmeshed as nylon lines snagged her gills. She spent the night tangled in a net attached to a buoy as the mistral-stirred water flowed around her, her fins nipped by the squid she had snapped at earlier.

Now, just after sunrise, she was being rudely hauled out of the water, over a pulley, and onto the deck of the *Salvia Regina*, the twenty-five-foot-long boat owned by fisherman Christophe Holtz.

Stopping the *Salvia Regina*'s electric winch, Holtz used a wooden-handled hook to free the *rascasse*'s spines from the gill net, which resembled a long rectangular badminton net. Holtz is a slender, raw-boned man, in his mid-forties, with a beaky, sunburned nose and forearms powerfully sinewed by twenty years of struggling with nets and buoys. Brushing a snot-like string of eggs from the fish's side, he tossed her towards a plastic crate full of other fish, missing by a couple of inches.

I gazed at the small pinkish-grey fish: she had batwinglike fins and inquisitive eyes that drooped with folds of freckled flesh, and was gasping her last in a bewildering world of light. Taking pity, I flipped her into the seawater-filled crate, but made the mistake of grasping her from above; one of the spines on her dorsal fin pierced my thumb.

A point of blood appeared. Almost instantly it felt like battery acid had been injected into my flesh, and I was reminded of the *rascasse*'s English name: the red scorpion fish. *Scorpaena scrofa*, as it is known to scientists, comes from the same family as the deadly stonefish – the bottom-dweller whose sting paralyses pearl divers – and the *rascasse* defends itself from predators with a similar strategy: by secreting a toxic protein through its spines.

'Ah, ça fait mal, hein?' (Hurts, doesn't it?), Holtz said appreciatively, and went back to pulling up the net. In his years of setting nets for rockfish – the spiky, variegated bottom-dwellers that go into the most celebrated soup of Provence, bouillabaisse – he has got used to their bites and barbs. When Holtz catches a weever, a dragon-like fish whose poison can send a grown man's blood pressure plummeting towards zero, he makes sure to snip off its venomous spines to save his clients a trip to A&E. A few minutes before, he had pulled up a thrashing, five-foot-long conger eel, which clamped itself to his waist with its small, powerful jaws.

'Qu'est-ce qu'il fait chier, celui-là!' (He's pissing me off, that one!), he muttered. Tearing the eel from his yellow overalls, he used a machete to cut it into bloody steaks. Conger is another essential ingredient in the making of bouillabaisse.

Reassured by Holtz's nonchalance, I did what John Wayne did when a rattler bit him: sucked and spat. Soon the pain was no worse than a bee sting, allowing me to continue my documentation of the morning's haul. Holtz had caught a hooded-eyed, silver-sided horse mackerel (tossed overboard); a comber, a slender fish striped with orange (a keeper); and the long-filamented John Dory (also a keeper), whose French name, Saint-Pierre, comes from the legend that the large black spots that mark its flanks are the imprint of Saint Peter's thumb and forefinger. There was a lot of bycatch: a hermit crab, a squatter whose claws protruded from the murex shell he had expropriated; a tiny squid, which shot out a jet of ink as Holtz freed it from the net; and several small, flat-sided sea bream.

'It's not worth it, massacring the little fish,' sighed Holtz, throwing the bream overboard. Behind his back the gulls following the boat snatched up everything that Holtz spared.

That morning, Holtz laid out a kilometre's worth of net for red mullet – if the weather held, he would return for it the following day – and pulled in two kilometres of net for rockfish like the *rascasse*. His day on the water had netted him two kilograms of fish.

'Fishing is like that,' Holtz said. 'It's all or nothing. Fortunately, though, it's not this bad every day! Otherwise I couldn't even pay for my diesel. I need to catch at least ten kilograms of *rascasse*, and lots of other fish on the side, for it to be a good day.' In October, always a productive month, he can pull up 250 kilograms of red mullet a day.

As we headed back to port, he ran through his overheads: diesel, 54 centimes (38 pence) a litre; his echo-sounding sonar, which shows the relief of the sea bottom, cost him €1,500 (£1,050); and this morning alone he had €6,000 (£4,200) worth of nets in the water, and they are expensive to repair. He pays the French government €1,600 (£1,120) every three months in licence fees; and then there is insurance, and the cost of maintenance. Yet after four hours of fishing, Holtz had caught just €6 (£4) worth of fish.

'Ten years ago there were eight boats like mine in La Ciotat,' said Holtz. 'Now there are four. The costs are going up. The restaurants in Marseilles that make bouillabaisse don't buy from local fishermen any more – only the tourists believe that. They get their fish delivered by wholesalers, who buy from the big industrial boats. Plus people here don't cook fish at home any more.

'Another thing: there aren't as many fish. Red mullet flees from pollution, and the waters are definitely polluted here. The style of fishing has changed, too; the nets are longer, we have better sonar.' He lifted his crate of rockfish into the back of his Renault estate car. 'The *rascasse*, though, that's not endangered: it will always be around.' He would sell some of his fish to a restaurant on the outskirts of Marseilles that made a *soupe de poisson* and the rest to a grandmother who was making bouillabaisse for her family that weekend.

I hoped Holtz was right about the *rascasse*. Pollution, overfishing and climate change are all changing the Mediterranean – as they are afflicting all the oceans of the world. But here another threat looms, one to which the smaller seas of the world are particularly susceptible. Looking back at the tangled pile of net on the dock, I saw little strands of green weed tangled in the mesh: it was *Posidonia*, the nutritious seagrass that forms the *rascasse*'s preferred hunting grounds. But I could also make out pieces of a darker brown plant in the net, something much more sinister: *Caulerpa racemosa*, one of the biological invaders, spread by man, that were already transforming the Mediterranean into a different sea – one that, in a couple of decades, even fishermen like Christophe Holtz may have trouble recognizing.

The Fish Soup of the Gods

Every European culture seems to have a soup, or stew, or some more or less liquidy concoction that captures the essence of the sea.

In the north of Europe they begin with butter. There is *cotriade*, the Breton stew of potatoes, onions, eel, hake and such 'blue' or oily fish as mackerel or anchovies; and the Belgian *waterzooi*, made with egg yolk and cream, julienned leeks and carrots, and eel, pike, bass and carp – the name means 'watery mess' in Flemish. The Normans have *matelote*, in which turbot, brill and oysters are flamed with Calvados and cooked in burbling apple cider. Nearer the Mediterranean olive oil is the fat of choice. The Basque *ttoro* is a spicy white-wine-based fish fumet poured boiling hot over chunks of monkfish, eel and gurnard, and then adorned with croutons and mussels; the *zarzuela de pescado* of mainland Catalonia is, literally, a 'musical comedy' of squid, flatfish, grouper and prawns. The Italians have many *zuppe di pesce*: the soffritto-based *caciucco* of Livorno, which also makes use of *rascasse*, as well as cuttlefish, octopi and prawns; and the Sardinian *burrida*, which is made with dogfish and skate and is linked in name alone to the Provençal *bourride*, an altogether more sophisticated concoction involving monkfish, egg yolks and the garlicky mayonnaise known as *aïoli*. (The recipe for the Jamaican version of bouilla-baisse is far more disturbing. Bony fish too small to fillet, all that is left in local waters after decades of overfishing, are boiled whole for hours; the scales and fins are then sieved out. The resulting broth is known as 'fish tea'.)

Finally, the Greeks have their *kakaviá* – a lemony soup made with rockfish such as *rascasse* boiled on a hot stove and served over toast in bowls – which, they claim, is the inspiration for the king of all fish soups, the bouillabaisse of Provence. But then, bouillabaisse has many creation myths. There is the soup-of-legend version: Venus, some Marseillais will tell you, laced the soup with the apocryphally soporific saffron to put her husband Vulcan to sleep in order to keep a tryst with Mars. There is the cod-etymology version: legend says it was invented as a Friday meal by the head of a convent – *une abbesse* – hence the name *bouill-* (the root of the verb 'to boil') plus *abbesse*, which we are meant to believe yields bouillabaisse. There is the heartwarm-ing folk tale: a ship sought shelter in a cove during a storm, and the cook improvised a soup of *rascasse*, cuttlefish, barnacles and whatever the crew could pluck from the shore; he entrusted a young mate to tell him, in good Provençal, when 'la bouillo baïsso souto la marquo d'oou bastoun' – that is, when the stock has boiled to below the mark of the stick. Those versions can be left to the folk academics who believe the word 'tip' derives from 'to insure promptness'. The word bouillabaisse, according to the French *Robert* dictionary, is probably a combination of *bouillir* (to boil) and the Provençal word *peis* (fish), hence *bouillepeis*, which, after some generations in the mouths of Midi, became bouillabaisse: a simple fish boil.

And that is exactly what bouillabaisse is: fish broth boiled furiously enough to achieve an amalgamation of gelatin and olive oil with the water and wine in the broth. For centuries fish-ermen caught rockfish, which, because they are unsightly and short on flesh, often remained unsold at the end of the day.

Rather than toss them back into the sea, they dropped them into a pot of water at a roiling boil – usually on a wood fire – with some roughly chopped garlic, olive oil and herbs gathered from the white limestone hillsides around Marseilles, and ate the resulting soup in their *cabanons*, the fishermen's huts that still dot the little coves just outside the city. In the popular tradition, bouillabaisse is cheap, delicious and infinitely varied: you can throw in a dragon-like weever, a tough and bony conger eel, a couple of little green crabs – whatever gets tangled in the nets. Though it is best to have a *rascasse*, ultimately it is the catch of the day that determines the flavour.

When the chefs of Marseilles, Martigues and Nice got their hands on bouillabaisse, they fancied up the recipe with saffron, the world's most expensive spice, and served it with a bowl of *rouille*, a garlic-pepper sauce thickened with bread crumbs. In 1830 William Makepeace Thackeray described eating 'a hotch-potch of all sorts of fishes' at Terré's tavern in Paris – a bastardized northern version involving red peppers, mussels, roach and dace – in his 'Ballad of Bouillabaisse'. It was the only thing about France he actually liked.

At some point the Gallic mania for codification, as well as the usual French culinary snobbery, got hold of bouillabaisse. The gastronome and Ritz chef Auguste Escoffier enshrined the soup in haute cuisine in his collection of five thousand recipes, *Le guide culinaire*. Middle-class home chefs used the version they found in the Bible of Provençal cooking, *La Cuisinière provençale*, by J. B. Reboul, which called for the classic combination of dried orange peel and saffron. Local chefs started serving it in two parts, starting with the *tournée de croutons* – the soup with toasted bread and *rouille* – and the fish course, throwing in a spiny lobster to make of it a bouillabaisse *royale*. And of course, they started charging more. A *lot* more. In Marseilles, it is impossible to find a bowl of bouillabaisse – a dish originally made with fish that cost less than vegetables, some seawater and stale bread – that costs less than €50 (£35).

In 1980, disgusted by the more touristy joints in Marseilles's Vieux-Port peddling 'real Marseilles fish soup/*echte Marseiller Fischsuppe*' made with such northern fish as turbot, cod and even salmon, a group of nineteen restaurateurs drew up the 'Marseilles Bouillabaisse Charter'. Starting with the lapidary 'It is impossible to normalize cooking,' the charter proceeds to normalize the making of bouillabaisse: it is a 'simple and familial' dish that nonetheless should be served with *rouille* and *aïoli*, made with saffron and fennel, and accompanied by croutons rubbed with garlic. The restaurateur is obliged to cut up the fish in front of the diners, and the broth and the fish have to be served separately. The charter then offers a list of fin and shellfish that *must* go into the mix. To wit, a minimum of four of the following: the *rascasse*, the venomous-spined weever, the conger eel (the same beast that attached itself to Christophe Holtz's overalls), the stargazer that buries itself on sandy bottoms, the *chapon* (simply a large *rascasse*), and the gorgeous galinette, with its lobster-red body and huge, electric-blue-green pectoral fins (and whose English name, gurnard or tub-fish, is entirely inappropriate for such a magnificent parakeet). Optionally, one can add any of the following: a John Dory, a *cigale de mer* (a flat lobster), a monkfish or a *langouste* (a spiny lobster).

Such culinary punctiliousness has always raised the ire of North Americans. For every Frenchman who has ever waved a finger and said, 'One cannot make a bouillabaisse in your country, you do not have the right fish,' there is an erudite American who does not like to be told what he can and cannot do. Food writer Waverley Root claimed the best bouillabaisse he ever had was at New York's Restaurant du Midi, 'before society discovered it'. A. J. Liebling took up eleven pages of the 27 October 1962 issue of the *New Yorker* to prove, through his correspondence with an ichthyologist, that a scorpion fish found off the coast of the United States was just as good as the Mediterranean *rascasse*. In his essential 1979 book *Unmentionable Cuisine*, Calvin W. Schwabe theorized that the venom in the *rascasse* acts as a fixative, setting flavour in a bouillabaisse the way musk and ambergris fix scents in perfume. Thus a bouillabaisse without a *rascasse* – as opposed to some washed-out New England scorpion fish – was indeed, as a Frenchman quoted in A. J. Liebling's opus put it, like a 'watch without a mainspring'.

In spite of the annoying exactitude of the Bouillabaisse Charter, I have to agree with the chefs of Marseilles: the only bouillabaisse worthy of the name is the one made with the nasty, poisonous little fish of the salty, tideless Mediterranean.

It has something to do, I figure, with the water.

Ain't What It Used to Be

Of the ten shell- and finfish listed in the Bouillabaisse Charter, three are in deep trouble. Monkfish caught by bottom-trawlers are, as I had learned in New York, to be avoided. As Mediterranean waters become warmer, the highly venomous weever is being chased out of its habitat by the arrival, from more southerly waters, of the voracious lizardfish, another bug-eyed bottom-dweller. If you are ever offered a *cigale de mer*, the crustacean with the molten-looking carapace, it is important to refuse: a protected species in France since 1992, the flat lobster is illegally hunted in marine-protected areas by scuba-diving poachers. The charter, in other words, actually invites restaurateurs to break the law. (The ninety-six known species of rockfish on North America's Pacific coast, by the way, are in far worse shape than the *rascasse*. Taken indiscriminately by trawls since the 1960s, the main commercial species are now down to 1 per cent of their original levels.)

131

Of course, the Marseillais have been saying things are not what they used to be for at least the last three hundred years. They will tell you the same thing about their own city: a kind of sunny, pastis-soaked nostalgia for less complicated times is the dominant civic mode. The coming of the TGV has put the capital only three hours away, and the hordes of Parisians the bullet train spills into the Gare St-Charles have been blamed for driving up prices. Since M. F. K. Fisher described it in *A Considerable Town*, the Vieux-Port – the pier-filled rectangular basin that is the real soul of the city – has lost much of its legendary grit. (Fisher confessed, incidentally, after eating 'one more bouillabaisse', that she was not a 'passionate devotee of the local attraction'. She also described that endearing, spiky little pug of a fish, the 'hideous fangy grey-pink' *rascasse*, as 'dour as hell to look at'.) 'The Good Old Beauvau', the waterfront hotel where Fisher invariably roomed in her visits between the 1930s and 1970s, has since been bought by the Mercure chain. The old Criée, the big fish market on the southern Quai, has become an avant-garde theatre, and the fishermen's trawlers that once moored outside have been replaced by the pleasure boats of the nouveau riche.

One part of the Vieux-Port whose grit has not entirely been polished away is the Quai des Belges, which hosts a small retail fish market every morning. In front of a dozen or so plastic tables set up on sawhorses, there is a bronze plaque set in the pavement that reads: 'Here / in about 600 BC / Greek sailors of Phocea came ashore. / They founded Marseilles, / from which civilization spread / throughout the / Western world.' It is precisely the civic swagger visitors expect from Marseilles, and the Quai des Belges is probably the only place left where vendors still foghorn their wares with the accent of Honorine, the salty fishwife of Marcel Pagnol's novels.

On a midsummer morning, they sweated beneath parasols and bellowed their spiels:

'Vé!' cried one, in the Italianate singsong of Midi, a patois that delights in adding terminal syllables. 'Com-me elle est bel-luh ma ras-cass-uh!' (How pretty my *rascasse* is!)

A particularly sun-wizened woman shouted: 'Les vi-van-tuhes aux prix des mor-tuhs!' ('The live ones for the same price as the dead!') Deftly whacking a twitching red mullet into still-ness before wrapping it in plastic, she told me she had been selling fish since she was seventeen. Her name was Nana, and though she must have been at least seventy, she was still a flirt.

'It's not like in the old days, *mon beau*,' she said. 'The people have changed. And the fish, there aren't as many as there used to be. It's the big boats, the ones that go out to sea, that get them all now. We only get the fish from the small boats that stay close to shore and catch nothing but rubbish. My trade, it's almost dead. Next year I'm going to quit.' (From the chuckles of her sunburnt neighbour, I gathered this was not the first time she had announced her retirement.)

Big trawlers used to come to the Vieux-Port, but these days the vendors on the Quai des Belges are licensed to sell only from boats forty feet in length or less. And, as fisherman Christophe Holtz told me, people just are not buying fresh fish like they used to.

'You can buy frozen bouillabaisse at Picard Surgelés now,' one of the fishmongers lamented, referring to a chain that special-izes in frozen, microwave-ready dinners. I noticed that some of the vendors were still advertising their wares in last century's currency: though you pay in euros, the plastic tags next to the *chapons*, sardines and sea bream still indicate the price in francs.

There is evidence that things in the Mediterranean may really have been better in the old days. The earliest indication of human presence in the area is the Cosquer cave, a grotto that can be reached only through an underwater passage. Along with the usual outlines of hands, its nineteen-thousand-year-old wall paintings depict a sea of plenty: seals, globular beings that may represent octopi, lots of fat fish, and a seabird, now extinct, known as the great auk. From Roman times until the nineteenth century, *madragues*, or fixed nets, were used to trap bluefin tuna near Marseilles. Perhaps because the currents changed, tuna stopped coming into shore: by 1728 the Monsignor de Belsunce was ordering public prayers to ask God to restore the sea to its former abundance. In 1840 nationalistic Provençal writers were already denouncing the use of the *gangui*, a type of net that raked the bottom, for taking up small and large fish indiscriminately. At the end of the nineteenth century, savants at the Académie de Marseille lamented the disappearance of fish that now sound like hallucinations: skates the size of barn doors, groupers that weighed up to sixty-five pounds, monkfish longer than a tall man. Relentless spearfishing by skin divers plagued the Mediterranean through most of the twentieth century; an American writer, Guy Gilpatric, made a name for himself by impaling grouper by lunging like a fencer. Modern scholars marvel at stories of fifteen-pound hake (the very largest now weigh less than five) and accounts of vast schools of sprats, another species vanished from Provençal shores.

After all these centuries of intensive fishing, the Mediterranean is indeed a diminished sea, stocked with juvenile fish. For the first time the European Union, under Maltese-born fisheries minister Joe Borg, is taking a tough stance on some forms of fishing: the drift nets that used to kill thousands of dolphins are now banned, and in 2005 bottom-trawling at a depth of more than a kilometre was forbidden. Enforcement has long been the EU's weak point, but France got a shock when, after years of letting their hake fishermen get away with bringing in undersize fish, Borg's ministry fined France €77 million (£54 million) – equivalent to four times the country's annual fisheries-management budget.

In spite of all this pressure, the Mediterranean still manages to support its remaining fishermen. From Gibraltar to Jordan, and from Syria to Spain, there are forty thousand boats work-ing the sea, and 80 per cent are small vessels less than forty feet in length. Mediterranean landings, about 1.5 million tonnes a year, account for only a fifth of the European total, but make up just over a third of the value of the total catch. In other words, by selling fresh fish to chefs and local markets – and even old ladies, in the case of Christophe Holtz – one hundred thousand fishermen throughout the twenty-one countries of the Mediter-ranean continue to make a living without exhausting the resource. True, nobody except the swordfish and tuna fishermen are really getting rich. But nor are they killing off their own trade, a feat the cod fishermen of Newfoundland managed in a single generation. Despite its troubles, the Mediterranean seems like a heartening exception to the worldwide rule of fisheries collapse: artisanal fishermen have learned to live in equilibrium with the sea that nourishes them, keeping the pots of *kakaviá* and bouillabaisse in one of the world's most fantastically varied seafood cultures boiling in the process.

Which may explain why there are still fishwives on the Quai des Belges hollering, in their timeless sing-song: 'Vé! Com-me elle est bel-luh ma ras-cass-uh!'

You're Soaking in It

It was not overfishing that was going to kill the Mediterranean. It was everything that was floating – and growing – in the super-heated water I was snorkelling in.

I had taken the battered and graffiti-daubed *train bleu*, which blasts its deafening whistle twice before entering the tunnels cut through the limestone cliffs of the Côte Bleue, to a beach west of Marseilles. Carrying cheap snorkel flippers past old men lob-bing *pétanque* balls in the shade of plane trees abuzz with cicadas, I skipped across the hot sand at Carry-le-Rouet. The beach was packed: topless women were having sun cream massaged into their backs by men in black Speedos, slender but for the solid pot-bellies you get from a lifetime diet of pastis and *panisse*. Weaving between the sunbathers on the thin strip of sand on the main beach, I rounded a point to a rocky stretch and found a hidden patch of sand where I could struggle into my snorkel gear with a minimum of oversight.

It was hot weather, even for July. Earlier in the week, the red flag banning swimming had gone up on several beaches around Marseilles. A reporter had taken a thermometer to the beach: the water temperature had reached 32 degrees Celsius; unheard of, even in the summer. Bathers came out of the water with stinging red eyes and later found crusty yellow sores covering their skin. Apparently a pipe had backed up at the Catalans beach, and all the sewage from Marseilles was pouring directly into the sea; warning of diarrhoea and meningitis, officials closed the beach for twenty-four hours and announced they would fine anybody caught in the water. (Even after the leaking cloaca had been repaired, the shallow, superhot water continued to smell rank; the mayor's office blustered: 'It's obvious, when ten thousand people are swimming at Pointe-Rouge, that the water is going to be dirty.') Meanwhile, a few hundred miles to the east, smacks of mauve stingers – hundreds of thousands of venomous jellyfish, which glow yellow at night – were inflicting painful, and in some cases fatal, stings at Italy's most exclusive beach resorts. Adriatic beaches are now regularly shut down by mucilage events and 'snot volcanoes', in which gelatinous columns of microbes rise from the sea bottom. This was what was becoming of the seashore in the age of global warming and flattening food pyramids, and it looked a lot like the Precambrian era, when microbes ruled. It is going to take some getting used to.

Carry-le-Rouet is home to the Parc Marin de la Côte Bleue,

one of the few marine reserves off the coast of France. The first such protected area – they are sometimes known as no-take zones – in the world was actually established near Marseilles in 1793. When it was reopened for exploitation in 1830, fishermen reported miraculous, multitonne catches of enormous hake. Globally, such protected areas have proven to be effective refuges for big fish. The coastal waters off Cape Canaveral, long off limits because of the space programme, now boast the only healthy population of trophy-size marlin, tuna and swordfish on the American east coast; the Great Barrier Reef, the Galápagos Islands and the waters off the northwest Hawaiian islands have also been made into marine reserves. In New Zealand, scientists have found that the marine environment thrived after a reserve was opened on an unremarkable stretch of coast: the density of rock lobsters in the protected area has increased by a factor of fifty and endangered red snapper flourishing. Fishermen who at first opposed the reserve have discovered that it acts as a nursery for commercial species in nearby waters. There are now thirty-one permanent marine reserves in New Zealand, covering 8 per cent of its coastal waters; the country's fishermen, convinced that such protected zones increased productivity, are campaigning to raise the amount to 30 per cent. (The only time the Atlantic has demonstrated such vitality in living memory was after the Second World War, when half of Europe's fishing vessels were sunk, and fish stocks were given a respite from fishermen. Whale populations bounced back and, for a brief period after the war, big fecund fish filled the Atlantic.) Though there are forty-seven such parks in the Mediterranean, they tend to be tiny, accounting for less than 1 per cent of the sea's total area.

The spot where I was snorkelling, the Parc Marin de la Côte Bleue, was typical: it was merely a 210-acre patch of ocean where fishing, scuba diving and boating had been banned. In spite of its modest size, this little park is also a success. I could see the red tips of a dozen snorkel tubes in the water before me, and the lifeguard who handed me a glossy pamphlet describing the Parc's species told me that it had become a haven for sea life. Walking backwards over slippery rocks, I immersed myself in water that felt close to body temperature, and flippered out a few dozen yards.

Soon I was floating over a meadow of seagrass, thousands of plants with blunt-tipped green fronds swaying in gentle currents. It was the same species I had seen in Christophe Holtz's nets, *Posidonia oceanica*, which was not a seaweed at all, but a flowering plant, one that occurs in only two places in the world: here in the Mediterranean, and off the southern shore of Australia. Herds of silvery striped salemas swished through the fronds; herbivorous fish, they browse on the *Posidonia* like cattle on wild grass. It is an incredibly rich habitat: cuttlefish come to reproduce here, rockfish leave their stony lairs to hunt among the fronds, and predatory groupers use it as a nursery; each square yard can harbour up to four thousand invertebrates. *Posidonia* at once nourishes the sea – an acre of dense meadow produces up to 8,500 gallons of oxygen a day – and serves as an important carbon sink, sequestering the atmospheric carbon dioxide that causes global warming. All through the Mediterranean, from the shoreline to a depth of about ninety feet, from Gibraltar to the Suez Canal, such *Posidonia* meadows provide productive habitat for the sea's most important seafood species; in decomposition, their dead fronds feed clams, oysters and mussels. The Mediterranean accounts for only 1 per cent of the world's water but, thanks in part to such rich seagrass habitats, it contains fully 7 per cent of its marine fauna. Without *Posidonia*, the Mediterranean would be a much poorer sea indeed.

A solitary sea bream approached my mask, darting away when I extended my hand. Catching sight of a glimmer of red on the bottom, I changed direction. I was hoping it was a *rascasse* lying in wait for prey. Taking a long suck through my snorkel, I held my breath and dived. A couple of yards from the bottom, though, as my cheeks were brushed by *Posidonia*, I realized it was a can of Coca-Cola. Surfacing, I briefly panicked as a clingy, floating mass wrapped itself around my face. It was no venomous stinger, but a waterlogged plastic bag printed with the name of a local *supermarché*.

It is an unfortunate truism: litter and pollution in Europe seem to increase in inverse proportion to one's distance from the Mediterranean. It is as though living in paradise inspires a perverse impulse to besmirch it. In Corfu, Naples and Dubrovnik, I have witnessed people dropping litter onto the ground with blithe disdain. In Cortiou, one of the most stunning of Marseilles's calanques – the steep-sided limestone fjords that begin only a fifteen-minute bus ride from the Vieux-Port – the civic aqueduct spews a spume of sewage out to sea. Until 1987, it was completely untreated. Even today, when all-too-frequent storms overwhelm the municipal water treatment centre and the streets of Marseilles become cataracts, the 'cacaduc', as it is ironically known, dumps the raw sewage of a conurbation of a million directly into the Mediterranean; the seabed nearby is well known for its high levels of polychlorinated biphenyls and heavy metals. This sea, like all the oceans of the world, is now filled with 'nurdles', tiny bits of plastic that get swallowed by jellyfish and salps, to be passed up the food chain to larger fish. (Present as little exfoliating beads in the body scrubs beloved by European women, nurdles get washed down bathtub drains to the sea, where they are soon coated in dioxins and other persistent organic pollutants.) Nobody knows what effect the 250 billion pounds of nurdles manufactured every year will have on sea life, or how long it will take them to break down – if they ever break down. A scientific vessel that trawled the waters off Marseilles discovered two hundred pieces of large litter per hectare, most of them plastic bags and bottles. The debris tangles and drowns sea mammals and turtles, chokes birds and fouls fishing gear. The researchers estimate that the Golfe de Lion, Marseilles's corner of the Mediterranean, now contains 175 million pieces of plastic litter.

Though the wastewater of Marseilles is chemically treated, the Liguro-Provenço-Catalan current, a westerly oceanic conveyor belt off the shore of Marseilles, ensures that Italy's pollution problems are also France's. All told, 48 per cent of coastal urban centres still dump their untreated wastewater straight into the Mediterranean, whose waters are renewed only by exchange with the Atlantic and the Indian Ocean, a cycle that takes up to 150 years to complete. What's more, eighty major rivers pour into this sea, carrying pollutants from two hundred petrochemical and energy installations. Marseilles also sits smack in the middle of the mouth of the Rhône River, which ferries hardcore industrial contaminants into the sea; its heavy metals are immunodepressive in fish, making them more likely to succumb to disease.

It is precisely here, and in similarly toxic river deltas in Greece and Italy, that many fish farms are located. One of the most popular products of Mediterranean aquaculture is sea bass. Rebranded as *branzino* in North America (to avoid confusion with politically incorrect Chilean sea bass), it has become popular with chefs for its moist, firm flesh. Mediterranean sea bass, as it should really be known, is almost inevitably a farmed fish whose flesh is marinated in the waters of Europe's most infamous chemical corridors.

Petroleum, meanwhile, is a never-ending problem; at any one time, two thousand vessels of one hundred tonnes or more can be found in the Mediterranean. During routine tank-washing and deballasting operations they leak oil, and combined with refinery waste, an estimated six hundred thousand tonnes of petroleum get dumped annually into the Mediterranean, the equivalent of sixteen Exxon-Valdez spills. If a really large wreckage happened in the Golfe de Lion – on the scale of, say, the

Prestige oil spill that dumped Russian crude off the Atlantic coast of Spain in 2002 – the tourist economy of the French Riviera could be in ruins for a decade.

Packing up my snorkel gear for the train ride home, I looked out to sea, past the small white motorboat that was patrolling the edge of the marine reserve. Somewhere out there, at a depth of sixty feet – beyond the range of my snorkel tube – lay a patch of seaweed that made all the gallons of oil and tonnes of raw sewage seem like the most trivial of irritants.

It went by the name *Caulerpa*, and it was first detected in French waters twenty years ago. If it was not brought under control soon, the bouillabaisse of Marseilles was going to become a very poor fish soup indeed.

L'Alga assassina

In 1988 a student diving in the waters just below the clifftop-perched Oceanographic Museum of Monaco discovered a fluorescent green algae growing in the muddy sea bottom. It was identified as *Caulerpa taxifolia* (*caulerpa* means 'creeping stem' in Greek), a species native to Australia. The patch was tiny. The student swam around it in less than a minute; he could have uprooted it by hand in less than an hour.

The origins of this curious invader were hardly a mystery. Cultivated for use in aquariums, this strain of *Caulerpa*, a particularly hardy, cold-resistant clone, had been imported from an aquarium in Stuttgart for use in the Monaco museum's fish tanks. It grew well; so well, in fact, that occasionally it had to be culled. As early as 1984, employees were seen dumping dustbins of freshly plucked *Caulerpa* out the aquarium windows into the sea.

In August 1989 Alexandre Meinesz, a specialist in algae from the University of Nice, used a dive scooter to explore the Monaco seabed. He was astounded to find that the patch covered almost two and a half acres of ocean floor. The sight was impressive – Meinesz described a 'magnificent meadow' – but it was also sterile; where the *Caulerpa* grew, no other plants were found. Unlike a field of *Posidonia*, which is richer in biodiversity than a tropical forest, the *Caulerpa* meadow was free of animal life. Analysing some samples, he found that the plants were toxic – they numbed the human tongue, and fish wouldn't touch them; what's more, all of them were male, clones of the original in Stuttgart. (Some scientists believe *Caulerpa* is the largest cloned organism on the planet.) Meinesz started warning journalists and politicians that the Mediterranean was facing a new biological invader, and the origin was almost certainly the Monaco aquarium.

The reaction of this august institution, which was founded in 1910 by Prince Albert I, a yachtsman and enthusiastic oceanographer, was not to its credit. The *Caulerpa* had been dumped into the sea when Jacques Cousteau, that great popularizer of oceanography, was director. His successor launched what amounted to a disinformation campaign: in all likelihood, he said, the algae was native to the Mediterranean; or perhaps it had come from the Red Sea through the Suez Canal. Whatever its origins, he maintained, it was certainly an improvement over the barren, polluted bottom that had formerly fronted the aquarium. Besides, it would probably die when the winter came. Charging the press with sensationalism – the papers had taken to calling *Caulerpa* 'the killer algae' and even 'the AIDS of the sea' – the director accused Meinesz of trying to drum up funding for his lab by exaggerating a minor curiosity of nature. He even boasted that he and the Prince of Monaco enjoyed eating the killer algae *beignet*-style: breaded and deep-fried, like a doughnut.

Clinging to fishermen's nets and the anchors of pleasure

boats, *Caulerpa* began its inexorable spread through the Mediterranean. By 1990 it was found in Toulon, France, eighty-five miles from Monaco. It reached the coast of Spain by 1992; in the same year it was found covering about 250 square yards of the bottom of the bay of Imperia, in Italy, where the local press dubbed it the '*alga assassina*'. Everywhere it appeared, people noted the same phenomenon: there were no other algae, no invertebrates and no fish. In winter, when storms ripped up the underwater beds, fishermen's nets became completely clogged with *Caulerpa* fragments and they had to be laid out in the sun for up to a month until the algae rotted away. The fishermen of Corsica filed a formal complaint against the Monaco aquarium, to no avail. Scientific studies confirmed that *Caulerpa* brought net declines in fish biomass and in mean fish sizes, as well as a drop-off in catches. Not only did cold winters fail to kill it; the original patches were becoming denser and healthier. By 1997, when *Caulerpa* reached Croatia, the entire coast of Monaco was dominated by a single organism.

It took five years for IFREMER, the French government's ocean and fisheries research institute, to acknowledge that *Caulerpa* might be a problem. By then it was an all-out plague, one that could not be eradicated, only controlled; when critical spots were threatened, as one French national marine park was, divers were dispatched to pull up the algae by hand. The strain of *Caulerpa taxifolia* from the Monaco aquarium – a single individual, cloned to infinity – can at present be found in six countries; from a single square yard, it has come to cover thirty-two thousand acres of Mediterranean seabed.

Caulerpa was discovered in Orange County and San Diego in 2000. It quickly smothered eelgrass beds, a crucial nursery habitat for halibut and spotted sand bass; scientists said it looked like AstroTurf, blanketing everything in uniform Day-Glo green. Within a couple of weeks of its detection, a team of marine biologists and resource managers consulted with Meinesz and

143

settled on an eradication technique: they smothered the invader by covering the *Caulerpa* patches with black tarp and pumping them full of liquid chlorine. The plan worked, but they had been lucky: the infestations had occurred in shallow lagoons. If they had happened in unsheltered coastal waters, such chemical treatments would have been impossible.

As the 'killer algae' progressed westward from Monaco via boat anchor and fishing net, the people of Marseilles braced for news of an outbreak. It never came. In 1997, however, a related species, *Caulerpa racemosa*, was found just outside the Vieux-Port. The new variety, smaller than *taxifolia*, is also toxic to fish, and turns the seabed into a barren prairie of crabgrass. Unlike *taxifolia*, it reproduces sexually, which means it can spread much faster than a clone. Moreover, it thrives in warmer water; the higher temperatures accompanying global warming are encouraging its spread.

'Invasive algae are worse than all the oil spills,' wrote Meinesz, 'against which society immediately puts to work all the means at its disposal. Nature suffers when oil is spilled, but it recovers. In this case, nobody is doing anything. The entire continental shelf of the Mediterranean is susceptible to these two kinds of algae.

'Sooner or later,' Meinesz predicted, 'they're going to dominate the entire sea.'

After only a few years, *Caulerpa racemosa* can be found off more than fifty miles of French coastline – it has even spread to the little Parc Marin where I went snorkelling – and more than 40 per cent of the infested waters are fishing areas. Patches have been recorded close to La Ciotat, which may explain the brown fronds I saw in Christophe Holtz's net, and it is now present in eleven Mediterranean countries, from Spain to Turkey. Scientists at Marseilles's Oceanographic Centre, impressed by how quickly *C. racemosa* spread to the Canary Islands in the northeast Atlantic, titled a 2005 paper 'Blitzkrieg in a Marine Invasion.'

At the Oceanographic Centre's marine station, dramatically sited on the oceanfront in a southern suburb of Marseilles, I met Jean-Georges Harmelin, a marine biologist and author of several books on the Mediterranean. Born in Marseilles, he has been swimming in local waters all his life; in fact, he had been for a dive that morning, making a rare sighting of the *cigale de mer*, the flat lobster that poachers hunt to keep the bouillabaisse pots boiling. Harmelin had seen decades' worth of changes in the sea around Marseilles. They had not always, he was quick to point out, been for the worse.

'Remember,' he told me, 'I knew the sewer at Cortiou *before* they installed the treatment station.' For much of the twentieth century, Marseilles was known as the filthiest port in France, if not the western Mediterranean. Typhoid outbreaks were common in the summer, and most homes had to boil their water. 'Strangely, there were actually *more* fish in that area then. They fed on the organic matter – the sewage. Certain line-fishermen even had reserved spots around the sewer mouth. Now they complain that the treatment centre has somehow poisoned the fish. The truth is, the fish simply left because there was not as much to eat as there was before.'

The beneficial seagrass *Posidonia*, he said, had been under attack for generations. It started with nineteenth-century pair-trawling, in which two sailboats would haul a net between them, systematically mowing down the seagrass fields. When, after the Second World War, people started washing with detergents – rather than traditional, and environmentally friendly, blocks of Savon de Marseille – the *Posidonia* fields retreated even further. In the space of only six years the area covered by *Caulerpa racemosa* has grown 350 per cent in the Gulf of Marseilles. *Posidonia*, which grows less than an inch a year, can not compete with the invader.

What concerned Harmelin the most was the radical increase in water temperature, and the new species it was bringing. Lately, he said, he felt like he was diving in a different sea – or at least a different part of the Mediterranean.

'It's a bit like Corsica, about thirty years ago. We're starting to see juvenile barracudas around the port of Marseilles. At Port-Cros, there's a band of six hundred of them, and they're getting bigger. We used to see sharks and big skates, lobsters and sea-spiders; they're very rare now. On the other hand, we're seeing more and more dentex, amberjack and salema.' (The latter are carp-like fish, and not particularly good eating.) 'The water temperature just below the lab was 29.2 degrees C yesterday. It's a historic record. The invertebrates, like the gorgonians, sea-fans and sponges are really suffering, and it's going to get worse. When you measure the average temperature of the deeper water, the long-term change is clear: there's been an increase of 0.8 C in thirty years. I hope it doesn't get worse. Around Marseilles we have red coral and gorgonians in very shallow water. If you go to Corsica, Greece or Turkey, you won't find such magnificent underwater landscapes. It's only possible because we have a certain climate – which is changing.'

I asked whether the so-called killer algae is a genuine threat.

'*Caulerpa racemosa* arrived in the Gulf of Marseilles all of a sudden,' said Harmelin. 'Its spores drift in the current, so there's nothing we can do to stop it spreading. The big problem with *Caulerpa taxifolia* and *racemosa* is that they monopolize the terrain. They carpet everything, darken the water, eliminate the native algae, and close up all the small crevices where rock-fish and crustaceans live. Unlike *Posidonia*, they are not a welcoming habitat for fish.' He showed me a photo he had taken of the sea floor completely covered with *Caulerpa taxifolia*, like a hideous low plush; a single clump of spidery *Posidonia* was stranded in the green carpet. For the *rascasse*, whose palette of colours goes from brown to orangey-red, the problem is clear:

146

in a field of *Posidonia*, it can easily camouflage itself from predators and prey. Against a field of *Caulerpa taxifolia*, it stands out like a can of Coca-Cola.

I told Harmelin that he sounded like a typical Marseillais: fatalistic, and apparently resigned to the changes affecting the Mediterranean.

He laughed. 'I was behind two old women in the post office yesterday. They were saying: "Things aren't what they used to be!" Well, Marseilles has existed for 2,600 years, and I get the feeling things were *never* what they used to be.

'As for the *chapon*,' said Harmelin, 'which is a very big *rascasse*, it's the best fish in existence, and it's still abundant. It has a superb taste. The true bouillabaisse was the one that poor fishermen made with fish they couldn't sell. But the "civilized" bouillabaisse you get at the charter restaurants – well, I don't eat it. It's too expensive.'

Harmelin chose to look on the bright side. 'You know,' he said with the slightest of shrugs, 'if one day the *chapons* and the lobsters do disappear, it may not be for the worst. Maybe then bouillabaisse will become an affordable, popular dish again.'

The Diversity Snatchers

Overfishing and pollution are conventionally fingered as the leading threats to the world's oceans. In the last decade or two, however, a new menace has emerged: invasive species. After habitat destruction, they are now the greatest cause of extinction worldwide. Experts in the emerging field of biological invasion fear that the world is entering a new era: the Homogecene, in which weedlike organisms, ferried around the world by human activity, drop a homogenizing shroud over a once diverse planet. If the trends of the last few years hold up, ecologists warn, a worldwide McDonald's ecosystem could emerge, in which a few metropolitan species – among them zebra mussels, brown snakes, giant Asian carp, kudzu, grey squirrels and *Caulerpa taxifolia* – overwhelm local environments and usurp much of the world's natural diversity. The Mediterranean, it turns out, is a staging area for some of the worst of these species.

There is nothing new about the phenomenon. Ever since humans have travelled, they have carried hitchhikers with them. The first recorded case of the unintentional introduction of an aquatic species dates to 1245, when Norse voyagers brought a soft-shelled clam to the waters of the North Sea on the sides of their wooden longships. Some species have been introduced intentionally, a form of ecological roulette that has had unintended consequences. In an experiment that started with a bucket and good intentions, the Nile perch, a gluttonous freshwater fish that can grow to enormous sizes, was slipped into Lake Victoria in the 1950s, where it thrived on the native cichlids, eventually causing the near extinction of hundreds of East African species. As the Academy Award-nominated documentary *Darwin's Nightmare* demonstrates, Nile perch fillets are being flown to European markets in planes that come back loaded with the weapons that fuel the social conflict engendered by the breakdown of the traditional fishing economy – a process that began with the introduction of the Nile perch.

It has been a long time since the earth's far-flung environments were hermetically sealed Edens. San Francisco Bay now has more exotic than native species: from Chinese mitten crabs that jam water-intake pipes, to the sea squirts that cover the bay floor with impenetrable yellow slime, more than two hundred non-native species have been identified. Even the animal life in the St Lawrence River – which flows an hour's walk from my Montreal apartment and was once home to walruses and the great auk – is now 60 per cent introduced exotics, brought by ships plying the seaway to the Great Lakes. When it comes to pristine ecosystems, we live in a fallen world, one whose baselines began to shift long ago.

What has changed most dramatically is the *rate* of species introductions. In the late nineteenth century, ships that once filled up with rocks, sand or steel started using a more supple form of ballast: water. The new steel-hulled vessels could suck up hundreds of thousands of gallons in one port, then dump their load in a harbour halfway around the world. A supertanker like the *Knock Knevis* – at a quarter of a mile long, the largest vessel in the world – can carry fifty different organisms in its ballast tanks, among them barnacles, bacteria, seaweed, diatoms, clams, isopods, shrimps, mussels and even good-sized fish. (Crew members of some such vessels drop hooks into the ballast tanks in search of lunch.) Ship traffic has increased by a factor of ten in the last half-century; eighty per cent of global trade is now conducted by ship.

The consequences are not limited to biodiversity loss. Perhaps not coincidentally, red tides, like ship traffic, are now ten times more common than they were half a century ago. Off the coast of Florida, blooms of a toxic algae called *Karenia brevis*, which used to occur once a decade, now happen almost every year and can last for months. A bloom is announced when tarpons, groupers and sea mammals such as manatees started washing up dead on local beaches. Collecting on wave crests and in sea foam, concentrated toxins are blown inshore, where they cause burning eyes, asthma, chronic sinus infections and pneumonia, even driving coast-dwellers to abandon their homes. (Surfers report that getting a mouthful of *Karenia brevis* was like being maced.) Ecologists believe such red tides are spread from ocean to ocean by ballast water.

The economic impact of the invaders is enormous. On any given day seven thousand different invasive species are hidden in the eleven billion tonnes of ballast water carried in the bellies of the world's ships. Too many succeed in implanting themselves in new environments. Baltic zebra mussels, pistachio-sized bivalves first identified in Russia in 1769, turned up in the Great Lakes in the 1980s, probably in the belly of a ship, and immediately made themselves at home. A car that was pulled out of Lake Erie after eight months was covered in a three-inch-thick layer of shells. Zebra mussels filter all the chlorophyll and nutrients out of lake-water, making life impossible for other living things. They block the water-intake canals of electricity companies and have to be blasted away with high-pressure hoses; they have now spread south to the Mississippi Delta. All told, invasive species are estimated to cost the US economy the equivalent of £67 *billion* a year.

Because it plays host to 30 per cent of the world's maritime traffic, the Mediterranean has become a hotspot for invaders. The four hundred introduced species in the sea already represent 5 per cent of its flora and fauna; over the last few years a new species' arrival has been recorded every four weeks. And this is a tragedy, because the Mediterranean is also the sea with the highest rate of endemism in the world. In other words, a greater variety of species is found in the Mediterranean and nowhere else than in any other sea in the world. Among them are the *rascasse*, the seagrass *Posidonia*, the flat lobster and the endangered monk seal. Given the onslaught of invaders, the marine reserves designed to protect them might prove to be useless.

Just how bad can a biological invasion get? The Black Sea, connected to the Mediterranean by the Bosporus, provides the textbook example. For centuries, this nearly landlocked body of water was famous for the schools of anchovies that supported both mackerel and tuna and the fishermen that chased them. But the Black Sea's forests of seagrass and kelp, which nurtured pipefish, isopods, shrimps and crabs – important food for larger species – were slowly killed off by pollution from Soviet and Turkish factories, and in 1982 the North American comb jelly,

Mnemiopsis leidyi, arrived in a ship's ballast tanks. This small translucent medusa survived by gobbling up zooplankton, including the tiny fry of anchovies. By 1994, when the voracious invader had driven the anchovy fishery to collapse – in turn pushing dolphins, sturgeons and monk seals to local extinction – it was estimated that 90 per cent of the total biomass of organisms in the Black Sea was a single species, the comb jelly.

In 2006 large populations of *Mnemiopsis leidyi* were discovered in the Baltic and North Seas. They were probably stowaways from the Mediterranean. By receiving so much of the world's marine traffic, this sea, a victim of invasion itself, has become an exporter of invaders, a kind of dispatching ground for the world's worst pest species. The toxic algae *Prorocentrum minimum*, first identified near Marseilles, is now causing red tides in Asia, Australia and the United States. The *Caulerpa taxifolia* that appeared in California in 2000 may have simply been dumped into the lagoons at Huntington Harbor and Agua Hedionda by an exotic fish lover cleaning his aquarium. But Alexandre Meinesz, the scientist who first raised the alarm about the species, notes a strange coincidence in his book *Killer Algae*. In an early, and failed, attempt to prove that *Caulerpa taxifolia* was in fact a haven for life, the Monaco Oceanographic Museum used the yachts of the Saudi prince Khaled to survey the ocean floor outside the museum. In 2000, the Prince's yachts, the *Golden Odyssey* and the *Golden Shadow*, sailed to San Diego to be repainted. Shortly thereafter, the same killer algae, which is known to survive long journeys in the anchor wells of yachts, made its first appearance in the United States.

'This is not the first time these ships were repainted there,' notes Meinesz. 'This sets one to dreaming,' he adds, elliptically and suggestively, before concluding there is no strong evidence to support a link between the simultaneous appearance of *Caulerpa* and Prince Khaled's yacht in San Diego County.

There is a way to stop the invaders in their tracks: through aggressive legislation. Ballast water could be superheated, turning a ship's tanks into a giant bouillabaisse of marine species, but this would be an imperfect solution at best as many organisms survive the heating process. The simplest method is to empty and refill the tanks on the high seas rather than in sensitive harbours and estuaries. (Since the zebra mussel invasion, this is now mandatory for any ship entering the Great Lakes, and it is set to become law in California in 2009.) Unfortunately changing ballast water at sea takes time, and time, in the shipping industry, is money. In most of the world, shipowners have successfully lobbied against laws limiting their role in spreading bio-invaders.

Thanks to the shipping industry, the world's slow creep into the Homogecene, an era promising ocean ecosystems dominated by jellyfish and toxic clones, continues.

A Final Bowl of Bouillabaisse

In *A Considerable Town*, M. F. K. Fisher predicted: 'The Mediterranean has fed us for so long that it is unlikely even current human stupidities of pollution and destruction will stop its generosity. As we learn respect instead of carelessness, its fish will swim more healthily than ever, and its shells will form closer to the shorelines again, and the salt-sweet weeds will wave lushly for the picking.' She wrote those words in 1977. She could not have anticipated a near future of chemical-marinated *branzino* farms, global-warming-induced jellyfish invasions, red tides spread by ballast water – and 'salt-sweet weeds' being replaced by a toxic algal clone.

Nonetheless, I was not going to leave town until I had learned how to make that fish soup of the gods, the bouillabaisse of Marseilles. After all, the next time I made it to the Mediterranean, the essential ingredients might have disappeared for good.

Christian Buffa, the chef at the Miramar, a restaurant that was one of the founding members of the Bouillabaisse Charter, agreed to divulge some of his secrets. We were cooking for a table of six for the lunch service. In the kitchen I was given a paper chef's toque, a burgundy-coloured apron, a knife, a pile of white onions and some bulbs of purple-husked garlic, and told to go to work cutting and dicing.

Buffa, who is in his early thirties, is part of the fifth generation of an Italian family who came to France in the First World War. (His charming eighty-year-old grandmother, whom I met in the dining room, told me the family once owned a fish shop in the Rue de la Dace.) A disciple of chefs Paul Bocuse and Roger Verger, Buffa is himself a disciplinarian: I tried to look elsewhere as he bawled out the sous-chef beside me for oversalting an *aïoli*. But to a foreigner with a notepad and questions, Buffa was kind and patient.

'Bouillabaisse is not technical,' he said. 'It's simple, but very good.' He poured half a cup of olive oil into a big two-handled pot on a gas stove, added the garlic – halved and roughly mashed with a knife while still in their husks – and fried the onions until they were transparent but not brown. He threw in some quartered tomatoes, fennel seeds and powdered saffron.

'Just put in a little at the beginning,' he advised. 'With saffron, you're better off using more at the end.'

Then came the rockfish, delivered, like all his fish, by a wholesaler that morning. (A shame, because the morning fish market at the Quai des Belges is less than a hundred yards from the restaurant.) There was a weever, a gurnard, the head of a John Dory, a couple of *rascasses* – about four pounds of fish in total. Covering them with water, he turned the heat to maximum to permit the amalgamation of the olive oil with the water and his secret ingredient, a glass of pastis. He let them boil at '*un feu d'enfer*, a hellish heat, uncovered. It was a little sad: the vivid pinks, reds, greys, and blues of the fish leached away in the boiling water. The consolation was that all their flavour – their very essence – was being concentrated in the stock. The rapid boil facilitates the process of emulsification: the individual oil droplets are coated with a stabilizing layer of gelatin from the flesh of the fish, ultimately giving bouillabaisse its velvety finish.

The stock was soon done. A little shockingly, the fish – bones, scales and all – went into a hand-cranked vegetable mill, where they were reduced to pulp. We poured the resulting liquid through a *chinoise*, a metal-mesh colander. 'When you eat bouillabaisse,' Buffa reminded me, 'first you eat this soup, with croutons and *rouille*. In a second time, you eat the whole fish, with more soup on top.'

The now-smooth stock was returned to the stovetop pot, and Buffa threw in a second set of fish: conger eel and a monkfish first, followed by a gurnard, another John Dory, and several *rascasses*. After a few minutes of boiling, he added some crabs and mussels. Finished with more saffron, the bouillabaisse took on a soulful burnt umber tone.

Lunch that day was good. I whipped lashings of *rouille* onto olive-oil-drenched croutons and let them soak up the reddish-brown bouillabaisse broth, which slid over the tongue with ambrosial viscosity. Buffa brought out the whole fish piled high on a metal tray, with the crabs' claws dangling over the edge – he had stuck a couple of still-smouldering twigs of burnt fennel among them – and I dug into the firm-fleshed conger and the delicate John Dory, though I made a point of avoiding the monkfish.

At the end of the meal I told Buffa I was surprised by some of his digressions from the charter. He had included potatoes, cooked separately so they would not disintegrate in the broth, a tradition associated more with Martigues than with Marseilles. And he had added red mullet and mussels, which were nowhere mentioned in the document – in fact, mussels were usually seen as a northern abomination.

'The mussels are more for appearance,' said Buffa, waving away my carping. 'There are a thousand and one ways to make bouillabaisse. In the end, what is really important is the *rascasse*; because they live in the rocks and are very tasty.'

There were clearly as many recipes for bouillabaisse as there were fish living under the rocks of the Mediterranean, but no chef should be allowed to have the last word on the authenticity of bouillabaisse. For me, it is the great author of detective novels, the late Jean-Claude Izzo – whose line-fishing detective Fabio Montale did for Marseilles what Raymond Chandler's Philip Marlowe did for the backstreets of Los Angeles – who best resolved the bouillabaisse controversy.

'To avoid angering anybody,' Izzo once told a reporter, 'I'd have to say that the best bouillabaisse is the one you prepare yourself.' (In Montale's case, one presumes, in a *cabanon* on the calanques, with a bottle of Lagavulin whisky within arm's reach.)

Outside, the sun was high over the Mediterranean, and bronzed children were jumping off white rocks into the blue waves, as a ferry headed past the Château d'If towards Tunisia. Perhaps it was the venom of the *rascasse*, but the bowl of bouillabaisse had tasted like the quintessence of the Mediterranean, with all its saltiness and sophistication, but none of its crude oil and heavy metals. The *rouille* had not been too spicy, and the combination of the saffron and the Bellet Blanc, a beautiful Niçois wine, left me dreamy and – shades of Vulcan – a little bit sleepy.

This is the Mediterranean – a sea of *bourride* and *burrida*, of *kakaviá* and *caciucco*, and of *zarzuela* and *zuppe* – that one day I hoped to describe to my grandchildren. I would start by telling them how to make a real bouillabaisse. You begin, I would tell them, with a fish called the *rascasse* . . .

5

PORTUGAL AND FRANCE -

SARDINES

'Fish She is Very Small'

I have to admit it: there were times when I wondered whether I should stop eating fish altogether.

Bottom-raking draggers off the coast of New England. Massive fish kills in the Chesapeake. The declining cod fisheries of the North Atlantic. Toxic clones in the Mediterranean. The more I learned about dead zones, invasive species, jellyfish-slimed beaches and rapacious supertrawlers, the harder it was not to get discouraged about the options open to a seafood lover determined to eat ethically.

Strangely, though, not halfway through my journey, I was more committed to a fish diet than ever. I had already learned some of the principles essential for navigating a seafood menu. I knew that the way a fish was caught is crucial: monkfish, Atlantic halibut and sole, orange roughy and other species typically fished with bottom-damaging trawls would never be a good choice. I knew that big-ticket predators, such as bluefin tuna and swordfish, are not only overfished, but also tend to concentrate toxins in their flesh. I had also learned about the parallel fishing industry whose pirate vessels are stripping the seas of, among other species, Chilean sea bass and Barents Sea cod. Most of all, in restaurants and fishmongers, I had started to ask a crucial question: where exactly did your catch of the day come from?

But now I was about to pick up the most important lesson of all. Fisheries scientists had shown me that our habit of eating high in the food chain – closer to the sharks than the oysters – was contributing to the worldwide collapse of fisheries. As satisfying as the protein hit of a tuna burger or salmon steak can be, I was beginning to view these often toxin-rich meals as, at the very most, occasional indulgences.

Besides, the oceans were clearly full of fantastic fish that fed low in the food chain. Travelling from Portugal to Brittany (on the west coast of France), I was about to learn that the seas' small fish, so unjustly neglected by chefs, were not only the healthiest, but also the tastiest, choices of all.

Bottomfeeding, it seemed, had its rewards.

The Wharf of Europe

On Lisbon's Rua do Arsenal, the last street in the Baixa neighbourhood before the waterfront where the Tagus River meets the Atlantic, two of the pillars of Portuguese cooking vie for space in a traveller's nostrils: the musty, protein-rich smell of dried *bacalhau* hanging in dark storefronts – ghostly swatches of splayed salt cod that have to be soaked in water for hours before they will swell to palatability – and the pungent onslaught of *sardinhas*, whose flesh roasts on the blackened grills of Lisbon's best restaurants. Starting on 13 June, the death day of San Antonio – the saint who preached to fish – the unmistakable smell of oily fish roasting over coals takes over the country. Traces of a good *sardinhada*, or sardine barbecue, will linger in your clothes longer than the smell of a cheap cigar.

The Portuguese like their fish big, but they also like them small. More to the point, they just *like* them: in this country of ten million, annual per capita seafood consumption is 57 kilograms, making the Portuguese the European Union's champion fish eaters. (Among Europeans, only Icelanders, whose economy depends on fishing, consume more: an astonishing 90 kilograms per person.) The Portuguese fish fetish is the result of a combination of history and geography. Portugal is the chin and jowls of the Iberian Peninsula, stubbornly set above Africa, with five hundred miles of coastline and very little hinterland; wherever you are in this country, the Atlantic is never very far. It is Portugal's heroic era of seafaring, during which it established outposts in India, Angola and China and gave birth to Brazil, that explained the spicy *piri-piri* sauce, the curry powders, and the cinnamon and saffron that occasionally accent an otherwise notably uninflected cuisine. It also explains the amount of seafood on local menus: on terrace tables, hinged copper pans called *cataplanas* are cracked like hubcap-sized oysters to reveal steaming stews of clams, hake or shrimp; stocky men dig into the hearty *açorda de marisco*, a mushy but extremely tasty lump of stale fried bread moistened with broth and studded with squid, mussels, shrimp and lots of garlic and fresh coriander.

Yet this nation of fishermen, the erstwhile wharf of Europe, now imports three times as much seafood as it exports – including stockfish from Iceland, cod from Norway and even sardines from Russia – running up a seafood trade deficit of €706 million (£494 million) in 2005 alone. What is true of Portugal also applies to Europe as a whole. Though the European Union is the world's second largest fishing power after China, it typically imports ten million tonnes of fish products a year, while exporting only six million – leading to an annual trade deficit of €10 billion (£7 billion). Europe, in other words, is consuming far more than its rightful share of the world's best protein.

Which is too bad, because European culinary traditions contain the seeds of a solution to the crisis in the oceans. Portugal, France and other developed nations should not be importing big fish like bluefin tuna, salmon and cod from distant oceans; instead, they should be spending more time learning to enjoy the small fish they already have, but insist on grinding up to make fishmeal, margarine, fertilizer, animal feed and even fuel oil.

Fish like the small, but quite beautiful, *sardinha*.

A Short History of Tiny Fish

For as long as there has been a Europe, the sardine has been a staple. The Greek word *sardonios* means 'of Sardinia', referring to the Mediterranean island where the silver-bellied fish are still abundant; it also bequeathed upon us the word *sardonic*, in reference to a Sardinian plant that produced facial convulsions 'resembling horrible laughter, usually followed by death'. The branching etymology is appropriate, as there has always been a mocking side to the Western relationship with sardines: they are considered too small to be taken seriously. Throughout Spain and as far away as Cuba, the end of the carnival season and fish-eating is still marked by the Ash Wednesday 'Burial of the Sardine', in which men dressed as women, and women dressed as men, carry huge papier-mâché sardines on a bier through the streets, wailing '¡Por qué!' with much sardonic sobbing.

The oldest known cookbook, the fifth-century AD *De re coquinaria* (On the Subject of Cooking), recommends a recipe for sardines stuffed with honey and almonds. The Romans developed ways of preserving their summer sardine catch in oil or salt so they could keep eating them through the winter, and Christopher Columbus carried sardines packed in four hundred barrels with him on his first voyage. But the real breakthrough in preserving sardines came in 1824 when Joseph Colin of Nantes developed the process for canning sardines in oil. Drawing on the heat sterilization technique of Nicolas Appert and the work of Englishman Peter Durand – who had replaced Appert's wide-necked champagne bottles with tin cans – Colin soaked his sardines in brine, gutted and guillotined them, and flash-fried them in oil. They were then packed gill-to-fin in oil-filled cans, which were in turn sterilized in vapour ovens. This system still produces the best sardines: in the coastal towns of Brittany, factories filled with nimble-fingered women pump out cans marked 'Connétable millésime 2007,' or 'First Sardine of the Season'. (As a general rule, avoid fish packed in sauce: like the spice in spicy tuna rolls, tomatoes are used to hide damaged and not-so-fresh fish.)

It is often alleged that there is no such thing as a sardine: the word is simply a generic term for small pelagic fishes – those living near the upper layer of the open sea – that magically become 'sardines' when lined up in a can. It is true that when it comes to canned fish, a kind of cladistic confusion reigns. Sardines belong to the *Clupeidae* family, which includes three hundred species of schooling fish, collectively constituting one of the ocean's most significant stocks of protein. According to the Codex Alimentarius, the United Nations' internationally recognized set of food guidelines, twenty-one different species can accurately be labelled sardines, among them sprats, pilchards, brisling, herring and menhaden. The Brunswick sardine, for example, is actually an Atlantic herring, and sprats (*Sprattus sprattus balticus*) are identical to brisling (the name they are known by in Norway, where they are eaten for breakfast). Off the Pacific coast of the Americas, the species that predominates is *Sardinops sagax*, identifiable by the single row of dark spots on its sides, and belonging to a genus as different from the European sardine, according to experts, as we are from the great apes.

The pilchard, which is regarded a little askance in Britain, is in fact a slightly more mature sardine; looked at another way, the sardine is merely a young pilchard. (Stargazey pie, in which pilchards are baked in a shallow dish so their heads poke out of the pastry, like so many scaly blackbirds, is a speciality of Cornwall.) Cornish pilchards are popular in northern Italy, where they are known, and prized, as *salicchie Inglesi* and eaten with polenta at Lent. Recently, the company Pilchard Works had the good idea of redubbing their product 'Cornish sardines' for the British market, and selling them at Waitrose and other retailers in cans illustrated with reproductions of paintings from the Newlyn School. Sales have reportedly improved since the name change.

People were preserving small fish, under a variety of names, long before French innovators started canning them in oil. In the Breton town of Douarnenez, where there is still a sizeable sardine fishery, archaeologists have uncovered sixteen stone receptacles, dating from the third century AD, that were used in the manufacture of *garum*, a sauce made of fermented anchovies and mackerel and a staple throughout the Roman Empire. The Japanese have their own fermented fish paste, a slimy mixture of squid or fish flesh, entrails and salt, called *shottsuru*. Well-aged anchovy or shrimp add the essential *umami* undertone to everything from Vietnamese *nuoc mam* and Thai *nam-plaa* to Worcestershire sauce and Gentleman's Relish.

Back home in my kitchen cupboard, there is a can of fish from a company called Club des Millionaires, which was founded in Montreal in 1908. (Thanks to inflation, there is now a Club des Billionaires line.) Its bilingual label sums up all the vagueness surrounding small fish. The can's sixteen to twenty-two fish, which were caught off Scotland, are identified as 'Brisling Sardines de Sprats', which covers a lot of bases. When it comes to the bewildering variety of pelagic fish that are put in cans, Millionaire's pidgin-Mediterranean motto probably suffices for too many consumers: 'FISH SHE IS VERY SMALL.'

But western Europeans know there is only one small fish that really qualifies for the title. That is the fat-flanked, oily-fleshed fish that schools off their coasts in the billions. According to the Codex Alimentarius, *Sardina pilchardus* is the only variety that can be sold without a geographic qualifier (such as 'Peruvian' or 'California' sardine). The more of them I ate, the more inclined I was to agree.

Whether eaten fresh, at a Portuguese beachside grill, or lifted from the can, still dripping with olive oil, it is the variety known simply, and accurately, as the 'sardine'.

Shooting Pigeons in a Bucket

On the deck of the *Mestre Comboio*, Captain Joaquim Paulo Leitão had no time for such hair-splitting. He knew exactly what he was chasing: a *sardinha*.

Squat and sunburnt, with a bristly head of swept-back black hair, Leitão is a survivor in an industry that has gone through hard times since the 1980s. We were standing on the bridge of his steel-hulled purse-seiner, a few miles offshore of Peniche, a fishing port north of Lisbon. Behind me a painted plaster Virgin of Fatima was bolted to the wall. Ahead and around us, all was azure: we were a cobalt spot in a sweep of turquoise Atlantic, the summer bluescape scumbled only by whitecaps and flashes of the thousands of white gulls and guillemots that had followed us from port.

By Portuguese standards, the seventy-five-foot-long *Mestre Comboio* – a dayboat that rarely goes out of sight of shore – is actually a pretty big vessel: 90 per cent of the nation's fishing fleet is still made up of boats less than forty feet in length. Things have changed since the days when Leitão's grandfather fished these waters in a fragile wooden *traineira*. Until the 1950s sardines were so abundant that catching them was more like harvesting grain than chasing fish. Sardines were then fished at night, when they rose to the surface, usually during the *ardora*, the dark of the moon, or, in a tradition that is thought to go back to Palaeolithic times, when Venus set beneath the horizon. After the Second World War, the Portuguese started outfitting their wooden boats with echo sounders and radiotelephones. By 1964 perhaps four hundred purse-seiners were competing for an apparently inexhaustible stock; in that year alone they took 164,000 tonnes. But catches started dropping, and by the 1980s there were half as many boats; by the end of the century, a fishery that had always been free and unregulated faced its first quotas. Leitão told me it is now forbidden to fish on weekends, to fish for more than 180 days a year, or to catch more than ten tonnes a day – a quota imposed not by Brussels, but by the Portuguese Producers Organization, one of many such voluntary fishermen's groups in Europe. In 2005 Portuguese fishermen took only 67,000 tonnes of sardines, much less than half the historic high. The day's catch could never be enough for Leitão: his handsome year-old boat, subsidized to the tune of €1 million (£700,000) by the EU, cost him a further million euros in loans, and he has a crew of eighteen relying on him.

Compared to other North Atlantic fish stocks, however, sardines are not overfished. According to Copenhagen's International Council for the Exploration of the Sea (ICES), the spawning stock biomass of sardines – that is, the combined weight of all the fish of reproductive age – off the Portuguese coast is 386,000 tonnes, an amount that is expected to increase. Leitão is not so sure.

'Every day it's a surprise,' he said, his eyes fixed on the sonar. 'Every day it's different. Sometimes we make good fishing. Sometimes we never see any sardines anywhere.' The big problem, he said – repeating a refrain I had heard in other waters – was the price of diesel. 'Today over one-half euro (35 pence) a litre. Very expensive. It's the big problem, in fishing in Portugal, in the world. The price of fuel.'

We had already sailed by the grim old fortress where political prisoners were held in the time of the dictator Salazar, passing the old men in broad black berets line-fishing off the boulders at the end of the breakwater. An hour went by before Leitão spotted a promising red blotch on the sonar, sixty feet to port. The process of purse-seining began: Leitão blew a whistle, a switch was released, and a skiff attached to the stern dropped into the water. Two shirtless crew members jumped into the skiff, started the motor and towed one end of the seine net away from the boat; the *Mestre Comboio* slowly powered forward, at less than a knot, Leitão's second in command turning the wheel. Eventually, the two boats met, having sketched a near perfect circle of yellow dots – the cork floats suspending the seine net – on the ocean's blue surface; lead weights pulled the bottom edge of the net down to four hundred feet. (In terms of scale, it was as if we had encircled all the pigeons in Venice's St Mark's Square with a fine-meshed, if roofless, corral that went well past the roof of the Campanile.) A hydraulic winch on the bow cinched the bottom of the net like a drawstring purse, even as the cork floats were pulled onto deck, reducing the circumference of the net. When the bottom was fully pursed, and the circle of cork floats had become an oval not much longer than the boat, Leitão signalled for the crewmen to stop the powerblock. As the edges of the net were pulled from the water, the hundred gulls bobbing in the water all seemed to cock their heads in our direction at once.

On every fishing boat there is a moment when even the most sun-wizened skipper looks like a boy with a Christmas stocking on his lap. It is the moment when the net is hauled up, the lobster trap breaks the surface, or the first hook of the longline appears, and he and the crew get to see whether the set was good, the bait was taken or a hundred thousand fish darted beneath the net's edge at the last minute. I watched Leitão, and for a second a smile almost crossed his serious Portuguese face, so unetched by laugh lines. He had done well: the net was slippery with countless silvery, flailing bodies. The grins on deck were unmistakable, if fleeting, as the crew lowered a landing net into the open-topped seine – a technique called brailing – to transfer the catch to the deck. (In industrial sardine fisheries, the fish are pumped into the hold with giant vacuum tubes, a process that can damage the fish.) Every time the pannier-like nets were winched aloft with a cry of '¡Viva!', shimmering scales tumbled through the air like tinsel settling in a snow-globe.

The ship's dog barked joyously as the crew layered the sardines in big plastic tubs between shovels-full of slivered ice. I was surprised at how few other species there were in the net. We had picked up only one hitchhiker, a five-foot-long sleeper shark, bleeding from its gills and flapping its last on the deck. The tendency of sardines and other small fish to school means that purse-seine captains can use sonar to track and encircle their prey accurately without bait or lures, reducing the bycatch of untargeted species. Compared to bottom-trawling, and even the gill-netting for the *rascasse* and other rockfish I had seen in the Mediterranean, purse-seining for small fish is positively surgical. It is also extremely economical in terms of fuel. Economists have calculated that fishing for sardines and other abundant coastal species produces far fewer greenhouse gases than the cultivation and transport of spinach.

I asked Leitão how many fish they had caught. In answer, he held up two fingers. Two tonnes – a respectable day's work. In his grandfather's time, the fishermen went out at night, and would set the nets at least twice. A single set is the standard today, and Leitão wanted to hurry back to port in time for the afternoon auction.

The *Mestre Comboio* moored at a dock right outside the auction house. Inside the long warehouselike building, men and women in slacks and polo shirts – the intermediate wholesalers who sold to restaurants and markets – were already seated on rows of seats in bleachers, eyes on digital auction clocks, as plastic tubs of sardines passed below them on a conveyor belt. The bidding, done Dutch-style, with descending prices, had already begun. The auctioneer, a young man in front of a laptop in a tiny booth, steadily lowered the price; each prospective buyer had a handset that looked like a Sputnik-era walkie-talkie, complete with plastic buttons and antennae. If nobody bid, Leitão would still get a guaranteed minimum, and his catch would be sold to make industrial fishmeal or oil.

But that was unlikely to happen. The day's catch was perfect for barbecuing, sooner rather than later. Somewhere in the room, a button on a handset had been pressed, and the auction stopped at €49 (£34) for a case of 22.5 kilograms. That meant Leitão would be getting €2.17 (£1.50) a kilogram, or €4,355 (just over £3,000) for two tonnes. Not bad for half a day's work. With that he would be able to pay his crew's wages, fill his tank with diesel and chip in a little to the monthly payments on his boat. Leitão shook my hand. It had been a good day, he told me. Not good enough, I noticed, to leave him with a lasting smile.

When we were still on the water, I had asked Leitão about the future of the family trade.

'Twenty years ago,' he had replied, 'there were forty boats in Peniche fishing sardines. Today, we have only twenty. Everybody emigrated: people went to the UK, France, Canada. There are still sardines, but it's not an easy life.' I asked him if he had kids. 'I have two children. The girl is thirteen. The boy is fifteen.'

Did his son, I wondered, want to become a fisherman?

Leitão's eyes widened, as though he didn't even want to contemplate the prospect of the family trade continuing any further into this millennium.

'No chance!' he replied, shooting a glance of what looked like mingled alarm and entreaty at the statue of the Virgin. 'He's a good student.'

Feeding the World

In every ocean of the world, there is a small fish that nourishes entire marine ecosystems and keeps dayboat captains like Joaquim Paulo Leitão working. Off the west coast of South America, in the Pacific waters fed by the cold Humboldt Current, it is a species called the anchoveta, a slender, silvery schooling fish that is netted in the billions, supplying, at times, half of the world's fishmeal. In the North Atlantic it is the blue whiting, ignored a generation ago, now caught by Norwegian boats to the tune of 2.6 million tonnes a year. In the North Sea it is the sand-eel, a skinny fish that spends half its life buried in the sea-bottom mud, and provides a crucial food source for seabirds, seals, cod and haddock.

The largest fishery along the Atlantic and Gulf coasts of the United States is for a species that few people have heard of: the menhaden, a plump plankton eater that has no teeth and emits a decidedly foul odour. Menhaden – aka mossbunker, aka pogy, aka shadine – has played an unheralded role in both ecology and American history, nourishing bluefin tuna and the Pilgrims alike. (The latter were taught by Native Americans to fertilize their corn with menhaden.) In the 1870s, the production of menhaden oil, used to keep factories lubricated, lamps burning and in the manufacture of soap, actually overtook whale oil in America. Thanks to their complex stomachs, they are a species, that, like immature sardines, can convert diatoms (microscopic algae) and other phytoplankton – including the algae that cause red tides and dead zones – into edible flesh. Capable of filtering four gallons of water a minute, and travelling in schools the size of five city blocks, menhaden are as efficient at cleansing the sea as the oysters of Chesapeake Bay.

As H. Bruce Franklin recounts in his book *The Most Important Fish in the Sea*, the entire menhaden fishery is now monopolized by a single company, Houston-based Omega Protein (whose predecessor, the Zapata Corporation, was co-founded by George H. W. Bush in 1953). The catch is so huge that, in terms of tonnage, it has turned the tiny town of Reedville, Virginia, into the United States' second largest fishing port. The fish's adult population is only 30 per cent of what it was in the mid-1960s, and a fully grown menhaden has not been seen north of Cape Cod since 1993. Even today, there is no catch limit on menhaden. In his book, Franklin argues that Omega Protein, which hunts menhaden with spotter planes, is overseeing the destruction of one of America's most venerable fisheries, and contributing to the ongoing collapse of Atlantic coast ecosystems.

Small- and medium-sized pelagic fish are known in fisheries literature as 'forage' fish because, like the hay and grass that fill the stomachs of livestock, they sustain and fatten the top-of-the-food-chain species that we in the developed world prefer to eat. Such little fish account for an astonishing 37 per cent of the world's total catch. Some see their fecundity – the immense gleans, shoals and schools that seem to exist only to nourish other species – as evidence of divine providence. Though their numbers are indeed prodigious, they are far from infinite. The United Nations' Food and Agriculture Organization now considers almost all forage fish populations, from Peruvian anchoveta to African sardinella, to be fully exploited – fished to the limit of their capacity to expand.

Throughout history, populations of forage fish have failed, driving entire ecosystems, and even economies, into ruin. It was the collapse of the enormous herring fishery in the early fifteenth century that provided the impetus for Europeans to cross the Atlantic in search of cod. Up until the middle of the last century California's sardine fishery was the greatest in the western hemisphere. In 1945, the year John Steinbeck's novel *Cannery Row* was published, five thousand people were employed in Monterey Bay, processing a quarter of a million tonnes of sardines.

'The purse-seiners waddle heavily into the bay blowing their whistles,' wrote Steinbeck, setting the scene. 'The whole street rumbles and groans and screams and rattles as the silver rivers of fish pour out of the boats, and the boats rise higher and higher in the water.' Only six years after the book appeared, the waterfront was silent as the entire Californian sardine catch dropped to a mere forty-five tonnes, and Cannery Row, and an entire way of life, was on its way to ruin.

Since the California sardine crash, marine biologists world-wide have teased out some of the processes and cycles that determine how many, and what kind of, small fish will end up in cans and feeding troughs from year to year. Since sardines depend on the ocean's production of plankton, which changes according to climatic conditions, their numbers can vary enormously; sometimes they abandon familiar coastal feeding grounds for decades. The key is often a phenomenon called coastal upwelling, in which offshore winds push surface water away from the land; the warm water is replaced by currents of cold, nutrient-rich water rising from the sea bottom. The cold currents bring with them nitrogen, phosphate and the diatoms – microscopic algae – that nourish larger surface phytoplankton, which in turn are gobbled up by anchovies, sardines and other small fish. Although such upwelling regions – among them coastal California, Peru and West Africa – account for only 1 per cent of the ocean's surface, they are crucial oases of life, providing fully a fifth of the world's total catch. A natural phenomenon such as El Niño – in which the cold, nutrient-rich water of the Humboldt Current off Peru's coast is replaced by warmer water that is low in nutrients – can shut down this oceanic dumbwaiter, causing stocks of anchoveta and other forage fish to collapse. The cascading effects can be legion: penguins and sea lions starve, coastal economies tank, commodity prices skyrocket.

According to Tim Wyatt, a marine ecologist who specializes in plankton and small fish at the Institute of Marine Studies in Vigo, Spain, the world's most productive upwelling regions are now being assailed by man-made problems.

'The existence of dead zones in some upwelling areas is well known, and similar zones are now appearing in many parts of the coastal ocean – the Mississippi Delta, the Po River in the Adriatic – as a result of cultural eutrophication.' In other words, all the nitrogen that is pouring into the oceans from sewage and agricultural runoff is causing more algae to grow, leading to vast dead zones. 'Some enrichment is of course acceptable,' explains Wyatt, 'because it increases fish production, but eventually grazer control of phytoplankton by sardines and other fish fails, and instead of being eaten, it dies, leading to decay, anoxia and larger dead zones.'

One such dead zone is occurring off the Atlantic shores of the African nation of Namibia. There, a stinking, oxygen-free anoxic zone fit for jellyfish and not much more has been growing from year to year. Sardines once filtered the excess algae from the water, but over the last decade European and Asian vessels have been removing ten million tonnes of the tiny fish a year. With its natural grazers gone, the algae sink to the bottom of the ocean and start rotting, and in so doing release deadly hydrogen sulphide. The toxic gas has in turn killed off two billion hake, a major food fish for Namibians. It is a striking example of one of the unintended consequences of overfishing.

While El Niños and other natural climatic cycles push stocks of small schooling fish into free fall, continued overfishing can cause a struggling population to die. Monterey Bay's Cannery Row, for example, might have weathered the natural downturn in sardine numbers in the 1950s if a hyperactive fleet had not been fishing them at over three times the sustainable level. North Sea herring populations crashed in the 1970s, after an all-too-efficient fleet of seiners netted them in their billions.

For Portuguese fishermen, who have long lived in harmony with sardine stocks, there is a new variable in the cycles of abundance and decline: global warming. Since the 1970s higher temperatures have led to sustained northerly winds off the coast of Portugal, increasing the rate of coastal upwelling. Rather than providing more food for fish, however, this rapid upwelling disturbs the water column, leading to the production of much smaller phytoplankton cells. They are too small, in fact, to directly nourish juvenile sardines, which are forced to turn to the far less numerous animal plankton to survive. In other words, thanks to global warming, the *increase* in upwelling, which normally enriches ecosystems with more plankton, is now leading to a *decline* in forage fish.

Another factor, according to Tim Wyatt, is that strong summer winds are driving currents that disperse larval sardines far and wide, separating them from the main schools and ending their chances of reaching maturity. Though natural cycles play a role, ultimately it is the combined impact of global warming and fishing that is driving sardine landings off the Iberian coast to historic lows; which is why Portugal now has to supplement its catch by importing sardines from Russia.

Fortunately, at least for somebody who is learning the

pleasures of eating down the food chain, the sardines of Europe are far from endangered. There is evidence, however, that they are moving north. As ocean temperatures rise, anchovies and sardines have lately been showing up as far away as Scotland. That is bad news for Captain Leitão, whose purse-seiner was hardly conceived for long voyages. But it should be good news for Britain: it is estimated there are 600,000 tonnes of mature sardines off the Cornish coast alone, a population local boats have barely touched.

Too bad England is so enamoured of the bland, wormy cod. If the nation develops a taste for pilchard, the fish of the North Atlantic may stand a fighting chance.

Why Small Is Delicious

An orange full moon hung low in the sky, and a half-dozen wooden *traineiras* listed in the shallow water of the old port, a net's toss away from my table. I was about to celebrate my day of fishing by sitting down to a plate of grilled sardines.

The Restaurante Mira Mar's menu was classic Portuguese seaside, with a good selection of fish from the lower end of the food chain, including blue whiting, grilled squid and horse mackerel. (Alas, they also sold swordfish and salmon, the latter undoubtedly from a farm.) Portuguese cooking is all freshness and simplicity: side salads tend to be nothing more than raw onions, tomatoes and lettuce, to be dressed using the plastic olive oil and vinegar dispensers on the table; potatoes are inevitably served peeled and boiled. Dinner typically comes with soft buns, black olives, sardine paste, a tub of soft, mild cheese and butter; the waiter bills you only for what you use.

My sardines were far from shrimpy: Portuguese sardines are famously fat and fleshy, and the smallest on my plate was eight inches long. By now, I had got pretty good at carving small fish: after notching the head and tail with my knife, I split the first fish and folded over the top fillet, turning the sardine into a symmetrical Rorschach, and lifted out the backbone. As I pressed my fork on the fillets, fat-jewelled juices seeped from the skin, which was still iridescent where it had not been charred on the grill. The flesh was firm, salty and white, and the flavour was pure protein, the healthiest kind you can eat: low in saturated fats, mercury and dioxins, sardines are also full of essential fatty acids.

Why do sardines taste so good? The flesh of ocean fish, it turns out, is particularly rich in amino acids. Amino acids are the building blocks of proteins; about half of them are considered essential, because the human body cannot manufacture them itself. In the cells of a fish they are also the particles that counterbalance the osmotic pressure of the salty ocean. While seawater is about 3 per cent salt by weight, animal cells are only 1 per cent dissolved minerals; to compensate, sea creatures have to be especially rich in amino acids. (The saltier the water, the more of these tasty substances a fish needs, which explains the relative blandness of trout and other freshwater fish, and the strong flavours of fish from salty seas like the Mediterranean.)

Sweet glycine, which sugars the flesh of lobsters and other crustaceans, is one particularly tasty amino acid. Then there is savoury glutamate, a fast excitatory neurotransmitter essential for thinking and remembering, and which also sets the human tongue reeling with pleasure. It is also the key flavour component of *umami* (a term that simply means 'delicious' in Japanese) and, along with sweet, salty, bitter and sour, is one of our five basic tastes. Most people have experienced pure *umami* in the form of monosodium glutamate – the notorious MSG of Chinese-restaurant syndrome – which was first extracted from kelp broth by a Japanese scientist in 1907. (Glutamate is also present in miso soup, cured Ibérico ham, Reggiano parmesan and salt-cured anchovies.) After getting a bad rap as a source of headaches, it is now slipped into processed foods under the alias 'hydrolysed vegetable protein'. Ounce for ounce, glutamate-rich ocean fish are demonstrably more savoury than meat: a fillet can have ten times as many flavourful amino acids as steak.

Fish, of course, can also taste and smell incredibly fishy, especially when they are no longer fresh. The substance responsible is smelly trimethylamine, which is produced when enzymes provoke a reaction with the fats in decaying fish flesh – resulting in the same smell as halitosis and some gynaecological infections.

In short, the reason the sardines on my plate, or what was left of them, tasted so good was because they had lived in the relatively clean and very salty waters of the open Atlantic, meaning their cells had to be full of glutamate and other amino acids to balance the salinity of their environment. (And because they were fresh-caught, their levels of another savoury substance, inosine monophosphate, whose levels peak shortly after death, made their *umami* flavour especially strong.)

Frankly, though, as I started on my sixth sardine, I was not preoccupied with chemistry. I was wondering whether I should make it an even dozen by ordering another plate; and, while I was at it, another half bottle of *vinho verde*, that addictive, sparkling white wine that easily compensates for all the gloom in the Portuguese temperament.

I was also realizing that eating down the food chain could be its own reward – and that turning fish as delicious as sardines into fertilizer, mascara and chickenfeed may be one of our epoch's more subtle and grievous crimes against nature.

The Real Soylent Green

In 1973, Hollywood released a notably cheesy science-fiction film called *Soylent Green*. In the near future of this Gyproc-dystopia, global warming has produced a year-round heatwave, most animals are extinct, and New York's population of forty million is kept alive by rations of Soylent Green, a synthetic foodstuff that the authorities claim is made by harvesting protein from the oceans. A stiff Charlton Heston, to his highly emotive horror, discovers the truth as he is chased by gun-toting guards through a sprawling factory. The authorities are euthanizing excess citizens and grinding up their corpses to make cheap protein to feed the masses. Bleeding his last in an over-crowded church, the dying hero howls an immortal piece of sci-fi kitsch: 'Soylent Green . . . is . . . PEOPLE!'

An attempt was once made to synthesize a legitimate version of Soylent Green. In the optimistic 1960s, when technocrats at the United Nations spoke of 'ploughing the seven seas', the US Congress authorized the National Marine Fisheries Service to manufacture a miracle food called 'fish protein concentrate'. Made from the ground-up bodies of small ocean species, FPC was a gritty supplement intended to balance the diet of more than a billion people around the world, at a cost of less than a penny a pound. A factory was built in Aberdeen, Washington, and production began in 1966, with Chile as the first target market. In the end, the FDA imposed so many conditions – including the stipulation that expensive top-of-the-food-chain hake be used, rather than cheap menhaden and herring – that the project became uneconomical. The factory shut down after only six years of production.

Perhaps it was a good thing fish protein concentrate never went into wide distribution. Its inventors had originally planned to use one of the world's most significant self-renewing sources of protein: the anchoveta fishery off the west coast of South America. In 1970 the anchoveta catch had reached 17 million tonnes (by weight, about a quarter of all the fish caught in the world). Three years later – the same year the FPC factory closed and *Soylent Green* was released – the anchoveta fishery unexpectedly collapsed, a victim of El Niño and overfishing. The anchoveta crash deprived American farmers of a key source of protein-rich feed for their livestock and ultimately drove up grain prices, contributing to the galloping inflation of the mid-1970s.

Anchoveta stocks have since recovered, and the enormous Peruvian fleet nets its entire catch of these sardine-like fish – six million tonnes in a good year – in just three months. Working at their peak, Peru's factories can process 7,500 tonnes of anchoveta an *hour*, rendering almost the entire catch into industrial products rather than food for local tables.

According to those who have tried it, the anchoveta makes pretty good eating. In 2006 a Peruvian marine mammal expert convinced thirty leading chefs in Peru to use the anchoveta as the basis for an entire banquet. Fisheries scientist Daniel Pauly recalled attending:

'Having had this wonderful meal,' said the director of the University of British Columbia's Fisheries Centre, 'which included anchoveta tempura, marinated fillet of anchoveta, a "soup with no name" and other delights, I can attest that anchoveta are tasty. And they contain omega-3 fatty acids, too!'

Sadly, only a tiny percentage of the world catch of these small and medium pelagic fish make it to our tables. Blue whiting, which can grow to fifteen inches in length, is traditionally prepared – steamed or poached – by Russian, Baltic and Icelandic chefs; yet Scandinavian vessels still catch millions of tonnes to grind into fishmeal. The roe of filter-feeding menhaden is traditionally prized in New England, and its grilled flesh, mixed with potatoes, makes great croquettes; yet Omega Protein turns the entire East Coast catch of this important filter feeder into fertilizer, chickenfeed and omega-3 supplements. Herring, of course, can be pickled, kippered, served with tatties, potted, made into rollmops, baked, or even soused; yet the North Sea stock was fished to collapse in the 1970s, mostly to make pig feed. Though many nations now prohibit the use of sardine-type fish for industrial purposes, South American anchoveta boats have been documented landing horse mackerel (a favourite in Japan) and juvenile pilchard as bycatch, then selling them for reduction into fishmeal and oil.

In other words, most of the world's tasty small fish never make it to the dinner table. Only three-tenths of 1 per cent of the Peruvian anchoveta catch goes for direct human consumption. The rest is used to fatten farmed animals, from swine to salmon, or in the manufacture of fertilizer, make-up, margarine, paint or linoleum. Meanwhile, South American coastal ecosystems are collapsing because this keystone species is being harvested at unsustainable rates, at a time when, according to the UN, a quarter of Peru's children are malnourished. Grinding up good table fish to make meal should be seen for what it is: an outrage not only against nature, but humanity.

As for sardines, the population off the west coast of North America has recovered since the days of *Cannery Row* – even as stocks on the Asian side of the Pacific are collapsing – but very few Pacific sardines ever reach our plates. The bulk of them are now frozen in blocks and sent to Japan, where they are used as bait for longliners.

'The notion that we can't eat mackerel, sardines, anchovies is a fiction invented by the fish-farming industry,' Daniel Pauly told me. 'People say, for example, "Ah, but Americans don't like anchovies or sardines." But believe me, somebody else in the world will eat them! To waste good fish by feeding them to farmed salmon and tuna doesn't make any kind of sense. These fish could provide humans with large quantities of protein, but we waste them by using them as raw material for fishmeal.'

Not only fishmeal but, in the most extreme case, fuel oil. After years of overfishing, in 2005 the Danish industrial fleet pushed a healthy population of 300 *billion* sand-eel, a skinny fish that spends half its life buried in the sea bottom, to the brink of collapse. The catch was going to a single rendering factory that in turn sold the excess fish oil to power stations.

In other words, they were burning edible fish to produce electricity – which, in a hungry world, makes about as much sense as grilling hamburgers with briquettes made out of beef.

The Shrinking Fish Stew

As much as there is to admire in European cultural traditions of eating small, flavourful fish, for too long the EU's fishing policies, particularly when it comes to Africa, have been worthy only of contempt.

A telling case study is what has happened to the national dish of Senegal, *thieboudienne*, a stew made with fresh and dried fish, vegetables such as manioc and pumpkin, and generally served with rice on the side. The main ingredient is traditionally grouper, a large reef fish once abundant off the coast of West Africa.

For decades, though, Europe has leased the right to fish off the shores of African nations, in deals called third-party fisheries agreements. Rapacious industrial trawlers have stripped the protein from the upwelling regions off the continental shelf, those richest in sea life. Ireland's *Atlantic Dawn*, the largest fishing boat in the world (at 475 feet in length, and with a crew of one hundred, it is on the scale of a good-sized destroyer), which works off the coast of Senegal and Mauritania, has been known to haul in 400 tonnes of small fish like mackerel and sardines a *day* – two hundred times what I saw the *Mestre Comboio* net.

While the third-party agreements that permit this onslaught put money in the pockets of a few shortsighted politicians, they do nothing for local fishermen. Traditionally, 50 per cent of the protein in the West African diet has come from fish, but over the last thirty years, overfishing by European vessels has halved regional populations of shrimp, squid and hake and has driven sawfish to local extinction. Grouper populations have also tanked, which means the Senegalese have taken to making *thieboudienne* with sardines. But West African politicians, protecting the interests of big vessels like the *Atlantic Dawn*, which was built with £47 million in cash and EU subsidies, have lately been preventing local sardine fishermen from going to sea, on the ground that coastal stocks are in decline. It all means that Senegalese cooks now have to import the main ingredient for their national dish from Europe at several times the old market price – and in cans.

Assuming, that is, they can find them. Much of the sardine catch off the coast of West Africa is now being sent to bluefin tuna fattening farms in Australia. Concentrated up the food chain, the protein that should be going to feed the world's poorest countries is ending up in the sushi bars of Los Angeles, London and Tokyo, in the form of bluefin tuna sashimi.

Back to the Future

'Small is beautiful' is a saying that applies not only to fish, but also to fisheries. The beauty of the dayboats I went out in – whether they were chasing lobster in Nova Scotia, rockfish near Marseilles or sardines in Portugal – is that they provide a decent living for their owners without stripping the seas. When there is a change in the abundance of lobster, *rascasses* or sardines, their captains can vary their effort, or change fishing gear to go after a different species (or, as in the case of oyster-dredging skipjack captain Wade Murphy of Chesapeake Bay, opt to pursue an entirely different prey: tourists).

A 2001 study of the Norwegian fishing sector found that although the nation's thirteen thousand small boats brought in less than half the catch of the nation's three hundred big industrial vessels, the value of the small-boat catch was higher – mostly because they were landing fish that people would pay good money to eat, while the big boats' catch was largely being made into fishmeal and oil. The small boats, meanwhile, provided work for almost six times as many fishermen as the large-scale fleet. Though none of the small-scale fishermen were buying mansions, they were not exhausting a limited resource either. The big boats, in contrast, made a few people very rich when the fishing was good – but had to be bailed out with government subsidies when fish stocks crashed or prices collapsed.

As European nations go, Portugal may come closest to embodying the ideal of small is beautiful; fully 40 per cent of the national catch is sardines, and 99 per cent of all landings go directly to tables rather than to rendering factories and feeding troughs. Portugal, of course, is far from blameless when it comes to what was happening to the oceans. As a huge importer of high-in-the-food-chain cod, the nation is contributing to the ongoing collapse of a major North Atlantic fishery, and the Canadian coast guard is still catching larger Portuguese vessels off the Grand Banks with holds full of illegal cod, plaice and Greenland halibut. That said, however, Portugal is nowhere near as rapacious as other European nations, for one simple reason:

Its boats, rather beautifully, are too small to do that much damage.

The Last Adventurers of Daily Life

My small fish binge ended, as it happened, in Concarneau, a fishing port on the west coast of France. Brittany was once home to the world's largest canning industry; in 1879 as many as 160 Breton factories were producing 82 million cans of sardines a year. Only two decades later the sardines began to bypass French shores and feed in the open seas, out of reach of the small coastal fleet. Two thousand dayboats were put out of work, the economy of Brittany was thrown into chaos, and in the ensuing crisis the port of Douarnenez became the first French city to elect a Communist mayor. (The city's harbour is still known for its red sails.) In the years that followed, the sardine market was taken over by Spain and Portugal, and still later by Algeria and Morocco. The Breton canning industry never really recovered.

In its *belle époque* heyday, Concarneau was the Cannery Row of France. In thirty factories around the port, women in white smocks packed cooked sardines in oil (a technique known in the seafood world as *à l'ancienne*). Still the fourth largest fishing port in France, Concarneau lives according to the rhythms of the tides, though these days its walled old town, set like a shrivelled oyster in a shell-shaped harbour, attracts more tourists than sailors, and the parking lot of the one remaining cannery is filled with tour buses.

On a late-summer evening, one of the last I spent in Europe, I watched half a dozen sardine boats brailing their catch from their holds into tubs in front of the *criée*, Concarneau's wholesale auction house. The survivors of a once-great industry, these dayboats were now outfished by the tuna boats that left Concarneau to hunt albacore off the coast of Spain, the Azores and as far away as Madagascar. My guide to the port was Simon Allain, the son of a fisherman and for years a cook aboard

Concarneau's industrial trawlers. As he walked me through the port, recounting local history that applied to much of Europe, he proved to be a philosopher of the fisheries.

'Up until the nineteen-thirties,' said Allain, 'there were two thousand boats in Concarneau, most of them fishing for sardines at the entrance to the port. The fishermen were illiterate, the sons of peasants; there were lots of fish, but not much money; it was the time of *pêche-survie*, fishing-to-survive. From the thirties until the eighties, it was the time of *pêche-profit*, fishing-for-profit. Everybody was a fisherman; you could earn more in two weeks in the seventies as a fisherman than as the CEO of a big corporation. Beginning in the nineties, we had to go farther and farther out to sea, and trawl ever deeper, to catch the same amount of fish. It was the time of *pêche-crise*, fishing-in-crisis, and we're still living through it. There are still boats, but we're scrapping many of them to reduce the catch. There are still fishermen, but too many are unemployed.'

We climbed up a ladder onto the deck of a big tuna boat. 'There are many reasons for the crisis in Concarneau,' said Allain. 'The globalization of markets means that sardines arrive from Peru, or tuna from the Philippines, at a price that defies all competition. At the same time the low price of farmed fish is lowering the price of wild-caught fish. Fishermen from other countries, Spain in particular, are willing to go out for a month at a time, in horrible conditions, for less than €4,000 (£2,800). Then there's the price of fuel.'

We were now in the cramped belly of the ship. 'A boat like this uses a hundred and eighty litres of diesel an hour,' said Allain, as we walked past its thousand-horsepower engine. 'It takes at least two litres of diesel to catch one kilogram of fish; at €0.50 (£0.35) a litre, which is the price of diesel today, it's almost not worth it. Finally, even if nobody wants to admit it, there's the increasing scarcity of the resource itself. When you put them all together, you get a social crisis.' It may also have explained why Allain was now working in the tourist industry, rather than making a fortune at sea.

Allain's love of the fishing life he grew up with – his father started as a mate on a fishing boat at the age of twelve – was clearly mixed with horror at what short-sightedness and greed had done to what should have been the ultimate renewable resource.

'Fishermen are hunters,' he said. 'Some people would even say they are predators. I'd add that they are lords, and probably among the last adventurers of daily life. They belong to the economy of the hunt, which goes back millennia. Except that three thousand years ago there were no echo sounders and GPS systems; obviously, with all this technological sophistication, the fish have a little trouble escaping. The difference between a fisherman and a farmer is that a fisherman has never sown a fish in the water. He's not responsible for the paternity of what he's caught. Fishermen are always subject to what I call the lottery-day syndrome, the hope that with the next set of the net they'll haul up the jackpot.'

As we returned to the deck of the tuna boat, Allain pointed to a small trawler moored at the wharf alongside the auction-eers' market. 'You see that rusty little ship? The other day, it came back from Ireland with a hold full of Atlantic emperor, a deep-sea fish that lives to be forty years old; they earned €213,000 (£149,100) in two weeks at sea. A fisherman is always going away like that, hoping to strike it rich. He doesn't see his life go by. His daughter is born; next thing he knows, she's getting married, and he says to himself, "Already!" His house is here on the ship, not there on the land.'

Given all the problems, I wondered, why was Europe still subsidizing the building of boats like the one we were on?

For Allain, the answer was simple: though half a century of fishing-for-profit has exhausted the fish off their own shores, there are still some left to catch off the coast of Africa. The steel behemoth we were on was brand-new, a 285-foot-long stern-trawler built with EU subsidies. The following day it would leave with a crew of thirty for a hundred days at sea, to trawl for albacore tuna halfway between the shores of West Africa and Brazil.

'Fishermen are hunters,' repeated Allain. 'And they will still be able to hunt for a few more years yet. But only if they put into practice – if it's not already too late – what an old Indian chief from your continent said years ago: "We not only inherit the earth from our ancestors, we also borrow it from our children." Though I like to add something we here in Brittany say: "Il ne faut pas tuer la vache avec le veau."'

Which means, quite simply, 'Don't kill the cow with the calf.'

The Bigness of Small

Big revelations sometimes come in small packages.

In Brittany I picked up a can of sardines packed in olive oil in a local supermarket. Though it was a little more expensive than I was used to paying, I didn't think much of it and tucked it away into my backpack.

But this was no ordinary can of FISH SHE IS VERY SMALL-style sardines: according to the label, they were 'Filets de sardines de Bolinche', *bolinche* being the local term for a purse-seine. They had been canned in the town of Douarnenez by a fishermen's cooperative called La Pointe de Penmarc'h, less than sixteen hours after they had been caught. There were several such co-operatives in Brittany, and they helped their members process and market their catch. Rather than blindly following the diktats issued by distant Brussels, they also set opening and closing dates for certain fisheries.

My sardines, it turns out, were caught by the *Wakan Tanka*

and landed at the port of Le Guilvenic on 7 October 2005. I knew this because the information was printed on the top of the can, next to the pull-tab. A quick Internet search turned up a site showing that the *Wakan Tanka* is a small wooden purse-seiner, with a 148-horsepower motor, painted a fetching blue and red – in other words, a dayboat. Another minute of surfing got me to the website of the International Council for the Exploration of the Sea, which indicated that sardine catches off the south coast of Brittany were currently sustainable. This was a can of sardines I could eat in good conscience.

For me, this was something of a revelation. Knowing the source of fish and their manner of harvesting – down to the boat that caught them, or the farm that raised them – was empowering for someone inclined to eat ethically. It allowed me to select seafood that did not come from overfished areas, or from regions notorious for unsound farming practices. I was starting to suspect that requiring companies to provide such information would go a long way towards curing the systemic ills of Big Seafood.

In France, of course, having this information is also a question of connoisseurship. Some French fish lovers treat well-canned sardines like fine wines. A small but dedicated sub-culture is devoted to *sardinopuxiphilia*, the collection of sardine tins, and some Parisian restaurants still serve sardines the traditional way: the can, already opened at the bottom, is placed on a plate with a purpose-built rectangular indentation, allowing you to admire the label. The flavour of canned sardines is actually thought to improve for up to seven years; aficionados recommend turning the can once every few months, like a good bottle of Champagne, to keep the oil seeping through the flesh.

One day, after my Douarnenez sardines had spent several months on a shelf, I lifted the boneless fillets from the can and dribbled a little of the herbed olive oil onto a slice of thick toast. I used the tines of a fork to mash the sardines' soft flesh into a pat of half-salted Breton butter, then smeared the still warm sourdough with the richest instant pâté imaginable. It was divine: bursting with glutamate and other flavourful free amino acids, loaded with omega-3s, and virtually free of environmental contaminants, sardines canned *à l'ancienne* instantly became my favourite midnight snack.

For me, there was no looking back. On my previous travels in Europe, I had learned to love Sicilian capers, Greek kalamata olives and sun-dried tomatoes from Puglia – all big tastes that came in small packages. The same, I now knew, applied to fish. When it came to eating seafood, I had learned the most important lesson of all:

Less is definitely more.

6

INDIA –

SHRIMP CURRY

Wave of Mutilation

Kanyakumari is as far south as you can go on the mainland of India: known to sailors as Cape Comorin, it is the bevelled culet of a jewel-shaped country, where the waters of the Indian Ocean, the Arabian Sea and the Bay of Bengal mingle in a billion turquoise facets beneath an equatorial sun. Depending on the currents, the beaches of Kanyakumari can be stained red, yellow or black, and sometimes all three; local souvenir vendors sell packs of tri-coloured sand, telling tourists the grains have washed all the way from the shores of Malaysia, Yemen and Burma. In a nation where cities can double as chakra points and rivers can be goddesses, land's end is bound to be a symbolically fraught patch of real estate, and Kanyakumari does not disappoint. Within a few hundred yards of the cape, you can visit the modernist temple where Gandhi's ashes rested before being scattered to the waves, ride a ferry to the gargantuan offshore statue of the Tamil saint and poet Tiruvalluvar, or simply sit in a beach chair with a Kingfisher beer and earn the right to brag you have seen the sun set over three distinct bodies of water.

On the day after Christmas 2004, when every guesthouse in Kanyakumari was filled with tourists and pilgrims, two clashing pieces of the earth's crust finally ended a millennia-long battle. The India plate yielded and abruptly slid under the Burma plate, lifting the seabed of the Indian Ocean by ten yards and displacing trillions of tons of rock. The resulting earthquake, the largest the world had felt in forty years, generated a force equivalent to twenty-three thousand Hiroshima-scale atomic bombs, caused the earth to vibrate at least half an inch on its axis, and triggered further earthquakes as far away as Alaska. From the quake's epicentre off the west coast of Sumatra, waves radiated outward at the speed of a jetliner. The Indian Ocean tsunami would redraw the coastline of Indonesia, temporarily submerge entire islands in the low-lying Maldives archipelago, and loom over some beaches in Thailand at the height of a three-storey building, draping the crowns of palm trees with cadavers.

At the Vivekananda Memorial, a crowd of tourists had got up early to watch the sunrise and were waiting for a ferry to take them the few hundred yards back to the Kanyakumari mainland. Just after 9:45 A.M. the first of the tsunami waves hit, in the form of a wall of churning water. The sky turned white as the wave slammed into the base of the Tiruvalluvar statue, sending spumes of seawater ninety feet into the air, as high as the saint's shoulders, and tossing ferries against the mainland pier as if they were toy boats in a bathtub.

The tourists at the Vivekananda Memorial were lucky that day; the waves washed up to their feet but did not overwhelm the platform on which they stood. Still, an Indian Air Force helicopter that arrived to evacuate them ten hours later was unable to land. It was the fisherpeople of Kanyakumari who rescued the stranded tourists that afternoon, braving still-treacherous waters to run continuous sorties in small boats. Eventually they would bring thirteen hundred people back to the mainland, even though they were coping with a tragedy of their own: most of their beachfront huts had been wiped out by the tsunami.

Up and down the Indian coast and throughout the thirteen Asian countries affected by the Indian Ocean tsunami, this was the pattern: beach-based fisherpeople died by the thousands in the initial impact, succumbed to disease in the weeks that followed or were left destitute by waves that shredded fishing nets and shattered homes and boats. In India, it was Tamil Nadu, the eastern coastal state that includes Kanyakumari, that bore the brunt of the waves.

Over a year after the waves struck, the village of Kottilpadu, the hardest hit in the district of Kanyakumari, was still struggling to recover. It was once a collection of terracotta-tiled houses that extended from the high-tide line to the palm trees behind the coastal road. When the surge came, people grabbed trees to keep from being carried inland; as the waters retreated, mothers watched helplessly as their children were snatched from their arms and carried out to sea.

Even now all that remained of many of Kottilpadu's houses were foundations filled with rainwater, or piles of bricks among drunken forests of leaning palms. On the beach, people were still living in temporary shelters; in the shade of a sheet metal hut stencilled 'House No. 18–4', a group of women in saris seated on the sand recalled the disaster in simple language.

'Tsunami full,' one said, gesturing towards the land to show how far inland the waves went. 'Seven hundred metres the water came. Two minutes it took to go into land; one minute to come back.'

Then the enumeration began. 'Four babies finished,' a stocky woman told me, rolling her eyes. 'Finished – died!'

A woman in a green sari said: 'Seven babies gone. One mother killed.'

The litany of loss continued: two brothers gone; one daughter vanished; mother–father finished. They were, of course, talking about their own children, their own parents. In Kottilpadu alone 480 houses were destroyed and 189 people were killed, most of them children; in a nearby mass grave, dug a few days after the disaster, the corpses had to be stacked one on top of the other.

Yet on the beach, two dozen men in hiked-up dhotis, exposed calf muscles knotted with effort, were straining to haul a seine net buoyed by plastic floats into the shore. For local aid workers, this return to the sea was a welcome sight. For two months after the tsunami fisherpeople were too traumatized to get back in the few boats that had remained undamaged. Gradually, however, as catamarans were replaced by donated fibre boats, the fisherpeople of Kottilpadu returned to the waters where the tropical seas meet.

The Indian Ocean tsunami, the most destructive in human history, disrupted shipping lanes, altered coastlines, exposed ancient submerged temples and left three hundred thousand people dead. Strangely, however, it may have been a minor incident compared to a slow-motion catastrophe that has been unfurling on the shorelines and creeks of Asia for the last two decades. Largely unnoticed in the West, and abetted by the collusion of trade organizations, loan-granting banks and foreign-exchange-hungry politicians, it is a disaster that is undoing the lives and livelihoods of tens of millions of coastal villagers – among the most powerless and voiceless members of many societies – in the name of ever-cheaper protein and all-you-can-eat meal deals.

The culprit, in this case, is not a tectonic plate shifting beneath the ocean floor but the arrival of a striped crustacean that swims backwards, lives in murky ponds, and is typically eaten breaded, with cocktail sauce, or grilled on the barbecue.

Mining Pink Gold

Shortly after the turn of the twenty-first century, shrimp surpassed canned tuna as the most popular seafood in the United States. With prices at an all-time low, by 2006 Americans were eating an average of 4.4 pounds of the stuff – a total of 1.3 billion pounds annually. Shrimp, which sells for as little as $4.99 (£2.45) a pound in some supermarkets, is available frozen in ten-pound bags at Wal-Mart, and year round on the menus of such unlikely retailers as Dairy Queen and International House of Pancakes. A single-chain restaurant operator, Darden, buys 44 million pounds of imported shrimp annually, and regularly features an Endless Shrimp special – bottomless plates of bottom-feeder, for as little as $14.99 (£7.35). (The Darden-owned Red Lobster chain, with 680 restaurants, is now the largest single end-user of seafood in North America.)

This shrimp boom is a worldwide phenomenon. McDonald's outlets in Tokyo promote the Sweet Chili EBI Filet Oset, a hamburger-style patty composed of rubbery pieces of fried shrimp. In London the sushi chain Yo! markets the Crunchy Prawn and Avocado Roll, and Marks & Spencer sells takeaway prawn-mayonnaise sandwiches on wholewheat bread at every major train station.* Frozen shrimp has been traded on commodity markets, alongside crude oil, pork bellies and plywood, for the last twenty-five years. Pound for pound, what was once a luxury food, or an occasional seaside indulgence, is now often cheaper than factory-farmed chicken.

* In the seafood business, the terms *shrimp* and *prawn* are interchangeable though *prawn* is favoured in Britain and Australia. Technically, *scampi* refers to a species of lobster, *Nephrops norvegicus*, also known as Dublin Bay prawn or Norway lobster. Under the special and separate rules of restaurant taxonomy, however, *scampi* has come to designate any large shrimp. *Butterfly shrimp* is not a distinct species, but any shrimp – or prawn – whose shell has been left on the tail segment, so the split flesh resembles a butterfly's wings.

There has been no miraculous crustacean population explosion in the oceans of the world. Little of the shrimp is being fished by Forrest Gumps on rusty trawlers in the Gulf of Mexico, and still less is caught sustainably in traps in the small fisheries in San Francisco Bay, the Gaspé Peninsula or Dublin Bay. Three-quarters of world shrimp production comes from such developing nations as Vietnam, India, Indonesia, Sri Lanka and especially China; the latter recently surpassed Thailand as the world's largest producer of shrimp. Since the mid-1980s, shrimp farming has been growing by 10 per cent a year, and shrimp exports from the developing world now amount to £4.25 billion annually. If you lined up all the shrimp farms in Thailand they would form a continuous band, nearly a thousand feet wide, around the country's seventeen hundred miles of coastline.

The simple fact is, if you are eating cheap shrimp today, it almost certainly comes from a turbid, pesticide-and-antibiotic-filled, virus-ridden pond in the tropical climes of one of the world's poorest countries.

Though Asians have raised shrimp using traditional methods for centuries, the industrial farming of shrimp began in earnest only in the 1970s, encouraged by the World Trade Organization and kick-started with loans from international financial institutions such as the Asian Development Bank. Shrimp is the 'pink gold' of the so-called blue revolution (the boosterish name for industrial aquaculture); the World Bank was a particularly enthusiastic backer, offering billions of pounds in loans as seed money to farmers in poor countries. In the early days even Greenpeace, the World Wide Fund for Nature and other environmental groups cautiously supported aquaculture.

'Fish is often the lowest cost animal protein,' one can read in a 2006 World Bank report with the biblical title *Changing the Face of the Waters*, 'and the world's growing food fish supply gap impacts disproportionately on the nutrition and health of the poor. Aquaculture must fill that growing supply gap.' For the Food and Agriculture Organization, the WTO and the World Bank, the blue revolution is a justifiable, and inevitable, panacea for world hunger that promises employment for the poor and cheap protein for all. 'Fish farming is a good and promising thing,' echoes the pro-free-trade newsmagazine the *Economist*, in an article titled 'A New Way to Feed the World'. 'It would be a calamity if rows about the environmental effects of fish farming prevented the development of a new industry.'

For those in the developing world who have watched the spread of shrimp farms with alarm, the 'rows' in question are matters of life and death. Father Thomas Kocherry is a Kanyakumari-based priest who has been working with fisherpeople for a quarter of a century. A member of the Redemptorists, founded in the eighteenth century by a Neapolitan bishop who lived among poor shepherds, Kocherry took the order's mission to heart: he worked as a fisherman for years, and regularly went to sea to haul nets with his parishioners. As chairman of the World Fishworkers Forum, which represents ten million fisherpeople in India, he has blocked roads, ports and railways; by his own reckoning, he has gone on seventeen hunger strikes. In one of his biggest triumphs, he led a nationwide fisheries strike that ended an Indian government proposal to allow thousands of foreign factory trawlers into local waters.

Kocherry's brick home, a few miles inland from Kottilpadu, is a simple two-storey affair he shares with another priest. He greeted me shirtless, a patterned blue lungi tied over his belly. In a fluorescent-lit living room, beneath a slowly turning ceiling fan, mice scampered beneath the sofa and lizards climbed the walls, but there was also a new Compaq computer with twin speakers whirring softly on an office desk. Kocherry was an interesting mix of third-world ascetic and jet-setting, Internet-connected activist.

His words came in a torrent, and he seemed impatient for me

to jot down his slogans: 'Gandhi said that we have enough resources for the *need* of us all, but not for the *greed* of us all,' he recited. 'And this is Thomas Kocherry's quotation: "The life of the planet, and the dependent health of humanity, cannot be sacrificed for the greed of a few."' Once we got that out of the way, he was eloquent and emphatic on the problems affecting fisherpeople.

'The tsunami,' he said, 'which was a disaster that happened in thirteen countries, is a good context to rethink our fishing and aquaculture policies. And the first priority should be helping people who undertake labour-intensive, beach-based fishing for their own survival.'

He believes Europeans and Americans do not understand the developing world context. Millions of fisherpeople in Asia live right on the seashore. They bring their catch back to the beach rather than the harbour, and tend to catch enough fish for their families, plus a small surplus. If the oceans are healthy, fishing is not only a sustainable trade, but can also keep them relatively prosperous – fisherpeople in India, though disdained as low-class, tend to earn a better living than factory or farm workers. But only, Kocherry insisted, when industrial trawlers and aqua-culture ponds are kept at bay. He believes that shrimp ponds in India, by monopolizing what were once shared resources like water, rice paddies and wild shrimp fry, have helped impover-ish fisherpeople. The aftermath of the tsunami was only hastening the process.

'Shrimp farming is what I call a rape-and-run industry,' said Kocherry. 'They rape the environment, make the maximum profit and move on. These rascals who rule the country will not be working in twenty years. But their victims, the fisherpeople, will be. After the tsunami, fisherpeople have simply been trying to survive; some go to the cities, some may go to the Persian Gulf countries to look for jobs. They are desperate. Any legislation should prioritize beach-based fisheries; and once their survival has been assured, we should allow medium-sized boats. For now it is aquaculture and the big trawlers that get the priority.'

What, I wondered, about the argument that fish farming is the only way to provide cheap protein to feed the world?

'Nonsense!' he thundered, banging the coffee table with his palm. 'They say they are increasing the amount of food products in the world, but it takes several kilograms of fresh fish, caught by industrial vessels, to make the feed to produce one kilogram of shrimp. I don't know who they are trying to bluff. It is only big people who benefit: merchants, landowners and exporters; the victims are the fisherpeople. The rich countries will *never* get their protein from fish farming sustainably. Intensive aquaculture should be banned all over the world. There is no justification for it. It is a destruction of the environment, and a poisonous food. I eat shrimp only if it comes from the sea – not these farms.'

Kanyakumari, explained Kocherry, was not the place to find shrimp farms; the real damage lay in the northern parts of Tamil Nadu. The next day he arranged for a neighbour with a car to drop me at the nearby town of Nagercoil, from which I endured a juddering eleven-hour overnight ride in a luggage-stacked sleeper bus to the city of Nagapattinam. It was the capital of a coastal district with the same name, where almost half of the disaster's 12,400 Indian deaths occurred. Boats had been washed a half-mile inland onto railway tracks. In one of the most affecting tragedies, fifty-two children died when the roof of an elementary school collapsed. Christian pilgrims from all over India had come to nearby Vailankanni to worship at a seaside church, India's largest, for Christmas; the waves left thousands of unidentifiable corpses, which were now buried in a field next to the municipal rubbish dump, marked with an obelisk and simple blue crosses. In the aftermath of the tsunami, Dalits, members of the caste once known as Untouchables, were given the job of transferring corpses to mass graves without the benefit of protective gloves or masks.

Yet somehow, thirteen months after the event, Nagapattinam, home to the largest trawling fleet on the Tamil Nadu coast, was coming back to life. Around my hotel fishing boats were being repaired in drydock, and in the harbour brilliantly coloured wooden trawlers – striped red, white, blue and yellow, their prows painted with almond-shaped eyes – bobbed gunwale to gunwale. In the market fishwives used old-fashioned scales to weigh the Indian Ocean catch of the day – the iridescent Indian mackerel, the saucer-shaped pomfret, the pink-eyed goat fish (and even, one afternoon, a leathery six-foot-long hammerhead shark). I saw few abandoned homes, and most of the damaged dwellings had been torn down to make room for temporary shelters, complexes of simple one-room shacks made of wood pulp or tin sheets, whose handpainted billboards read like a roster of the world's aid organizations.

The people of Nagapattinam had got back on their feet with a certain amount of pride. The Indian government refused an offer of tsunami relief money from other countries; when Hare Krishnas came offering vegetarian meals but refused to help with nets or catamarans for catching fish, local fisherpeople sent them packing. Truckloads of clothing, sent by well-meaning donors in Europe and North America, were left on the beach, because Indian fisherpeople refuse to wear cast-off clothes. Officially the Indian government had offered a package consisting of bedsheets, rice, kerosene, clothing and a one-time payment of 4,000 rupees (£50) to each tsunami-affected family, but over a year after the disaster, even this minimum had not reached many coastal fisherpeople, particularly Dalits and other members of what are still called the 'backward castes'. It was the non-governmental organizations, more than elected representatives, that had helped the people of Nagapattinam recover. As many as 450 NGOs were registered to operate in the district –

so many that they need a coordinating centre to divvy up the turf – and so far they had brought in £320 million in aid. Slowly but surely, the tsunami damage was being repaired.

In contrast, the impact of aquaculture was all the more insidious because it was taking place behind the scenes, hidden from the main roads. I hired a driver and an interpreter, and late one morning we piled into an Ambassador, the Indian remake of the stodgy 1956 British Morris Oxford, a car that calls to mind a bowler hat on wheels. Much of our progress southward along East Coast Road was over dried yellow rice stalks; Kumar, my interpreter, explained that they had been placed on the corrugated asphalt by farmers, which allowed tyres to do the work of grinding the husks into animal feed. The Nagapattinam district is considered the granary of Tamil Nadu: bounded by the mouth of the Kollidam River to the north and a point of land called Kodikarrai to the south, it projects like the surface of a steam iron into the Bay of Bengal. The land, parched in the dry season, is a crazy quilt of fields, stitched with rivers and canals. It is Nagapattinam's low-lying topography – it rarely rises to more than a few dozen feet above sea level – that allowed tsunami waters to penetrate up to two miles inland.

We left the Ambassador next to a narrow canal a few miles inland from the pilgrimage site of Vailankanni, and approached a shrimp farm. It was a small operation, with only four ponds, each about the size of an Olympic-style swimming pool. Bunds, or embankments, had been built up out of the sun-bleached earth to contain the water that was pumped from a brackish canal. The water was greenish-brown, turbid and opaque from suspended plankton, less bistro aquarium than fetid pond. A skinny-legged boy with a bowl haircut came over to meet us, offering a shy smile. He told us he was sixteen years old and worked for the shrimp farmer. Pulling a square fabric screen from the shallow water, he lifted two shrimp out of the pond. Trapping them beneath his palm before they could flip back into the water, he presented the shrimp to us. (Kumar, not a seafood lover, leaped back a foot from the wriggling catch.) Their translucent bodies were striped brown; the biggest of them was four inches long.

'They are still small,' the boy told us. 'They won't be ready for another month.'

In this part of the world, shrimp are harvested every six months, and an operation of this size, if all goes well, will yield one hundred thousand shrimp a year. As we talked, an older man, in a starched white shirt, slacks and sandals, approached us along the bund with nervous strides. It was the owner, a bald middle-aged man. When I explained I was researching shrimp farms, he smiled and invited us into his office, a small hut piled with muddy rakes and dented filing cabinets.

This was his family's land, he explained. The rice paddies that surrounded the fields also belonged to him. He sent his shrimp to Chennai, the state capital, where they were processed in a factory, which in turn exported them to the United States and Europe. He could not tell us which restaurants or supermarkets might sell them. When he started in the business in 1992, a kilogram of shrimp would earn him 450 rupees (£5.60); this year he got less than half that. The feed alone cost 50 rupees a kilogram (£0.62), and the shrimp had to be fed four or five times a day. He gestured to plastic sacks labelled 'CP Aquaculture Prawn Feed' piled in the corner. The only way he had been able to survive was by starting an agency that sold shrimp feed to other farmers.

'Nowadays,' he sighed, 'there is no profit.' Since the tsunami, poaching had also become a problem; he had had to string razor wire around the ponds and hire guards to prevent local fisherpeople and labourers from stealing the stock.

Nonetheless he tried to remain optimistic, if only for the sake of his eight employees. He presented me with a business card with his e-mail address and earnestly hoped I could connect him with a seafood importer in Canada.

Before we left, I asked if he used any chemicals in the ponds. 'No, no!' he protested. 'No chemicals! No antibiotics! All natural.' I pointed to one of the drained ponds whose cracked surface was covered with a white powdery residue.

'Yes, yes,' he said. 'This is true. But this is only a bleaching powder, to prepare the pond before it is filled.' The smile had left his face, and he showed us the door; the interview was over.

As we walked back to the car, Kumar laughed. 'No chemicals! That is a lie.' We walked past the paddy field; the stalks nearest the shrimp ponds were crooked and yellow. He swept his hand over the rice fields. 'Come back in two or three years,' he said, 'and all these will be dead.'

All-You-Can-Eat Antibiotics

There is nothing natural about the shrimp that are raised for export in Tamil Nadu and throughout Asia. From hatchery to deep-fryer, they are as much a product of industrial agriculture as McDonald's Chicken McNuggets.

In the wild, shrimp occupy a niche in almost every aquatic environment. On coral reefs in shallow tropical waters, the snapping shrimp stuns its prey by clamping shut its outsized claw, generating a jet of water and a cracking sound so intense that submarines have used it as a screen to hide from sonar. Ten thousand feet beneath the ocean's surface, blind white shrimp swarm around hydrothermic vents that belch bacteria and superheated seawater. Some species, like the trap-caught spot prawns of the British Columbia coast, begin life as males, and change sex as they age. Tiny brine shrimp eschew the ocean but thrive in brackish estuaries (and for decades in children's aquariums, in the form of those 'real live fun-pets', Sea-Monkeys). All told, there are two thousand known species of shrimp, ranging in size from a fraction of an inch to a foot in length.

Two hundred kinds of shrimp are exploited for human consumption, about twenty of which are available in North America. Among them are the grass shrimp – once netted by Asian fishermen for export to China – that live in San Francisco Bay; the pink shrimp known as hoppers in South Carolina; and the sweet and petite cold-water northern shrimp, *Pandalus borealis*, called *crevettes de Matane* in Quebec and Maine shrimp in the United States. When it comes to farmed shrimp, the selection is even more limited; in Ecuador and Brazil, as in most of Asia, *Penaeus vannamei*, or whiteleg shrimp, is favoured. If you prefer your shrimp popcorn-style, all-you-can-eat or packaged with cocktail sauce in a convenient tray, you are almost certainly eating the fast-growing *Penaeus monodon*, the giant tiger shrimp, so called because of its striped tail and ability to quickly grow to a length of up to twelve inches.

The Japanese biologist Motosaku Fujinaga is credited with being the father of modern shrimp aquaculture. In the 1930s he was the first to bring cultured shrimp fry to market size in the lab, and in 1963 he set up his own shrimp farm, using large ponds on discarded salt beds and feeding the growing shrimp chopped bycatch and discarded fish. Starting in 1958, a government lab in Galveston, Texas, developed techniques for culturing plankton that they used to feed larval shrimp; hybrid forms of 'Galveston Hatchery Technology' and the system developed by Fujinaga are now being used from backyards in the Philippines to farms in the Sonoran Desert.

Shrimp farmers in Tamil Nadu buy larvae that are grown from eggs in local hatcheries or else from fishermen who wade through estuaries using fine-meshed mosquito nets to scoop up shrimp fry. The 'mother' prawn, which can lay up to fourteen thousand eggs at a time, is especially coveted. Catching one is like hitting the jackpot, as farm-owners will pay £105 – the equivalent of four months' wages for a shrimp factory worker – for a single egg-bearing female. (Illegal smuggling of mother prawns from state to state is now a lucrative black market trade.) The bycatch is enormous: for every shrimp fry caught in a mosquito net, 160 fry of other species are discarded.

The waste does not stop there. Among the main ingredients in the prawn pellets made by CP Aquaculture (whose feed bags I saw piled in the shrimp farm's office) are fish and squid meal. It takes at least two pounds of ground-up wild fish flesh – milled with cod liver oil, vitamins, broken rice and attractants – to produce one pound of farmed shrimp flesh. (More advanced formulations now use synthetic attractants, crystalline amino acids and soybeans.) As Father Kocherry insists, shrimp aquaculture does not increase world food security: when shrimp are fattened with wild fish, the net amount of protein in the world can only decrease. Aquaculture has even turned crustaceans into cannibals: the second major ingredient in CP's feed is ground-up shrimp heads.

Farmed shrimp succumb to, and carry, a malignant palette of maladies. Black-splinter disease, brown gills, white spot virus and sky-blue discoloration have all wiped out Asian shrimp crops at one time or another, and a disease called *colita roja*, or little red tail, plagues the Latin American industry. Were it not for the frequent application of heavy-duty chemicals, shrimp would not survive a single season in the overcrowded, artificial setting of an aquaculture pond.

According to Tamil Nadu's fisheries department, a dry pond should be prepared by spreading urea and superphosphate to encourage plankton growth. Once the pond has been filled with brackish water, generally pumped from a nearby creek, it is typically covered with diesel oil to kill off any insect larvae. The water is then treated with a piscicide – a substance that poisons any competing aquatic life – such as chlorine or rotenone; the latter has been strongly linked to Parkinson's disease in humans. (The use of rotenone to rid the lakes and streams of the United States of unwanted fish, in order to provide the fly-casting lobby with an endless supply of rainbow trout, is one of the twentieth century's great unheralded crimes against biodiversity.) As the shrimp grow, the water is treated with pesticides and more piscicides, but by far the gravest area of concern is the use of antibiotics to ward off disease. Acutely toxic to other marine organisms, they can cause contact dermatitis in the shrimp farm employees who administer them. When the plug is pulled on the ponds at the end of the growing season, hundreds of pounds of shrimp remain marinating in the toxic mud at the bottom, and pickers have to be hired to scoop up the stranded shrimp.

Farmers, like the man Kumar and I met, naturally deny they use antibiotics, knowing full well they are banned in important export markets. When shrimp are tested, however – and the FDA checks less than 2 per cent of seafood imported into the United States – prohibited chemicals are still found. In Louisiana, which does rigorous testing of its own, the antibiotic chloramphenicol, known to cause leukaemia and aplastic anaemia, was found in 9 per cent of all samples. In 2007, the European Union rejected shipments of Indian shrimp from six major exporters because they tested positive for chloramphenicol and nitrofurans, another powerful antibiotic and a suspected carcinogen; meanwhile, Japan insisted that all shrimp imported from India be certified by government labs after several consignments were found to be contaminated with nitrofurans. Food safety experts have discovered that some people who believe they have shellfish allergies are actually exhibiting reactions, like itching and swelling, to antibiotic residues in farmed species.

A good indicator of antibiotic use, even if the chemicals have already been eliminated from the tissue of the shrimp, is the presence of antibiotic-resistant pathogens, such as typhoid and salmonella. Researchers at Mississippi State bought thirteen brands of imported ready-to-eat shrimp – some packaged with cocktail sauce – and found 162 separate species of bacteria, showing resistance to ten different antibiotics, including chloramphenicol. Their conclusion: consumers, particularly those with depressed immune systems, are probably better off *cooking* ready-to-eat shrimp.

'The shrimp farmers *all* use antibiotics,' Jesu Rethinam, the director of a Nagapattinam-based voluntary group helping fisherpeople after the tsunami, told me. 'You only have to look in local supply shops, where all these chemicals are available. But they very cleverly stop seven days before harvesting. After a week the chemicals can't be detected in tests. But they are still dumped into creeks, backwaters and the sea, in the form of effluents.'

The adulteration of shrimp does not end at the pond. Like scallops and even some wild salmon, shrimp are routinely soaked in a solution of sodium tripolyphosphate, or STPP, a suspected neurotoxicant, still legal in the United States, that prevents seafood from drying out in transit and boosts product weight. Borax, best known as a hand cleaner and insecticide, is used to preserve the colour of shrimp in some countries. The most unscrupulous companies use caustic soda to chemically burn tiger shrimp a customer-pleasing pink.

Wild-caught shrimp tend to be sweet and juicy, filled with glutamate, glycine and other flavourful, naturally occurring amino acids. At best, the farmed and frozen imported product tastes like rubbery extruded artificial crab meat. If, however, your shrimp have been rescued from the mud at the bottom of an Asian pond, you might pick up overtones of diesel oil, chlorine, rotten shrimp feed – and perhaps the slightest soupçon of carcinogenic antibiotic.

Bon appétit.

Mangrove Desperadoes

Eating farmed shrimp may be risky for consumers, but for those forced to accommodate the blue revolution in their backyards, ill-regulated shrimp farms are proving to be deadly.

The Muthupet mangrove forest lies at the southern tip of the Nagapattinam District, where six tributaries of the great Cauvery River form two lagoons before emptying into the Bay of Bengal. In the popular imagination, such mangroves have always had a dubious reputation. They were the 'swampland' sold to country bumpkins by Florida sharpies, so much economically useless real estate infested with crocs and rattlers; Singapore, Bombay and Hong Kong were painstakingly expanded by beating back mangrove swamps. Yet they are among the most productive ecosystems left on earth, as well as the most efficient carbon sinks we know of, sequestering the gases that cause global warming in their foliage. Like the rainforests, they are also highly threatened; every year, 2 per cent of the world's mangroves are cut down. One study has found that up to 38 per cent of mangrove loss worldwide can be attributed to shrimp farming. In Ecuador, a major supplier of farmed shrimp to American chain restaurants, almost 70 per cent of mangroves have been razed since the coming of shrimp farms. In all, 3.7 million acres of tropical mangroves, an area the size of Hawaii, have been turned into shrimp farms.

The former warden of the Muthupet forest, G. Ramamurthi, agreed to take me on a tour. He was a small man with big glasses, whose voice rarely rose above a hoarse whisper. Forced to retire because of poor health, Ramamurthi has remained an enthusiastic naturalist. Already, as we buzz down the shallow Korai River in a small wooden motorboat, he has pointed out fiddler crabs and mud lobsters, a kingfisher in the treetops and a white-ruffed Brahmanic kite wheeling overhead, as well as dozens of milkfish that flashed silver as they leaped from the water.

Technically this is protected land, but Muthupet is no untouchable Yellowstone or Jasper National Park; the mangroves also sustain a large human population. At the dock, fishermen were busy beheading wild white shrimp spread on plastic bags and weighing them with hand-held scales; out on the water, shirtless fishermen waded chest-deep with mosquito nets in search of wild shrimp. Behind us a herd of cattle forded the stream. As we approached the lagoon dock, the tillerman lifted the outboard motor to prevent the propellers from cutting a line of buoys laid out to mark the position of crab traps. In all, three thousand families from neighbouring villages earned a living fishing the waters around the forest.

Stepping ashore, we followed a wooden boardwalk through the mangrove forest. In the Cretaceous landscape of waxy leaved trees, whose aerial roots splayed like thousands of pairs of chopsticks into the water, the only sound was the dripping of water and the scuttling of crabs. The mangrove's decomposing leaves, Ramamurthi explained, provide nutrients for bottom-feeders, and fish come in from the sea to lay their eggs in the safe haven of the root network. This mangrove forest, the largest in South India, supports six different species of shrimp, eight kinds of mangrove trees and seventy-three species of fish. Waterbirds visit the mangroves on their migratory routes. Other, harder-to-find species are lurking about: cobras and civets, horseshoe bats and flying foxes, as well as plenty of medicinal plants, useful for curing snakebites and kidney ailments.

As we motored back along the Korai River to the pier, Ramamurthi pointed to a brick embankment, strung with razor wire, on which we could see thatched huts, most of them bristling with television antennae. They were the offices, toolsheds and guardhouses of some of the area's 150 shrimp farms, which suck up clean water and pour effluents into drainage canals illegally cut through the mangroves. Sixty per cent of the original thirty-two thousand acres of mangrove in Muthupet have been degraded by illegal grazing, poaching and tree-cutting. The shrimp farms, said Ramamurthi, have had the worst impact.

The captain of our little boat, who was also a fisherman, exploded when he realized we were talking about the shrimp farms.

'Every year there are fewer and fewer wild shrimp,' he said angrily, as he clutched the tiller. 'It is because of pollution from the shrimp farms. We used to find sea bass, carp, tilapias and blacktails here, but they are delicate, and now they die when they are quite small. We have to go farther and farther out to sea to find them. More and more, it is not worth it, because diesel fuel is so expensive. It is all their fault.' He swept one hand towards the shrimp farms.

My host invited me for chai and ginger snaps on the veranda of his bungalow, which his great-grandfather had built of bamboo and palm. A heart attack had forced Ramamurthi to retire from his job as forest warden; now he teaches naturopathy and environmental studies to college students.

'Mangroves form a natural barrier against cyclones and tsunamis,' he told me. 'On the day of the tsunami, hundreds of mangrove trees near the ocean were uprooted, but there was no tidal effect, or change in the water level, around Muthupet. Up the coast, there was devastation. The mangroves prevented the incoming of the water.'

The villagers who lived behind the mangroves suffered next to no loss of life. The complex root systems absorbed the force of the incoming waves, and distributed the water into the lagoon and tidal creeks of the wetlands; by the time the tsunami reached coastal hamlets, some of them only fifty yards from the edge of the forest, all its power had dissipated. Throughout the Asian countries hit by the tsunami, the pattern was the same: where there were mangroves, lives were saved. Where mangroves had been cut down, people died. The state government of neighbouring Kerala, noticing that the tsunami's impact had been particularly severe near cities where mangroves were destroyed, has since sponsored a 340 million-rupee (£4.25 million) programme of mangrove restoration.

Gradually the porch filled with a half-dozen Tamil-speaking fishermen and farmers from local villages. Ramamurthi had invited them to talk about the shrimp farms. Salty effluent from the ponds was pouring into the forest, they said, making the groundwater undrinkable and killing the mangroves. They had lost forty species of edible fish since the shrimp farms appeared, and the catch was down to 20 per cent of what it had been before shrimp farms came. The coastal people were very poor, they explained, but the shrimp farm owners were 'big money people' who bribed government officials. After only four or five years of operation, the shrimp farmers moved on, leaving local people to clean up their mess.

I was surrounded, it turned out, by wanted men, desperadoes of the swamplands. They had tried to convince the district collector, the highest government official in Nagapattinam, to remove the shrimp farms, but when no action was taken, they took matters in their own hands. Men, women and children stormed a local shrimp farm, using shovels and hoes to break the embankments and release the shrimp into the sea. The police jailed seventy-eight of the men in a distant town for forty-five days, but six of them escaped. I asked one of them if he was still worried about the police.

'If they come looking for me,' he said, puffing out his chest, 'I will cover myself with kerosene and set myself ablaze.' His friends laughed at his bravado.

By law, the shrimp ponds bordering the Muthupet mangroves should never have been dug. In 1996 the Supreme Court of India banned new development within half a kilometre of the high-tide mark and specifically forbade converting agricultural land, forests and mangroves into shrimp ponds. But India, as it is frequently remarked, is a country with a lot of laws but not much enforcement. Tamil Nadu, unlike neighbouring Kerala, got around the issue by never bothering to mark the high-tide line. One state fisheries minister, eager to promote shrimp farming in his central Indian district, went so far as to declare freshwater prawns a vegetarian food. 'Like eggs,' the minister said, 'the protein content in prawns is very high. Both are covered in shells.' (Vegetarian Hindus and Jains were not impressed by his absurd argument, which further equated eggs with shrimp because they both get hard when they are boiled.)

The federal government, in contrast to the Supreme Court, saw exported shrimp as a great potential source of hard currency. An important minister, it was whispered, owned shares in shrimp farms, and the state was thought to be using tsunami recovery as a way to clear the shores to make way for more shrimp farms and tourist facilities. In Nagapattinam and Chennai, tsunami-stricken fishing families had been offered keys to new concrete homes, several miles inland. Commentators saw it as a cynical use of the tsunami as a pretext for clearing the beaches of their most troublesome inhabitants, the fisherpeople. Few of them wanted to leave the seashore, the age-old source of their livelihood.

Almost all of the shrimp farms in Tamil Nadu, Ramamurthi pointed out, were established illegally, when the Supreme Court order was still in place. Technically, then, the fisherpeople who broke the embankments in Muthupet were merely enforcing the law.

'We will win the case,' predicted Ramamurthi. 'The collector of this district himself said it was a people's operation, not a criminal activity.'

In the meantime, he said, local shrimp farmers were in trouble, because the shrimp were dying from the incurable white spot virus. The fishermen said they were happy that disease might drive the shrimp farms from their backyard; but they were also worried the virus would spread to the wild fish and shrimp in the mangroves, on which they depended for a living. They were right to be concerned; elsewhere in the world, pathogens had already leaped out of shrimp ponds. In the 1990s a flesh-eating virus had spread from Mexican shrimp farms to the wild, wiping out the fishery for blue shrimp in the upper Gulf of California. And pathogens may have already made the jump from shrimp to human beings: an epidemic of antibiotic-resistant cholera has been documented among Ecuadorean shrimp farm workers.

'Our people don't eat the farmed shrimp,' Ramamurthi told me. 'We believe that if you eat them continuously, you will have problems with asthma and cancer. We take only natural shrimp and fish. They are tastier and more healthy. Maybe eating farmed shrimp wouldn't be so bad for *you*, because you eat fruit, salad and other things. But fish and shrimp is almost all that we eat, so we suffer more.'

With a chuckle, he added: 'In Europe and America you can kill the poisons by drinking Coca-Cola.'

Delenda est India

It is clear who pays the highest price for shrimp farming: those unfortunate enough to live in coastal regions suitable for aquaculture. But who, apart from retailers and restaurant chains, is profiting from the blue revolution?

In Tamil Nadu it is rarely the individual farmer, who has to cope with low prices and high feed costs, and, sooner or later, will almost certainly see his investment wiped out by disease. Nor is the blue revolution benefiting some new rural workforce. In spite of the much-vaunted burgeoning of the Indian middle class – the nation now boasts one-third of the world's software engineers – India still remains home to a quarter of the world's undernourished. What India is rich in is manpower, and the nation's great challenge is feeding a population of over a billion, two-thirds of whom are still employed in agriculture. An acre of rice paddy provides employment for fourteen people; at best, an acre of shrimp ponds employs one person. On the afternoon I visited the shrimp farm near Vailankanni, I saw a single worker – a sixteen-year-old boy – supervising four ponds. Though more workers would be employed during the brief harvesting period, the farms hardly provide steady work.

The owners of the processing plants in Chennai and Pondicherry are only slightly better off. They rely on a work-force of young women, mostly from the neighbouring state of Kerala, who are willing to work twelve-hour days, and on festival days, in order to send money back to their families. A big plant might employ fifteen hundred women, who sleep in hostels on the site and spend their days beheading and deveining the shrimp. The average monthly wage for women, I had learned, was 1,590 rupees (£20), at least a third less than men were getting for doing similar work. Even while paying such slave wages, the exporters – facing tariffs and competition from China – are going through troubled times. There were once sixty in the state; now there are only fifteen.

The one Asian company that is profiting from the shrimp boom is the Charoen Pokphand Group, whose feed bags I had seen at the shrimp farm near Vailankanni. The CP Group is a Thai multinational which, among other things, owns the 7-Eleven franchise in Thailand, supplies chicken to KFCs throughout China, farms tilapia in the military dictatorship of Burma and has introduced American-style battery chicken farming to Asia. Founded as a feedstuffs business by four sons born to Chinese immigrants in Thailand, CP was taken over by the youngest, Dhanin Chearavanont, who took over from his older brothers and built CP into the Nestlé of Asia. The CP Group is now a stable of 250 companies with a hundred thousand employees in twenty countries, and it is one of the world's top five animal feed producers. It has utterly transformed the landscape of Thailand – a Senate committee found that the company had encroached on mangrove forests in Rayong Province – making shrimp ponds ubiquitous in that country.

Shrimp farms are far too susceptible to disease to make their ownership profitable. It makes more sense to allow individual farmers to assume the risk, and these days the CP Group makes its profit by selling prawn feed and shrimp fry to farmers. If white spot disease destroyed the entire shrimp industry in Tamil Nadu tomorrow, the company could simply source its shrimp from Orissa, Andra Pradesh or Sri Lanka. In fact, the CP Group is sufficiently diversified that it could probably survive the collapse of an entire sector. Though the 2005 outbreak of the avian flu sent its poultry sales into free fall, CP's profits from farmed shrimp in that year rose 400 per cent.

Before I left Tamil Nadu, Kumar told me there was one more place I needed to visit. We left Nagapattinam one afternoon and drove north to a village called Thirunagari. It is in an area considered the rice bowl of southern India; scientific methods of irrigation have been used there as far back as the eighth century AD, and in the late 1960s it was the launch pad for the 'Grow More Food' programme, a precursor to the green revolution.

But Thirunagari has lately become a victim of the blue revolution. At a village office local farmers showed me a map of the Uppanar River, which flowed past twenty shrimp farms on its way from Thirunagari to the Bay of Bengal.

'Our village is going to die,' said Sellapan, a farmer and retired bank employee who has lived in Thirunagari all his life. 'The population is about four thousand, but already in half of the village there is no cultivation. The boys and girls are migrating to cities like Coimbatore, Kerala and Karnataka to look for employment. The groundwater has become totally polluted, and there's a famine of drinking water. Shrimp farms have destroyed the cultivatable land, which has to be abandoned. The shrimp have come down with diseases, but the owners have brought in experts, and they are managing the problem with antibiotics. In fact, the government is giving out leases to new farms.'

Have attempts been made, I asked, to stop them?

'Yes. The Supreme Court gave clear-cut orders for the farms to be removed, but they were ignored by corruptible local officials. We believe all these farms should be removed. Otherwise our people cannot live here. It is a matter of life and death.'

We got back in the Ambassador and drove to the banks of the Uppanar River, dominated by the now-familiar sight of shrimp farm embankments surrounded by razor wire, and thatched tool huts extending to the horizon.

Sellapan pointed to an island in the middle of the river.

'These were all fertile coastal lands, which used to be rice paddies. The island you see has been converted into shrimp farms. Before it was grazing lands for the village animals.'

At a rice paddy adjoining a shrimp pond, the stalks were yellow and leaning at all angles; the ground was marshy; and unhealthy-looking white and green blooms of algae grew in the stagnant water. The adjoining field, separated by a ditch filled with brown sludge, was a wasteland of cracked dried mud. A woman in an orange sari saw us and strode up. Her name was Kamala, and she was the owner of this land.

'She says that this is her land,' said Sellapan, interpreting her rapid-fire Tamil. 'Her late husband went to Singapore about fifty years ago and made the money to buy this land. Now the prawn farms have come, and she has lost everything. Her land is becoming a desert. It is totally destroyed. She has become a pauper.'

We walked past a little tin bucket filled with green crabs. She collected them out of habit, she told us, but now they were too poisonous to eat.

As we walked towards a clutch of palm-tree-shaded huts, Sellapan explained that we were in a part of Thirunagari called Riverbank Street. The people here were Dalits who long ago converted to Christianity. I was quickly surrounded by villagers. The men hung back with their arms crossed, shy smiles on their faces. When Sellapan explained I was writing about the shrimp farms, an older woman with a pair of thick bifocals stepped forward.

'She is a rice farmer,' Sellapan said. 'She says: we don't want the shrimp farms here. We cannot cultivate our land any more; it has become a burden to us. We used to eat the fish in the river, but now it is contaminated, and we have to buy sea fish from fishmongers.'

A little boy handed me an old whisky bottle filled with water. It was milky brown, practically opaque with suspended sediment. I touched it with the tip of my tongue, and had to spit; it was as salty as seawater. It had come from Riverbank Street's only well. The groundwater, Sellapan explained, had been contaminated by seepage from the brackish water of the shrimp ponds and was undrinkable.

'Now they have to walk two or three kilometres to get their water,' said Sellapan. He pointed to a palm tree. 'There are no more coconuts in the trees – the water has killed them.' The tree's crowns were indeed barren. A hundred yards from us I could see the blinding white surface of a drained shrimp pond; a goat with concave sides was browsing on a patch of weeds on the embankment.

'The animals are all sick. Many have died from mysterious diseases. The people too are sick.' A man lifted up his lungi and showed me patches of white, psoriatic skin on his thighs; he said it came from wading in the river in search of fish near the shrimp ponds.

As I was shown more sores and patches of dry skin on

slender arms and legs, the old woman with the thick glasses took my notepad and wrote in it, in a schoolgirlish hand: 'Dysentery. Ulcer. Womitting. Itching. Breathing problem.' All of them, Sellapan explained, were maladies that had afflicted the people of Riverbank Street since the shrimp farms arrived.

'By law the ponds should be a thousand metres away from any dwelling,' he said. 'But these are only a hundred and fifty metres away.' I asked who owned them. 'The owner is a local policeman. There is his shelter.' He pointed to a thatched hut. 'He owns ten hectares. He is supposed to *enforce* the law, but he is *breaking* the law.'

As we walked back to the Ambassador, passing Riverbank Street's largest structure, a small white-walled Pentecostal church with a cross-shaped window cut into its brick wall, I started to pay attention to the dwellings. They were all mud huts, covered with coconut fronds as roofing. The entrances of many were covered with plastic bags. Approaching, I saw that they were the same kind of bags I had noticed in the office of the shrimp farm near Vailankanni. On top one read, 'Nasa Prawn Feed', and under a picture of a shrimp was the logo of the Thai multinational CP Aquaculture. These plastic bags, used to rain-proof roofs, were probably the only tangible benefit the people of Riverbank Street had derived from the blue revolution.

The Uppanar River, once a source of fish for the community, was now a source of water for shrimp ponds and a dumping place for their untreated effluent. Groundwater levels had been depleted to supply the ponds with fresh water; rice paddies have been contaminated; and pasturage for animals appropriated. As fresh water was pumped out of the ground, salt water seeps in, causing the land itself to become saline and unusable. Though the tsunami waters did penetrate this far inland, they alone were not responsible for the level of salinity.

A team from the nearby Kumbakonam Government College

analysed the soil from eighteen shrimp farms near Thirunagari and found levels of salinity, phosphates and total suspended solids to be well above levels permitted by the government. Shrimp farming, they concluded, 'would have a definite impact on the surface and subsurface water quality . . . most of the land nearby shrimp culture ponds is polluted due to this activity.'

Duong Van Ni, a hydrologist at Cantho University in Vietnam, a country with its own shrimp-farming problem, puts it even more succinctly: 'Shrimp farming is so damaging to the environment and so polluting to the soil, trees and water that it will be the last form of agriculture. After it, you can do nothing.'

Aquaculture in India has been likened to a modern-day enclosure movement. What was once shared land, used by all, is now cordoned off with razor-wire for the profit of a few. In eighteenth-century Britain the fencing-off of common land to provide pasturage for private landowners led to a massive displacement of its rural population, eventually creating the sprawling slums of Victorian London. The same process is happening in twenty-first-century India and throughout Asia – this time in the name not of sheep, but shrimp. Fields and coastal waters that once supported a large population of farmers and fisherpeople are both claimed and contaminated by aquaculture, an industry that has created a casualized wage-labour force – mostly employed in feed mills and processing plants – whose future work is at the mercy of viruses such as white spot. The tsunami aftermath is also providing the authorities with a good opportunity to clear the coast of fisherpeople, those troublesome folk whose presence, and protests, impede the digging of more shrimp ponds. Advocates insist shrimp farming is the only way to increase food security in a hungry world. Too bad the poor of India rarely get to eat farmed shrimp; it is a luxury food, exported to the developed world.

India's slums, home to one hundred million people, are the largest in Asia. Many forces have created them: drought, hydroelectric dams, sectarian conflict. Aquaculture is the latest. Suddenly, the shanty towns next to the runways of Bombay's airport, my touch-down point in India, seemed directly linked to the prawn curry being served to rich Indians and foreigners in Maharaja Class on the jetliners that taxi past them.

It reminded me of Rome's revenge on Carthage. After selling the city's inhabitants into slavery, the Romans razed what was left of it, ploughed the land and sowed salt in the furrows so nothing would grow for generations. Unless extremely high environmental standards are implemented, observed and rigorously enforced – the kind of standards Europeans and North Americans would expect if they had shrimp ponds in their own backyards – this kind of Roman revenge is what the blue revolution has in store for Asia.

No Shrimp Is Good Shrimp

What, then, is a shrimp lover to do?

To begin with: be very, very careful.

If the shrimp in your supermarket display case glisten unnaturally, or if they taste soapy even after being cooked, they have probably been treated with STPP, or sodium tripolyphosphate, the suspected neurotoxicant used to prevent drying. (Shrimp naturally contain high levels of phosphates, which makes detecting STPP difficult. An exaggeratedly salty taste is also a good tip-off to the presence of STPP, though some processors in the United States have been charged with masking the taste with saccharin.) A grainy substance coating the shell could mean the shrimp has been treated with caustic borax, to prevent discoloration. If the flesh looks yellow, particularly near the head, then the shrimp has already started to go bad before being frozen. Finally, take a whiff; if the shrimp smell briny, like seawater, they are probably safe, but an odour of ammonia means they have already started to rot.

Personally, I have sworn off eating intensively farmed shrimp. I agree with the Indians I met, who consider it a poisonous food and refuse to touch it. Cheap farmed shrimp, I now believe, is one of the worst seafood choices out there.

Attempts are being made to farm shrimp ethically. A company in Florida has developed antibiotic-free organic shrimp; and in Mexico's Sonoran Desert, far from the Pacific, they use closed-system aquaculture, which does not pollute coastal environments.

If you are concerned about your health, wild-caught shrimp is clearly a better choice than farmed. Unfortunately, most wild-caught shrimp come with a terrible environmental price: like monkfish, they are caught with trawls that drag the sea bottom, and the bycatch can be enormous. For every pound of shrimp caught by trawlers, *ten* pounds of other fish are typically thrown overboard, dead or dying.

Besides, it is pretty hard to find a restaurant that serves wild-caught shrimp. Major American seafood suppliers consistently prefer foreign-farmed shrimp to domestic wild-caught product; 85 per cent of the shrimp sold in the United States, for example, is now imported. A vice president of Darden, Red Lobster's parent company, testified before a federal trade commission: 'We will not sell our guests broken shrimp, shrimp that has been treated with *excessive* amounts of STPP, or shrimp that is off odour or has black spots.' (The italics are mine.) More important, the wild-caught product was not uniform enough for Red Lobster. 'It is critical that we serve [our guests] the same shrimp size each time they order the same menu entrée or appetizer.' Lobbied by southern shrimp fishermen, the commission decided that foreign farmers were dumping their low-priced shrimp in the United States, and slapped tariffs as high as 85 per cent on individual exporters. The tariffs, however, have not proven onerous enough to disrupt supply chains. Annually, one billion pounds of frozen shrimp are still imported into the United States – a volume that would make a shrimp cocktail the size of the 108-storey-high Sears Tower.

In the final analysis, you are better off buying – ordering, *demanding* – shrimp that has been caught in traps, the way lobsters are. That means paying attention to names and seasons; for example, the spot prawns of Canada's west coast are best in late spring and early summer. Pink hoppers are wild-caught in the Gulf of Mexico from October to May. The small northern shrimp, *Pandalus borealis*, is in season from November to May in Britain, and is currently experiencing a boom now that the cod that once preyed upon them are gone.

For me, shrimp has become what it was for people of my grandparents' generation: not some cheap Miracle Gro-spiked protein but an occasional seaside luxury.

One, however, that I am happy to go out of my way to indulge in.

A Decent Plate of Prawn Curry

Since arriving in Tamil Nadu, I had not had a single serving of shrimp.

Not that I dislike shrimp. When they are fresh, their sweet saltiness and the way they burst in the mouth when they are cooked just right make them the perfect ingredient in a Chinese stir-fry, a Thai lemongrass soup or an Indian curry. It was just that lately, and for obvious reasons, I had lost my appetite.

Fortunately in some places shrimp are still caught, and even raised, the traditional way – and I was not leaving India before I had tried a decent plate of shrimp curry. Leaving behind the desert scrubland of Tamil Nadu, I took an overnight train across the mountain range called the Western Ghats and woke up on the lush coastal plains of Kerala, on the western shore of India.

The state is a remarkably pleasant place to visit. I hitched a ride on the back of a motorcycle to Alleppey and shamelessly talked three Dutch women into letting me tag along on their tour of the backwaters, that network of canals, lagoons and streams between the Lakshadweep Sea and the Western Ghats. We spent a night on a fifty-year-old *kettuvallam*, a boat made from planks of jackfruit trees sewn together with coconut fibre and waterproofed with sardine oil, with a canopied parlour to provide respite from the midday sun. Assembling the makings of a dinner was easy. Two fishermen paddled up to the boat in a canoe with 'Vembanad Fish Counter' painted on the side. They held up shrimp the size of large crayfish, their swimmerets still twitching, for our inspection. At first we balked at the price: at a thousand rupees (£12) a kilogram, it was more than twice what we would have paid for frozen back home, and for India it seemed obscenely expensive. But we did not regret the decision. That night, as the sun set and the mosquito coils were lit, we ate mackerel marinated in lime, poppadoms and puffy red Kerala rice, beetroots fried with ginger, followed by the pièce de résistance, wild-caught prawn curry. The meaty shrimp, cooked by our chef, Anandan, tasted more like miniature lobster than the rubbery shrimp I was used to. Washed down with coconut toddy – fermented coconut milk, sour and slightly fizzy, with a deceptively strong alcoholic kick to it – and accompanied by the mournful sound of men's voices raised in song in the paddy fields, those backwater shrimp made up for a lot of reheated chapatis and Indian railway station lentils.

The Kerala coast has not been spared from overfishing. In the coastal town of Kochi one of the prime tourist photo-ops is the Chinese fishing nets: cantilevered wooden-framed contraptions, counterweighted with dangling stones, that call to mind the animated skeletons of giant whales. Fishermen have been dipping the nets into the harbour since the fourteenth century. One afternoon I asked if could join in the fishing. It took six of us, pulling thick cords with all our might, to lower the crooked ninety-foot-long spine and raise the net from the water. Running to the end of the platform, we inspected the catch in the dripping net: a baby swordfish, two striped tigerfish, a red snapper, a few flat fish with spots and spines, several thrashing mullets and a tiny crab; fifteen fish, all of them undersize.

Relaxing with a bidi (cheap cigarette) before the next pull on the net, moustached Michael told me he had been doing the work for the last eighteen years.

'There were many more fish when I started,' he said. Even ten years ago they could get more than one hundred pounds of fish from the sea in as little as four hours; now, a twelve-hour-day might net them only thirty-five pounds. It was almost not worth it, Michael said, flipping a scrawny tigerfish to a stray cat, who pounced on it with practised paws. Fortunately, he could still make a living charging tourists to take pictures of him while he worked.

Kerala, unlike Tamil Nadu, has been spared the worst depredations of the blue revolution. Shrimp are farmed here, but the old-fashioned way. Under the *pokkali* system, marshy coastal land was used for rice paddies from June to October. The rest of the year, when ocean water floods the land, the same fields are used to raise shrimp, much of it for local consumption.

I visited a large shrimp farm south of Kochi. Surrounded by healthy mangroves, the ponds were several times the size of those in Tamil Nadu and were bordered by low palm-tree-and-grass-covered embankments. Jacob Pediacal, a fisherman who lived on the land and supervised the ponds, waded a few feet into the bluish-green water and, twisting like a shot-putter, tossed a net into the air; it formed an almost perfect circle before splashing flat onto the surface, the lead weights on its perimeter pulling it to the bottom. Retreating to the bank, he hauled on the line, drawing the net in. He had caught half a dozen large tiger shrimp and two pearl spots, edible fish that share the ponds with the shrimp. (In Tamil Nadu's industrial ponds, antibiotics and piscicides would have killed off other species.)

My host in Kochi, V. P. Paul, explained that he was part owner of the land, but that Pediacal, who had been living there for forty years, got most of the profit from the ponds. Paul occasionally came to pick up some shrimp for his wife. 'Antibiotics and chemicals aren't allowed in Kerala,' he said. 'There would be protests.' Besides, the number of shrimp in the ponds is low compared to the intensive operations I saw in Tamil Nadu, and without overcrowding, there is less risk of disease. None of the shrimp are for export; they manage to sell their shrimp at local markets, for about 250 rupees (£3.10) a kilogram.

We took our catch back to Paul's house. His wife, Nimmy, who had been profiled in the *New York Times* for the cooking classes she runs out of their home, had a feast in store for us. I watched carefully as she showed me how to make *chemeen molee*, or prawn curry. Heating a little coconut oil over a gas flame, she tossed in peppercorns crushed on a piece of polished granite, a pinch of the yellowest turmeric, a few green chilli leaves, garlic, ginger and a lot of onion, until the smell rising from the pan made me feel faint with desire. Her assistant, nicknamed Baby, had beheaded, peeled and deveined the shrimp after soaking them in water several times.

'You wash and wash the shrimp until the water is crystal clear,' Nimmy told me. 'I don't trust anybody. I wash my meat, I wash my fish.' After five minutes of sautéeing, she threw in well-soaked cashews and a cup of thin milk from the coconuts from her garden, finishing it all with thicker coconut milk and a little vinegar.

Lunch, the biggest meal of the day in Kerala, was a feast. We had *kari meen*, the pearl spot fish from the pond, cooked with a mild but intricate curry powder; *palappams*, lacy, golden-rimmed rice pancakes, made with semolina, rice flour and coconut milk; and another fish curry made with a green mango that Paul and I had snagged from a tree in the garden. This is a Christian household, where alcohol is consumed, so sips of white wine from Bangalore accompanied the seafood. The pale pink shrimp, bathed in coconut milk, were exquisite, their sweet-tasting glycines balanced by the citrusy tang conveyed by a few black pieces of tamarind. Lunch was over all too quickly.

It was about as far from an endless deep-fried popcorn shrimp special as you could get. Admittedly, compared to the farmed, chemical-suffused product, the shrimp I had in Kerala – both in the backwaters and in Nimmy Paul's kitchen – were expensive. But in Tamil Nadu, I got a glimpse of the real bill we were paying for the industrial product. It included the destruc-tion of mangroves and paddy fields, the fouling of drinking water with heavy-duty chemicals, the infection of wild fish with antibiotic-resistant pathogens, and the undermining of tradi-tional fishing economies that could support millions. Not to mention the impact the stuff had on the immune system of any-body unfortunate enough to get hooked on it.

Cheap shrimp, I now knew, was a meal I could no longer afford.

7

CHINA –

Buddha Jump over the Wall

It is the eve of the Year of the Golden Pig, and in Shanghai – China's business boomtown – eating fish is both an emblem and an augury of prosperity. The inhabitants of this coastal city of eighteen million spend more money on seafood than anybody else in China. If this holiday season is anything like the last, the Shanghainese will go through 57,000 tonnes of seafood over the next ten days – as much as the Republic of Ireland consumes in an entire year.

The Yu Chi Shark's Fin Bird's Nest Restaurant is an excellent place to view that ultimate apex predator, man, in full feeding frenzy. Located in a glass and steel office building whose lobby has been turned into a kind of rococo palace of ivory-hued marble and gold-capitalled columns, it is, like many seafood palaces in China, a monument to questionable taste. A canary-yellow Ferrari Modena is on display on the sidewalk in front of the revolving door. A grand piano sits, unplayed, on a pedestal beneath a multitiered incandescent chandelier. The soundtrack

223

is provided by teenage Cantopop singers keening and cavorting on countless flat screens.

But you don't come to a restaurant like this for the decor; you come for the seafood, and the selection at Yu Chi is fantastic. Plates of jellyfish salad and smoked fish with caramelized skin are crowded in display cases lit by halogen lamps. In metal soup tureens, broth churns with tentacles, fins and eyes. Ziggurats formed by dozens of stacked aquariums are overseen by young attendants holding long-handled dip nets, ready to scoop up the electric blue or iridescent orange reef fish of your choice. Much of the food available is alive and still moving. Hairy crabs with bound claws twitch on shaved ice. Giant bullfrogs make green mesh bags pulsate. Bird-beaked tortoises try to scrabble out of plastic tubs. Shiny-carapaced water beetles skitter and swarm over each other. In the luxury food section, the huge fin of a basking shark has been wrapped with a festive red ribbon. For sheer biodiversity, the Yu Chi restaurant rivals the Shanghai Ocean Aquarium – with the difference that here you can eat everything you see.

Upstairs, on the balconies of the mezzanine, the enablers and architects of Shanghai's economic boom are turning red-faced as they finish gold-labelled bottles of *baijiu*, China's indigenous sorghum-and-kerosene-flavoured hooch. It is considered auspicious, at this time of year, to order more than you could ever eat; on most tables, there is hardly room for another plate. As the diners eat crustaceans the Chinese way, their hands are soon covered with sauce, oil and bits of shrimp or crab meat; the fingers become tools for conveying flavour to the mouth. The most stubborn molluscs, from thumb-splitting razor-shell clams to finicky mantis shrimps, are cracked open, sucked and quickly reduced to oily heaps of shell fragments and claws.

For anybody curious to sample the sea's bounty, the Yu Chi Restaurant offers an opportunity to explore the oceanic food pyramid, trophic level by trophic level. From all-too-abundant jellyfish (at the second trophic level), to nearly endangered sharks (that feed near the fifth and top level), you can find it all here.

At Yu Chi, of course, there is no menu. You just point, and the kitchen will kill it for you. Every dish, it turns out, comes with a story.

Jellyfish Salad (Trophic Level 2.0)

Jellyfish, those net-clogging, back-stinging, beach-fouling bags of gelatin, are severely underrated as food. Low in calories, they are loaded with magnesium and skin-nourishing collagen, vitamins A and B, and a protein similar to the one found in egg whites. Present in all oceans, jellyfish feature in the cuisines of only a few cultures. The Vietnamese enjoy *goi sua* made from strips of jellyfish marinated in wine vinegar, coriander and the fermented fish sauce called *nuoc mam*. The Koreans make a dish called *hae-pa-ri neng-chae* by soaking salted jellyfish until it swells, then covering it in a mustard and garlic sauce.

As humans wipe out the upper levels of the food chain, these primordial blobs are taking over the oceans. Global warming is turning coastal waters hotter and less salty, ideal habitats for smacks of jellyfish that make some of the world's most popular tourist beaches – most recently in Spain and Italy – unswimmable during prime summer months. Late in 2007, a ten-square-mile flotilla of mauve stingers, a species more commonly seen in the Mediterranean, overwhelmed Northern Ireland's only salmon farm, killing all one hundred thousand fish. Meanwhile, fishermen worldwide are now hauling in 450,000 tonnes of jellyfish annually, more than twice the catch of a decade ago; especially big harvests came from the Bering, South China and Black seas. In some overfished areas, like off the coast of

Namibia, the total biomass of jellyfish exceeds all other fish by a factor of three. If we all ate jellyfish for breakfast, lunch and dinner, it would barely put a dent in the population.

Japanese fishermen have recently had to contend with a persistent infestation of *echizen kurage*, monstrous 200-kilogram creatures that can be as wide as a man is tall. Known as Nomura's jellyfish, they tear apart fixed nets and are toxic enough to turn the flesh of any fish they touch an unmarketable white.

Japanese scientists lay the blame for this invasion directly on China. Up the Yangtze River from Shanghai, the world's largest hydroelectric project, the Three Gorges Dam, has increased the amount of phosphorus and nitrogen in the waters off China, creating an ideal breeding ground for jellyfish. In the summer of 2005 half a billion were estimated to be floating from the shores of China to the Sea of Japan *every day*, eventually forming a ring of jelly around the entire nation. The citizens of Fukui, a northern Japanese island, coped by marketing souvenir cookies flavoured with powdered jellyfish. A professor from Japan's National Fisheries University went on a fact-finding mission to China, returning with ten different ways to prepare Nomura's jellyfish. ('Making them a popular food,' he opined, 'is the best way to solve the problem.')

Fortunately, the Chinese already eat jellyfish; in fact, they have been part of the local cuisine for centuries. In Shanghai's markets, where the jellyfish section is often as big as the crisp aisle in a Western supermarket, the going rate for just over a pound of dried Nomura's jellyfish is 25 yuan (£1.65). Almost every restaurant serves jellyfish prepared some way: tossed with shredded turnip; dripping with oil or vinegar; stir-fried with ginger.

Jellyfish flesh itself is flavourless, but it is an excellent medium for conveying flavour. At Yu Chi the jellyfish appetizer is first parboiled to rid it of any toxins, allowed to chill, and then is lightly dressed with chilli-spiked sesame oil and sprinkled with sesame seeds. Cut into strips that glisten in the light, the rubber-band-like flesh offers infinitesimal resistance – much like the sesame seeds – before yielding to the teeth. It is not a filling meal; you would have to consume several plates before you were sated.

Given the state of the oceans, perhaps eating jellyfish, those pests on the beaches of the world, should be looked upon as a public service, like swatting malarial mosquitoes.

Braised Abalone (Trophic Level 2.0)

At Yu Chi, an abalone adheres to the walls of a small glass aquarium with its single sluglike foot, waiting to be selected by a diner. Viewed from above, an abalone resembles a moving rock; it is actually a gastropod that can scuttle at an impressive speed by moulding its single foot into four 'legs' to escape starfish and other predators. When grazing on kelp, it sits up, like a koala chewing on eucalyptus. In Asia the abalone's slightly rubbery flesh is considered an aphrodisiac. Its shell, which is shaped like a human ear with a serially pierced rim, has a gorgeous nacreous interior. The abalone is the world's most prized shellfish.

The wild abalone trade has created underworld fortunes in South Africa. Fisheries officers there drive armoured vehicles to protect themselves from automatic-weapon-toting gangs of poachers. Sprawling Chinese-owned homes in Durban, Johannesburg and Cape Town have been discovered hiding clandestine abalone-drying-and-canning factories. In the alchemical accounting of the international seafood trade, China manages to import twice as much Australian abalone as Australians are legally allowed to harvest every year. If poaching continues at its current rate, the abalone is expected to be all but extinct off the coast of Africa by 2010. The best ones, from Japan, are also the biggest, and can sell for £1,940 a kilogram.

Which is stupid, because overfished wild abalone are in no way superior to farmed abalone. It happens to be easier, for the moment, to prise a wild abalone off a rock with a crowbar than to grow one. Like oyster farming, abalone aquaculture is environmentally sustainable – their grazing actually encourages kelp growth – and produces an excellent product. California, whose white abalone was the first marine invertebrate to receive federal protection as an endangered species, now has fifteen abalone farms; and a hatchery and farm for *ormeaux*, as they are called in France, has been set up in Brittany. Though it takes about three years to bring an abalone to market size, the existence of this nascent industry should make an ethical eater's choice much easier.

But only farmed abalone is a reliably good choice. Which puts all of the abalone in Shanghai, which is inevitably poached or wild-caught, off limits.

Sea Cucumber in Soy-Sweetened Sauce (Trophic Level 2.3)

At the bottom of a tide pool the sea cucumber looks like a cross between a hedgehog and a slender Chinatown aubergine. When importuned, it shrinks into a phimotic oval covered with blunt spines. When *really* importuned, it pukes up its guts. (Auto-evisceration, in which a sea creature extrudes its entrails through its anus, works on the theory that a cormorant or other attacker will favour the tasty entrails over whatever is left. The sea cucumber, like the lizard that leaves its tail beneath a cat's paw, simply grows a new set of innards.) In Malaysia, where this legendary self-regenerating power has created a cottage industry of sea-cucumber-fortified toothpaste, massage cream and soft drinks, it is known as the *gamat*. In Catalonia, where sea cucumber is eaten broiled, it is known as the *espardenya*, or sandal of the sea. In Naples it is rudely but evocatively referred to as the *cazzo di mare*, or cock of the sea.

After being boiled to restore its elasticity, the sea cucumber looks exactly as appetizing as a swollen, heavily bruised banana slug. Slipping over the tongue, its flesh feels like jellyfish, but slimier; soy-sweetened sauce gives it most of its flavour. (*Konowata*, the salted and fermented sea cucumber intestines that are among Japan's most prized delicacies, are truly pungent.) The chewing is endless and finally a little tedious. Sea cucumber is one of those Asian foods that is all about texture. The bill for a whole sea cucumber, expertly prepared, is 880 yuan, or £56, a week and a half's wages for the average factory worker in Shanghai.

Sea cucumbers owe their expense to their rarity. There are forty edible species, and they have been severely overfished in the Philippines, India and Egypt. After South Pacific sea cucumber beds were stripped, the trade turned to the Galápagos Islands; by 1992 Ecuadorean divers had collected thirty million sea cucumbers, knocking out a staple food for cormorants, penguins and all kinds of fish. Canada has just authorized a trawl fishery for sea cucumbers on its east coast, and Indonesian pirates are stripping the north coast of Australia to keep Chinese restaurants supplied with the stuff. The trade is still completely unregulated.

In other words, just because something is at the bottom rung of the food chain does not mean it is abundant. Even bottom-feeders can be overfished.

Drunken Tiger Shrimp (Trophic Level 2.6)

The Cantonese of southern China joke about their voraciousness: they like to say if it has four legs, and isn't a table, they'll eat it. Three Scream Mice is a classic dish. The first scream comes when you pick up one of the live baby mice with your chopsticks, the second when you dip it in sauce, the third when you bite down.

According to the Shanghainese food scholar Jiang Liyang, eating live food is common practice in rural China. He cites villagers in Henan Province who pour boiling water over a living donkey and cut off the bits they want to eat. ('Chinese people trust in the idiom that "A thing is valued if it is rare,"' adds Jiang. 'Some think eating strange and precious things shows their wealth and social status.') When it comes to cruel seafood, the South Koreans trump even the Chinese: *san nak-ji* is a dish in which a live octopus is taken from the tank, chopped to bits and rushed to the table with its tentacles still writhing. You have to make sure to chew them thoroughly, or the suckers will adhere to the walls of your oesophagus.

Zhui xia, 'drunken' shrimp marinated in alcohol, is a rather common dish in China. In Shanghai's restaurants, however, the shrimp are served very much alive. The waitress brings a Pyrex dish with at least two dozen greenish-grey shrimp, their swimmerets and antennae twitching in a piping hot broth of chilli peppers, orange slices and high-alcohol-content rice wine. At first the overstimulated animals leap about, and only the glass lid prevents them from jumping onto the table; then their antennae start waving woozily. After about ten minutes they lapse into an alcoholic coma. Prodding with chopsticks may revive them, and they have been known to bite overanxious diners on the lips. Which only seems fair.

The variety served in Shanghai restaurants is the tiger shrimp, which is inevitably farmed in ponds. One can only imagine all the antibiotics and pesticides being excreted from their dying bodies.

When eating drunken shrimp, it is customary to be quite drunk.

Salt-Cured Carp Marinated in Rice Wine (Trophic Level 3.0)

Carp may be the best seafood choice at the Yu Chi Restaurant. Like tilapia, carp is a vegetarian fish: it thrives on recycled table and farmyard scraps. The domestic industry is uniquely sustainable; rarely exported, most carp goes to feed the local population. In fact, fish farming was invented in China three thousand years ago, when the waste from cultivating silkworms was fed to carp in small freshwater ponds.

The water was a lot cleaner back then. Though China is now home to 1.3 billion people – 22 per cent of the world's population – it has only 8 per cent of the world's water. Three-quarters of the rivers that run through Chinese cities are so dirty they cannot be used for fishing or drinking. Every year twenty thousand tons of heavy metals and eight hundred tons of cyanide end up in Chinese waters.

Where do all these pollutants go? To the sea. The United Nations has already declared the coastal estuaries of the Yellow and Yangtze rivers dead zones, so polluted that they are devoid of life. Every spring the East China Sea, on which Shanghai is located, is hit by enormous algae blooms, and many of them harbour paralysing toxins; eighty-two such red tides occurred in 2005 alone, affecting an area of ocean almost the size of

Taiwan. The Yangtze delta, where Shanghai is located, is now considered the biggest source of marine pollution in the Pacific.

Worryingly, for any sane seafood lover, the world's most polluted nation is also its single greatest source of table fish. Fish here grow and feed in some of the most direly contaminated water this planet has ever seen. Three-quarters of China's lakes are now polluted with algae or choked of oxygen by dead zones. A serious industrial accident causes severe contamination of river water somewhere in the country every *three* days, and the list of the products involved – arsenic, nitrobenzene, cyanide – reads like a poisoner's handbook.

While carp tends to remain in China, such high-value carnivorous species as shrimp, turbot, cod, grouper and eel are exported to Europe and North America. China supplied America with 68,000 tonnes of shrimp in 2006, beating out Thailand as the world's leading shrimp exporter. (The phenomenon is a relatively new one: according to the FAO's figures, it took a *single year* for China to more than double its shrimp-producing capacity.) All told, China now supplies 70 per cent of the planet's farmed fish. In the United States just over one in every five fish on the market now comes from China.

The FDA routinely rejects Chinese seafood products for containing salmonella and listeria pathogens, nitrofurans, the carcinogenic antibiotic chloramphenicol, or veterinary drugs, or simply for being 'filthy' or 'poisonous'. In 2007, however, outcry over contaminated imports got so bad that the FDA announced that it was banning several kinds of seafood imported from China, among them shrimp, catfish, eel and basa (a kind of catfish). Targeting certain foods from China is nothing more than a stopgap: the United States imports millions of pounds of seafood from Thailand, Indonesia, India and other Asian countries, all of which have their own problems with banned drugs and water quality. Of the 860,000 separate seafood shipments imported into the United States in 2006, a mere 1.3 per cent were physically inspected and only 0.59 per cent ever made it into a lab for more rigorous testing; according to industry insiders, fresh fish, which is prone to spoilage, is *never* inspected. Worryingly, the FDA does not yet test for some of the chemicals most commonly used in Asian aquaculture. A Chinese investigative reporter found that in southern provinces such as Fujian and Guangxi, licensed veterinarians routinely sold antibiotics not yet tested for in North America and Europe to any fish farmer who asked. An FDA study analysing samples from fish farms found that the salmonella frequently detected in Asian farmed fish came from faecal bacteria in the grow-out ponds. The fish, in other words, were bathing in shit, from both humans and livestock. In 2006, cancer became China's leading killer, and health officials put the blame squarely on pollution and pesticides.

The European Union, in contrast, physically inspects at least 20 per cent of all imported seafood, and when an individual product is proving problematic – when they are finding too much salmonella in Vietnamese shrimp, for example – inspection increases to 100 per cent, until the problem is resolved. Japan, which inspects 12.3 per cent of its seafood, has a similar policy. The Canadian Food Inspection Agency also targets problem products and regions; in 2006 they inspected a quarter of all shipments from China, and found that 12 per cent were in violation, mostly for antibiotic residues. Sometimes the situation gets so bad that seafood has to be banned until the exporting country brings its standards up to snuff. When seafood from Bangladesh was proving particularly unsafe – inspectors found nails and other metals packed with shrimp to boost the weight, as well as mercury droplets and astronomical levels of antibiotic residues – the EU completely banned Bangladeshi seafood for several months. Unfortunately, the closing of European doors makes other countries vulnerable to a practice known as 'port shopping', in which containers of frozen seafood rejected in one port are simply shipped to jurisdictions with less rigorous inspection. After discovering shocking conditions in Pakistani seaports in 2006, the EU completely banned Pakistani seafood. In response, the country simply started exporting seafood to the United States.

In fact, there is now no need to export carp from China to the United States; the Asian carp now thrives wild in American rivers. In the 1970s, catfish farmers in the American South imported the species to clean the algae from their ponds, but thousands escaped in the Mississippi floods of 1993. A carp can eat half its body weight in food in a day, and quickly reach weights of sixty pounds; giant leaping carp now regularly break the noses and arms of boaters on the Mississippi. Asian carp have already taken out the bottom of the food chain in some tributaries, gobbling up the small plankton eaters that other species rely on, starving out native species of fish. The invaders are inexorably moving north, and a single electric fence on the Chicago River is all that is preventing Asian carp from reaching the Great Lakes.

So, at home or abroad, eat your carp. Like dining on jellyfish, it is a public service.

Napoleon Wrasse, Sautéed with Preserved Chillis (Trophic Level 4.0)

Napoleon wrasse live around coral reefs, reaching weights of four hundred pounds and lengths of six feet. Scuba divers are fond of them because they act like curious, friendly dogs, accepting food out of outstretched palms. Bulbous-headed, beady-eyed curmudgeons, they have the inflated lips of collagen-crazed Hollywood starlets. Those lips are especially coveted in Chinese restaurants, where they can fetch £125 a serving.

A single Napoleon wrasse, seared alive and presented with its heart exposed, recently sold for £1,320 in a Hong Kong restaurant. As the fortunes of mainland China have improved, so the wrasse's have declined; between 1995 and 2003 the species was fished to 1 per cent of its former population levels.

Napoleon wrasse, like giant groupers, yellow croakers and other reef fish, are caught with some of the most destructive fishing methods devised by man. Blast-fishing was the first: American soldiers stationed in the Pacific during the Second World War realized that tossing a grenade onto a coral reef would stun hundreds of fish, which could then be scooped up when they floated to the surface. Switching to dynamite, fishermen blasted reefs like Pedro Blanco, on the Chinese mainland opposite Hong Kong, into smithereens: it is now a dead seascape of split rocks and sea urchins. Throughout Asia the fines imposed for such acts of destruction are laughable: while a Philippine fisherman can earn £35 a day on the reefs, the maximum fine for blast-fishing is less than £5. Only Indonesia has passed laws banning dynamite fishing.

For decades the reef fish market has been driven by Chinese gourmands. In the 1950s the local waters off Hong Kong supplied 90 per cent of the city's demand. Gradually, as pollution and overfishing took their toll, merchants started sourcing their fish from farther afield. A new, equally destructive technique has since been developed: cyanide-fishing. A diver puts a couple of crushed sodium cyanide tablets into a squeeze bottle and squirts the cloud of poison at a coral head. The stunned prey can then be scooped up with a net; if it hides in the reef, the diver tears apart the coral with his hands. The fish are collected and kept alive in shallow atolls; buyers fly in from Hong Kong, Taiwan, Singapore – and now mainland China – to pick out the best. While a dynamited reef can regrow, dosing coral with cyanide usually kills it. Algae and bacteria colonize the compromised reef, and a few weeks later, the coral dies. (It is estimated that for every reef fish caught with cyanide, a square metre of coral is wiped out.) Cyanide remains in the fish's flesh only for a short period, so there is no danger that fishmongers will accidentally poison their clients. It can, however, be fatal for the fishermen: many are paralysed when they accidentally swim through a cloud of cyanide.

Starting in the 1970s, the zone of destruction from cyanide-fishing radiated outward from its epicentre in Hong Kong, taking in Indonesia, Malaysia, the Philippines and even the Maldives, three thousand miles to the west. The Dong Sha Atoll, a stunning, almost perfect ring of white sand and coral two hundred miles southeast of Hong Kong, was once a nursery for many of the juvenile fish in the South China Sea. After 250 tonnes of cyanide and five tonnes of dynamite were used to destroy every square inch of the atoll, it became an aquatic desert. Divers now report going for miles without seeing a single fish.

Worldwide, coral reefs are already dying because of pollution and rising water temperatures. Dynamiting them and poisoning them is extremely shortsighted. The world's coral reefs harbour a quarter of all known marine fish. When the reefs disappear, so too will the fish – and with them the restaurants, like Yu Chi, that specialize in serving them.

Hong Kong started the trend, but today it is mainland China that sustain destructive fishing. In 2006 scientists discovered a new ecosystem off the west coast of Papua, which they called the Bird's Head Seascape. Populated by leatherback turtles, killer whales and coral colonies that are uniquely protected from bleaching because of the region's lower water temperatures, Bird's Head has been dubbed a species factory. As soon as Bird's Head was discovered, Chinese and Korean fishing vessels started lobbying for access. Scientists estimate that commercial fishermen, using dynamite and cyanide, could wipe out the area's riches in only five years. All told, fifty-two life-forms new to science – including the flasher wrasse and a kind of nocturnal shark that walks along the sea floor on its fins – have been discovered in its waters.

Some of them will undoubtedly end up in the tanks of the Yu Chi Restaurant.

Buddha Jump Over the Wall, Made with Fins from Blue Shark (Trophic Level 4.2)

As the ocean's apex predators, sharks sit at the top of the food chain, among the planet's most ancient and successful hunters. Slow to reach sexual maturity, many sharks produce only one or two pups every one to three years. Sharks range in size from the cigar shark, about the size of a Cuban panatela, to the largest fish in the sea, the whale shark, which is the length of a city bus. Great white sharks, as seen in *Jaws*, can survive with stingray spines stuck into their brain cavities and still swallow whole seals in a single gulp. Yet even they are no match for the real king of the food chain, the Asian gourmand.

The most expensive bowl of soup you can buy at the Yu Chi Restaurant is one known as Buddha Jump Over the Wall, made with rare red abalone, sea cucumber and braised shark fin. The name comes from an apocryphal story: a Buddhist monk – and in some versions, Siddhartha Gautama himself – was so intrigued by the odour of the simmering broth coming from a courtyard that he vaulted a wall to investigate. In the Chinatowns of San Francisco and London, a single small bowl can go for over £100. At Yu Chi the soup is a steal at 268 yuan, or £18.

For most of the twentieth century, shark fin soup was a regional Cantonese dish, derided by party officials in Beijing as an elitist indulgence. Now that China seems to have embraced self-indulgence, shark fin is consumed everywhere the nouveau riche can be found. China is now thought to consume 12,000 tonnes of shark fin a year, worth about £1.6 billion. The trade is driving global shark populations to collapse. Of the four hundred species of shark known in the world, eighty-three are endangered. Twenty are expected to become extinct in the next decade.

In a covered section of Shanghai's sprawling Tongchuan seafood market, among the abalone and jellyfish dealers, an entire street of shops is devoted to shark fins. Neatly sacked in plastic and stacked in cubicles, the fins come from every ocean. There are fins from mako and porbeagle sharks, and the bleached white dorsal fins of *Prionace glauca*, the blue shark, a species classified as near-threatened by the World Conservation Union. They are sold for £100 a kilogram to Shanghai's big hotels.

In a practice called finning, living sharks have their pectoral and dorsal fins cut from their bodies with heated metal blades. Given the difference in price between shark meat (which sells for 25 pence a pound) and the fins (which can wholesale for seven hundred times more), fishermen have no incentive to fill their boats with difficult-to-preserve corpses. The sharks are kicked back into the ocean, alive and bleeding; it can take them days to die. A paper published in *Ecology Letters* in 2006, based on a survey of the shark fin market in Hong Kong, estimated that 38 million sharks are killed annually for their fins alone. Every year, three hundred thousand sharks are taken in the Galápagos National Park, the world's third-largest marine reserve, even though shark hunting is technically banned there.

Director Ang Lee, martial arts movie star Jackie Chan, the President of Taiwan and basketball star Yao Ming (formerly of the Shanghai Sharks) have all made impassioned public service announcements entreating their fellow Chinese not to eat shark fin soup. In 2005 the University of Hong Kong and the newly opened Hong Kong Disneyland announced they would stop serving the dish. While seventeen countries, including the

United States, Australia and Canada, now ban finning, China still imports one-third of its shark fins from the European Union. Spain, the worst offender, is currently lobbying the European Parliament for even weaker restrictions on finning.

Scientists have long wondered what the disappearance of sharks would mean for the oceans. In the North Atlantic we are about to find out. 'Large sharks have been functionally eliminated from the east coast of the US,' according to Julia Baum, a researcher at Halifax's Dalhousie University, 'meaning they can no longer perform their ecosystem role as top predators.' Until the 1960s whitetip sharks, 350-pound fish with distinctive white markings on their fins, were the most abundant large animals remaining on the planet. Forty years later they have all but disappeared from the Gulf of Mexico. Up the length of the Atlantic coast, the story is the same: since 1972, bull, dusky, smooth and hammerhead shark populations have all been fished to 1 per cent of their former levels. Scientists liken it to the herds of buffalo vanishing from the Great Plains, unnoticed. The immediate impact has been dramatic. With their chief predators gone, small skates and rays are thriving. An estimated forty million cownose rays now live off the East Coast, and the population is increasing by 8 per cent a year. In their migration south to Florida, the rays have routed local populations of oysters and soft-shell clams, and they have driven North Carolina's century-old bay scallop fishery to collapse.

'This tragedy is caused by continuing overfishing,' wrote the chief author of the study, the late fisheries scientist Ransom Myers of Dalhousie University, 'and the demand for a single luxury item – shark fin soup. For this species to survive we need to reduce fishing effort by half and have a global ban on shark finning.'

Shark fin soup is not especially tasty. The dried flesh of the fins must be boiled for twenty hours, until the cartilage breaks down into thin, needlelike strands, like tough vermicelli. The only detectable flavour comes from other ingredients in the broth, like mushrooms and scallops. Nor is the soup particularly good for you. Most shark fins are treated with hydrogen peroxide to bleach them a marketable white, and they are so laden with mercury that you might as well be chewing on a thermometer.

In China shark fin soup is about as high as you can go on the food chain. But the closer to the top you get, the worse things look, both for your own health and for the health of the oceans. Banqueting on Napoleon wrasse and shark fin is what it looks like: pure decadence, the desperate feasting of despoilers, who really don't care if there's anything left over for the generations that follow.

Bill, Please

At the Yu Chi Restaurant, the feast that ushers in the Year of the Golden Pig is over. The plates, piled with barely touched vegetables and half-eaten fish, are being cleared away by waitresses in golden tunics. Outside, the streets and alleys are resonating with the playful blasts of a billion firecrackers. Tonight they sound like the echoes of the detonations that are tearing apart the coral reefs of the Pacific.

The future of the oceans may lie in the hands of the Chinese. Asia now consumes two-thirds of the world's seafood, and lately China has been outbidding Japan on world markets for such basic commodities as Alaskan pollock and farmed salmon. China has a fishing fleet of 280,000 boats, the largest in the world, and its distant-water fleet is present in the waters of West Africa, Russia, New Zealand, Peru and Iran – in every ocean in the world.

Though China drives the market for black fish, its distant-water fleet is still small compared to those of Japan, Korea and Taiwan, which are especially notorious for illegal, unreported and unregulated (IUU) fishing. (Among the European nations, Spain, which has almost no important fishing grounds within its two-hundred-mile limit, is the worst offender.) Pirate vessels can purchase flags of convenience online, from Mongolia, Panama, Liberia and other countries that are not signatories to international fishing agreements. Fish are offloaded at sea onto larger transport vessels, which land the catch in places like Las Palmas, on Spain's Canary Islands, where there are virtually no port controls. From such ports of convenience the fish are re-exported to Europe or Asia. In all, 2,800 vessels, about 15 per cent of the world's large-boat fleet, currently fish under flags of convenience, and at least one in five, and perhaps as many as one in three, fish caught in the world now come from these IUU fisheries. Now that bluefin tuna has a street value of £9.50 an ounce in Tokyo, and Chilean sea bass sells for up to £500 for a single fish, we have reached the point where seafood can rival some controlled substances in value. Shady mafias, from Libyan bluefin poachers to Azerbaijani caviar gangsters, have emerged to circumvent the international laws designed to control such valuable commodities.

Chinese demand is rightly blamed for keeping IUU fishing alive and well. Four hundred million people live in China's coastal areas alone – four times the population of Japan – and as their prosperity increases, so does their taste for seafood. In 1980 average annual Chinese seafood consumption was 5 kilograms per capita; a little over twenty years later the figure quintupled to 25 kilograms. Even if seafood consumption does not rise, population increases mean the Chinese will be going through 37 million tonnes of seafood a year by 2020. Currently, all the oceans and fish farms of the world produce only 140 million tonnes.

Until recently, eating raw fish the Japanese way was unknown in China. But in Shanghai and Beijing, hundreds of restaurants now offer conveyor-belt sea urchin roe, raw flounder and octopus on rice at five *yuan* (33 pence) a plate.

The newly affluent Chinese, in other words, are developing a taste for sushi. And that is very bad news for the fish of the world.

8

JAPAN -
BLUEFIN TUNA SASHIMI

Sorry, Charlie

No other market comes close to Tokyo's Tsukiji. It is Billingsgate by way of *Blade Runner*, a Fulton stocked by Captain Nemo.

Nothing can prepare a jet-lagged visitor for the sensory shock of Tsukiji at four-thirty in the morning. Leaving the quiet, pre-dawn streets of Ginza, one walks into an incandescent-lit dream city, where gruff men carrying hooked gaffs and cutlass-length knives load dripping tuna crates onto gas-powered flatbed carts, and the frozen heads of eight-hundred-pound tunas go skidding across concrete floors to the sound of staccato laughter. It is like stumbling on the backstage to all of Tokyo's kabuki and geisha glamour, to find that behind the fabled politesse and precision lies the world's biggest abattoir-cum-deportation camp: an Auschwitz for fish. Tsukiji is a fifty-five-acre city of fifty thousand souls, with its own banks and post offices, a liquor store and a library, a place whose economy is entirely focused on moving seafood. In an average day, Tsukiji sells five million pounds of seafood. In two weeks of operation, it sells more than

London's Billingsgate does in a year. And in a year it wholesales £2.5 billion worth of seafood, an amount equivalent to the gross domestic product of Fiji.

Set on the banks of the Sumida River, in the oldest part of Tokyo, Tsukiji's main hall, a 1930s-vintage building curved like a plumber's elbow joint, is as cavernous as a European railway station. It would be a menagerie fit for an emperor – if most of the specimens on display were not destined to end up on some chef's chopping block later in the day. According to Theodore Bestor, an American anthropologist whose book *Tsukiji: The Fish Market at the Center of the World* is the single best introduction to the market, of the two thousand species of fish in Japanese waters, at least four hundred are available at Tsukiji's 1,677 wholesalers' stalls. Identifying them all would tax the skills of even the worldliest taxonomist.

Wandering down the narrow aisles, dodging men in wetsuits pulling wheelbarrows stacked with Styrofoam hung with tentacles, I hardly knew what to do with my gaze. I eyed the still-living giant crabs, their claws tied with rubber bands, next to tubs full of tiny *chirimen*, dried baby sardines served as bar snacks. I ogled glistening purple and cream-coloured folds of monkfish liver next to tubs full of *dozeu*, or freshwater loach, a cross-between a snake and a catfish. And I frankly gawked at Taiwanese eels soaking in tubs of their own blood, phallic geoducks from Ishikawa prefecture, the convoluted intestines of the ocean sunfish, and champagne-bubble-sized herring roe on green kelp, flown in from British Columbia. I was attracted by the Day-Glo orange of the exophthalmic alfonsino, amazed by the extravagance of £15-an-ounce sea-slug caviar, and repulsed by the sight of a yellowtail being killed with a spike to its head and a metal wire driven into the marrow of its spine. Halfbeaks and arkshells; cuttlefish and cutlassfish; sea robins and horse mackerel – for a voyeuristic seafood lover, Tsukiji is heaven on earth. (For the still-living, gape-eyed octopi taking in the scene from behind aquarium glass, in contrast, it must have been a Boschian vista of hell.)

My guides to Tsukiji, Naoto and 'Radio-Controlled' Eiza, were retired seafood importers, who offered a wry running commentary on their old stomping grounds. (Given his nickname, I had vaguely hoped Eiza would sport antennae and be guided through the market by remote. In fact, he was a middle-aged man in a shapeless jacket who owed his nickname to the fact that he was 'crazy about radio-controlled model aeroplanes'.) We started in the outer market, a warren of sushi restaurants and shops selling sake, hand-forged knives and fresh wasabi. At the Namiyoke Jinja, the market's shinto shrine, Naoto and Eiza showed me how to bow twice and clap my hands next to votive stones dedicated to sushi, eggs and shellfish.

'Here, fishermen, sushi chefs and fish dealers come to make an apology for all the fish they have slaughtered,' explained Eiza.

Inside the market building Naoto played a cat-and-mouse game with two young women carrying clipboards, peering around the corner into a refrigerated room before we entered. 'The Tokyo Metropolitan Government officials can be lousy people,' he explained, 'and sometimes they try to kick us out of this place.' The room was filled with boxes of *uni*, or sea urchin roe. The apricot-hued blobs, arranged in spruce boxes, looked as precious as gemstones.

'What we call *bafun*, or "horseshit" sea urchin, is considered the best. You should look for *uni* that is bright orange or golden in colour,' said Eiza, who once imported the roe for a living. 'There is sea urchin from California, Canada and Chile, but of course the domestic quality, from Hokkaido, is number one!' A one-hundred-gram box from northern Japan could sell for 7,000 yen (£31).

My opinionated guides hurried me to a fluorescent-lit hall, where the day's main event was about to begin: the tuna auctions. Hundreds of bluefin tuna were lined up on wooden pallets. Their bodies were as sleek as streamlined zeppelins, glossy scales shading from the silver-grey of their bellies to electric blue at the lateral line and to navy near the dorsal fin. These lustrous corpses had already become commodities: slit open at the belly, they had been stickered with flags indicating their provenance and numbered with red paint, the lower figures indicating a higher expected value at auction. Using metal gaffs, serious-looking men lifted flaps gouged in the orangish-red hued flesh near the tail, looking for signs of *yake*, the 'burn' that mars the flesh when a bluefin struggles too strenuously against the fisherman. Fingering the flap, they rubbed their thumbs and forefingers together to check the slipperiness. The fattier the better, said Eiza.

The clangs of a hand bell echoed through the room. Fish number one was up for sale, a 550-pound frozen giant from Iran. Buyers put on baseball caps with plastic tags showing their licence numbers and formed a loose semi-circle around the auctioneer as he mounted a stool. The spiel began: shouting out numbers, the auctioneer rhythmically bobbed at the knees, his face reddening with the effort. The buyers remained stoical, occasionally holding up a hand to make a bid. (In *teyari*, the bidding is done silently, with upheld fingers; ties are broken with *janken*, a form of rock–paper–scissors.) It was all over in less than ten seconds. The winning bidder made a hurried notation on a clipboard, permitting himself only the slightest of thin-lipped smiles at his victory. The auctioneer, meanwhile, was already dragging his stool over to fish number two, a smaller bluefin caught off Cape Cod. In the next half-hour two hundred tuna would be auctioned off. And this auction was just one of scores happening throughout Tsukiji: upstairs, sea urchin roe was being bid upon; in concrete sheds, hundreds of buyers were packed on wooden bleachers to compete for domestic *kuruma* shrimp; outdoors on the quays, dealers in tall rubber boots were making offers on swordfish and marlin from the Atlantic. (Some fish still arrive at Tsukiji by boat, but most are now trucked from Narita Airport, which fish merchants jokingly refer to as Japan's biggest fishing port.) For a good percentage of the fish, Tsukiji is just a hub where the price is fixed: in an extravagant outlay of fossil fuel, much of the fish will go straight back to the airport, to be jetted to some of the most expensive restaurants in Sydney, Vancouver and New York.

'The winning bidder paid eight thousand yen a kilogram for fish number one,' said Naoto, keying a few numbers into a calculator. 'At two hundred forty-eight kilograms, that's almost two million yen.' Or £8,675 for a single fish. 'And that is a low price,' he added. 'Bluefin are much more expensive in December.'

In fact, the first bluefin of the year, whose purchase brings much prestige, are the most expensive fish on the planet. In 2001 a 445-pound bluefin sold for 20 million yen, £85,000 at the then-current rate of exchange. (The buyer subsequently went bankrupt.) Pound for pound, bluefin can be more valuable than even rhinoceros horns or elephant tusks. Given the prices, fishermen worldwide flout quotas and risk conviction to catch them: harpoon the right thousand-pounder, after all, and you could be sending your kid to Harvard. The times, however, are changing. A decade ago, Naoto said, the bluefins were the size of cows. Now, the biggest of them are only the size of steamer trunks.

The Iranian bluefin was hoisted onto a *koguruma*, a handcart with steel wheels. We followed the prize fish across an alley, dodging diesel-powered turret trucks, to the main market stall of Hicho, an intermediate wholesaler specializing in tuna. We arrived in time to witness the *maguro no kaiwa*: literally, the 'conversation of the tuna', in which master cutters reduce the giant fish to sashimi. (With frozen bluefin, the conversation is a bit perfunctory: it is simply cut into five-kilogram blocks with a bandsaw.) It took three apprentices to hoist the tuna onto a four-legged wooden chopping block. Using a knife with a wooden handle and a yard-long blade engraved with the name of a sword maker who once armed the samurai, the master sawed back and forth, pressing down on a cloth to apply pressure to the top of the blade.

To make the final cut, he pulled out a new knife, this one with a blade longer than a tall man's arm, and under its razorlike edge the bluefin fell into two pieces. The halves were transferred to a new cutting board and further subdivided. Reduced to saleable pyramids thinly striated with whorls of fat, the flesh was a striking oxblood red. The prime cut, called *toro*, from the belly meat found beneath the pectoral fin, was paler; it is considered the tenderloin of the tuna. The very best cut of *toro* is the fatty *jabara* ('snake's stomach'), cut from the bottom of the belly. For connoisseurs, a slice of *jabara* from a bluefin caught off the northern tip of Honshu Island is the apotheosis of seafood.

Hicho would sell the *toro* from today's Iranian bluefin to sushi shops for 18,400 yen (£80) a kilogram; the restaurants would mark up the price by at least 100 per cent, meaning a single serving of *toro* might cost at least £8. In Tokyo's very best restaurants, however, you could expect to pay considerably more. Hicho's owner, Tsunenori Iida, handed me a slip of paper with the address of a restaurant in Ginza, one of dozens he supplied. I trusted he knew the scene; Iida was a seventh-generation fishmonger whose family had been wholesaling fish in Tokyo since 1800.

'Ginza sushi shops are the best in Japan,' Iida told me, 'and Kanetanaka, next to the kabuki theatre, is one of the best restaurants in Ginza.' It was certainly one of the most prestigious: patronized by company presidents and their geisha escorts, Kanetanaka in the 1980s welcomed the likes of Henry Kissinger and Jimmy Carter, and a single diner's bill – with *toro* as the centrepiece – typically ran to £400. These days you can enjoy the *kaiseki* menu there for a quarter of the price. (With the decline of the yen, the world's most expensive sushi restaurants are now found in London and Manhattan.) Reservations at

Kanetanaka still had to be made several weeks in advance. I did not stand a chance of getting in.

Fortunately, there are three hundred thousand eating establishments in Tokyo, and *toro* seemed to be available in a rather high percentage of them. Within a few city blocks of Tsukiji, there are dozens, perhaps hundreds, of hole-in-the-wall sushi joints. Which was a good thing: after visiting the market, I was hungry enough to eat a giant bluefin.

Japan, I had already decided, would be an auspicious place to abandon my culinary scruples. This is the nation where baby pigs are delivered by caesarean so diners can enjoy the pinkest pork without fear of trichinosis; where living baby eels are cooked into blocks of tofu, and the adult ones are nailed to a cutting board by the eye before being skinned alive. Japan, home of the poisonous pufferfish buffet, is no place to come with a closed mind – let alone a closed mouth. Depending on your convictions, Japan's seafood culture is either a testament to an island culture's refinement, or the ultimate manifestation of the human greed that could empty the seas of their big fish within our lifetimes.

There was only one way to find out. For the duration of my stay in Japan, I would suspend moral judgement and experience whatever the local seafood culture threw my way. A civilization with such a long history of drawing sustenance from the sea, I figured, could surely teach the world something about balancing conservation and gourmandize.

Every new thing you eat, the Japanese say, adds seventy-five days to your life. Judging from what I saw at Tsukiji that morning, I had a lot of living ahead of me.

Bluefin for Breakfast

In spite of serious competition from China, the Japanese are still the world's leading fish eaters, going through 61 kilograms of seafood each a year – almost four times the global average of 16 kilograms – the equivalent of six pieces of sushi per person a day, every day of the year. For most Japanese, the notion that changes in the oceans might force them to change their eating habits is not only far-fetched; it is unthinkable. One in every ten fish caught in the world is consumed in Japan.

For reasons historical, cultural and geographical, this should come as no surprise. Japan, an archipelago with little arable land, is located in the North Pacific, one of the world's most nutrient-rich oceans. Until the nineteenth century, Buddhist and Shintoist principles discouraged the eating of four-legged animals, a prohibition that, unlike in Korea and China, even ordinary people obeyed. (Ingenious gourmands, of course, found ways around the religious strictures: wild boar, for example, was rebranded as 'mountain whale'.) Before the Second World War, Japan was the world's leading fishing nation, and artisanal fisherpeople still work in thousands of small ports dotted along the coasts.

Over the centuries, seafood has become interwoven into every aspect of Japanese life. On grocery store shelves, there are rows of fish-flavoured baby food, served in jars labelled with cartoon images of smiling flounder, cod and salmon. Children watch the adventures of the cartoon Anpan-Men, whose heroes, Mr Winkle and Tendon-Man (Mr Shrimp and Rice Bowl) – *unlike* Spongebob Squarepants – are actually edible. Sports teams, such as the Hiroshima Carp, are named after fish. Seafood is the subject of travelogues (among them the best-selling *Rotary Sushi around the World*), and such manga as Mitsuo Hashimoto's *Tsukiji Uogashi*. Seafood even has a place in sex: *nyotaimori*, or naked sushi, involves using chopsticks to pick sushi off a sex partner's body; a *maguro*, or tuna, is a woman who remains passive during intercourse (an allusion to the fact that tuna swim stiff-spined, moving only their caudal fins to swim). 'Tentacle porn', in which women are violently penetrated by cartoon cephalopods, is a popular sub-genre of anime and manga; the first known example, showing a pair of octopi ravishing a pearl diver, is a woodcut dating from 1820.

Of all the kinds of fish eaten in Japan, tuna is the most prized. Annually, the Japanese consume about 600,000 tonnes, a third of the world's supply. At the tip of the tuna pyramid is bluefin, which is sometimes called *hon-maguro*, or 'true tuna'. Eighty per cent of the world's bluefin ends up in Japan.

For all its mystique, bluefin is not hard to find in Tokyo. A breakfast of *toro* at Yamahura, for example, a restaurant in a narrow alley a few hundred yards from Tsukiji's wholesalers, is a steal. Stooping beneath the *noren*, the cloth curtains, I sat down at a long counter and ordered the *maguro-don*. The owner – a stoop-shouldered woman with a chain-smoker's bark who looked like she could outgrunt even the roughest fishdealer – brought me a bowl of rice covered with six slices of cherry-red, iron-rich *akami* (the regular cut of bluefin from the upper body), topped with three slices of the paler *toro*. The rice was spiked with wasabi, and there were layers of thinly sliced ginger and seaweed hidden beneath the *akami*. The pinkness of the *toro* contrasted with the glistening green and white of the thinly sliced cucumber and the sprig of green *shiso*, or perilla leaf, a fresh herb whose leaves taste like peppery basil. (It is excellent, my interpreter Yumi told me, with uncooked squid.)

I ate the *toro* plain, without any soy sauce. It slid over the tongue, cool and moist, melting from the heat of my body alone, slowly dissolving into segments separated by the thin layers of marbled fat. *Toro* is, as the French say, *longue en bouche*: the flavour develops in the mouth, playing over the tongue as *umami*, salty and sweet taste receptors are stimulated; it is halfway between a *demi-sel* Breton butter and an unctuous steak tartare. I suddenly understood what all the fuss was about. Bluefin has as much in common with canned skipjack as Aberdeen Angus beef does with the ground round on top of a chilli hot dog. The bill for breakfast, including miso soup and salted aubergines, was 1,600 yen (£7). At that price, I could afford to eat bluefin at least a couple of times a week.

The more I learned about bluefin, though, the more I was inclined to think my first taste of *toro* would also be my last.

The Dodo of the Seas

Ernest Hemingway saw his first bluefin in the harbour of Vigo in northwestern Spain in 1921. It was a six-footer chasing sardines that broke the water with a 'boiling crash' and fell back 'with the noise of a horse driving off a dock'. Anyone good enough to land one of these great fish, Hemingway decided, would 'enter unabashed into the presence of the very elder gods'.

Bluefin are among the most impressive fish in the sea. Starting life as microscopic larvae, they can grow up to fifteen feet in length and reach weights of fifteen hundred pounds. Like sharks, they have to swim continuously to breathe; like mammals, they are warm-blooded, relying on a network of veins and arteries called the *rete mirabile* – the 'wonderful network' – to thermoregulate their muscles and eyes, an adaptation that extends their range from the equator to the Arctic. (In fact, there are three distinct bluefin species: the southern, the Atlantic and the Pacific bluefin. A single giant of the last species was tracked crossing the Pacific Ocean three times, covering a total of twenty-five thousand miles.) Ferociously efficient hunting machines, they boast binocular vision and fibrous, sickle-shaped tails that can beat at thirty cycles per second, so fast they are a blur to the human eye. Their torpedo-shaped bodies are three-quarters muscle. Capable of sprinting at fifty miles per hour, bluefin have been observed hunting in schools shaped like parabolas to cut down on friction, and shooting into the air to escape killer whales.

Traditional fishing methods, though sometimes bloody, at least limited the slaughter of these magnificent animals. In a technique used in the Mediterranean for three millennia, migrating bluefin are herded into successively smaller offshore nets, until they reach the 'death chamber', where they are speared with ten-foot-long gaffs. (Sicilians call the resulting slaughter the *mattanza*.) For decades the bluefin fishermen of Cape Cod harpooned the bluefin from the pulpits of small boats, in heaving seas and with little financial reward. Until a generation ago, Atlantic bluefin on the American east coast were sold for pennies a pound to make pet food, and specimens caught by sportfishermen were often buried with a bulldozer.

Technological and economic changes have transformed the fishery from a fair fight between fisherman and a powerful predator into a wholesale harvest. Harpoons were electrified, which meant the fish were more likely to be killed instantly and retrieved. In the 1960s purse-seiners – like the sardine boat I had been on in Portugal – arrived on the scene, vessels that could take three hundred fish in a single haul of the net, as many as a single harpooner used to take in a decade. In a process Italians called the 'flying *mattanza*', purse-seiners in the Mediterranean and Atlantic started working in tandem with spotter planes, Cessna-sized craft whose pilots used radio to guide captains to their prey.

Meanwhile in Japan tastes were changing. Bluefin had long been dismissed as *neko-matagi*, fish that even a cat would disdain; its fattiness meant it tended to go bad quickly. The coming of refrigerators after the Second World War allowed the taste for bluefin to spread. In 1972 a Japan Air Lines employee arranged for a giant bluefin, caught by a fisherman off Canada's Prince Edward Island, to be packed in ice and urethane and flown via DC-8 from John F. Kennedy Airport to Tokyo's Haneda Airport, from there to be auctioned at Tsukiji. Pioneering New England fish dealers followed suit, flying bluefin out of Boston's Logan Airport. At roughly the same time President Nixon took the dollar off the gold standard, boosting the yen and making Atlantic bluefin cheaper for the Japanese to buy. By the 1980s, sushi and sashimi, formerly eaten only on special occasions, had become everyday meals, as Japan's bubble economy permitted even the junior salaryman to eat out several times a week. From nickel-a-pound pet food in 1970, bluefin became a cash cow, netting Cape Cod's fishermen $18 (£9) a pound only two decades later. A long gold rush, facilitated by the globalization of sushi, had begun.

It was soon apparent, however, that there were only so many bluefin in the seas. The International Commission for the Conservation of Atlantic Tunas (ICCAT, pronounced EYE-cat), was established in 1966 to manage tuna stocks. Among its forty-two members are South Korea and Japan, countries with no Atlantic coastline but that buy, or fish for, Atlantic tuna. Most scientists regard the commission with scorn. American marine biologist Carl Safina, who called the bluefin the 'most purposely mismanaged large animal in the world', also proposed that ICCAT be redubbed the 'International Conspiracy to Catch All the Tuna'. It is one of many such regional fisheries management organizations that purport to manage the world's most valuable fish.

ICCAT's main order of business seems to be dividing up the resource pie and letting fishermen know how many bluefin they can catch. In 2007, for example, ICCAT's own scientific committee recommended that the catch for the eastern Atlantic and Mediterranean be limited to 15,000 tonnes. ICCAT, as usual, ignored its own scientists and set a quota twice as high. The World Wildlife Fund (WWF) called it 'a collapse plan, rather than a recovery plan', and a mockery of the scientists' work.

The quota might have been reasonable if the tuna-fishing

nations of the world were in fact observing the commission's limits. But Spain consistently overfishes, as does France. Libya, whose catch is officially restricted to 1,400 tonnes, is thought to be taking six times that amount. All told, the WWF estimated the 2006 catch was at least 30 per cent over quota. Many tuna, of course, never even make it into the official statistics. Frozen at sea, they are landed in such 'inspection-friendly' countries as China and Vietnam before arriving in Tsukiji. After almost four decades of being subjected to this multinational fishery, Atlantic bluefin numbers have declined by nearly 90 per cent.

Fish species, unlike land animals and marine mammals, rarely reach the point of complete extinction. The effort it takes to hunt down the last of their number, in terms of fuel and days at sea, is just not worth it. But thanks to the rarity premium paid by wealthy gourmands, hunting some species to actual, rather than just commercial, extinction is a real possibility. The Caspian sturgeon, pushed to the brink by poachers seeking beluga caviar, is one example. Abalone, stripped from the inter-tidal zones of California by divers and selling for £39 a plate in American restaurants, is another. The Atlantic bluefin may prove to be the most dramatic. For several years now, the WWF has been calling for a three-year closure of the Atlantic and Mediterranean fisheries. Like the cod off European coasts, the bluefin tuna needs a break if it is going to survive.

At Tsukiji the names I saw on the 'coffins', the crates in which tuna are shipped, hinted at the latest development in the bluefin story. 'Caladeros del Mediterraneo' I read on a crate that had been shipped from Murcia in Spain. Others had been sent air express by Qantas from Australia, or from Istanbul or Zagreb. All were products of a new kind of fish farming. In 1993 a Croatian-Australian fisherman named Dinko Lukin launched the bluefin-fattening industry. Purse-seiners encircle southern bluefin migrating across the Great Australian Bight in miles-wide nets and haul them, still alive, back to the coast at the painfully slow rate of two knots. (Easily spooked bluefin tend to panic and break their necks against the nets if they are hauled too quickly. Even so, 10 per cent die during the towing process.) They are then transferred to cages, hundreds of yards in diameter, where they are fattened up until they reach market size. Thanks to bluefin fattening, Port Lincoln, once a forgotten south coast fishing village, now has Australia's highest concentration of millionaires. Its streets are filled with Mercedes and Humvees, and a hotel has been built to accommodate Japanese inspectors. Lukin's concept has since spread to six continents. The Spanish were early adopters of bluefin ranching; Turkey and Libya signed on soon afterwards; and Croatia accounts for 20 per cent of bluefin production in the Mediterranean. Bluefin are now being fattened from Baja California to the Canary Islands.

For entrepreneurs, these ranches are a brilliant innovation. For the bluefin, they are a disaster. Tuna are typically caught at thirty-five pounds and fattened until they double in weight, a process that takes five months. Ranching removes immature bluefin from the wild, before they have a chance to spawn. While two pounds of fish go into the feed that makes one pound of farmed shrimp, for the voracious bluefin, the ratio is closer to twenty to one. Picky eaters, bluefin have to be stuffed with sardines, herrings and anchovies – often shipped frozen from the west coast of the Americas – fish that could better go to feed the world's poor. The farms are nothing more than a ploy to derive maximum profit from the bluefin, while still abiding by quotas set by ICCAT and other fisheries-management organizations.

Japan is the ultimate destination for the fattened tuna. In late summer, Japanese reefer ships queue up in the ports of the Mediterranean to buy the ranches' entire output. The tuna-ranching industry also accounts for the affordability of my *toro* at the Yamahura Restaurant: a regular supply of what should be considered an endangered fish keeps prices low. You will not find ranch-fattened tuna in such high-grade sushi restaurants as Kanetanaka: because they get little exercise, their flesh is considered inferior in flavour, fat content and firmness.

In the summer of 2006 Greenpeace and the World Wide Fund for Nature set out to confront Mediterranean tuna fishermen. They were surprised to find boats returning to port with empty holds, which meant the bluefin ranchers had nothing to fatten. Only 2,500 tonnes of bluefin were caught in the Mediterranean that year, versus 16,200 tonnes ten years before.

According to Barbara Block, 'the mystery, and the problem that's making management difficult is taking an animal that is using the entire North Atlantic as its range and making policies that the forty-two nations that fish it will follow.' Block, a marine biologist at Stanford University, has tagged fifteen hundred Atlantic bluefin, surgically implanting microprocessors capable of recording information on the fish's position and its feeding habits for up to four years. It has long been known that Atlantic bluefin spawn in the Mediterranean and the Gulf of Mexico. Block's research has proved that the two stocks mix: 38 per cent of the tagged bluefin she released in the west were later found in the east. In other words, bluefin farms in Croatia may well be causing the decline of the summer catch off Cape Cod. For Block, the bottom line is that bluefin are being caught far too young.

'Our data show they spawn for the first time, on average, at close to eleven and a half years. We probably shouldn't be catching them until they're larger, until they've spawned at least twice.' American fishermen are part of the problem. Technically there is no targeted fishery for bluefin in their Gulf of Mexico spawning grounds, but longliners chasing albacore, bigeye and yellowfin are allowed to keep one bluefin for every tonne of fish they land. Block believes even this is too much. 'If they could set aside ninety, or even sixty, days every year for the bluefin to spawn without having to interact with fishing lines, there's a lot of evidence that we could actually help the stocks recover.'

A more decisive move would be to list bluefin as an endangered species under the Convention on International Trade in Endangered Species, or CITES. The southern bluefin is already listed as 'critically endangered' on the World Conservation Union's Red List, but a CITES listing would actually restrict international trade and end the daily spectacle of the bluefin auctions in Tsukiji. Such a move has already stemmed the trade in elephant ivory, tiger bones and rhino horns. In 1992 Carl Safina lobbied for a CITES listing, encouraging Sweden to make the proposal to ICCAT. (Bluefin were fished out in Scandinavian waters decades ago.) The listing was shot down after politicking by Japan and the United States.

Judging from the evidence I had seen in my travels, we have a long way to go before bluefin is stricken from the menus of the world. *Toro* is still considered the apotheosis of seafood almost everywhere in the world. At Nobu in London's Park Lane, a single serving of *o-toro* sashimi went for £5.25; in Manhattan, I gave up counting the number of restaurants – from David Pasternack's Esca to Laurent Tourondel's BLT Fish – that had some form of *toro* on the menu. According to Kim Jong-il's former chef, bluefin from Tsukiji is one of the dictator's favourite meals, and in the wake of North Korean nuclear tests the Japanese government considered an export ban on bluefin to hit Kim where it hurt – in his ample belly. Though its boosters call it the black truffle of tuna, or the foie gras of the Med, bluefin is more likely to become the dodo of the seas.

Did I regret my bluefin breakfast? Well, I was willing to try anything once – if only to cross it off my list. But to tell the truth, I was having a little trouble digesting this particular meal. Bluefin are magnificent apex predators, ones that happen to live in the ocean. Dining on them is like ordering sashimi of Bengal tiger – decadent and more than a little amoral.

Author, chef and food travel show host Anthony Bourdain has done a lot to popularize *toro* in the West. He sang its praises in his book *Kitchen Confidential,* and ate it lightly seared and served with sweet-and-sour sauce in his gastronomic travelogue *A Cook's Tour*. In his collection *The Nasty Bits* he refers to yet another meal of bluefin as 'once-in-a-lifetime *toro*'.

That just about nails it. And I had just had *my* once-in-a-lifetime *toro* experience. There were, I figured, better ways to add seventy-five days to my life.

The Linear Automat

'*Irrasshaimassee!*' the young waitress cried as I entered. A dozen voices picked up the refrain, like jovial robots, volume knobs set on eleven.

The slow leak that is Japanese politesse – the sing-song '*one-gaishimasu*' of the free tissue distributors in the streets, the honorific greetings at the cash register – gives way to something more effervescent in the Tokyo sushi bar. I took a seat against the wall, joining a line of clients waiting for a stool at the popular Asakusa restaurant Maguro-Bito, or 'Tuna-Humans'. We were lined up neat as sardines in a can: it was as though we had sat on a conveyor belt ourselves, shifting one seat to our left every time a spot became free in front of the conveyor belt that snaked around the sushi chefs. This was *kaiten-zushi*, or rotary sushi, where the automat meets Charlie Chaplin's *Modern Times*.

Rotary sushi was born when an Osaka restaurateur, Yoshiaki Shiraishi, was looking for a way to increase the traffic in his sushi bar; his epiphany came on a tour of an Asahi beer plant, where he saw beer bottles passing on a conveyor belt. In 1958 Shiraishi opened his first Genroku Sushi restaurant, tinkering until he found the perfect conveyor belt speed: three inches per second, fast enough so that customers did not get impatient, slow enough so that airflow did not dry out the fish. Launched by massive exposure at the Osaka World Fair in 1970, the concept has been a lasting success: there are now 3,500 *kaiten-zushi* restaurants in Japan, including sushi that chugs by on little trains or floats along countertop creeks.

Finally, it was my turn to eat. A smiling waiter showed me to my stool, next to an elderly woman and her escort, who had already amassed two dozen plates between them. I ran through the sushi bar's many rules in my head. Never rub your chopsticks together – it is considered impolite – nor use them to pick up the *nigiri sushi*. Instead, use your thumb and first two fingers to dip the sushi fish-side down in the soy. Then, pressing the fish, rather than the rice, to the tongue, eat it in one bite; grains of rice floating in your soy will be seen as a badge of shame. You should not put wasabi in the soy sauce – it destroys the delicate flavour – nor should you gobble up the pickled ginger as if it were salad; instead, use it to cleanse the palate between dishes. Miso should be eaten at the end of a meal, not before. Never gesture or point with chopsticks in your hand (more rudeness) and, whatever you do, '*DO NOT PLACE YOUR CHOPSTICKS STRAIGHT UP IN THE RICE.*' As the Japan National Tourist Organization's website notes, 'This is how rice is served to the dead.'

Fortunately, with rotary sushi, the potential for missteps is minimized. You just grab whatever parades in front of you; no need to fear linguistic slips. The lady next to me demonstrated that the powder in the ceramic jar before me was not wasabi but dehydrated green tea, to be added to one of the cups of hot water passing by at a slower rate beneath the sushi. The plates, colour-coded by price, were tightly packed; pulling one out took finesse. (The *toro*, which occupied the place of honour on the gold-rimmed plate, was the most expensive.) The waitress brought a tall glass of cold *biru*, and I was off.

What was most striking was the variety. Such Western chains as the UK's Yo! Sushi and Moshi Moshi offer a familiar array of salmon rolls and *futomaki*, all covered by hygienic plastic domes. Maguro-Bito, in contrast, was a mini-Tsukiji on parade. Day-Glo orange *uni*, poised in spiny black sea urchin shells preceded sectioned octopus tentacles on a black metal plate. There were things slippery and wet: snow-white scallop and greyish abalone. There was the raw, of course, but there was also the cooked: grilled eel and whole cuttlefish. Unidentifiable translucent tentacles burst out of a seaweed wrapper, followed by an ovoid pale green mollusc I had no idea how to open. I started with the mild, little pockets of tofu stuffed with rice, dared the conger eel, and worked my way up to the *uni*. In twenty minutes I had amassed ten plates. When I was finished, I waved down a busboy, who ran a hand-held scanner down the pile of plates – two blue plates at the bottom standing for the beer – which spat out a curling receipt. Paying my bill at the cash register, I ceded my place to the next tuna-human; the conveyor belt continued. I was in and out in less than half an hour, for less than ten pounds.

Kaiten-zushi is hardly some modern perversion of a venerable tradition. Sushi has always been fast food. The technique of preserving fish by packing it in rice came to Japan in the seventh century AD, probably from cultures along the Mekong River; the fermented rice was traditionally discarded before the fish was eaten. In about 1600 rice vinegar was invented, which, when splashed on sushi rice, approximated the sought-after taste of fermentation. Sometime in the 1820s Yohei Hanaya, the owner of a sushi shop in Tokyo (then known as Edo), noticed his clients were too impatient to wait for the traditional pressing of the fish in a wooden box. He started shaping vinegar-flavoured rice with his hands and topping it with raw, and sometimes partially cooked, fish; this was the first *nigiri* sushi, the form that has since conquered the world. (The term sushi refers not to fish, which is known as *sakana*, but to the vinegared rice itself – which is why you can correctly order *tamago*, or omelette, sushi. *Nigiri* means 'hand moulded', while sashimi refers to raw meat in any form.) For purists, Edomae-style sushi – literally, 'in front of Edo', or caught in Tokyo Bay – preferably served on a *hinoki* counter, the same cypress used to make emperors' coffins, is still the only kind worthy of the name.

Recently, however, the urban stretches of landfill-afflicted Tokyo Bay have become so polluted that any chef who dared to serve his sushi Edomae-style would soon send his clientele to their sickbeds.

Shopping for the £18 Mackerel

Fat-marbled *toro*; sake-saturated *dozeu*; conveyor-belt *uni* – though familiar enough menu items in Tokyo, such dishes are hardly daily fare in the average Japanese household. To get some insight into day-to-day seafood culture, I took a subway ride to Futako-Tamagawa, an upmarket bedroom community an hour west of central Tokyo. At the subway turnstiles I met Elizabeth Andoh, an American-born food writer and anthropologist who teaches classes in Japanese cuisine at her cooking school, A Taste of Culture. Andoh, who had married a Japanese man in 1968, began our whirlwind tour of Tokyo supermarkets – there were several within a few hundred yards of the subway station – at an inexpensive chain called Tokyu Hands.

'What is the first thing you notice?' Andoh asked, as we paused in the seafood section. Evidently an adherent of the Socratic method, she tended to answer her own questions: 'It's the *variety*. I'd estimate there are thirty-five kinds of fresh fish here on any given day.' At least. The seafood section took up two long walls and several aisles.

Even in this bargain chain, the quality and selection in the fish department surpassed what you'd find in a large Marks & Spencer or Whole Foods. There was a whole section devoted to dried cuttlefish and *chirimen*, sardines used as beer snacks. (Said Andoh: 'A mouthful of those has as much calcium as two glasses of milk; thanks to *chirimen*, every time I get my bone density taken at the doctor's, I'm off the chart.') For the homemaker-in-a-hurry there were open bins of frozen mixed seafood, sold in bulk, to be used for stir-fries or atop ramen noodles. There was *bonito*, dried skipjack tuna that has been smoked and deliberately infected with a mould to enhance its flavour, in a hermetically sealed '*freshu-pakku*' – for making soup stock. ('When I first came to Japan, every home had a box with a blade and a drawer underneath it. You'd wake up in the morning not to the sound of coffee beans being ground, but to the scraping of dried *bonito* against the blade.') The canned seafood section, which featured mackerel, sabrefish, sardines, kingfish and crab, often in a soy or miso broth, made me want to fill a shopping bag right away.

'Meat, in contrast, gets very little space,' said Andoh, pointing to a single wall of steaks and poultry. 'There's chicken, beef and pork. End of discussion.'

What impressed me most was the amount of information available to Japanese seafood consumers. We walked a few hundred yards to the doors of Puresee, a midmarket supermarket chain. Already there was a change in price, presentation and variety: an entire floor refrigerator was filled with a murky rainbow of fish eggs, including glistening, caramel-hued dried mullet roe. The label on a pack of tuna showed the packaging date, the sell-by date and the facts that it was sashimi-grade and could be consumed without the application of heat. Here, as at Tokyu Hands, a green-rimmed blackboard hung above the sushi selection, indicating whether each kind of fish arrived fresh or frozen, whether it was farmed or wild-caught, and where exactly on the globe it came from.

'This board tells you the shrimp came from Canada,' said Andoh, 'and it has been defrosted. The *kampachi*, a kind of yellowtail, came from Miyazaki Prefecture; it's fresh, but was farmed. The chart, which is required by law, presumes you can identify the kind of fish just by looking at it.

'The notion of *terroir* is very strong in Japan, and of course it also applies to seafood. This is *seki-aji*, for example,' said Andoh. Reading the label, I did a double-take: the price, 4,038 yen (£18), was what you might pay for a vintage Burgundy from France. In this case, it was the price tag for a single ten-inch-long horse mackerel. '*Seki-aji* is caught in a certain area, at a certain time in their life cycle, at a certain time of year. The Japanese are very aware of the food that fish feed on, the temperature of the water, whether they're sweatin' it out, or whether they've already spawned. All this, they know, can have an impact on taste and availability. For example, this sticker refers to *shun*, or seasonality, meaning that this is the magic time of year when this horse mackerel is going to taste its very best.'

The attention to quality exceeded anything I had seen in Western supermarkets. Andoh explained that whole, line-caught fish were always displayed the same way, with the head to the left. Could I guess why? she asked. (By then I had learned that if I waited a beat, the answer would come on its own.) 'It's because fish hungry enough to snap at bait are more likely to be full of gastric juices, and if their bodies are shifted frequently in transit, the acidic liquid may seep into the flesh, causing "belly burn", those gaping sections you sometimes see in fillets.'

Added Andoh: 'This way of displaying fish, tail to the right, belly forward, is your guarantee that from the time they're taken out of the water to the time they land up on your plate, they've been in a single position.'

Our final stop, the food section of a department store called Takashimaya, was more Harrods than Safeway or Sainsbury's. A pair of melons in a wooden box set the tone: the selling price was £150. (When my jaw dropped, Andoh explained that such a gift would be given on very special occasions, to the family, for example, of a sick friend.) Women dressed in Chanel and carrying Louis Vuitton handbags comparison shopped for marinated *kasu zuke* cod and the perfect cut of salmon. The seafood section would enrapture an Escoffier and confound a Cousteau: in the aisles you could find the meaty cheek of sea bream, swordfish smeared with the milky lees of sake, and blocks of sea gelatin served with tart mustard miso. And of course, occupying pride of place, were take-home packs of *toro* from Turkey, gorgeous pale red chunks, beneath an image of a giant bluefin leaping out of the water.

I asked Andoh whether overfishing and the potential disappearance of ocean fish were issues the Japanese paid attention to.

'It's hardly a calling card of discussion here,' she replied. 'Your well-educated college grad in the United States certainly has more environmental concern than his equivalent in Japan.' Sometimes, she conceded, the differences could be shocking to Westerners. *Iki-zukuri*, for example, is a style of cooking where the fish is still alive on the chopping board and can still be twitching when you put it in your mouth.

'It dates from before the time there was refrigeration,' explained Andoh. 'It was one way to be sure that your fish was going to be flappingly fresh. But I don't view the average Japanese as having a sense of entitlement about natural resources. I think it's more a question of valuing ingenuity; the Japanese imagination is captured by the ability to control the environment and manipulate the food chain. The driving force, I think, is culinary finesse rather than cruelty to animals.'

I am not sure I agree. Swallowing live fish, that fraternity house rite of passage in North America, is a fixture in Japanese haute cuisine. It is known as *odori gui*, or 'dancing-eating'. The fact that such practices are collectively known as *zankoku ryori*, 'cruel cuisine', suggests there is some cultural ambivalence towards eating living food.

Admittedly, the Japanese find many Western practices abhorrent, though the issue tends to be more about connoisseurship than cruelty. Alaskan fishermen had to be taught by experts from Tsukiji to stop unloading their salmon with pitchforks, which lacerated the fillets. In the United States high-grade tuna is treated with carbon monoxide before it is frozen, to prevent it from turning brown – such tuna can be left in a car boot for a year and it will still be lollipop red – a practice that is completely banned in Japan. Some Japanese companies are even experimenting with acupuncture to keep fish alive, relaxed and fresh during the shipping process. Dismayed about such foreign abominations as mashed kipper and crispy-bacon sushi and cream-cheese-stuffed Philadelphia rolls, Japan's agriculture minister in 2006 launched a certification plan for foreign restaurants to ensure authentic sushi was being served abroad.

Not that all Japanese cuisine belongs on a pedestal. This is the home, after all, of the sea-urchin-roe-and-mayonnaise-covered pizza, rubbery beef *kare-raisu* ('curry-rice') covered with slurries of flavourless brown curry sauce, and the stale white bun stuffed with cold yakisoba noodles. Thanking Andoh for the tour, I stopped for my favourite Japanese snack food. *Takoyaki* are piping-hot balls of dough encasing a bit of octopus tentacle, flavoured with ginger, scallions, *bonito* flakes and a sickly sweet brown sauce. I called them octo-balls: they were cheap, delicious and a little nasty – one of the ocean's most intelligent hunters reduced to high-calorie street food. Just such a *takoyaki* stand displayed my all-time favourite example of a genre called suicide food. For me it expressed something ineffably Japanese – at once cute and carnivorous – about local attitudes to food.

The sign showed a cartoon octopus, with a chef's headband and a shaker in one of its tentacles, grinning broadly as it poured salt over its own head.

'Save Them, Eat Them!'

It was five P.M., and I had a worm's-eye view of rush-hour Tokyo. From my below-street-level seat in a Shibuya restaurant, I watched the crowd: knots of knock-kneed schoolgirls with Hello Kitty baubles dangling from their mobile phones; a yakuza with mirrored shades and a punch perm; junior executives with jet-black faux-hawks and patent-leather shoes; a woman in a kimono and wooden geta (clog) carrying a Yorkshire terrier festooned with pink bows; even a young sumo hipster, the earbuds of his iPod tucked beneath a helmet-like *chonmage* hairdo. As their numbers thickened, they dodged one another with the precision of a school of tuna-spooked sardines.

Thanks to cryptic Japanese addresses, it had taken me an hour to find the restaurant. I got caught in the tides of humanity at a diagonal crosswalk, ducked into what I thought was an Internet café but turned out to be a *soapland* – a bathhouse where young women provided stressed salarymen happy endings – and then passed and re-passed the Panda Restaurant (an establishment I hoped had nothing to do with Ling Ling and her kin). Finally, on the ground floor of the 109 Building, I found my goal: the Kujiraya Restaurant.

Very slowly, very clearly, the maître d' had said to me, in phonetically perfect English: '*This – is – a – whale – meat – restaurant.*'

When I nodded sagely, he had smiled in relief, escorted me to my table and left me alone to study the menu. At Kujiraya you could order whale meat tempura, sliced raw whale tongue and heart, boiled whale caudal fin, gristle of a whale's upper jaw, and the intimidating '5 kinds of whale dainty bits'. At least, I reflected, they used the whole animal. I pressed a buzzer for service, a waitress appeared, and I placed my order for whale sashimi.

For many people, the dinner I was about to have was as morally reprehensible as eating bush meat, live monkey brains or human flesh. While whales have not been considered food in the West for several centuries, the Japanese have been hunting them for eight thousand years, since at least the prehistoric Jomon period. Considered not mammals, but very big fish, they were long exempted from the Buddhist ban on meat eating. In shortage-ridden post-Second World War Japan, half of all the meat consumed came from whales.

Globally, industrial whaling came to an end in 1986, when the International Whaling Commission (IWC) imposed a hard-won moratorium. It had been time for a ban: in the twentieth century alone half a million whales had been slaughtered in the North Pacific, and two million in the southern hemisphere. Some ecologists now put the pre-whaling population of hump-back whales at 240 million; today only 12,000 remain. In the case of the blue whale, the largest animal on the globe, there are only 1,400 left in the entire world. Though some whale populations have recovered since the beginning of the moratorium, the most optimistic estimates put populations at only 14 per cent of former levels.

The Japanese continue to kill whales under the IWC's scientific whaling programme, which allows about a thousand whales a year to be harpooned for 'scientific purposes'. This is nonsense, and everybody knows it: the Japanese are contributing nothing new to human knowledge by dissecting these animals. As only 1 per cent of the population still eats whale meat on a regular basis, the government has amassed enormous stockpiles of frozen flesh. Deep-fried whale meat has been slipped into school lunchboxes, and in 2006 a Tokyo company was caught grinding it into dog food. Bureaucrats have employed vendors to go to hip youth hangouts to hand out free whale sushi rolls, promoting whale consumption with such Orwellian Newspeak slogans as 'Save Them, Eat Them!'

In spite of the lack of a market for whale meat, the Japanese are strenuously campaigning to have the ban overthrown. Since 1998, they have persuaded nineteen new countries to join the IWC. (The organization, which includes landlocked Mongolia and Switzerland, has been compared to the Eurovision Song Contest for its corruptibility.) In 2006, after buying the help of the tiny nations of Antigua, Dominica and Grenada in exchange for £150 million in aid, Japan finally got the 50 per cent of votes it needed to set the IWC's agenda. Antiwhaling activists fear that the twenty-year-old moratorium will be overturned by the end of the decade.

Japanese bureaucrats employ some truly specious reasoning to justify their position: they claim that since whales eat many times more fish than humans do, they are responsible for fish stock collapses. According to this logic, humans are doing the fish of the world a favour by hunting whales.

While it is true that marine mammals eat ten times as many fish as humans, in fact we are rarely competing for the same kinds of fish. Computer models run by marine biologist Kristin Kaschner at the University of British Columbia in 2004 showed that 99 per cent of marine mammal feeding takes place where little or no fishing occurred. Sperm whales, for example, spend most of their time chasing after oceanic squid, a species whose flesh is too laden with ammonia for humans to eat.

It is Japan's nationalist politicians, the same men who want to remove references to East Asian comfort women and wartime slavery from textbooks, who most fervently support whaling. One Japanese fisheries minister famously urged whaling ships to blow Greenpeace Zodiacs out of the water, and liked to refer to whales as the 'cockroaches of the sea'. Whaling is seen as a symbol of identity; to defend whaling is to refuse to be cowed by foreigners. One hundred and fifty years ago, the pro-whalers can correctly point out, free-trade-pushing Americans forced Japan to open its ports so Westerners could stop to provision their own whaling ships; after the Second World War, General MacArthur and his occupying army encouraged the Japanese to eat whale meat. Westerners, many Japanese believe, suffer not only from amnesia but also, encouraged by such films as *Free Willy*, a weak-minded anthropomorphism. After all, Japanese people do not tell Australians to stop killing hundreds of thousands of kangaroos a year; Belgians to stay away from horse steaks; or Canadians to lay off their bison burgers.

The Japanese are right about one thing: not all whales are endangered. The only kind of whale meat I saw for sale – in the form of bloody ten-kilogram rectangles at Tsukiji market, and cellophane-wrapped steaks at the upmarket Takashimaya department store – were from the species called minke. Thanks to the moratorium, minke populations have recovered; it is thought that as many as a million of them now live in the southern hemisphere alone. I can believe it: in a single afternoon's flight in a Cessna the year before, I had counted forty minke, fin and humpback whales breaching and blowing off the west coast of British Columbia.

My dinner arrived: seven pieces of minke whale sashimi, cut into thin rectangles and arranged on the round plate *sugimori* style – leaning against each other like *sugi*, or cedar trees. Spotlighted by recessed halogen, the meat was almost oxblood red, shot through with veins of white fat. I suppose, if I were a young vegan, this would be the ultimate horror, all the more so because of the impeccable presentation. But I am not as earnest as I used to be.

Whale was not what I expected. I had imagined myself chewing a hunk of gummy blubber, but the cut was lean, and the taste was closer to rare bloody beef than fish. Whale was dense meat, reminiscent of venison, but with a slight aftertaste of liver. Frankly, though, it was nothing special – tuna tartare was tastier – and mine was still a little frozen in the middle.

As I chewed, I found I was already trying to rationalize my meal. After all, compared to ordering overfished bluefin, the caviar from sturgeon or any of the endangered delicacies served in Michelin-starred restaurants in the West every night of the week, ordering minke whale from the vast stocks in Japan is no more than a minor transgression. Surely it is a venial rather than a mortal sin, the moral equivalent of buying a second-hand fur coat.

But I failed to convince myself. Pushing the plate away, I wondered if hell has a special media room for the overly curious writer.

(Looking back, it is fortunate that I did not develop a taste for whale meat while in Japan. Like many marine mammals, whales are often infected with *Brucella*. Shortly after my trip to Tokyo, the *Marine Pollution Bulletin* revealed that 38 per cent of minke whales sampled in Japan were found to contain the pathogen, which causes a disease that in humans leads to fever, muscle pain, spontaneous abortions and inflammation of the testes. What's more, whale flesh can contain so much mercury that even one meal of organ meat can cause acute intoxication. I am glad I did not order those 'dainty bits' mentioned on the menu.)

The bill, I found, was telling: only 2,200 yen (£9.60) for a dinner set that included shiitake mushrooms, radishlike daikon, rice, and a salad of tofu and dried *chirimen*. Thanks to the government stockpile of 'scientific' meat, going for whale was an unusually cheap night out in Tokyo.

The other clients at Kujiraya that evening were grey-haired businessmen. One was clearly introducing a younger colleague to the dish he ate when he was a child. The restaurant, which opened in 1950, was an institution, and I was not particularly shocked that these old gentlemen were enjoying a dinner of their childhood staple. It was a case not of thrill-seeking for its own sake, but of genuine nostalgia. Nor do I have any problem with traditional communities like the Norwegians of the Lofoten Islands, or the Inupiat of Alaska, who have been whaling sustainably for generations. Whales are indeed intelligent creatures; but so are octopi, and you do not see Greenpeace storming many Greek tavernas.

With that said, the industrial slaughter of whales is as unnecessary as it is deplorable. Synthetics long ago replaced the oils and other products rendered from whale carcasses, and, given the levels of mercury and other pollutants in whale flesh, feeding it to schoolchildren is an abomination. Obscenely, the slaughter of whales in the twentieth century was largely revived to make margarine. As long as a nationalist agenda sets the course for national whaling policy, and Japan sets the agenda at the IWC, there is every reason to oppose the slaughter.

As a nation, Japan is clearly in conflict about the issue of whaling: according to the *Economist*, the Japanese derive more profit from the tourism associated with whale-watching than they do from the heavily subsidized whale-hunting industry. However, by putting the entire country on the defensive, the more strident antiwhalers have transformed what should become a global issue – the crisis in the oceans, of concern to all nations – into a matter of misplaced national pride. In the long run the globalization of the Japanese-born sushi trend is more of a threat to the oceans than all the whalers combined.

The imminent disappearance of any of the less media-empowered species – sharks, deep-sea fish, and most urgently, the bluefin tuna – is far more likely, and will be no less of a tragedy. They may not be as charismatic as whales, but they are in a lot more trouble.

What Man Has Wrought with Nature

'People in Japan,' Arata Izawa told me, 'aren't even aware of the danger of the extinction of bluefin tuna.'

I had met Izawa, the marine programme officer for the World Wide Fund for Nature in Japan, in the organization's cluttered offices in a high-rise near the Tokyo Tower. Izawa was uniquely qualified for his position: a marine biologist who had a master's degree in fishery resource management in Okinawa, he had once worked for a firm that imported tuna from the Philippines, where he witnessed first-hand the shark fin fishery. ('I know from real-life experience how they report the catch,' he says. 'They would just write down any number they wanted.') His biggest challenge, he said, was to communicate the need to stop overfishing to a nation that did not particularly want to hear the news.

'Some people are worried that they might not be able to eat as much bluefin and other fish in the future,' said Izawa, 'but the media certainly don't talk about animals dying and the problem of bycatch.' He showed me a WWF survey that had polled Japanese consumers about what they looked at when they bought fish. While 80 per cent of those surveyed said they took the price of fish into consideration, 72 per cent looked at place of origin and 38 per cent took into account its seasonality, a mere 5.5 per cent considered the environmental impact of the fishery.

'Fishermen,' explained Izawa, 'are romanticized heroes of our history. Though whaling is only a small percentage of total fisheries production, the Ministry of Fisheries says if we don't protect whaling, we won't be able to protect other traditional fisheries.' By taking too strong a stand on overfishing, the WWF would be associated with Western nations that were attacking whaling – and the very essence of Japanese identity.

'If the WWF puts bluefin on the "to avoid" list, then consumers won't trust us. I have to be very tactful in the stance I take.' Izawa preferred to choose his battles: he had got supermarket chains to buy fish certified by the Marine Stewardship Council (MSC), the organization that labels ethically caught fish, even convincing chain stores to retail MSC-labelled snow crab and flathead flounder.

'The Japanese,' writes Donald Richie, a lifelong observer of Japan, 'sees himself as an adapter, an ameliorator, a partner. It is not what nature has wrought that excites admiration, but what man has wrought with what nature has wrought.' Izawa agreed that the Japanese were optimistic about technology's ability to solve any natural crisis. And Japan has had very real success in improving upon nature. Japanese scientists bred the first shrimp in captivity, and it was Japan Air Lines that developed the anaerobic technology that allowed live fish to be shipped around the world in a state of suspended animation. In 2002 Hidemi Kumai, a scientist at Kinki University in Wakayama, succeeded in hatching bluefin tuna larvae, the first time such a feat had been achieved in the lab.

According to Stanford tuna researcher Barbara Block, it is a development that deserves to be taken seriously: 'I think it's exciting that Kinki University has learned to take the tuna through the life cycle. It's a great vision to imagine a day when bluefin could be farmed. If they can develop sustainable ways to farm that don't pollute the environment, then I'm all for it.'

It may be the only way to end the gold rush on these magnificent predators in the wild. Lab-spawned bluefin are already being sold in Tokyo department stores, albeit for two-thirds the price of wild-caught tuna.

Izawa understood why it was cheaper. 'Farmed tuna is just too fatty; it's not really delicious. Before, when you ate wild-caught *toro*, it made you feel special.'

Wait a minute, I interrupted. *You* eat bluefin?

'Sometimes,' he replied. 'But I don't eat sushi every day. When I do have it, it's only one piece of *toro*.' And only, he added, if it is wild-caught.

Interesting, I thought, that Izawa, part of an organization that campaigned to save bluefin, was not averse to dining on them from time to time. When it comes to seafood, the Japanese really are a breed apart.

Forget About It, Charlie

My fortnight of eating dangerously had been interesting, to say the least. In addition to sampling *toro*, minke whale, *natto* (fermented soybeans – they look like snot) and *basashi* (chewy horse-meat sashimi – it tastes like whale), I had knelt on tatami mats in the Asakusa neighbourhood and eaten dozens of whole *dozeu*, or loach, a kind of freshwater eel whose bones are softened in a marinade of sake and miso. (Butter-soft and rich in protein, *dozeu* are reputed to stoke the sex drive.) Counting all the new kinds of sushi I had eaten, and presuming that the Japanese proverb about novel foods holds true, I had extended my life span by a total of two years and eighteen days.

But I was also considering crossing a rather important category of food fish off my list: namely tuna, and not just bluefin, but most major species. Whether it comes from a can or the hands of an accomplished sushi chef, tuna, I was learning, is one of the worst seafood choices you can make.

Tuna, of course, is a confusingly generic term for many kinds of fish. There are at least fifty tuna and tunalike species, not to mention the many fish in the mackerel family whose common names include tuna. The flesh of larger, longer-lived species – among them albacore, bigeye and yellowfin – tend to be dangerously high in mercury, the heavy metal notorious for causing cognitive disabilities.* Bluefin in particular is one kind of brain food that actually makes you stupider. A single serving typically contains over one part per million of mercury, about sixty times more than a similar-sized serving of sardines. By breakfasting on bluefin, I had consumed 350 per cent of my safe weekly limit of mercury in a single shot.

The health issues are only the start. The way almost all species of tuna are caught is cause for concern. The 'dolphin-friendly' logo you see on canned tuna in the United States is no guarantee of good fishing practices. In the eastern Pacific dolphins have never really stopped dying for the canned tuna industry – 1,461 of them were killed by purse-seiners in 2004 alone, though this was a big improvement over the hundreds of thousands that used to die before the label appeared. Yet purse-seines are positively benign compared to longlining, the most common method of catching tuna. Longliners snag and kill sharks, swordfish, seabirds and turtles. According to sustainable seafood organizations, the only ethical tuna choices are species caught by trollers or hand-lines.

But when was the last time you saw a can of tuna that told you how the fish inside was caught? Tuna canners in Europe and North America are not even required to tell consumers what *species* is in the can. And in North America, while the label indicates the exact amount of saturated fat in the can, it does not tell you which ocean the fish inside has come from. Of all the varieties on sale, only non-longline-caught skipjack (marketed as 'light') tuna, which is low in mercury and relatively abundant in the oceans, can conceivably be considered a healthy, sustainable choice.

I hated to do it, but until the industry started indicating

---

* A single, six-ounce can of albacore, typically sold as 'white tuna', exceeds the US Environmental Protection Agency's limit by 30 per cent. A can of skipjack, a smaller, short-lived species sold as 'light tuna', is a better choice, at 60 per cent under the EPA limit.

where the tuna it sold came from and how it was caught, I would be crossing tuna off my list.

The Freeing of the *Fugu*

Since I arrived in Japan, many fish had died for my eating pleasure. On my last afternoon in Tokyo I decided to give the fish a chance to get even. I accepted an invitation to dine on *fugu*, aka the notorious, and poisonous, pufferfish.

Fugu contains tetrodotoxin, a poison akin to curare, one milligram of which is enough to kill thirty adults. In Tokyo's eight hundred pufferfish restaurants, where you can wash down pan-seared *fugu* fillets with sake flavoured by toasted *fugu* fins, government-certified chefs dispose of toxic bits of pufferfish flesh as if they were medical waste. Even so, there are several *fugu* fatalities a year, particularly among fishermen who insist on eating the *fugu*'s organs. The fish's best-known victim was Bando Mitsugoro, a kabuki actor, who died after forcing a Kyoto restaurant-owner to serve him four helpings of the liver; the chef was given an eight-year suspended sentence.

Fugu poisoning generally kicks in twenty minutes after dining. The mouth goes dry, the eyes lose their focus, and the muscles, including those that animate the lungs, are paralysed. The victim asphyxiates slowly, fully aware of the stupid death he is dying.

Katsundo Kaneko, the director of the Tokyo Marine Products Wholesalers Association, and my guide to Tsukiji Market one morning, had invited me to the Pufferfish Memorial Service. Every year the market's *fugu* wholesalers gather to pay tribute to the souls of all the fish their trade has forced them to dispatch. In the sea urchin auction halls of Tsukiji, I bowed deeply and presented Kaneko-san with a bottle of champagne in thanks for

277

the invitation. Taking our seats among inspectors in rubber boots and auctioneers with plastic badges, we listened as their bosses, dressed in three-button suits, perorated about the vagaries of the fish wholesaling business. A Shinto priest in a golden headdress eventually approached a single *fugu* floating in an aquarium behind the lectern, lit a candle, rang a bell and started chanting a guttural prayer.

Naturally, a buffet of *fugu* followed the ceremony.

Standing at a long table spread with *nigiri* sushi, sashimi and cooked *fugu*, I smiled at my neighbours as I picked out a lunch of potentially toxic tidbits. The pan-seared *fugu* was white and curled at the edges, like trout that had been fried in a pan. The *fugu* sashimi were sliced thin and arranged in a flower shape, like some kind of carpaccio carnation. I took a few pieces of each, then loaded my plate with more conventional sushi. Around the room, two hundred other people were already washing down their pufferfish with big gulps of Asahi beer. I did not see anybody writhing on the floor. (Or pretending to. The classic *fugu* restaurant joke, much loathed by chefs, involves dropping your chopsticks and clawing at your chest.) I shrugged and took my first bite.

For an ocean species, pufferfish is surprisingly bland. The *fugu* sashimi had a rubbery texture, halfway between carp and squid. The cooked fillets tasted a little like perch and were about as exciting. But then, I noticed an unexpected sensation: a few minutes after I had cleared my plate, my tongue started to tingle. Panicking a little, I mentioned it to my interpreter, who introduced me to the head of the *fugu* wholesalers' association, busy working on his own plate of pufferfish. Hearing of my plight, he laughed heartily. The numbness, he explained, came from small but harmless traces of poison on the skin and fins; it was entirely normal.

Mollified if not fully reassured, I followed my fellow diners as plastic tubs of live pufferfish were wheeled through the empty aisles of Tsukiji. Trailed by stray cats, we halted at the concrete banks of the Sumida River. A market official in a black suit upended a bottle of sake into the river and tossed a few clumps of cooked rice after it for good measure. As the monk and a robed acolyte chanted monotonously, the official scooped a large *fugu* from the tank and tossed it into the river. The entire crowd gathered around to do the same, and soon *fugu* were flying through the air.

I was not sure if we were doing these fish a favour. The Sumida was a notoriously polluted watercourse, and when I peeked over the edge into the murky water, I saw an empty can floating in the current, and seagulls were diving to scoop up the *fugu* while they were still stunned. One burly fellow threw his *fugu* overhand as though it were a football, so it went spiralling through the air. However, I felt a strong urge to liberate at least one fish so it would have a fighting chance to make it out of Tokyo Bay. Picking a midsized *fugu*, I cupped its slippery belly in my palms. It was surprisingly heavy. Looking up at me with its round, dark eyes, it was as cute as a Pokémon, minus the annoying squeaks. I walked to the river, watching my *fugu* gasp through its rectangular mouth.

The Japanese may be the world's most voracious consumers of seafood, and their ambivalence about bluefin tuna and whaling can be shocking to Westerners, but any society whose relationship with seafood is this complex, and ancient, should be given a little credit. I had seen fish dealers bowing before the Namiyoke Shrine on their way to work, as well as the inscription on the rock at the market entrance from the Association of Sushi Suppliers that reads: 'We have pleased many humans with fine sushi but we must also stop to console the souls of the fish.' We in the West rarely show such reverence for the sea life that sustains us. When was the last time you saw a bishop or rabbi asking for forgiveness from the souls of departed halibut at your local fish market?

And there are signs the Japanese are becoming more aware of the crisis in the oceans. As reports of the disastrous 2006 bluefin season in the Atlantic and Mediterranean spread, Wal-Mart-owned Seiyu, one of Japan's largest retailers, announced it would stop selling European-caught bluefin in over two hundred supermarkets. Some sushi chefs took to replacing *toro* with venison and horse meat. Then in 2007 Japan surprised the world by voluntarily cutting its own share of the eastern Atlantic bluefin catch by 23 per cent. After admitting it had exceeded its quota for southern bluefin by 1,800 tonnes in 2005 – an Australian audit found they had hidden as much as £3.5 billion worth of bluefin over ten years – they agreed to halve their quota starting in 2007.

Once the world starts to wake up to the crisis in the oceans, the Japanese will not be slow in coming up with solutions. They cannot afford to. When it comes to seafood, Japan just has too much to lose.

Giving my *fugu* a final pat, I let it slip into the slate-coloured water as smoothly as I could. It quickly disappeared beneath the surface of the Sumida River.

When I last glimpsed it, it was heading in the direction of the Pacific Ocean.

9

BRITISH COLUMBIA –
GRILLED SALMON

An Economy of Scales

At this point in my travels, I had heard all the arguments of the proponents of fish farming.

There is no need, according to the boosters of aquaculture, to worry about the future of seafood. Thanks to technology, we are already living in a brave new world of cheap protein.

Take salmon, for instance. Once it was a delicacy for the rich. Because of aquaculture, it has become one of the most popular seafoods in the United States, surpassed only by shrimp and canned tuna; twenty-three million Americans eat salmon at least once a month. In Britain, where consumers bought £432 million pounds of the fish in 2007, the farm-gate value of salmon routinely drops below one pound a kilogram – less than the price of chicken. Rich in omega-3s, low in saturated fat, what was once a seasonal delicacy has become the alternative to beef or poultry in a million inflight meals.

According to this optimistic script, the old hunter-gatherer of the seas, the fisherman, is already being supplanted by a more advanced figure, the symbol of a new era of ocean stewardship: the fish farmer. Forty-three per cent of the fish eaten in the world are now farmed, according to the United Nations, and the industry has been growing by an astonishing 9 per cent a year for the last three decades. By 2010 world aquaculture output is expected to surpass beef production.

Just as the green revolution of the 1960s stymied the doom-sayers who predicted population growth would outstrip the land's ability to produce food, the blue revolution will harness the full potential of the oceans and keep the world – the popu-lation of which is expected to reach eight billion by the year 2025 – fed with a predictable supply of high-quality marine pro-tein. As a not insignificant fringe benefit, the most important populations of wild food fish – salmon, tuna, shrimp, cod and halibut – will be saved from extinction. Who needs to hunt them, after all, when you can grow them?

There is just one problem with this proposition, as people on the west coast of Canada are discovering. The fish farmers are emptying the very oceans they claim to be saving.

Down on the Fish Farm

'I'm a second-generation fish farmer,' said John Holder. 'For me, this isn't a job; it's a career. I'm proud of what I do.'

We were standing on the floating metal catwalk of a fish farm in Salmon Inlet, one of a network of narrow fjords gouged into the Pacific coast of Canada, a forty-five-minute ferry ride and an hour's drive northwest of Vancouver. It was a miserable day in paradise: clouds were tangled like sheep's wool in the fir trees that plunged from the hillsides on either side of the inlet, as a relentless winter rain drenched the optimistically named Sun-shine Coast. Holder, dressed in camouflage cargo pants and faded

lumberjack's plaids, was responsible for the day-to-day operations on this and two other salmon farms. Next to him was
Justin Henry, who had a master's degree in aquaculture and
supervised the company's salmon from the time they were fry
in the hatchery to the moment their gills were cut in the processing plant.

Site 9, which floated a couple of hundred yards from the
shore, was typical of such operations on the coast of British
Columbia. It consisted of an aluminium-sided outbuilding that
served as crew's quarters, a warehouse stacked with one-tonne
bags of feed, and the site's offices. Alongside it were a dozen net
cages, each sixty-five feet to a side, in two rows of six. Metal catwalks buoyed by plastic floats ran around the perimeter. It
looked like a half-dozen tennis courts had been airlifted from a
swank suburb and dropped intact into the middle of a pristine
inlet. The net cages, which dangled a hundred feet beneath the
surface, were attached to the bottom by concrete anchors; they
were surprisingly capacious, each capable of holding 60,000
fish. Site 9, which was a relatively small operation, was stocking
only 200,000 salmon, but some of the biggest farms could hold
well over a million.

'You get a much better look with polarized lenses,' Holder
said, handing me a pair of wraparound sunglasses. With the glare
from the surface cut, the glistening silver backs of thousands of
Atlantic salmon leaped into view. Their movements were nervous: netted and confined, fish that evolution intended for
purposeful forward movement darted among each other frenet-
ically. Every once in a while one flipped itself into the air before
us, as if it could no longer stand being in its native element.

Now twenty-eight months old, the salmon at Site 9 weighed
about six and a half pounds, and were still three months from
their optimum weight of thirteen pounds. The only way they
would bulk up in time would be through constant feeding,
and providing that food was the main duty of the farm's

employees. A burly First Nations man in his early twenties –
with the exception of Holder, all the employees looked to be college age – plunged a plastic boat bailer into a pail of brown
pellets and scattered them over the surface with a flick of the
wrist, provoking a frenzy in the pen as the salmon snapped up
their lunch. All the while, his eyes were fixed on a black and
white television monitor linked to an underwater camera
angled upwards from the bottom of the net. When too many
pellets appeared on the screen, it meant the fish had stopped
feeding, and he could move on to the next pen.

'When the fish are really eating hard, we'll use the automatic
feeder,' said Holder. The machines, which look like artificial
snow blowers, could empty a one-tonne feed bag in less than a
minute and a half. A big farm could go through £10,000 worth
of pellets in a day.

I asked them about the waste that accumulates beneath
salmon farms, a mixture of fish faeces and any feed that has
fallen through the nets. (According to biologists, a farm of this
size releases faecal matter equivalent to the untreated sewage
from a city of 65,000 people.)

'You cannot compare human sewage and fish waste!' snapped
Holder. 'It's inert carbon material. Salmon are cold-blooded
animals – they just don't have the bacteria that human waste
does.' When I asked about antibiotics and pesticides, used to
treat salmon for diseases and parasites, Henry stepped in. 'Sediment is just not an issue on this farm. Sechelt Inlet is very deep,
with a hard bottom and fast currents. Every year we do sediment
samples, and there is no deposit whatsoever.' (Which probably
meant the waste was gathering somewhere else in the inlet. Not,
I hoped, in the shorefront scallop and oyster farms I saw on our
boat ride to the farm.)

How, I wondered, did they keep predators under control? It
is well known that penning up this many fish in one spot can
attract everything from grizzly bears to killer whales. The year

before, British Columbian salmon farmers had shot seventy-eight harbour seals, and over the years they had killed 350 Steller's sea lions, recently declared a species of special concern by Canada's Committee on the Status of Endangered Wildlife. In a single incident in 2007, fifty-one California sea lions were trapped and drowned in a three-layered net cage on the west coast of Vancouver Island.

'We don't even have a rifle on site,' Henry replied. 'We've got bird nets to keep seagulls and ravens out, and at night we switch on the electric nets to keep the predators out. Once they've been shocked, they think twice about coming back.'

What, then, about escapes? Scientists claim that farmed salmon can spread disease to wild salmon or take over their spawning grounds.

'We lose a fish here and there,' admitted Henry. 'But it's way down from what it used to be. I think the whole industry has been pretty good lately. Government regulations have changed, and the nets are much stronger than they used to be.' (Just behind Henry's back I could see a hole in the net the size of a dinner plate, mended with a much finer grade of netting. Two men in scuba gear were on the other end of the catwalk, diving to repair holes.)

Curious to hear insiders' answers to the criticisms most commonly voiced about the industry, I kept up my relentless questioning. If it weren't for artificial colourants added to the feed, the flesh of farmed salmon would be a repulsive grey or an unappetizing yellow. Weren't such additives, I asked, bad for your health?

Henry had an answer for that, too: 'We use a carotenoid pigment called astaxanthin. Sockeye get it naturally in their diet from krill. We add the *identical* pigment to their diet. It's just a synthetic version of it. It's like taking a pill to get your vitamin C instead of eating an orange.'

Holder scooped a handful of salmon feed from one of the

bags. Each pellet was seven millimetres in width, perfectly cylindrical, a little brown nugget of heat-treated, extruded fish kibble. 'There's nothing wrong with the feed at all,' he said. 'It's just protein. You can try it.'

I took a bite and immediately gagged; the taste reminded me of the oil from a can of anchovies that had been sitting on the counter in a heatwave: rancid and nauseating. I spat it into my hand before I could swallow.

'Yeah,' said Holder with a smirk. 'It's not that tasty. It's more for fish than people.'

I asked about a recent report that claimed there are so many toxins in farmed salmon that you should avoid eating it more than once a month.

Holder looked outraged. 'I eat farmed salmon three or four times a week! I won't even buy wild fish, because I think there's too much overfishing going on. I've actually walked out of restaurants because they don't serve farmed fish.' His father, he explained, farmed trout and salmon for over three decades. Defending the family trade was in his blood.

Justin Henry, the aquaculture technician, agreed. 'It's true that there are slightly fewer contaminants in wild salmon. But when you look at it objectively, the levels are so low that PCBs and dioxins in farmed salmon are really a non-issue. You get more of those chemicals from beef. I have a four-and-a-half-year-old son, and I let him eat farmed salmon all the time.'

Artificial colourants; escapes; pollution; toxins – the industry, it seemed, had all the worrisome issues discussed in the media under control. Viewed from the catwalks of Site 9, the critics appeared to be radically out of touch with the people who actually live and work on the coast. For men like Holder and Henry, salmon farms provided not only the possibility of long-term employment but also an affordable dinner.

'There's no such thing as agriculture without impact,' admitted Henry, as he shuttled me back to shore. 'You just have to make sure it's at an acceptable level. And I think our industry's done a pretty good job.'

Until recently Holder and Henry were employees of Target Marine Products, the last major salmon-farming company in British Columbia still owned by Canadians; but the week before my visit a Norwegian company had bought the operation, bringing its total farm sites on the coast to seventeen. Almost the entire salmon-farming industry on the west coast of Canada is now owned by three European multinationals.

After Henry dropped me on the dock at Porpoise Bay, I ran into the new owner of Site 9, who was climbing onto the float of a seaplane bound for Vancouver Island. Per Grieg is the managing director of the seafood division of a family business founded in Norway in 1884. Aquaculture is only one of this multinational's many activities; the Grieg Group is also one of the world's largest shipowners and shipbrokers.

A couple of hours earlier, in the offices of Target Marine's hatchery, I had chatted briefly with Grieg. He was in Canada, he said, to make a lightning tour of the salmon farms he had just acquired. A tall man in his forties, with pale blue Scandinavian eyes and the firmest of handshakes, he was clearly enjoying his Canadian wilderness adventure and waxed enthusiastically about Grieg's prospects on the west coast.

Pointing to a wall map of the province's fjordlike coastline, he told me, with a glint in his eye: 'British Columbia is currently producing only seventy thousand tonnes of Atlantic salmon a year. You could easily do much better. You could produce as much as Norway does and even more. You should have the goal of producing at least a million tonnes a year!'

Norway's 850 salmon farms currently produce 450,000 tonnes of farmed salmon a year. For British Columbia to reach a million tonnes, virtually every major river, inlet and channel from the forty-ninth parallel to the Alaska Panhandle would have to be occupied by a netcage. A single farm, like Site 9, may seem like something the vast Canadian wilderness can handle, but the cumulative impact of hundreds of such farms would be something else altogether.

My guides to Site 9 had not mentioned a few key facts about the potential impact of farms. In Norway salmon farming has led to rampant waterborne diseases and the deliberate poisoning of entire rivers, and contributed to the virtual extinction of the native salmon population. That, many people believe, is why the Norwegians came to Canada in the first place: after ravaging their own coastline, they needed virgin territory to exploit.

Far from sparing wild fish populations, industrial-scale aquaculture could administer the *coup de grâce* that finishes them off for ever. Some think that, only three hundred miles to the north of Site 9, the death blow to wild Pacific salmon is already being dealt.

From King of Fish to Spam of the Sea

Salmon refers not to one fish but to many, a fact reflected by all the names that get attached to them. Most salmon are anadromous: they start life in fresh water as *alevins*, become free-swimming *fry* or *parr* once they've absorbed their egg sacs, and undergo a radical metamorphosis into *smolts* that allows them to survive in salt water; finally they return to fresh water to spawn and die, often to the very stream where they were born. (Male Pacifics that spawn a year earlier than their cohorts are called *jacks*; the one in ten Atlantics that live to spawn again are known as *kelts*; and yearling Atlantic salmon, which until the mid-nineteenth century were thought to be a different species, are called *grilse*.) Twenty million years ago there was only one kind of salmon, but the cooling of the Arctic Ocean split the habitat of this prototypical fish so that it evolved into two different genera: *Oncorhynchus*, the Pacific salmon, and *Salmo*, the Atlantic salmon. Periods of glaciation in turn isolated and sub-divided the Pacific genus into eleven species, namely: chinook, chum, coho, pink, sockeye and kokanee (the latter live in land-locked lakes); cutthroat, golden and Apache trout; and their Asian cousins, amago and masu. Long since extinct is *Oncorhynchus rastrosus*, the sabertooth salmon, a monster that could weigh 350 pounds.

Europe's rivers were once filled with salmon. The oldest known depiction of a fish is a 25,000-year-old carving of an Atlantic salmon, found on the ceiling of a cave in France's Périg-ord region, one hundred miles from the nearest coast. Caesar's legionnaires caught salmon in what is now central London, and salmon rivers in Britain have been regulated since the days of Richard the Lionheart. Traditionally anybody building a dam or similar structure had to leave a hole the width of a well-fed three-year-old-pig – the King's Gap – to allow the fish to pass. As Industrial Revolution factories started spilling effluent into British rivers, however, the salmon began to disappear. It is believed that King George IV paid a guinea a pound to eat the last salmon caught in the Thames. By the 1850s salmon were such a luxury – as expensive, in relative terms, as shark fin soup is in Shanghai today – that poaching became widespread. By the mid-twentieth century salmon were extinct in Germany, Bel-gium and the Netherlands and had been all but eliminated from other western European countries. The only places with healthy populations are Ireland, Iceland, Norway and Scotland – all northern, Atlantic-girded lands with convoluted shorelines.

Before the *Mayflower* dropped anchor off the fishhook that is Cape Cod, the eastern seaboard of North America supported a population of twelve million salmon. In Atlantic Canada salmon on the Miramichi River were so abundant that they kept early French settlers awake with the noise they made throwing them-selves out of the water. But mill dams and overfishing made short work of local salmon runs, and by 1846 salmon were commercially extinct in New England. In spite of hatcheries, which have released 120 million smolts into the wild over the last 140 years, salmon stubbornly refuse to return to the northeastern United States; in Maine, only the Penobscot River still sees a few hundred returning wild salmon a year. Today, from Norway to New England, less than half a million Atlantic salmon are left in the wild. In many of New Brunswick's rivers 80 per cent of the Atlantics that return are actually escaped farm fish.

Pacific salmon are in much better shape – a good thing, too, because without salmon, a keystone species, the Pacific Northwest would be a far poorer place. When the glaciers receded after the last ice age, the west coast of North America was barren of life. Nutrients from the ocean arrived en masse when salmon, which had survived the glaciation in coastal refugia, swam up rivers and died by the millions, often hundreds of miles inland. Their decomposing bodies provided the nutrients that allowed plants to take root. The great temperate rain forests of British Columbia, with their stands of millennial Sitka spruce, red cedar and Douglas firs, owe their existence to the rotting bodies of these nomadic fish. (In turn, the complex hydrology of the forest provides salmon with the gravel they need for spawning, and tree canopies distribute nutrients over the breadth of the stream for alevins; that is why, too often, logging around salmon streams kills off entire runs.)

Salmon were the vehicle by which the biological riches of the North Pacific – the immense productivity of krill and plankton – were spread to the land. Even today a third of the nitrogen in the valley bottom forests of British Columbia is of marine origin, and trees along salmon streams grow three times as fast as their counterparts inland. Salmon provide 90 per cent of the carbon and nitrogen in Alaskan brown bears' diets. The entire food chain depends on them; even deer have been known to eat their spawned out carcasses. Salmon nitrogen has been found in the cells of mountain goats in the Rocky Mountains.

With the coming of the Europeans, Pacific salmon were harassed by fishermen at sea and increasingly deprived of spawning habitat in rivers. The gold rush of the 1860s killed off California's salmon runs, as hydraulic mining, a technique that involved blasting gravel with pressurized water, choked spawning streams with sediment. Relentless dam building condemned the great salmon runs on the Columbia River. Government hatcheries were set up to restore dwindling runs, but the hatchery fish tend to outcompete wild stocks, negatively affecting the gene pool and further decreasing salmon stocks.

Though precontact aboriginal fishermen were astonishingly efficient – northwest coast natives caught an estimated 127 million pounds of salmon a year – they seem to have instinctively understood the principle of maximum sustainable yield, never reducing the biomass below half its original level, a practice that ensured that salmon runs persisted and even increased. By the end of the twentieth century, Canadian and American fishermen, overseen by bureaucrats, were taking up to 90 per cent of the salmon in some runs. The most recent estimates put salmon returns to Pacific Northwest rivers down to 7 per cent of their historic levels. From California to British Columbia, 232 distinct salmon populations have become extinct. Only Alaska, which has had a policy of releasing 50 per cent of all salmon caught in nets since 1924, continues to have healthy runs.

When I was a boy growing up in Vancouver, salmon could only mean one thing: wild Pacific salmon. A neighbour of ours owned a salmon troller, and when he started fishing in the 1960s, seven thousand small boats were selling their catch to a hundred processing plants up and down the BC coast. By the time he retired at the turn of the century, only three thousand boats were left, supplying their catch to a mere half-dozen factories. New technology now means that a much reduced fleet can take a year's quota in a matter of days. Though wild salmon is getting scarcer, and fishermen are going out of business, salmon is cheaper than ever. My mother remembers paying $20 (about £10) for a fillet of sockeye in a local supermarket in the 1980s; the wholesale price for much of that decade hovered around $9 (£4.40) a pound. Late in 2007, Safeway was *retailing* salmon fillets for $5.99 (£2.95) a pound.

What happened in the interim? Aquaculture came to the west coast.

Salmon, once the king of fish, worshipped by First Nations people as a provider of wealth and coveted by English royalty, has become the Spam of the Sea. There is a simple explanation for this sudden dethroning: the invasion of the Atlantics.

How the Atlantics Took Over the Pacific

The first salmon farmers were motivated by good intentions. In the 1960s, thanks to overfishing, acid rain, overdamming and development, Atlantic salmon were no longer returning to Scandinavian streams to spawn. Rather than exhaust the remaining stocks of wild fish, fish farmers decided to raise their own. Inspired by the success of Danish trout farmers, Norwegians decided that sheltered fjords with a constant supply of cold, oxygen-rich water were tailor-made for aquaculture.

They ran into problems from the start. Swedish juvenile trout, brought to Norway to enhance local populations, infested farmed Atlantic salmon with a nasty parasite called *Gyrodactylus salaris*, which feeds by attaching its mouth to its host and secreting a digestive enzyme that dissolves scales and skin. The parasite soon spread to wild salmon; finally the government decided to flood twenty-four rivers with the pesticide rotenone – the same chemical used to cleanse shrimp ponds in India –

ridding them of all animal life. (The parasite has since recolonized several of the affected rivers.) Furunculosis, a disease that covers fish with bluish pus-filled boils, was found in 550 farms by 1992 and eventually spread to seventy-four rivers. Millions of salmon escaped from pens that were damaged during storms. In a single breakout 630,000 farmed fish were released into the ocean, outnumbering all the wild Atlantics left on earth. Farmed traits have long since infiltrated the gene pool: 80 per cent of the fish in some Norwegian rivers are now of farmed origin – which is a problem, because fast-growing farmed salmon steal nesting spots from their wild cousins but then lay deformed, nonviable eggs. In Norway, the country that pioneered modern salmon aquaculture, farms have now been banned in eight fjords for fear of killing off the last remaining wild fish.

Some Norwegian farmers adapted, spacing their farms apart and reconfiguring their facilities. Others looked abroad for new coasts to colonize. On the west coast of the United States, Americans were wary: only a handful of salmon farms have ever been licensed in Washington State while Alaska, whose economy depends on its wild fisheries, has long had a zero-tolerance policy for salmon farms. (They do, however, allow salmon ranching, in which about 1.5 million fish are fattened in pens every year until they are big enough to be released in the wild.) Scotland had already experienced problems with escapes and disease, particularly in the sea lochs of the west coast; only Canada seemed ripe for the picking.

'We are very strict about the quality and the environmental questions [in Norway],' Jon Lilletun, a Norwegian parliamentarian, explained to a Canadian committee in 1990. 'Therefore, some of the fish farmers went to Canada. They said, "We want bigger fish farms; we can do as we like".'

In British Columbia idealistic small operators, among them doctors, hippies and even one of the founders of Greenpeace, started running small salmon farms in the 1970s. These pioneers faced many problems. In the relatively warm waters off the Sunshine Coast – where I visited Site 9 – predators, disease and summer algae blooms wiped out entire farms. The real crisis came in 1989, when Emperor Hirohito died, and many Japanese stopped eating salmon and other luxury foods as a sign of respect, temporarily eliminating a major market. Meanwhile overproduction in Norway had created a 30,000-tonne stock of frozen product, known in Scandinavia as the *laksberg*, or salmon mountain. Wholesale prices dropped by 40 per cent worldwide, and British Columbia's farmers could no longer afford to pay off their loans. Norwegian and Dutch corporations swooped down on Canada's west coast, buying operations from dozens of farmers on the verge of bankruptcy.

The Europeans' honeymoon in Canada was short-lived. In 1995, a left-of-centre provincial government announced a moratorium on new salmon farms; in response, the European companies started cramming more fish into the existing pens, so that farms designed to hold a quarter of a million fish were stocking five times that amount. Eventually, frustrated by their inability to expand in Canada, they turned to another hemisphere. Since the 1990s, the industry has been booming in Chile: blessed with a long, temperate-water coastline, lax environmental regulations and workers who would accept £16 for a forty-eight-hour week, the country also had no wild salmon of its own. (Thanks to aquaculture, however, the rivers of the Andes now support a thriving population of escaped farmed salmon.) The big problem is geographical: Santiago's airport is a long way from Miami International, and jet fuel adds to the cost of each fillet. Canadian salmon, in contrast, can be shipped south in tractor-trailers. Though Chile is now the world's largest producer, exporting £830 million worth annually, BC's farmed salmon industry was revived when a business-friendly provincial government lifted the moratorium on new licences. By 2002 British Columbia was back in the salmon-farming business.

In the late 1980s there were fifty fish farm companies in British Columbia, most of them run by locals. Twenty years later only one Canadian-owned venture, a small Vancouver Island outfit specializing in organic salmon, was still in business. In 2006, the Norwegian giant Pan Fish bought its main competitor, a subsidiary of the Dutch company Nutreco, for £785 million, in the process creating the world's largest salmon-farming company. Rebranded Marine Harvest, this Oslo-head-quartered multinational now operates seventy sites in British Columbia. Their closest competitor is Mainstream, which has thirty sites. Both Mainstream and EWOS, the world's biggest fish-feed manufacturer, are divisions of Cermaq (a contraction of 'cereals and marine aquaculture') whose biggest shareholder is the Norwegian government. Grieg Seafood – the new owner of Site 9 – is the up-and-comer in the industry, with seventeen sites in the province. Over the next decade the provincial government is expected to approve ten new sites a year, doubling the industry's footprint in British Columbia.

Concentration of ownership has been good for the Europeans. Globally, three players control a £160-million-a-year industry, which allows for vertical integration and further cost-cutting: Mainstream, for example, can feed its farmed salmon EWOS-manufactured pellets, and ship them to market on Cermaq's own trucks. Most of Mainstream's BC farms are located in Clayoquot Sound, a UNESCO biosphere reserve that is home to some of the planet's hugest old-growth trees. It is now possible to kayak for two days to the heart of a Pacific coast rain forest, only to find the automated feeders of a Norwegian-government-controlled fish farm noisily blowing pellets to a million Atlantic salmon.

The great mystery is what British Columbia stands to gain from salmon farming. The profits go to bank accounts in Oslo; licensing fees are laughably low; and company presidents do not have to pay Canadian income tax. Employment is minimal and short-term – the farms are mostly staffed by teenagers and people in their twenties – and as the industry becomes increasingly automated, the ratio of jobs to pounds of fillet produced constantly decreases.

What the province stands to lose, however, is becoming all too evident: its remaining stocks of wild salmon.

Guerrilla Science

The Broughton Archipelago is the last place you would expect, or hope, to find a twenty-first-century industrial activity. Leaving the northeastern edge of Vancouver Island in a Beaver – the floatplane that is the workhorse of the west coast – I was reminded of how gorgeous the British Columbian wilderness could be: the archipelago looked like a jigsaw puzzle flung over the surface of the sea, with snaking channels and serrated sounds separating its scattered pieces. As we flew in the direction of snow-capped mountains, I was also reminded of how much the local economy depended on the quick buck of resource extraction: the hillsides, furrowed with cutblocks and stripped of trees, looked as if they had been buzzed by King Kong's hair clippers.

The Beaver was on the milk run, touching down at dots on the map that had at most a few dozen year-round inhabitants. At Sullivan Bay, a little community of floating houses, the slick round head of a sea lion popped up to watch as we unloaded crates of pipes and shingles. Bald eagles eyed us from the treetops at the logging camp at East Seymour. Swooping low over Kingcome Inlet, we spooked a herd of wild cattle, before touching down on the river, where two Tsawataineuk men in mirrored shades roared up to the dock in a powerboat to pick up the mail. Dipping a wing over Knight Inlet, the pilot pointed out the curved wake of a pod of a dozen Pacific white-sided dolphins as their bodies arced above the water's surface. The Broughton Archipelago, home to sea otters, great blue herons and until recently a resident population of humpback and killer whales, is one of the richest pockets of biodiversity on the coast. In the 1960s, 144 streams in the area had healthy Pacific salmon populations. Today, only six do.

The Beaver finally dropped me west of Gilford Island. A small power boat sidled up to our floats, and Alexandra Morton, who calls herself a guerrilla scientist, welcomed me into the cabin. An affable, middle-aged marine biologist originally from New England, Morton had begun her career studying killer whales at a San Diego aquarium. She came to the Broughton Archipelago to pursue her dream of studying a pod of killer whales in the wild. She bought a floathouse and started a family. Then the salmon farmers came.

'I arrived here in 1984,' said Morton. 'The salmon farms came three years later. I thought they were a great idea. I offered myself up as a welcome wagon. I let the industry know if there were any women who wanted to know about school and shopping, I'd be glad to help.' But Morton had second thoughts when the salmon farmers began to use acoustic harassment devices to drive away predators, killing her dream of studying killer whales.

'The first time I heard them, I actually had my headset on, with a microphone in the water. I turned on the tape machine, and I was like: "Waaaah!" I had to tear off the headphones; it was that loud.' The underwater noisemaking devices produced a sustained and deafening cricketlike chirp that drove away seals, sea lions and otters. (The devices have since been banned.) Unfortunately they also permanently scared off the resident pods of killer whales. 'One family after the next came out, experienced the noise and never came back.' Morton was left wondering how she could be a whale researcher without any whales to study.

We motored into Sir Edmond Bay. Ringed by evergreens, the small inlet would have been idyllic if not for the farm owned by Mainstream, the Norwegian-government-controlled multinational, anchored in the middle of it. The main building bristled with dishes for pulling in satellite TV signals. A generator kept the computers and automatic feeders running. A loudspeaker blared announcements to the staff. Sir Edmond Bay had once been a prime prawn-fishing spot for one of Morton's neighbours, but after the farm arrived, his traps began to come up covered with a yellow sludge of rotting feed and faeces.

Though the wild prawns were gone, there were now a million full grown Atlantic salmon in Sir Edmond Bay, nearly ready for processing. And this was just one of many farms. Even though the Broughton Archipelago is an officially designated provincial park, there were twenty-six other salmon farms like this one scattered among its bays and channels. Grieg Seafood was the latest company to be granted a permit.

'The way this industry operates here is completely as bullies,' said Morton. 'The government asked my neighbours, the old-time fishermen, where they wanted the fish farms. They showed us a map divided into green, yellow and red zones. For the red zones, they said they weren't even going to accept applications. Six months later more farms were placed in the red zones than anywhere else! One of my neighbours is a cod fisherman. He said, "Alex, it's uncanny. They put every one of their farms in one of my hotspots!"'

The farms, locals believed, brought disease to wild fish. For the first time in living memory the Broughton's coho salmon stocks were covered with pus-filled boils. All the nutrients being added to the water led to toxic algae blooms. Fishermen reported pulling up groundfish covered with lesions and tumours; they found rock sole and turbot with growths that looked like palm trees sprouting out of their eyeballs. First Nations people, who had been practising aquaculture in the

Broughton for hundreds of years, if not millennia, in purpose-built clam gardens, reported the most disturbing changes. Beaches near the farms, they discovered, were knee-deep in black mud and smelled like sewers.

'Before the farms came, there were plenty of healthy clam beaches,' said Bill Cranmer, chief of the Namgis First Nation, which claims the Broughton as part of its traditional territory. 'We're finding that the ones from beaches near the salmon farms have a kind of dark brown colour to them, with black tinges. You just can't eat them.'

To make matters worse, the newly arrived Atlantics were not staying in their pens. Morton visited the boats of local fishermen and in six weeks found they had caught 10,826 escapees from the farms. The results of autopsies, which she published in the *Alaska Fishery Research Bulletin*, showed that 14 per cent of them had shrimp, herring or sticklebacks in their stomachs – proving that they were not only feeding, but also surviving for weeks in the wild.

In spite of the disease, the pollution and the escapes, Morton told me she might have been willing to accept the farms – if it weren't for the sea lice.

One day a Scottish tourist at a fishing lodge near her floathouse asked her, 'Do you have the scourge of the sea lice yet?' In Scotland, he explained, when the salmon farms came, sea lice started appearing in great quantities on wild fish. He had seen some of the same parasites on the fish he had just caught in the Broughton. Alarmed, Morton took out a dip net and pulled up smolts that were bleeding from the eyeballs and the base of the fins. Many of them were covered with dozens of brown flecks – sea lice. Normally little silver rockets, the infested pink salmon were emaciated, and swam lethargically.

Morton handed me a vial containing a preserved two-inch-long pink salmon smolt, covered with at least twenty chilli-pepper-seed-sized flecks; each was a sea louse. When they reach

adulthood, feeding on mucus and scales, the lice look like miniature horseshoe crabs, with bodies as wide as thumbtacks; the
females trail long white strands of eggs. A full-grown salmon
can survive infestation by dozens of sea lice, but the parasites
exhaust the juvenile fish, and soon kill them off.

Outside a harbour seal poked its head above water to watch
Morton as she threw a fine-meshed net overboard. Today she
was trawling for sea lice; she had a hunch it would be easy to
find their free-floating larvae at this time of year, when the water
was clearer, and she strongly suspected they would be more
abundant near the farm. (It was a perfect example of what she
called 'guerrilla science': though her work is published in peer-
reviewed journals, often she conducts research on her own,
without the support of any institution.)

Every March pink salmon, the smallest of the Pacific species,
descend from local rivers, usually in their millions. They are
exceedingly fragile; unlike most salmon, pinks arrive in salt
water without a protective covering of scales, and they use the
nutrient-rich waters of the Broughton Archipelago to fatten up
before heading to the open sea. Since the arrival of the farms,
however, they have been spending their first year of life in the
vicinity of tens of millions of sea-lice-infested Atlantic salmon.

'They're like these little tadpoles,' said Morton. 'There are so
many they blacken huge areas; it's like a river of these tiny brave
fish. They feed predators, and when they die and decompose,
they feed the entire ecosystem. I see pinks as being like wilde-
beest in Africa or herring in the Atlantic: a sacred species, put
on the planet to feed the masses. They can survive huge harvests,
and as long as you give them a place to spawn and let them go
to sea, they'll still make it.' In 2000 two million pinks spawned
in the rivers of the Broughton. Since they return in two-year
cycles, government scientists predicted 2002 would be a boom
year, with up to 3.6 million returning. But only 147,000 did – a
97 per cent population crash.

The industry denied all responsibility, claiming the low numbers were due to natural variation; they pointed out that pink returns climbed in the years that followed. (Morton believed that this was only because the government forced them to fallow four farms at critical points on the pinks' migration route.) Most scientists not affiliated with the government agreed that sea lice had been the culprits, massively infesting the pinks as they swam near the salmon farms. One study showed fish farms amplified sea lice numbers 33,000 times over ambient levels, resulting in an infestation rate seventy-three times greater than normal, and that abnormally high sea lice levels could be found up to nineteen miles away from farms.

'There's no question that lice will kill fish,' Paddy Gargan, a former director of Ireland's Central Fisheries Board, testified before a Canadian committee on sustainable aquaculture. 'The presence of salmon farming has had serious consequences for wild salmon and sea trout stocks in Ireland, Scotland and Norway. There are papers published in Norway indicating that ninety-five per cent of the juvenile salmon are killed by sea lice in their migration.' In fact, Ireland's sea trout, a species closely related to salmon, were almost driven to extinction by sea lice. Stocks have only recently recovered, after farms were forced to change management practices, and government scientists in Ireland now inspect the farms for sea lice fourteen times a year. In British Columbia, inspectors generally make only one annual visit. For the rest of the year monitoring is up to the salmon farmers themselves.

Treatments for sea lice can be as damaging to the environment as the parasites are to wild salmon. When the lice first hit, farmers used a powerful pesticide similar to the sheep dip used to rid livestock of stubborn ticks; it has since been banned. The only brand now permitted in Canada is Slice, or emamectin benzoate. Though Slice is not technically approved (even its manufacturer lists it as a 'marine toxin'), veterinarians can obtain a special emergency-only permit to add the poison to salmon feed. Slice works by disrupting the nervous system of invertebrates – when administered in large doses to rats and dogs, it causes tremors, spine and brain deterioration, and muscle atrophy. It has already been shown to kill off krill, shrimp, crabs and other crustaceans. The owner of a lobster pound in New Brunswick claimed that after a nearby farm was treated for sea lice, he lost ten thousand pounds of lobster. These days 'emergency' permits for Slice are dispensed all too frequently.

Morton laid out a wrinkled map on the table in her boat's cabin. Each salmon farm on the British Columbia coast was represented by a red sticker. In the sheltered waters to the east of Vancouver Island, the chart was poxed with crimson dots.

'Vancouver Island and the mainland form a funnel through which one-third of the salmon in BC pass on their way to the Fraser River,' she told me. 'All the way down, there are belts of salmon farms. It's like the fish are going through a sieve, and anything going on in those farms – bacteria, sea lice, whatever – will get passed on to them.' In other words, along the main migratory route of one of the world's largest remaining wild salmon populations, the BC government has consented to allow the existence of what, in Morton's vivid words, are essentially sea-lice ranches.

'For salmon pathogens,' she said, with a sad smile, 'this is the best thing that's happened since the glaciers receded.'

How to Grow a Salmon

A farmed salmon fillet, like chicken nuggets or bacon from a factory-farmed pig, is a product of industrial agriculture, exposed to chemicals at every step of its manufacture. Most of the approximately 200 million salmon being grown in farms around the world are descended from forty original Norwegian stocks, genetically selected to be docile in their pens. In British Columbia, they are likely to be the fast-growing MOWI brand, named after Thor Mowinckel, the founder of Marine Harvest.

A farmed salmon's life begins in a hatchery, where a female is killed and cut open, and her fourteen thousand or so eggs are squeezed out and manually mixed with the milt from the male. Eggs are prone to disease, so they are soaked in an iodine-based disinfectant called Ovadine to kill off any viruses or bacteria, and washed with Formalin to kill fungus. The latter, a formalde-hyde-based preservative listed as a 'known human carcinogen' by the World Health Organization, is considered preferable to malachite green, a toxic fungicide that was for a long time the industry standard. Canada banned the use of malachite green in 1992 when it was found to cause liver tumours and birth defects, but it is still widely used on farmed fish in Chile and China. In spite of the ban, in 2005 the Canadian Food Inspec-tion Agency (CFIA) detected malachite green in 310,000 salmon from British Columbia's Stolt Sea Farm. According to the *Vancouver Sun*, the company, now owned by Marine Harvest, coped by shipping their salmon to Japan, where testing is not as rigorous.

As in an indoor marijuana grow-op, artificial light is used in a hatchery to speed growth. Lamps are switched on and off in cycles that mimic accelerated winters and summers, nudging salmon fry to the smolt stage in less than half the time it takes in the wild. The growing fish are transferred to ever-larger tanks, and, one by one, injected via syringe to vaccinate them against the diseases they are likely to encounter in the saltwater environment.

When, at about three ounces, the fish have completed the smoltification process (the physiological changes that allow them to live in saltwater), they are loaded into live-haul barges and towed to the net pens, like the ones at Site 9, where they are fattened until they reach market size. Underwater lights are often used to fool the fish into thinking it is summer, the time of year when they eat the most. The lights tend to attract herring, which are small enough to swim in and out of the mesh. These free-swimming fish are considered a potential disease vector; scientists are concerned they could pick up pathogens from the salmon and spread them to the wild.

To prevent the growth of mussels, seaweed and algae, the nets are treated with an anti-fouling paint originally formulated to make the hulls of boats so poisonous that even barnacles would not stick to them. The industry standard for years was a tin-based paint that caused reproductive failure and growth abnormalities in shellfish in surrounding waters. Banned in the 1980s, it has been replaced by copper-based Flexgard, which is shipped in containers marked with a skull and crossbones and a label that warns: 'Toxic to aquatic organisms.' Every few months the anti-foulant flakes off the nets into the water and they have to be repainted. Many people questioned whether such poisons should be used around food fish, and a 2007 study documented how sediments around a Scottish salmon farm showed extremely high levels of zinc, copper and cadmium contamination, mostly from anti-fouling paints.

After thirty months, when the salmon weigh between eleven and thirteen pounds, they are ready to be taken to market. Towed to the processing plant in specially modified vessels, they are killed with a pneumatic stunner, or dropped into a tank containing carbon dioxide, which slows their metabolism so they are easier to handle. After their gills are cut and they are bled, the salmon are run through automatic filleters that spit out spines and fins, leaving two boneless fillets ready for market. (Fish that go to market whole are simply decapitated and gutted.)

From there, the salmon are transported by truck and ferry to

Vancouver. Eighty-nine per cent of the salmon farmed in British Columbia is shipped, by truck or plane, to the United States.

A fish that was swimming in Salmon Inlet in the morning can be sitting on a plate in Los Angeles, covered in sherry mango reduction and served with a glass of Chardonnay, by six P.M. the next day.

Big-City Problems

The biggest salmon farms on the west coast hold 1.3 million fish, at densities of twenty-two pounds per cubic yard – which means the salmon can be packed more tightly than battery hens on a factory farm. In terms of population density, it is as if British Columbia's coast has welcomed Bombay and all its shanty towns.

The environmental impact of having so many fish concentrated in one place is hotly disputed. Critics say that the faeces and uneaten feed that drop through the net cages consume oxygen as they decompose, making it impossible for prawns, eels, sea urchins or even starfish to survive. The provincial government disagrees, reporting on its official aquaculture website: 'According to divers who examine the environment under fish farms, vibrant communities of organisms often flourish there, due to the addition of organic material from the farm.' Biologists acknowledge there is indeed life beneath salmon farms. It tends to be a single species: the primitive, commercially useless bristle worm, which is able to survive in a low-oxygen environment.

Even their supporters have to concede one thing: salmon farms, like overpopulated cities, can be hotbeds of disease. Between 2001 and 2003 infectious hematopoietic necrosis (IHN), a virus that kills salmon fry and leaves adult survivors with spinal deformities, reached epidemic proportions. (Some of the thirty-six affected farms had to be quarantined: boots and work clothes were burned, and supplies were dropped to fish farm workers by helicopter.) In 2003 furunculosis and bacterial kidney disease hit the farms, forcing farmers to boost the amount of antibiotics they use in the feed. A particularly sinister disease called kudoa now afflicts one in every five BC farmed salmon. Caused by a parasite related to jellyfish, it is undetectable when the fish are alive, but liquefies their muscle tissue after death. Slitting a kudoa-infected salmon causes its flesh to pour out like jelly.

Disposing of the morts, as dead salmon are known, has been a public relations disaster for the industry. When First Nations groups prevented a barge loaded with 1.6 million smolts killed by IHN from docking, it wandered the coast like a plague ship, while local newspapers spread their front pages with photographs of the overflowing tubs of salmon that had been topped with formic acid to keep the maggots down. (The festering corpses were finally turned into fertilizer.) When a farm operated by Grieg Seafood threatened to sink under the weight of salmon killed by a toxic algae bloom, Canada's Department of Fisheries and Oceans (DFO) gave them an emergency permit to dump a quarter of a million fish into the open ocean. Because of prevailing summer currents, the two-mile-long slick of rotting Atlantics soon washed back to shore, where their corpses were picked over by crows and gulls. Local natives were outraged: for fear of disease, they had to stop eating seagull eggs, a seasonal delicacy.

If salmon farms were hermetically sealed from the rest of the world, disease might not be an issue. In reality, they are as leaky as colanders. Since the industry arrived in British Columbia, at least 1.5 million farmed salmon are thought to have escaped into the wild.

Salmon farmers maintain that escapes are no longer an issue.

Even if farmed salmon did manage to get out of their net cages, salmon farmers have long insisted, they would not survive in the wild for more than a day before being snapped up by an otter or seal. And if, by some fluke, they did make it into a river, they would fail to spawn. Besides, they note, being a different species, Atlantics pose no threat to the genetic integrity of Pacific salmon. Recently, they have been able to point to encouraging statistics: while 43,895 salmon escaped in 2004, the provincial government was happy to report only 64 broke out the following year.

'Those numbers are fiction,' John Volpe, an ecologist at the University of Victoria, told me. 'What they refer to are *reported* escapes. The industry would have us believe there's only one escape for every three-quarters of a million fish. Around the world, in Norway, Chile and the UK, the actual average is one escape for every three hundred fish.' (Close to a million salmon and trout escaped from Norwegian farms in 2006.) 'Now, either Canadians are the best darn salmon farmers in the world, or perhaps our reporting structure leaves a little to be desired. I've talked to a lot of divers over the years who work at the farms, and to the person they've said, we could be repairing the net cages seven days a week, there's no way we could keep up with all the holes in them.'

Volpe has firsthand evidence of the escapes. He and his graduate students have put on snorkels and fins, and found that escaped Atlantics are already present in seventy-seven separate rivers – every major drainage area on Vancouver Island. Even if disease were not an issue, Volpe believes, escaped Atlantics would be bad news for the wild Pacific fish. They particularly threaten steelhead, a cousin of the salmon and a popular sport fish.

'Both Atlantics and steelhead are big-water, fast-water fish – they like to spawn in the same rivers,' said Volpe. 'Steelhead aren't doing well in BC, so if a female steelhead ends up spawning with an Atlantic salmon then the steelhead female's contribution to a population that desperately needs her is all of a sudden gone.' The biggest issue, Volpe believes, is competition in resource-poor rivers. If enough Atlantic salmon escaped, they could monopolize the food and habitat that native fish need to survive.

Volpe's research also put to rest the industry's contention that Atlantics were incapable of reproducing in the wild. 'We actually captured wild reared Atlantics in three rivers. In two of them, there were multiple-year classes' – different generations – 'which showed this wasn't a one-off thing.'

Volpe and his team are about to start on an ambitious study of the distribution of feral Atlantic salmon. Escaped farmed salmon, it turns out, are already spreading north: Alaskan fishermen have caught hundreds of escaped Atlantics in the Bering Sea.

Meanwhile the industry is experimenting with transgenic fish, made by combining salmon DNA with an antifreeze gene from a fish called the ocean pout, which tricks salmon into producing growth hormone year-round. The advantage is clear: transgenic salmon reach market size in less than a year rather than the usual thirty months. Conservationists are horrified, because if these fast-growing 'Frankenfish', as they have been dubbed, ever escape into the wild, they could outcompete wild fish for mates and habitat. One scientist has predicted that escaped transgenics could drive a wild population a thousand times larger to extinction in less than forty generations.

For some technocrats, the utter disappearance of wild fish may be a mere historical footnote. Scientists looking for sources of protein for long space flights have already devised a way to grow chunks of fish flesh in the lab. Using a piece of fish protein as a starter, they bathe it in a culture of fats, around which the new flesh assembles. The result is home-grown fillets, already deboned.

Who needs wild fish, after all, when you can grow them in a lab?

It Don't Add Up

Salmon farms are offshore feedlots for converting brown pellets into edible, pink-hued flesh. What goes into the pellets eventually ends up in our bodies – often in a more concentrated form.

Two major feed manufacturers supply these brown pellets, controlling 80 per cent of the salmon feed market: EWOS, which is controlled by the Norwegian government, and the Dutch-owned Skretting. Their plastic sacks can be found piled on pallets in salmon farms up and down the BC coast (and too often, washed up on remote beaches). The information on the labels of these feed-filled bags – each of which weighs a tonne – appears straightforward and clinical, breaking the pellets down into percentages of crude protein, fat and fibre, noting the amount of ash, moisture and vitamins that have been added.

The biggest question mark hovers over ingredient number one on the feed bags: crude protein. In the wild, salmon are top-of-the-food-chain predators, subsisting, at various times in their life cycle, on plankton, krill, squid and smaller fish. Industrial aquaculture, however, has turned them into consumers of some of the nastier by-products of land animals. Salmon feed contains 'poultry meal', an industrial product made from the intestines, undeveloped eggs, spray-dried blood, necks, and feet of poultry – in the jargon of the trade, all the 'nonfood parts' left over after processing. Normally indigestible feathers are hydrolysed to make a dusty powder called feather meal; chicken manure – a potentially rich source of tapeworms, salmonella and arsenic – is also a key ingredient in salmon feed. The rendering industry likes to boast they use everything in a chicken but its squawk.

The bulk of the protein in the diet of farmed salmon, however, comes from fishmeal and fish oil. As I learned in Portugal, fishermen worldwide are granted huge quotas to catch sardines, anchovies, blue whiting and other perfectly edible small fish. Unlike cows, sheep and the other animals we raise for food, salmon are a carnivorous species. About 30 million tonnes of wild fish – about a third of the world's total catch – goes towards making fishmeal and oil, with anywhere from 3.1 to 4.9 million tonnes of that total going directly to the farmed salmon industry. Farming salmon is akin to nourishing tigers and lions with beef and pork, and then butchering the great cats to make hamburger meat.

Salmon farmers insist they now use less wild protein than ever; in the industry's early days, the feed conversion ratio was two to one, which means that a salmon would have to eat two pounds of pellets over the course of its life to add a single pound to its body weight. Now that feed manufacturers are adding more vegetable oil to pellets – often in the form of genetically modified rapeseed oil – the ratio has dropped to 1.2 to one. (Putting more vegetable oil in feed, incidentally, makes the health benefits of salmon evaporate. Because there is less fish oil in their diet, farmed salmon typically have much lower levels of omega-3 fatty acids than wild salmon.) Such ratios are misleading, however, because they refer to the weight of the pellets rather than to the amount of wild fish used. Feedmaker Skretting, for example, admits that it takes 2.45 pounds of wild fish to make a pound of salmon flesh; analysts put the industry average closer to 3.9 pounds. Though salmon represent a small minority of the total output of the world's farmed seafood, they now consume 15 per cent of the fishmeal and 51 per cent of the fish oil destined for aquaculture.

Catching little fish to feed big fish inevitably decreases the net amount of protein available to the world. If industry optimists are right and the amount of salmon grown in the world doubles to two million tonnes by the year 2010, we might soon be facing catastrophic crashes of the stocks of anchovies, sandeels and other species that are at the foundation of oceanic food chains.

The most sinister ingredient in salmon pellets is the crustacean called krill. These translucent shrimplike invertebrates are a keystone species in the oceans of the world, filtering the minute phytoplankton that other species are unable to process and sequestering atmospheric carbon through their faeces, which sinks to the sea floor. In the Southern Ocean around Antarctica, krill biomass is already in sharp decline as global warming decreases the sea ice coverage that provides habitat for the plankton the krill need to survive. Yet enormous vessels from six different countries are vacuuming up krill; a single vessel from Norway, the *Saga Sea*, now takes 120,000 tonnes a year, and such giant seafood companies as Pacific Andes and Ocean Trawlers are outfitting vessels to join the harvest. Though the fishery has been banned on the west coast of the United States, a 500-tonne annual quota is still allocated in British Columbia. The main consumer of krill is the aquaculture industry; feed pellets are coated in the krill to make them more palatable to farmed fish. If the demands of fish farming increase, it could have a severe impact on a species that feeds everything in the oceans from anchovetas and penguins to blue whales.

'If you raise herbivores like tilapia, oysters and carp, as they do in Asia,' fisheries scientist Daniel Pauly explained to me in his office at the University of British Columbia, 'then you are making a net addition of seafood to the world. But in the West, when we talk about aquaculture, we are talking about salmon, bluefin, eel. These are actually operations for fattening carnivores. We feed them cheaper fish to produce a luxury item.'

Some forms of aquaculture benefit the environment; raising

oysters in Chesapeake Bay, for example, cleans the water and turns plankton into edible flesh.

Salmon farming is clearly not one of them.

You Are What They Eat

While farming salmon is bad for the oceans, eating farmed salmon can be hazardous to your health. For example: beware sushi, gravlax or ceviche made with Chilean salmon. In South America smolts are raised in freshwater lakes rather than in hatcheries, and native species pass parasites to the juvenile salmon before they are taken to the net pens. Brazil recently traced several cases of tapeworms in humans back to the eating of raw farmed salmon from Chile.

On the upside, salmon, being relatively short-lived fish, are low in mercury. The good news, unfortunately, ends there.

Were it not for artificial colourants, the flesh of farmed salmon would be an unappetizing grey, yellow or khaki. In the wild, salmon owe their pink hue to krill and shrimp, which contain the organic pigments astaxanthin and canthaxanthin. In salmon farms, artificial versions, synthesized from algae or yeast, are added directly to the feed. Pharmaceutical giant Hoffman-La Roche makes a convenient colour chart – like those used to select paint colours in hardware stores – called the SalmoFan, which allows farmers to choose shades of flesh between pale salmon pink (#20) and bright orange-red (#34). These colourants, as my salmon farm guides rightly pointed out, are chemically similar isomers of the natural substances; they are even sold in American health food stores as supplements. But the United Kingdom removed canthaxanthin self-tanning pills from the market in 1987 because the pigment has a tendency to accumulate in the retina; children's eyes were found to be especially vulnerable. Because of this issue, the European Union recently reduced the amount permitted in animal feed by a factor of three. In 2003 Washington State consumers won a lawsuit that forced Safeway and two other supermarket chains to put 'colour added' labels on farmed salmon packages nationwide.

Artificial colourants are only the start. When bacteria sickens salmon, farmers add antibiotics and other medications directly to their feed to control the outbreak. During the epidemics of 2003, salmon feed in British Columbia was spiked with 55,000 pounds of antibiotics. After antibiotic use, a waiting period before harvest is meant to guarantee that no residues remain, but the Canadian Food Inspection Agency continues to find traces in salmon; every year up to 400 tonnes of farmed BC salmon and 1,000 tonnes of New Brunswick salmon are estimated to go to market with residues above what Health Canada recommends. In sensitive individuals, even small amounts of antibiotics can trigger serious allergic reactions.

Most worryingly, a group of researchers led by Ronald Hites of Indiana University has published a series of papers – the first appeared in the leading peer-reviewed journal *Science* in 2004 – on industrial toxins in farmed salmon. Analysing two tonnes of salmon bought in stores from Edinburgh to Seattle, they found that farmed salmon contained up to ten times more persistent organic pollutants (POPs) than do wild salmon. The chemicals in question, among the most toxic known to man, include the dioxins produced by coal-burning utilities and smelters (the most infamous being Agent Orange) and the polychlorinated biphenyls (PCBs) used in paints, pesticides and even carbonless copy paper. Banned since the 1970s, these contaminants continue to show up in the food we eat. All are suspected carcinogens; most cause behavioural, growth and learning disorders.

Using standards set by the Environmental Protection Agency,

Hites and his team concluded that, because of the POPs concentrated in their feed, 'The vast majority of farm-raised salmon should be consumed at one meal or less per month.' In the case of Scottish salmon, the authors advised anyone wishing to avoid cancer to have no more than three farmed salmon meals a *year*.

When news of these results caused salmon sales to plummet by a quarter of a million pounds worldwide, the industry went into damage control. Coached by Hill & Knowlton – a New York-based firm that at various times has been hired to manicure the images of Enron, Three Mile Island and the Tobacco Institute – the BC Salmon Farmers' Association accused the authors of applying the wrong standards: FDA guidelines, they said, which allow forty times more toxins, would have been more appropriate. Co-author David Carpenter, noting that these standards had not been revised since 1984, responded: 'I do not believe that the FDA guidelines in any way, shape or form are protective of human health.' Swallowing hard, the industry had to hope the public would eventually forget the report.

If you must buy farmed salmon, according to food safety writer Marion Nestle, you should grill or broil the fish until the juices run off, then remove the skin. That way, she writes in her book *What to Eat*, you can get rid of much of the toxin-conveying fat and with it half of the PCBs. (Rather than being forced to treat your dinner like a biotoxin, though, you might want to consider choosing some other fish to eat altogether.)

Organic farmed salmon would be a good option, if the term organic had any meaning at all. When it comes to farmed salmon in North America, there is no Health Canada or USDA seal of approval; antibiotic- and colourant-fed salmon can be packed 60,000 into a pen and still legitimately be called 'organic'. In Europe standards are stricter. The Soil Association in the United Kingdom, for example, stipulates organic salmon must be fed with meal made from the filleting waste of fish caught for human consumption, and artificial colourants such as canthaxanthin are prohibited. Farmers are permitted, however, to treat the fish with veterinary chemicals, including heavy-duty sea-lice treatments.

For the time being, wild Pacific salmon are probably your safest choice. (Remember that if a salmon in your local store is labelled 'Atlantic', it almost certainly comes from a farm; wild Atlantic salmon are now as rare as bluefin tuna.) Though many wild Pacific salmon runs are in rough shape, some BC fisheries are sustainably managed; sockeye and pink, which also feed low in the food chain and are thus lower in persistent organic pollutants, tend to be a good choice. As are salmon from the Alaskan fishery; much of the canned salmon available in supermarkets comes from north of 55 degrees. Unfortunately, mislabelling – the seafood industry's besetting sin – is also rampant in the wild salmon section. In a cross-country survey of American supermarkets, *Consumer Reports* found that 56 per cent of salmon fillets – for which their researchers paid up to $15.62 (£7.65) a pound – were labelled as wild-caught when they were in fact farmed.

Personally, I cannot face another piece of farmed salmon. The herringbone pattern of flesh, barely held together by creamy, saliva-gooey fat – the vehicle for some of the worst toxins known to humanity – has lately been making me choke.

Fortunately chefs in Vancouver, BC's largest city, are at the forefront of the sustainable seafood movement. I had come to the Blue Water Café, a seafood restaurant in an old brick and fir-beam warehouse in Vancouver's Yaletown, to sample Frank Pabst's Unsung Heroes menu. The chef, who was committed to serving ethically caught seafood, was highlighting what used to be considered trash fish and bait; the catch of the day included herring roe on kelp, a sesame-soaked jellyfish salad, and lightly cooked slices of mackerel served with savoy cabbage and red beets. Some of the proceeds went to the Vancouver

Aquarium's Ocean Wise programme, which promotes the idea of eating down the food chain.

As I tried to decide between the live sea urchin in ponzu sauce and herring topped with *crème fraiche*, the waiter tempted me up a trophic level or two with a well-placed word about the night's special, a hook-and-line caught 'winter spring salmon'. This is the evocatively oxymoronic name given to late-run chinook; there had been an opening of a few days, he explained, and they were serving a whole tail, grilled and garnished with sprigs of thyme and oregano and just a bit of lemon. I did not ask the price. I had to have it.

A few minutes later there was a chinook tail on my plate, skin, bones and all. The flesh was not Day-Glo orange, but healthily pink: salmon-coloured, in fact. It was firm, well-muscled, juicy but not oily, and lower in the fat that makes eating Atlantic fillets such a chore. It was to farmed salmon as venison is to ground beef. It was the taste of my childhood – it was the essence of British Columbia – and I did not want it to end.

I had forgotten: *that* was what a salmon was supposed to taste like.

Fish Out of Water

At their worst, salmon farms are like pig farms at sea, emitting a toxic cloud of pollutants and parasites into the ocean. But few people I talked to, even the most adamant critics of the current industry, are actually opposed to the idea of fish farming. Most just think there is a better way of going about it.

Changing a few operating procedures would considerably decrease the industry's negative impact. Rather than specifically targeting small forage fish, salmon feed makers could use the estimated 28 million tonnes of bycatch that are now discarded by the world's fisheries, as well as the scrap left over from fish for human consumption. Lowering stocking densities could obviate the use of antibiotics and treatments for parasites. These procedures, already standard in organic cod farms in Scotland, are ignored by the industry because they would raise the price of the finished product. In North America, salmon aquaculture is predicated on keeping up a constant supply of cheap fish.

Before visiting Site 9 on the Sunshine Coast, I was given a tour of a salmon hatchery. The owner had just sold his salmon-farming operation to the Norwegians, but he wanted to show me a part of the business over which he had retained control. Inside a gloomy hangar, we climbed a ladder onto a catwalk that took us over huge circular tanks, open at the top. Beneath us swam hundreds of living fossils, like ghostly sharks, many of them over six feet long. We were looking at sturgeons, fish that have changed little in two hundred million years. Long and scaleless, the sturgeons had a ridge of bony, dinosaurlike scutes along their backs and four barbs around their mouths to help them sense food on murky river bottoms. The hatchery manager was raising them for their roe, which he figured he could sell for $60 (£29) an ounce. His dream was to serve farmed sturgeon caviar at the opening ceremonies at Vancouver's 2010 Winter Olympics.

'We've been using this technology for seven years, and I love it,' the manager told me. 'The control it affords us. About ninety-seven per cent of the water is recirculated, and all the uneaten feed and faeces go to a septic tank, so nothing is released into the ocean; it's taken to a sewage plant. The water is then stripped of carbon dioxide, and we supersaturate it with oxygen, and it goes back into the tanks.'

We were hundreds of yards from the shore. There were two thousand of these huge animals in the hangar. Each tank looked as if it could hold twenty times as many salmon.

I was looking at a closed-containment system. Such systems

are already being used to raise turbot in France, shrimp in the Mexican desert, bluefin in Japan. Members of the fish farming industry claim such tanks were too expensive to raise farmed salmon. But here was one of them, fully functioning, saving its owner money because of its efficiency. Experts estimated that, in the long run, using land-based closed-containment systems would add only 30 per cent to the price of each salmon fillet.

If it meant there would still be wild chinook salmon twenty years from now, that was a premium I would be happy to pay.

No Rocket Scientists

It is a mystery to many, given the controversy the issue generates, why the governments of Canada and British Columbia seem so committed to the salmon-farming industry. It provides direct employment for only 1,900 people in BC, and contributes about $87 million (£42 million) to the provincial economy. In contrast, the marine sports fishery employs 4,700 and generates $134 million (£66 million) for the province. Yet, because of sea lice, aquaculture has the potential to eliminate the very fish on which the lucrative sports fishery relies.

Perhaps, for the powers that be, wild salmon are an inconvenient presence on the west coast. Salmon fishermen certainly are. Take Billy Proctor, a fisherman who has lived in the Broughton Archipelago for fifty years. His father, who emigrated from Scotland, drowned when Proctor was still a boy. His widowed mother became a fish buyer, living in a floathouse that was towed around the raincoast to follow the fishing boats. Proctor's love affair with fish started at the age of four, when he used to sit on the beach with water up to his nostrils, observing their underwater habits. He bought his first troller at the age of seventeen, and soon became a high liner, a top-catching fishboat

captain. Now in his seventies, he is a fisherman with a conser-
vationist's ethos, and an opinionated, and widely respected,
defender of the raincoast.

'Jeez, I must look like the wreck of the Hesperus,' said Proctor, glancing down at his half-buttoned mackinaw jacket, as I
snapped his photo outside Billy's Museum. The wooden building was stocked with trade beads, old bottles, seal teeth and
other treasures of a life of beachcombing; on the dock, Proctor
gave me a tour of the *Ocean Dawn*, a beautiful forty-five-year-
old white-and-blue troller, with complex rigging for trailing
lures and hooks for salmon and other fish.

In his time, Proctor had witnessed a fair amount of human
stupidity. He watched as whalers came to the Broughton in the
early 1950s and shot the resident humpbacks one by one –
the same whales he had rowed alongside and caressed as a boy.
A few years later he saw Forest Service planes crisscrossing the
area for a full week, spraying the land with thousands of gallons
of DDT, even as juvenile salmon swam down local rivers.
Shortly afterwards, he saw people carrying poisoned salmon
from local riverbanks by the wheelbarrow-load. He witnessed
big companies like BC Packers using powerful Mercury lights, a
technique called pit-lamping, to attract herring, and then
scooping up billions of the forage fish in their seine nets – and
with them, entire runs of juvenile salmon. He remembered the
year the federal government set the sockeye salmon quota at 1.7
million fish, based on a previous year's unusually high catch, so
that eight hundred fishboats were eventually competing for fish
that no longer existed. Later, when he tried to restore the coho
population in a local river by starting a hatchery, Proctor saw
the salmon he had released with his own hands come back with
pus-filled boils, infested by the furunculosis that was then
raging in the salmon farms.

He invited me into his tin-roofed home, which was heated by
a wood stove and solar panels. Inside, we were enclosed by heavy

beams and boards made of alder, fir, yew, and red and yellow cedar. Sitting at his big round dining-room table, Proctor reflected on what had happened to all the once-abundant wild salmon.

'There were so many factors,' he said. 'Habitat damage from all the logging. Big deep seines. Letting trollers catch too many on the west coast of Vancouver Island. That was the demise of the salmon.' The farms were the last straw. 'Now you've got about seventeen million Atlantic salmon on the BC coast breeding lice all winter. You don't have to be a rocket scientist to see there's a problem.' Before the farms came, he got $4.60 (£2.25) a pound for a big chinook. Lately the price of wild-caught salmon had dropped to $1.60 (78 pence). Around the world the availability of the cheap farmed product has almost destroyed the market for quality wild salmon. Who, Proctor wondered, was going to pay that much for a wild fish, when he could get a fillet that looked about the same for a third of the price?

His daughter, whose house next door he helped build, worked on one of the salmon farms for nine years. She was tough, he said; she forced the employees who tossed their cigarette butts into the net pens to fish them out with a dip net, and she kicked them off the computers when they were watching too much Internet porn.

'She wasn't very popular, but she did grow good fish. But she quit when they started putting too many fish in the pens – that's when they got more diseases and more lice. Stands to reason. Christ, those fish in the bottom of the pens are swimming around in their own shit. It's just a big cloud going down ninety feet.'

I told Proctor about the sturgeon tanks I had seen, and asked if he thought a similar approach could be taken to farming salmon.

'There's no doubt in my mind we have to have fish farms, because there isn't enough fish in the oceans to feed the world's

population. It could work, too, if they had it on land, in concrete or aluminium closed-containment tanks. It would take
them a bit to set it up, but it would be a hell of a lot cheaper to
operate in the long run. All the government has got to say is that
you've got to put your farms on land, and it would be done
tomorrow.'

At the very least, Proctor said, salmon farms should not be so
close together. Twenty-seven sites in the Broughton Archipelago
were just too many. The government should do what the Norwegian government forced their farmers to do after a parasite
decimated their farms: space the farms far apart and, if necessary, ban them when they overlapped with runs of wild salmon.

Why, I asked, wasn't it happening?

'Christ, I think they *want* to get rid of the wild salmon,' he
said. 'Once the salmon are gone, they can log, they can mine,
they can dam rivers, they can do anything they like. I can't think
of any other reason they're doing what they're doing. Most of
the commercial fishermen think that's the reason why too.'

It is a theory you hear a lot on the BC coast. The omnipresent
protected salmon streams, which reach like a network of capil-
laries into the province's every ecosystem, are rumoured to
stand in the way of oil and mining exploration, logging operations and even the damming of the Fraser River, a megaproject
that would allow the province to sell billions of dollars of electricity to the United States. A far-sighted – if terribly cynical –
government might adopt a long-term strategy favouring policies that promoted salmon aquaculture, to the detriment of the
wild stocks.

That might explain why the province's Liberal Party had
received so many campaign contributions from salmon-farming
companies over the years, and why a provincial minister – the
same one who lifted the moratorium on new permits – resigned
from his post after a police inquiry into an allegation that he
had tipped off a salmon farm that they were about to be

investigated for escapes. It might also account for why $110 million (£54 million) has been poured into research on and subsidies for aquaculture in recent years, while habitat monitoring and enforcement – the only things that prevent logging companies from destroying salmon streams – got only $600,000 (£295,000) in 2005. (With only six full-time staff at the Department of Fisheries and Oceans charged with policing all of BC and Yukon, each enforcement officer is now responsible for patrolling 93,000 square miles.) It would explain why, when it was re-elected, the Liberal government eliminated Fisheries Renewal BC, an organization that funded the restoration of wild-salmon habitat and stock enhancement. Finally, it would explain why, when the federal DFO came to investigate sea lice after the collapse of the pink runs, it arrived three weeks late, used gear that knocked the lice right off the fish and trawled miles from any fish farm. Though they caught only seven fish, they were apparently still able to announce that sea lice were not a problem in the Broughton Archipelago.

It is only a theory, of course – one that everybody who cares about wild salmon and the coast, and all those who make their living from fishing, hope is not true.

I told Proctor that I had definitively crossed farmed salmon off the list of seafood I was willing to eat. I asked him whether he ate the stuff himself. He looked me dead in the eye and said:

'I'd go pick through shit with the chickens first.'

10
NOVA SCOTIA -
FISH STICKS

Fast Fish, Slow Fish

With its streets lined with the stately, shipshape Victorian homes of defunct sea captains, and a waterside fronted by brightly painted wooden warehouses, Lunenburg is still a perfect Nova Scotian picture postcard of a fishing town. Founded in 1753, in the same wave of immigration that brought the Hanoverian Dutch to Pennsylvania, Lunenburg was long famous for its rivalry with Gloucester, Massachusetts. For years the competing ports sent sleek sailing ships to the Grand Banks in search of cod, and races between such schooners as the Yankee *Henry Ford* and the Canuck *Bluenose* became maritime legends. Until the 1930s the port thrummed with activity as factories turned cod into salt fish to be shipped to Portugal, Spain and the Caribbean.

These days there are only a few real fishing boats left in the harbour, and they work the lower end of the food chain, dragging for scallops, or seining for what is left of small fish like mackerel and herring. A replica of the *Bluenose* – the two-masted schooner pictured on the Canadian dime (10-cent piece) – is moored in the harbour, covered by tarps, awaiting the summer tourist season.

A few miles from the Lunenburg waterfront, the High Liner factory sits alone on a sheltered bay, a sprawling relic of the days of peak fish. In its mid-1960s heyday, when it was known as National Sea Products, the company owned fifty-two vessels, had seven thousand employees, and subsidiaries in Argentina, Australia, Portugal and the United States. When the building's cornerstone was laid on 7 June 1963, it was the biggest fish processing plant on the continent. Kept supplied by twenty trawlers, the Lunenburg plant could process 80 million pounds of fish a year. The cod, halibut and haddock of the Atlantic that arrived at the factory's docks were poured down aluminium conveyor belts, and were carried by forklifts to the processing lines at the rate of 50,000 pounds an hour, emerging at the other end as frozen fillets or fish sticks (as fish fingers are known in North America). From there, they were loaded on to trucks or Canadian National railcars, for shipment to distant markets.

'The northern cod, which was the main part of the fishery, was projected to go to a half million metric tonnes,' Ron Whynacht, the company's vice-president of business development, told me. 'At the time it seemed like there was no end to the fish. Now there isn't any.'

How much of their cod, I asked, still came from local waters?

'Surprisingly little,' said Whynacht. 'A little of our cod comes from Newfoundland, and some of our haddock from Nova Scotia, but mostly it comes from the Barents Sea, north of Russia.'

After pulling all the big fish it could out of the Atlantic, High Liner has turned its back on the ocean that once fed it. In the last decade the company has sold off its entire fishing fleet. Unprocessed fish, transported from abroad by container ship, are now unloaded from eighteen-wheelers, and leave the factory the same way they came: by highway. High Liner buys wild

Pacific salmon from Alaska, and farmed Atlantic salmon from Chile. They get their basa, a catfish native to the Mekong River, from farms in Vietnam, and their tilapia from aquaculture operations in Indonesia. The pollock that goes into their fish sticks comes from the Bering Sea, west of Alaska. Though there is a booming scallop industry on the nearby Scotian shelf, High Liner largely sources their scallops from farms in Asia and South America. Once a corporation that harvested North Atlantic fish to sell around the world, High Liner has transformed itself into a buyer and packager of the world's fish, for shipment to North American supermarkets.

'Anything that is high labour content, like putting salmon on skewers, is done in China,' explained Whynacht. 'Why do we send them to China? Because they have very affordable labour there.' The huge Chinese factories have payrolls in the tens of thousands, and the employees work for one tenth of the wages Canadians receive.

On the day I visited the High Liner factory, whose floor vibrated with the din of deep-fryers and blast freezers, the morning shift was working on a run of Captain's Grill Lemon Pepper Fillets. The frozen tilapia had already been filleted in China; here they were being defrosted, grilled, coated with sauce and then refrozen. Two middle-aged women in hairnets sat on stools before a conveyor belt, using long batons that looked like outsized chopsticks to separate any fillets that had stuck together in the bowels of the machinery. In another room, frozen breaded cod fillets destined for the United States were dropping down a corkscrew chute into plastic bags. A few technicians in white coats wandered around, checking the oil levels in a deep-fryer; otherwise the production line was almost completely automated. In the developed world, fish processing is not the big employer it used to be. High Liner directly employs only six hundred people worldwide, less than a tenth of its peak fish payroll.

High Liner's fish sticks are now made from pollock that is caught, filleted, chopped up and frozen in factory vessels on the Bering Sea. Trucked across Canada, it arrives at High Liner in the form of frozen pre-minced blocks with the skin and fat already removed. By the time the blocks get to this factory, where they are sawn into oblong portions, covered in batter and bread, and deep-fried, they have already travelled 4,300 miles. In the worst-case scenario a salmon farmed on the Chilean coast could be sent by container ship to Dalian, China, to be filleted, then shipped back across the Pacific to Vancouver. From there it would cross Canada by truck, be processed and packaged in Lunenburg, and go right back out the door. If it ended up in a supermarket in, say, San Diego, that salmon would have travelled 22,300 miles, a distance close to the circumference of the earth.

Captain High Liner, the bearded, blue-eyed trawlerman in a turtleneck sweater who appears on every box of frozen fish, is the public face of the company. (A 'high liner', in fishing slang, is a top-catching captain.) High Liner, which bought the processing business of Newfoundland's Fishery Products International late in 2007, is now Canada's largest seafood company, selling almost half the frozen fish on the country's supermarket shelves. In the United States, it is second only to Gorton's of Gloucester – a company now owned by Nippon Suisan, one of the largest marine products companies in Japan. High Liner sells the leading frozen processed seafood brand in Wal-Mart; its Fisherboy fish sticks are available in supermarkets from Seattle to Mexico City. (Captain High Liner's British cousin was of course the shanty-singing Capitain Birds Eye, but the High Liner company's present day counterpart is Grimsby-based Young's Seafood, which claims to sell 40 per cent of the seafood eaten in the United Kingdom.)

I asked Ron Whynacht about the identity of the company's mascot.

'He's Captain High Liner!' he replied. 'In a globalized indus-try like seafood, the idea that there's a living person involved, somebody you can be comfortable with, is so important.' Not of woman born, the captain, like the Gorton's Fisherman and the UK's Captain Birds Eye, issued fully formed from the mind of an advertising executive.

In the days when High Liner had a fishing fleet, real captains stood at the helm of every one of its trawlers, close-cropped, clean-shaven Maritimers with names like Gislasson, Whiffen and Mitchell. After the Second World War the old hook-and-line schooner fishery, in which swift two-masters raced to the Grand Banks in search of cod, did not stand a chance against National Sea Products' fleet of diesel-powered 150-foot-long trawlers. Vessels like these were so good at raking the Atlantic clean they ended the fishing careers of the *Bluenose* and her sister ships, turning them into relics for the tourists.

Fishing with two-masters was labour-intensive, but it also kept thousands of people from Newfoundland to Cape Cod employed, and ensured that Lunenburg and other seaports were real communities, rather than heritage photo-ops for summer day-trippers. In the end the captains of the new trawlers proved too good at their work. In their efficiency, they first killed off the schooners, then put an end to the northern cod.

And once the cod were gone, High Liner had no more use for the captains themselves. Only *the* Captain – that old salt smil-ing from every box of fish sticks – remains.

The Global Fish Stick

In my travels, I have made a point of eating locally caught fish. For most consumers, however, seafood is no longer something that comes fresh from a nearby body of water. It comes from a freezer, and looks more like a finger, a stick or a patty than any-thing that has ever lived in the ocean. The seafood most people eat these days is a pure product of industry.

It took new technology to bring seafood to the masses. In 1912, an eccentric Brooklynite moved his young family to Muddy Bay, Labrador, in the Canadian Arctic. Clarence Birds-eye, sick of low wages in New York, had come north to trap fur. He had not anticipated the long Canadian winters, and to feed his wife and infant son he sought advice from the natives. An expert ice-fisher, Garland Lethbridge, showed the young green-horn how to dip just-caught fish into salt water, whose freezing point is lower than fresh water; they froze quickly and could be thawed out, good as new, even weeks later. Birdseye used the same technique on cabbage, filling his baby's basin with salt water – and, to his wife's consternation, the family bathtub with pickerel (small pike). Long ice crystals tend to form when food is frozen slowly, cutting it apart when it thaws and making it mushy. But quick-freezing prevents ice crystals from forming, and Birdseye found when his frozen fish was thawed it looked and tasted almost as good as fresh-caught.

Birdseye later moved his family to the fishing port of Gloucester, where he founded a company called General Seafoods. Like Lunenburg, the Massachusetts town had built its prosperity on salted cod, but filleting machines had come to Gloucester in 1921, and the preserved product was losing its popularity. Birdseye, after figuring out how further to hasten the quick-freeze process by pressing food between metal plates, sold the secret, and his company, to the Postum Company. They renamed Birdseye's company General Foods.

The new quick-freeze technology, combined with cod ready-cut by automatic filleters, led to a new American staple, the frozen fish fillet. In 1953 the Birds Eye Division of General Foods launched a new product: the breaded fish stick. A pack of ten cost 49 cents, and took only twelve minutes to cook. Soon,

Americans were eating 1.1 billion fish sticks a year. (Fish fingers were introduced to the British in 1955 as 'a new, delicious way to buy fish, which takes the time, trouble and smell out of preparing our favourite foods'.) Fish sticks are technology's triumph over that most perishable of products, seafood. As long as they are kept frozen, they will stay edible for months, and can be shipped anywhere in the world. By covering fish in oily batter, the new technique also turned a healthy, naturally low-fat form of protein into a cholesterol-and-saturated-fat-laden brand of fast food.

The new technology brought quick-frozen fish to the home. Just as significantly, it brought the world's seafood to the shopping centres and food courts of America, ushering in a new phase for seafood: the era of fast fish.

From the Fork to the Pond

In 2006, Americans consumed 2.2 million tonnes of seafood, about 7.5 kilograms per person. Eighty-three per cent of that total was imported. The bulk of it was shipped frozen, like the raw materials I saw in the High Liner plant, by container ship and trailer truck, from distant oceans. Transporting this fish to dinner tables consumes an enormous amount of fossil fuels. Bringing a single five-kilogram farmed salmon to the consumer, for example, is estimated to consume 23 litres of petrol.

Fifty per cent of the American seafood supply is eaten in restaurants, representing sales of $47 billion (£23 billion) a year. Much of that total is eaten in fast-food or midmarket restaurants – places like Joe's Crab Shack, Long John Silver's, McCormick & Schmick's, Bonefish Grill and Bubba Gump's, seafood specialists that compete for customers in the suburbs of America. The most successful of them is the 'family style' seafood chain Red Lobster, which numbers 680 outlets in the United States and Canada, with 63,000 employees serving 145 million clients, racking up sales of $2.58 billion (£1.26 billion) in 2006. The chain that claims to have introduced Middle America to calamari and snow crab, and is known for its all-you-can-eat shrimp and crab specials, has become the single largest end-user of seafood in North America.

Decorated with cast-iron lobster-claw door-handles, upended rowboats, model schooners, aquariums of live 'Maine Lobsters' and cavorting crustaceans on its upholstery, as well as a menu printed with images of lighthouses and shrimp boats, the average Red Lobster outlet apparently aspires to be a strip-mall version of a New England fish shack. In fact, the first Red Lobster was opened in 1968 in Lakeland, a Florida town fifty miles from the nearest coast, and the chain is now headquartered in landlocked Orlando. In Maine, the one state with a flourishing lobster industry, there are no Red Lobster outlets at all.

Only a tiny percentage of Red Lobster's purchasing budget goes to American fishermen; the seafood it serves now comes from around the world. The Darden Restaurant Group, Red Lobster's parent company, buys 45 million kilograms of seafood a year, for which it pays an estimated three-quarters of a billion dollars (£365 million). It is one of the few companies that, rather than relying on US-based importers, buys directly from overseas suppliers – from storefront operations like Ronald's Seafood, a Bahamas-based wholesaler of rock lobster, to the enormous Thai Union Frozen Products, a £350-million-a-year frozen shrimp and canned tuna giant listed on the Bangkok Stock Exchange. From its Orlando headquarters, and a procurement office in Singapore, Darden's purchasing staff oversee the sourcing of seafood from thirty different countries.

At a trade show in Boston, a Louisiana shrimp-boat captain stood up and criticized the chain for what he saw as its misleading advertising:

'Red Lobster is trying to deceive their customers into thinking they are eating local shrimp off the boat,' he told the chain's executives. He was sick, he said, of seeing posters at Red Lobster showing shrimping boats. His colleagues' boats had been repossessed by the banks because they could no longer compete against cheap farmed shrimp served by chain restaurants. 'If they are so proud of the shrimp farms they source from,' he added, 'they ought to have a picture in the restaurant of the guy working alongside the [shrimp] pond. But they don't, not one of them.'

I had seen what shrimp ponds in India looked like, and there was no way any restaurant would want to share the image of dying rice fields and sick villagers with its customers. In a world of globalized seafood, following the trail from your fork back to the hook or the pond can lead to some pretty ugly places. One of the chain restaurants' leading suppliers of cheap shrimp is Ecuador, where 70 per cent of mangrove forests have been cut down to make way for shrimp ponds, destroying the livelihood of traditional fishing communities. American shrimp fishermen have accused Thailand, another big supplier of frozen shrimp, of using child labourers in their factories.

The most troubling species served in many chain restaurants is spiny lobster, a crustacean native to the waters off Nicaragua and Honduras. The dive fishery there is known for its brutal conditions. With decrepit scuba equipment and minimal training, the divers, most of them Miskito Indians, suffer from pressure-related maladies: collapsed spinal cords, destroyed nerve endings, and the paralysis that comes with the bends, the excruciating decompression sickness caused by nitrogen bubbles in the blood. More than five hundred Miskito divers are affected by the bends every year, all in the name of getting cheap lobster to bib-wearing customers.

It is all a pretty good argument for knowing where your seafood comes from. But that has never been in the interests of the seafood industry. In an attempt to improve fish's status as the ultimate mystery meat, the US government made country of origin labelling (COOL) laws mandatory for seafood in 2005. Zealously opposed by such seafood trade organizations as the National Fisheries Institute, the laws apply only to seafood sold in supermarkets. Processed seafood, such as breaded and cooked shrimp (which accounts for half of the shrimp sold in grocery stores), is exempt. Nor do COOL laws affect small businesses or restaurants, which is why chain restaurants such as Red Lobster are not obliged to tell their clients where their shrimp, or anything else on their menus, comes from.

At a shrimp conference in London in 2006, the vice-president of seafood purchasing at Darden waxed enthusiastically about how consumers were embracing the health-giving benefits of fish. He displayed graphs that predicted the United States alone would need a billion additional pounds of seafood by 2025. If the industry could only push global shrimp consumption to about two pounds per person, he mused, it would create a demand for 14 billion pounds of product. He concluded: 'We have a very big future growth opportunity.'

Indeed. According to United Nations figures, population growth means the world will need an additional 25 million tonnes of farmed seafood by 2015. If at least some of that seafood is going to be sustainably and ethically harvested, consumers are going to have to start asking a fundamental question, the one I got used to asking in my travels:

Where, exactly, did this fish come from? And refusing to take 'I'm not sure' for an answer.

Filet-O-Fish and the Bluewash

Not all mass-market seafood comes from unsustainable stocks. Take, for example, the surprising case of McDonald's Filet-O-Fish sandwich.

The sandwich's creator, Lou Groen, owned a McDonald's franchise in a heavily Catholic section of Cincinnati. He found he was losing sales during Lent, and every Friday of the year, to Big Boy, a competing chain that marketed a fish sandwich. In 1962, Groen showed McDonald's president Ray Kroc a fish patty of his own invention. Kroc insisted on selling the fish sandwich alongside his own pet project, the Hula Burger, made with a cheese-topped slice of pineapple on a cold bun. Not surprisingly, Groen's Filet-O-Fish, served with homemade tartar sauce, was what sold. The only change he had to make was replacing expensive halibut with cheaper cod, a move that made the 25-cent fish burger profitable. When declining catches off Newfoundland made cod too expensive, the chain then substituted a fish called pollock.

Pollock is a two- to three-foot-long schooling species, scooped up by enormous factory trawlers in the Bering Sea off Alaska. In the bowels of the ship, the fish are filleted and deep-skinned – their fat and skin removed, leaving only white flesh – and then frozen into 7.5-kilogram blocks, often minutes after being caught. The frozen pollock blocks are then sold to converters, such as LD Foods in Wisconsin and Gorton's of Gloucester, which saw them into patty-sized portions (meaning a single patty can contain the flesh of several individual pollock). They are then breaded and prefried. Alaskan pollock goes into 90 per cent of the three hundred million Filet-O-Fishes McDonald's sells in North America every year. It is also the main ingredient in the fish sandwiches sold by Arby's, Dairy Queen and Burger King.

McDonald's chose its fish wisely. The Alaskan pollock fishery is the largest in the United States, and stocks are still abundant; in a good year pollock can account for 8 per cent of all the fish caught in the world. Like sardines, they live in the middle of the water column, which means destructive bottom-trawls do not have to be used in their capture. Moreover, the Alaskan pollock fishery is certified as sustainable by the Marine Stewardship

Council (the MSC), the single most credible independent certifier of fisheries in the world.

The council's blue and white label is familiar to fish buyers in the United Kingdom, where much of the fish sold by Marks & Spencer, Waitrose and other retailers comes from MSC-certified fisheries, but it is still not well known in North America. Created in 1997 in a unique collaboration between the consumer food brand giant Unilever (owner of Birds Eye and Knorr) and the World Wide Fund for Nature (WWF), the council has long since been cut loose as an independent entity. The MSC criteria are laudable: for a fishery to be certified, it cannot deplete fish stocks, harm the overall structure or diversity of the ecosystem, or contravene local or international laws or standards. As of January 2008, the council had certified twenty-six fisheries around the world as sustainable, from Cornwall's tiny handline mackerel fishery to such giants as Alaska's wild salmon and pollock fisheries, and the retail value of over one thousand MSC-certified products topped £250 million.

Among environmentalists, the MSC is controversial. Its certifications, some argue, make no provisions for marine reserves or no-take zones, which biologists agree are the key to ensuring long-term sustainability and biodiversity. The council has certified the New Zealand hoki fishery (hoki is an alternative source of fish for fast-food sandwiches), even though it failed to comply with New Zealand's own fisheries act, and stocks have undergone rapid decline since 2001. Some environmentalists question the MSC's certification of the Alaskan pollock fishery, which they blame for a decline in the population of Steller's sea lions, an endangered species. In 2008, there were signs that even this mighty fishery was succumbing to overfishing: the National Marine Fisheries Service revealed that stocks off Alaska had dropped by half in a single year, and Greenpeace was calling for sustainable seafood advocates to put pollock on their red lists.

McDonald's, interestingly, has never bothered to advertise the fact that its Filet-O-Fish comes from sustainably fished pollock stocks. That is allegedly because the chain does not want to pay royalties for the use of MSC's eco-label.

Oddly enough, in North America it is a retailer, rather than consumer demand, that is driving the move towards sustainable seafood. And not just any retailer. In 2006 the Marine Steward-ship Council got a major boost when Wal-Mart announced it would endeavour to sell mostly council-certified seafood within the next five years. Environmentalists expressed hope that the power of Wal-Mart, the world's biggest retailer, would trans-form the seafood industry. It is definitely going to transform the MSC, though perhaps not for the better. Critics pointed out that Wal-Mart's past nods towards social responsibility – including their notorious promise to sell products 'Made in the USA' in the 1980s – were empty gestures, inevitably trumped by the chain's true philosophy: 'Always Low Prices, Always.' They also worried that conflicts of interest could lead the council to lower its standards for certification. (In 2006, for example, the MSC received an £880,000 grant – their London office initially refused to disclose the total amount to me – from the Walton Family Foundation, a private philanthropical organization endowed by Wal-Mart's founder.) The most strident critics accuse the certification scheme of being a greenwash: a way for industry to disarm all accusations of harming the environment by slapping a too-easily obtained eco-label on seafood that may well come from compromised ecosystems.

Similar certification schemes are being devised for farmed seafood. Red Lobster, for example, supports the Global Aqua-culture Alliance (GAA). The Missouri-based organization certified shrimp and fish farms around the world with its Best Aquaculture Practices (BAP) label. Mangrove campaigners and other environmentalists have criticized the GAA for failing to include local communities in its consultation process, allowing the building of farms on crucial salt flats, and lacking a realistic programme for restoring mangroves.

In January 2008, after four years of activity, only forty-three farms worldwide had qualified for the GAA's seal of approval. To put this number in perspective: in Bangladesh alone, a country that is not even one of the world's top five shrimp exporters, there are 50,000 shrimp farms. (The MSC, in contrast, has certified 6 per cent of the volume of the world's wild-caught fish.) Some critics believe that such certification schemes risk becoming a bluewash – a convenient greenwash for the 'blue revolution' – providing a seal of approval that makes seafood retailers look good, while having very little impact on their day-to-day operations.

'The Global Aquaculture Alliance programme was created by industry, for industry,' says Jason Clay, of the World Wide Fund for Nature. 'The main investors were companies like Darden, CP Aquaculture and some of the major shrimp-farming companies. It's kind of like having the fox guard the chicken-house.'

As vice-president of the WWF's Center for Conservation, Clay has been campaigning to develop an alternative, independent certification system for aquaculture since 1999 and has been instrumental in getting industry to collaborate on standards for salmon, tilapia, catfish, shrimp and just about every other species that can be farmed.

'It's common knowledge,' says Clay, 'that the ones that develop the standards shouldn't be the ones that implement them.' Once the criteria have been agreed upon, Clay plans on stepping down and handing over operations to the Marine Stewardship Council, or another independent organization. The first certified species will likely be farm-raised catfish.

However, until the day when such reliable eco-labels are commonplace for both wild-caught and farmed species, fish lovers will be adrift in a world of questionable seafood.

The Big Picture

In a world of poorly labelled, unsustainably harvested and even potentially toxic seafood, would it not make more sense to swear off the stuff altogether?

Perhaps. But I prefer the alternative: get informed and eat sensibly. To a person, all the ecologists and fisheries scientists I met in my travels told me they still eat seafood. They just choose their meals very, very carefully.

While in Nova Scotia, I was curious to check some of my conclusions about eating ethically with an expert. With thirteen colleagues from Europe and the United States, marine ecologist Boris Worm was the author of the study that appeared in *Science* in 2006 projecting the collapse of all of the world's major fisheries in the next forty years. Based at Dalhousie University in Halifax, he is responsible for a series of papers in leading peer-reviewed journals that catalogue the impact of declining biodiversity in the world's oceans. With his colleague, the late Ransom Myers, he was among the first to highlight the worldwide collapse of the stocks of such large predators as bluefin tuna, swordfish and sharks.

I met Worm and his wife Heike Lotze in the biology building on the Dalhousie campus. Originally from Germany, they fell in love with, and in, Canada. They make a striking couple: Worm is slender, curly-haired, soft-spoken; Lotze is tall and elegant, with long brown hair. Lotze's specialty is historical research: her studies of coastal regions – including such big estuaries as Chesapeake Bay – have been instrumental in revealing the big picture about the global loss in marine biodiversity.

'We extracted the data from eight hundred papers and studies,' Lotze explained, 'and looked at twelve different estuaries and coastal seas, everything from FAO catch records to sediment cores and archaeological data going back a thousand years. What you see is that changes in diversity really started happening in 1800, when the industrialization of fishing begins.' Since 1950, 29 per cent of exploited fish and invertebrate stocks around the world have been fished to 10 per cent of their former numbers. Extending the timeline back a thousand years, 38 per cent of the world's exploited marine species have collapsed, and 7 per cent of them – including blue walleye, Steller's sea cow and Chinese river dolphins – have become extinct. Though the paper offered succinct numbers on just how badly the spread of humanity around the globe has affected life in the oceans, it attracted the attention of the world media because it was the first to project the observed loss of biodiversity into the future.

'I was overseeing a student exam when I analysed the numbers on my laptop,' said Worm, 'and I just got this sinking feeling as the numbers came in. It was a really profound moment.' He saw 'just a smooth line going down', with the collapse of all world fisheries occurring by 2048.

In spite of all the bad news, both Worm and Lotze confessed they had not stopped eating fish. While earning his masters degree, Worm lived in a cabin in a Nova Scotian fishing village, where crab and lobster fishermen were his neighbours; there, he developed a taste for the seafood of the North Atlantic.

Lotze had some errands to run, but I talked Worm into accompanying me on an expedition to the place most people get their seafood: the supermarket.

At Sea at the Fish Counter

We drove a few blocks to a sprawling, high-ceilinged supermarket called the Atlantic Superstore, which is owned by Loblaw's, Canada's biggest grocery chain.

In the seafood department, which consisted of a dozen floor refrigerators and freezers and a counter with fillets and whole fish spread on ice, Worm reached into an open fridge and pulled out a package of smoked salmon.

'"Naturally hardwood smoked", he said, reading the label. '"Naturally" is the first word you read. But it comes from the Bay of Fundy, in New Brunswick, and the indigenous salmon there are almost extinct. They're actually on the endangered species list. So this has to be farmed, but nowhere on the package does it say so.' He pointed to a package of smoked sockeye from British Columbia, labelled 'wild'.

'If it doesn't say "wild", which is a selling point, you can pretty much assume it's farmed. I talked to a fish farmer about the artificial colour they put in farmed salmon and trout; he told me one company has a monopoly on the food colouring, and it's incredibly expensive, like twenty or thirty per cent of the production cost.'

We strolled the aisles, Worm commenting on anything that caught his eye.

On a package labelled King Crab:

'Look at the ingredients list. It is actually Alaskan pollock, water, conjack flour, carageenan, artificial flavouring and a little bit of crab, but they can still call it king crab. This is a whole section of fake crab meat. I suppose you're meant to put it in salad. I would never eat it: it's too processed.'

On a package of generic fish sticks:

'"Made from minced fish fillets." It says pollock, cod, haddock, ocean perch – it could be any one of those. It also says "Product of Canada", but the fish have probably travelled all the way to China for processing. I've never eaten a fish stick in my life. I don't even know what they taste like.'

On a package of salted cod bits:

'In Germany I once gave a talk at a seniors' home. They remembered fish being a poor man's food after World War II;

that was all people could afford. They said they thought the cod they were getting now was baby cod; a whole fish could only feed one person. Before, a whole cod could feed a football team.'

On the canned tuna aisle:

'One thing that maddens me is the marketing of seafood. You should eat fish with a consciousness that it's wildlife, knowing where it comes from. But look at this can: they call tuna "Chicken of the Sea". It couldn't be any farther from that: they are actually the wolves of the sea. I don't eat any canned tuna.'

Something caught Worm's eye at the fresh fish counter.

'Here is red snapper, for $9.89 (£4.82) a pound. Sorry, sir,' said Worm, addressing a young employee in an apron and cap. 'Where does the red snapper come from?'

'I'm not sure,' said the counterman, glancing at the plastic sign planted in the chipped ice.

'Is it from Florida?' asked Worm.

'Probably . . .'

Worm whispered to me: 'Red snapper is the most endangered species in the Gulf of Mexico.

'And where does your sea bass come from?'

'It's not local, I know that.'

Worm guessed it was branzino, probably farmed in the Mediterranean.

'What kind of tuna do you have today?' pursued Worm. The counterman said it was bluefin, marked down to $16.99 (£8.30) from $19 a pound (£9.30).

Worm whistled in surprise. Even here in Halifax, a supermarket was selling the fetish fish of Japan, one of the most endangered species in the sea.

'Sometimes bluefin is caught locally,' Worm told me, 'but this time of year, it probably comes from somewhere else.'

Again the fishmonger did not know where it had been caught.

'Well, we're pretty much through here,' said Worm.

We left the counter without buying a thing. Was there anything, I wondered, that Worm might consider buying?

He pointed to a package of small rose-coloured shrimp in a freezer.

'This is the only species of shrimp I eat, *Pandalus borealis*, the northern shrimp. They're seeking Marine Stewardship Council certification for the fishery because it has very little bycatch, which is unusual for trawled shrimp, and it's done on muddy bottoms, which is less harmful to the sea floor. As far as shrimp goes, this is as good as it gets.

'When I have a craving for salmon,' he continued, leading me back to the canned fish aisle, 'I go for wild canned sockeye from Alaska, which is an MSC-certified fishery. You can see where it's fished, because it's stamped into the top of the can: "Salmon, Alaska, USA."'

'And this is tilapia,' he said, holding up a package of frozen fillets. 'I really like tilapia. It's a very good fish. It's farmed mostly, in land-based ponds, so it doesn't pollute the marine environment, and it usually doesn't have a major fishmeal component in its diet. Trout, though they're a carnivorous species, are also raised in land-based ponds, so they are also relatively nonpolluting.'

As we walked back to the car, Worm admitted he never buys his seafood at a supermarket, but prefers to shop at a local fisherman's co-op, where he can get his dinner fresh from the boats. Sometimes he makes a special trip to a local farmer's market where a Polish woman makes a to-die-for herring in cream sauce. The herring off Nova Scotia, he said, are still in good shape.

'I really have to know where my fish is coming from. That's why I like to buy directly from the fishermen.'

We left the supermarket having experienced what consumers outside of the UK and Japan go through every time they try to buy fish: inadequate labelling and underinformed staff – a horrible dearth of information.

Worm confessed he was surprised by how bad the situation was. Unlike Europe, Canada and the United States do not require their seafood to be labelled wild or farmed. Unlike Japan, retailers in North America need give no indication of whether a fish is in season, or post an information board listing where each species has been caught, and whether it is fresh or has been previously frozen. And though the United States requires fish retailers to label fish with its country of origin, that indicates only the place it was processed, and rarely has anything to do with which ocean it was caught in. The frozen cod that I saw at the High Liner factory, destined for the United States, was labelled 'Product of Canada', even though it was likely caught in the Barents Sea, north of Russia. For a North American consumer, noted Worm, it is very difficult to shop ethically. Labelling laws, he believed, have to be a lot stronger.

Worm and I ended our evening at a seafood restaurant in Halifax harbour. As we perused the menu, we simultaneously pulled out seafood-choice wallet cards. (Worm had collaborated on the Seafood Choices card, the Canadian version of the Monterey Bay Aquarium's Seafood Watch card.) Going through the menu – tonight's specials included chemical-laden farmed salmon, overfished Atlantic halibut and bottom-trawled scallops – Worm looked dispirited and was about to order an appetizer of goat cheese-stuffed artichoke hearts. Then he spied a pasta dish, and asked the waiter if he could have his noodles without any scallops or salmon.

'You mean only with lobster?' asked the waiter. 'Okay' – he gave Worm a look – 'but you're not going to get a ton of it.'

'I eat local lobster,' Worm explained. 'It's an unusual fishery because it's been small-scale and sustainable for one hundred and fifty years.'

The waiter brought Worm his plate of linguine, adorned with

a few scraps of lobster meat. (At least it looked like lobster meat. For all we knew, it could have been monkfish.)

Our quest for ethical seafood in one of the east coast's great ports had been discouraging, to say the least. In the absence of strong laws demanding accurate labelling, I asked Worm, what was a seafood lover to do?

'Ask questions,' he replied, picking at his dinner. 'Always ask questions – it's the only way. We have to become conscious about the fish we're eating. I mean, we do that with other products. We'll look at the list of ingredients, and make choices that help the environment and are good for our health and the health of our children. We need to apply the same standards to seafood.'

The Slowest Fish

As I stood on a bay south of Halifax, looking past the multi-coloured buoys that marked a thousand lobster traps, I was not thinking about where my next seafood dinner would come from. After a year and a half of travel, I was remembering all the people I had encountered who made a living from the sea: a skipjack captain in the Chesapeake, a trawlerman on the picked over North Sea, the crew of a sardine boat in Portugal, the beach-based fisherpeople on the disaster-stricken Indian Ocean, an opinionated salmon troller in the North Pacific. As my guide to the port of Concarneau put it, fishermen really are the 'last adventurers of daily life', among the few remaining full-time hunters in a world of fields and farmers. Those who continue to fish are reminders of the time that humanity, limited less by ambition than by the limits of sail power and the vagaries of weather, lived in harmony with seas that seemed inexhaustible in their bounty.

In the context of failing ecosystems and the industrialization of fishing, I wondered what would become of the two hundred million people around the world who still earn their living from fishing. There was an argument to be made that the world's fisheries do not need to employ fewer people. In the developed world especially, they should be employing far *more*.

In the unilateral arms race against the fish, our neutron bombs have already been deployed: the bottom-trawls that can devastate seamounts, the longlines that trail dozens of miles of hooks, the giant purse-seine nets big enough to easily pull in half a dozen *Trafalgar*-class nuclear submarines. Fishing technology has got too good: captains now use translucent monofilament fishing line invented by the Dupont Corporation, contour maps generated by side-scan sonar equipment, and Doppler radar to detect the thermoclines richest in sea life. Perhaps the solution is not to develop bigger and more efficient vessels, but to step back from the precipice of extinction and reclaim, and revalorize, older technology. Intentional inefficiency may be anathema to our notions of progress, but it has happened throughout human history, and it is happening right now.

There is Chesapeake Bay, where long ago the watermen of Maryland chose to spare the wild oyster population by fishing only with sail-powered skipjacks. The relatively fish-poor Mediterranean continues to support one hundred thousand fishermen in small boats, and with them a fantastically varied array of seafood-based cuisines. In the North Atlantic, established fishermen have agreed to stick with the time-consuming and low-tech system of traps and pots, even though a team of scuba divers could easily clean out an entire bay full of lobsters in a couple of weeks. In India, activist Thomas Kocherry showed me how fisherpeople had organized to resist the foreign super-trawlers that can kill off entire coastal communities. And here in Nova Scotia, swordfishermen have preserved the daring harpoon fishery, even though nets and longlines can get the job done far more efficiently. Just as automation means that aquaculture operations need fewer employees as time goes on, the increasing efficiency of supertrawlers means the number of people employed per kilogram of fish harvested is always dropping. What needs to be favoured, in our policies and patterns of subsidies and penalties, is *true* sustainability: fisheries that sustain both oceans and human communities.

Lately, government policies have focused on diminishing the number of working fishermen. But decommissioning and scrapping fishing vessels to reduce the overcapacity of fleets are likely to be unpopular tactics – no politician wants to be responsible for sending a lifelong cod fisherman's trawler to the scrapyard. (And too often, decommissioned vessels end up being sold to countries in the developing world, meaning the overfishing problem is merely relocated to a distant ocean.) There is an easier way to end the insane imbalance of power between fishing fleets and their prey. It is simply to stop lavishing outlandish subsidies on the fishing industry. Governments worldwide are still paying fishermen to build new boats: I had gone fishing on a year-old Portuguese sardine boat in Peniche, built with almost a million euros in subsidies, and toured a brand-new tuna trawler in the port of Concarneau – both vessels built with money from European taxpayers. According to Ussif Rashid Sumaila, of the University of British Columbia's Fisheries Centre, the world pays its fishermen £17 billion in subsidies a year just to keep them on the water. Of that total, at least £10 billion are what Sumaila calls 'bad' subsidies: money that goes directly to pay for fuel and the building of new boats. The amount of overfishing in the world, Sumaila believes, is directly proportionate to the amount of money governments give fishermen to keep fishing. Once these artificial supports are removed – restoring fishing to the free market from whence it came – some of the most destructive fisheries in the world, like the profligate high-seas bottom-trawling industry and the distant-water fleets operating off Africa, would suddenly become unprofitable. By all means, says Sumaila, keep giving fishermen 'good' subsidies to provide unemployment relief, retrain workers, and even sink old trawlers to create artificial reefs. But remove the bad. No taxpayer should be forced to contribute a penny of tax money towards the destruction of the oceans. Once governments stop giving the industry a free ride, the bad economics of sailing halfway around the world to scoop up fish on the brink of extinction will help curtail the worst excesses of the fishing industry. In 2007, 125 scientists signed a letter that urged the World Trade Organization to scale back subsidies to the world's fishing fleets.

At the Fisheries Centre Daniel Pauly told me that he and his colleagues dream of a 'slow fish' movement, similar to the 'slow food' movement born in Italy, which would see fleet capacity reduced, the rate of fishing slowed, and government support going to coastal fishermen in small boats rather than big industrial vessels.

'Small-scale fisheries,' Pauly believes, 'should not be favoured over large-scale operations because of romantic notions of rugged small operators battling both the elements and anonymous corporations.' They should be supported, he insists, 'because of the scientific evidence available to confirm the common-sense inference that local fishers, if given privileged access, will tend to avoid trashing their local stocks, while foreign fishers do not have such motivation.'

From this perspective, small-scale fisheries are not messy, inefficient leftovers from a pre-industrial age, but nimble and efficient, responding quickly to changes in species abundance, while using far less fuel to catch fish than industrial fisheries. 'Slow' fisheries would not produce vast fortunes, but they would allow a large number of people to live very well. They would also keep coastal communities alive, a not insignificant advantage in an era increasingly concerned with the integrity of frontiers.

I think 'slow fish' has equal potential as a gastronomic movement. Slow fish, after all, are what I have been seeking since I started my journey. Slow fish are fresh sardines brought to port by dayboat, and eaten barbecued an olive pit's throw from the Atlantic. Slow fish are what goes into the bouillabaisse pot – the ugly, rock-loving species that fishermen used to keep for themselves (along with fennel, potatoes and a good slug of pastis). With slow fish, it is not always the species that matters, but how it gets to your table. Slow fish are often caught in traps or on fishing lines, but never in drift nets or bottom-trawls. Slow fish are very often bottom-feeders, healthily low on the food chain, but high in flavour. A slow fish can be a kippered herring staining wax paper translucent, eaten overlooking the docks of a North Sea fishing port. It can even be a Belon oyster that ends its life a few yards from where it was cultured, and whose shell is tossed back into the sea to provide habitat for new generations. Slow fish are those caught in the Chinese fishing nets of Kerala, where it takes half a dozen men straining with all their might to haul up the catch. And a slow fisherman is one who plans on fishing for a long time, long enough to make a downpayment on a home, start a family and teach his kids to fish – slowly.

I looked towards the little breakwater on the bay, where two old men were dangling hooks in the water. I had seen their kind around the world, the old fellows whiling away the day by fishing, hoping against hope for a nibble from whatever fish were left in the sea.

It reminded me that the slowest fish of all – even when it happens to be very swift indeed – is always the one you catch yourself.

CONCLUSION

Compared to the other seemingly intractable challenges facing humanity – the spread of HIV in Africa, anthropogenic global warming, the end of oil – the crises in the world's fisheries may be rather easy to resolve. We don't need to synthesize new drugs, invent complex carbon-sequestration technology, or discover new means of generating energy. In fact, among fisheries scientists and ecologists, there is a growing consensus about exactly which steps to take.

What Needs to Be Done

To prevent the destruction of fragile seamounts, some of the last refuges of biodiversity in the oceans, bottom-trawling has to be banned on the high seas. To stem the spread of invasive species, which are turning once diverse ecosystems into homogenous environments, cargo ships must be obliged to change their ballast water at sea, rather than in fragile lagoons, harbours and estuaries. To limit overfishing, fish that are now discarded as bycatch should be landed and used rather than thrown overboard, dead. European and Asian countries must stop taking advantage of weak regimes and plundering the coastal seas of Africa. And top-of-the-food-chain species like bluefin tuna and sharks, which control oceanic food webs in ways we still do not understand, need to be protected using international instruments such as the Convention on International Trade in Endangered Species.

To stem pirate fishing, enforcement officers need access to the best satellite technology, enough horsepower to catch perpetrators, and wages high enough to discourage corruption and bribery; diplomatic pressure must be used to shut down ports that allow the trans-shipment of illegal fish; and international laws should be changed to prevent the widespread use of flags of convenience. Politicians and members of the fishing industry can no longer be in charge of setting quotas; truly independent councils need the authority to manage fisheries based on the best scientific evidence available. Our food safety authorities need to be given the resources to monitor seafood, and real power to ban imported and domestic products that are consistently in violation of food safety standards.

Finally, communities need to think hard about the benefits, if any, of allowing industrial aquaculture in their backyards. The pillaging of the ocean's resources, from krill to anchovies, in order to fatten salmon, shrimp and bluefin tuna may well be driving ocean ecosystems to collapse; international financing organizations have got to stop funding the farming of carnivorous species in the Third World.

Policy makers could enact most of these changes overnight; all that is standing in the way is a lack of political will. Other problems afflicting the oceans, unfortunately, are not so easily resolved. The sewage, agricultural runoff, acidification and rising temperatures that are creating dead zones, bleaching coral reefs and poisoning estuaries are chronic problems; it is estimated it will take 100,000 years for the carbon humans have emitted into the atmosphere so far to be absorbed by the seas. Such issues will require long-term action – which can only start with a major adjustment in our attitudes towards the oceans.

'Right now,' says fisheries critic Daniel Pauly, 'we see the seas as some sort of superstore where we don't have to pay.' The oceans have served as our grocery stores but also as sewers for our cities, and as rubbish dumps for heavy industry. They are no longer up to playing their role as catch-all for humanity's waste.

A good start, believes Pauly, would be the creation of a system of marine reserves (also known as marine-protected areas), the equivalent of national parks on land. As things stand now, fishing is allowed everywhere, except for the tiny number of areas where it is limited (often only to certain kinds of fishing gear or at specific times of the year).

Even in the United States – where a marine reserve the size of Germany has been created off the northwest Hawaiian islands, and twenty-nine marine reserves are planned off the California coast – only 1 per cent of coastal waters are protected, versus 10 per cent of the country's land. Though 5 per cent of Canada's coastal waters are now technically off limits, in two-thirds of these marine-protected areas enforcement is non-existent. The World Wide Fund for Nature wants to see 20 per cent of the world's oceans made into no-take zones by 2020, an initiative Pauly supports. Globally, 12 per cent of the world's land is now contained in protected areas; only three-fifths of 1 per cent of the world's oceans are so protected.

'On land we say that you cannot hunt anywhere except those areas that are designated for hunting,' Pauly told me. 'That is what we need for the fisheries: as a default mode, the oceans have to be closed to exploitation, with only a few areas open to fishing.' Rather than further privatizing the oceans by granting quotas to giant fishing corporations, it may be time to start viewing these waters as a genuine public trust – instead of as the last frontiers of free enterprise, open to anybody who happens to have a boat and a net.

Of all the proposed solutions to the crisis in the oceans, the spread of marine reserves is the most promising. The few already in existence have had a staggeringly positive effect. They serve as nursery spots for fish and invertebrates, and their riches tend to spill over into adjoining areas. Crucially, supporting marine reserves makes for good strategy. A politician who champions them might alienate a small number of fishermen, but this would be more than compensated for by those cheering him for providing them, and their children, with a glimpse of what the oceans once looked like – before fishing caused environmental baselines to start shifting. South Africa has already committed to protecting 20 per cent of its territorial waters. In New Zealand, which has a large network of such reserves, fishermen are now among their strongest supporters.

In the uproar surrounding Boris Worm's paper projecting the collapse of world fisheries by 2048, the media neglected to mention a positive side to the paper. Worm and his colleagues found that the parts of the ocean protected by no-take zones and marine reserves experienced a 23 per cent increase in biodiversity. The recovery often happened in only a few years.

In other words, if we can give the oceans even a bit of a break, there is hope for the future.

What We Need to Know

Wallet cards and eco-labels, though great tools, are only a beginning. One of the most effective measures for empowering consumers would also be the simplest to enact: policy makers need to demand more transparency from the dangerously opaque seafood industry. As long as consumers are kept in the dark about where their fish come from, they will never be able to make sound purchasing decisions.

At the very least, labelling standards in North America and continental Europe need to meet those already current in Japan. Supermarkets need to inform their clients whether their fish is wild-caught or farm-raised, whether it is being sold preserved, previously frozen or fresh, and most important, where it was caught (or if it is a product of aquaculture, where it was raised). A package should mention the method of capture – whether it was caught by hand-line, in a trap or by a trawl – and the species should be prominently displayed. ('Chunk light' is not a species of tuna, and 'fish stick' is not a taxonomic division.) For obvious reasons, seafood sellers don't want to include any more information than they have to: an informed consumer might be inclined to avoid canned albacore tuna caught in the eastern Pacific, where purse seines scoop up sea turtles and tropical fish, or fish sticks made with cod that came from the pirate-infested Barents Sea. The Marine Stewardship Council is already eco-labelling wild-caught fish, but a reliable, independent organization is also needed to certify farmed fish.

When it is commercially advantageous, retailers have shown themselves to be perfectly capable of identifying the provenance of their products. The can of sardines I bought in Brittany had the name of the vessel that caught them printed on top; in thirty seconds of Googling, I was able to find a picture of the fishing boat that caught my lunch (and determine that it was fishing sustainable stocks). A British Columbia company has found a way to label hatchery-raised fish with bar codes and chemical tracers that indicate exactly which river a salmon comes from. Sophisticated labelling technology is *already* being used in European waters. As I had seen with the boxes of cod at London's Billingsgate Market, trawlers rely on a computerized system called Seatrace, which labels every box of fish and shellfish, stamping them with the date and time of the catch, the species and weight, and the part of the ocean they come from. Such traceability needs to be extended all the way to the fish counter.

If untraceable seafood remains the norm – if waiters and fish-mongers cannot tell you where the fish you are buying comes from – then all the wallet cards and public awareness campaigns in the world will do nothing to help the oceans.

What's Left to Eat

Can changing the kind of seafood we eat really help the oceans?

The answer is, emphatically, yes.

For me, choosing fish ignorantly is no longer an option. In too many cases I found that following the line connecting the fish on my plate to the hook or net that caught it – or the aquaculture pond it was grown in – led directly to a scene of devastation. Roasted monkfish in New York led to the Atlantic sea floor reduced to mud by bottom-trawls. Steamed wrasse in Shanghai, to corals poisoned by cyanide and ripped apart by dynamite. Popcorn shrimp in the strip malls of America, to dead mangrove forests and poisoned drinking water in some of the world's poorest countries. Around the world there is one force driving this rout: the human appetite, abetted by all the destructive industries that have arisen to serve it.

So yes, what you choose to have for dinner matters. And when a hot chef chooses to put a deep-sea fish like orange roughy on the menu, it matters. When a food writer raves about another kill-me-now *toro* dinner, without bothering to mention bluefin is close to extinction, it matters. When a procurement agent for a supermarket chain sources his flounder or halibut from an overfished stock, it matters. And when we buy fish without caring enough to find out where it came from – well, when you multiply that decision by a couple of billion mouths, then it really, really matters.

The question remains: given all that is happening to the oceans, is there anything left for an ethically inclined seafood-lover to eat?

There is. Quite a lot, in fact. In spite of all I have learned about persistent organic pollutants and the residues of banned anti-biotics; about dementia-inducing mercury and retina-clogging artificial pigments; about fishing down food webs and our hunting of the last big predator fish to near-extinction – in spite of all the bad news, I have not sworn off seafood. In fact, I eat it at least four times a week, more often than I did before starting my journey. For every fish I have crossed off my list, I have added several more.

That is the appeal of seafood. The variety is endless. Like loving Burgundies or savouring raw-milk cheeses, fish-eating demands connoisseurship – just as cooking fish well calls for expertise. The combinations of flavourful amino acids in fish are limitless; the ways fish are transformed by marinating and cooking endlessly surprising. That is the reason seafood cookery is often considered the pinnacle of gastronomy: it is always challenging, never routine. A committed piscivore, though often sated, will never be bored for long.

And after a year and a half of fish-eating, I feel pretty damn good. In spite of months of dining dangerously, from downing oysters in R months to participating in a poisonous pufferfish buffet, I have not experienced anything worse than a short-lived stomachache or two. And since I started taking two purified omega-3 capsules a day, I feel as if I have a whole new brain. (It may be true: the old, omega-6 fatty acids in my neurons have been swapped for high-quality omega-3s, which promote elasticity and better nerve transmission.) My energy is high, and my mood is excellent. My body feels different too, as though my fat and muscle have been redistributed to more useful places; as I navigate among the land-animal-eating hordes, I feel lean and swift, like a tuna darting among sea cows. Later in life I may experience other benefits: omega-3s, by lowering the immune system's inflammatory response, are thought to decrease the incidence of cancer and heart disease, and, by preventing clots, the risk of strokes. Public health officials are increasingly on my side: the American Heart Association advises those with cardio-vascular disease to eat at least two servings of fish a week, especially such oily fish as mackerel, trout, herring and sardines. A Swedish study has shown that men who eat sardines twice a week are 50 per cent less likely to develop prostate cancer. The British Food Standards Agency now recommends eating fish twice a week – even for pregnant women.

With that said, the kind of fish I eat has completely changed. My list of permissible seafood is now criss-crossed with emphatic black marks. All the brain-boosting omega-3s in the ocean, I now know, will not compensate for the potential nerve damage that comes from ingesting the mercury in such long-lived species as swordfish, tuna, tilefish and grouper. I have learned there are enough dangerous dioxins and PCBs in many forms of industrially farmed seafood to significantly increase my risk of cancer. I now avoid eel, shrimp, catfish and other farmed species imported from the developing world; the pres-sures to boost productivity abroad, and the lack of good inspection at home, guarantee that you will eventually get a dose of dangerous antibiotics and pesticides.

I have stopped eating other kinds of seafood because I have seen exactly how much their exploitation is costing the planet. The idea of ordering bottom-trawled orange roughy or monkfish is as ethically repugnant to me as eating bushmeat or monkey brains. The sight of prettily pink farmed salmon in a seafood case now inevitably conjures up images of sea-lice-infested smolts and the potential extermination of wild chinook, coho and pink salmon. (Thanks to what I saw in British Columbia, if I am offered the choice between beef or salmon on a long flight, I'd rather go hungry.) And as much as I used to enjoy shrimp, I now rarely touch the stuff. If it is the product of aquaculture, I hear the voices of the villagers I met in Tamil Nadu, listing all the illnesses that come from living in close proximity to shrimp ponds. If it is caught in the wild, I see tons of bycatch – from skates to sharks – pouring onto the deck of a trawler.

After circling the globe, I have come home a convinced bottomfeeder. The big fish, I now know, need a break. I am going to lay off the upper levels of the food chain, especially the big predator species – tuna, cod, grouper, shark, swordfish – that in many areas have been fished to 10 per cent of their historic levels. Giving them up will not be too much of a sacrifice – my body doesn't need the toxins that come from eating that high in the food chain. Continuing to eat them would mean hastening the arrival of a future of unpredictable trophic cascades and extinctions – and, eventually, peanut-butter and jellyfish sandwiches.

Fortunately, for every top-of-the-food-chain species I have crossed off my list, I have added several from lower down. I now get excited about sardines, especially if they are fresh-caught and barbecued, or canned *à l'ancienne* and spread on buttered sourdough. I will make a long detour to patronize a restaurant that creatively serves sea urchin, mackerel or squid; and I have discovered a world of fantastically flavourful clams, quahogs, razorshells and mussels. I have learned the pleasures of taking a couple of days to assemble the ingredients for the perfect fish soup. I do not have to go through life without fish and chips: line-caught haddock can be a sustainable choice, and one I actually prefer to cod. To my surprise, I am happy to eat fast-food sandwiches made with sustainably fished Alaskan pollock. I have learned the pleasures of oak-smoked kippers, herring in cream sauce and sake-marinated sablefish. I now seek out oily fish like anchovies and mackerel – so high in omega-3s, so low in toxins. And if I see a jellyfish salad on a menu, it is my policy to order it.

Frankly, though, right now I am more excited about the idea of a meal I've been imagining for a while. It will involve a dozen raw Belon oyster, sprinkled with a little bit of pepper, followed by a perfectly cooked Atlantic lobster, its sweet flesh dipped in melted butter.

Sure, there is virtue in eating at the lower end of the food chain. But there is more pleasure – which is why I am proud to call myself a bottomfeeder.

APPENDIX

ADVICE ON CHOOSING SEAFOOD

When choosing fish, knowledge is power. Even for experienced shoppers, though, deciding what to buy can be a quandary. A species that is sustainably fished one season can be in trouble the next, and more and more kinds of fish are being farmed, some in questionable conditions. Fortunately, tools are available for anybody determined to eat seafood healthily and ethically. They range from regional seafood-choice wallet cards (which are typically updated twice a year), to websites that can be consulted via mobile phone at a restaurant or fish market.

Web Sites

www.fishonline.org (or search for 'FishOnline')

The Marine Conservation Society (MCS), a British charity founded in 1977, has made its pocket Good Fish Guide available online. It divides leading seafood species available in Britain into 'Fish to Avoid' and 'Fish to Eat'. You can download and print out a wallet-sized version, or simply enter the name of a species in their searchable database, which ranks seafood from 1 ('to eat') to 5 ('to avoid'). The site is a constantly updated, one-stop resource, with extensive documentation on the criteria for rating each kind of seafood, pages illustrating the problems associated with various types of fishing gear, and a chart showing the best time of the year to buy individual species. The site can also be consulted by mobile phone.

In 2007, the MCS also began listing supermarkets, fishmongers and even fish farms that sell sustainable seafood, ranking restaurants and pubs on a scale of 1 to 4. You can consult the ever-expanding list at: www.fishonline.org/buying_eating/seafoodlistings.php.

www.msc.org (or search for 'Marine Stewardship Council')

This independent organization assesses capture fisheries (for wild-caught, as opposed to farmed, seafood) around the world, certifying those that meet its standards. Though environmentalists have questioned some certifications (particularly of the large New Zealand hoki and the Alaska pollock fisheries), the MSC is still the best eco-label on the shelves. Check their website for information on twenty sustainably run fisheries worldwide, and look for their blue-and-white eco-label, now found in Marks & Spencer, Asda, Waitrose, Sainsbury's and most other leading retailers.

www.fishbase.org (or search for 'FishBase')

A fish can go by many names, and these aliases can be the bane of seafood buying. An international group of research institutions has created a searchable database, originally intended for scientists, of thirty thousand fish species worldwide. Entering an unfamiliar name in one of 200 languages (say, 'squeteague') will direct you to a list of common and Latin names (in this case, 'weakfish', *Cynoscion regalis*). From there you will be linked to a page with a description and photo and information about its habitat and ecology as well as access to more information. The FishBase team has also put together an easy-to-use website (www.seafood.guide) that presents seafood guides from different countries in a format optimized for Internet-enabled mobile phones.

www.iucnredlist.org (or search for 'World Conservation Union')

This Switzerland-based conservation organization's website offers a searchable database of its red list of threatened species; think twice about buying marine species listed as 'VU' (Vulnerable) and especially

'EN' (Endangered) or 'CR' (Critically Endangered). It is a good first stop to check the status of marine species.

www.gotmercury.org (or search for 'Got Mercury')

This simple calculator determines the amount of mercury you are getting from seafood. Enter the names of the fish, your weight and the serving sizes per week, and the site will calculate the percentage of safe weekly allowance of mercury you are getting, following US Environmental Protection Agency standards. (In contrast, the FDA's standard for permissible mercury, 1 part per million, is among the highest in the world; Thailand, for example, allows half as much mercury in its fish, and Britain only 0.3 parts per million.) The site is interesting to play with: a single six-ounce can of albacore tuna, for example, gives you 130 per cent of your weekly limit, but you would have to eat 8.5 pounds of sardines, or thirty-six cans, to get the same dose.

Principles to Follow When Buying Seafood

When you are far from the seashore, cheap seafood is suspect seafood. It was probably farmed, and may have gone through several cycles of freezing and rethawing before getting to your table.

Avoid fish that has travelled too far. The more fuel used to ship it, the less inclined you should be to buy it.

Avoid long-lived predator fish (sharks, swordfish, Chilean sea bass, tuna), which tend to have the highest levels of mercury.

Avoid farmed shrimp, tuna, salmon and other species that are fattened with other fish; they tend to have higher levels of dioxins and other persistent organic pollutants. Favour tilapia, carp, catfish and other species that are fed vegetable, rather than animal, protein.

In North America and Europe, opt for domestically farmed seafood. (Standards on additives, water quality and environmental impact tend to be higher.)

If you have a choice, favour organically farmed salmon, cod and trout; stocking densities are lower, and they tend to be treated with fewer chemicals.

Finally, opt for seafood at the lower end of the food chain, from mackerel down to oysters. Bottomfeeding is better for your health and for the long-term health of the oceans.

Questions to Ask Your Waiter or Fishmonger

(It should take no more than three to make an informed choice.)

Question 1: Do you know if this fish was wild-caught or farmed? If it was *wild-caught*:

Question 2: Do you know which ocean it came from, and if so, which country and port it was landed in?

Question 3: How was it caught? (with a hook and line? a trawl net?)

And if it was *farmed*:

Question 2: Was this fish farmed domestically, or was it imported?

Question 3, *if imported*: Which country was it imported from?

If you can find fishmongers or restaurateurs who know and care enough to answer your questions, stick with them.

Fishing Methods:
The Good, the Not-So-Good and the Really Ugly

Unless you know how your fish are caught, choosing them intelligently will be impossible. No fishing comes without impact. The gear used, whether it is a bent coat-pin at the end of a string or a bottom-trawl big enough to net the Ritz, inevitably determines its effect on the environment. The following list roughly follows fishermen's rankings of various types of gear, from least to greatest impact, as reported in the paper 'Shifting Gears' (in *Further Reading*, p. 388).

THE GOOD

Hook and Line

Few fishing methods have a lower impact than a baited hook at the end of a line; the wrong species can be tossed back, usually quickly enough so that it will survive the experience. Hook-and-line-caught fish are also referred to as pole-caught or handline-caught; not to be confused with longline-caught.

Trolls

British Columbia fisherman Billy Proctor spent much of his fishing career trolling for salmon in his beautiful boat the *Ocean Dawn*. Such trollers, which trail elaborate cat's cradles of lines, are used to catch mahi-mahi, Pacific salmon and albacore tuna. Trolling results in little bycatch: as with a hook and line, a fisherman who catches the wrong species can unhook it and throw it back.

Harpoons and Scuba

In terms of limiting bycatch, harpooning is an excellent, and genuinely sporting, technique, used by skilled fishermen to catch tuna, swordfish and other big-game fish. Skin and scuba divers (as in 'diver-caught abalone', 'wreck-caught grouper') also target their catch. Such techniques can be abused: harpooning has been industrialized by whalers, and scuba divers have stripped entire bays of lobsters and other invertebrates.

Purse Seines

The Portuguese sardine boat the *Mestre Comboio* is an example of a purse-seiner. Using echo-sounding sonar, such boats can target schools of fish, from tiny anchovies to giant tuna, and surround them with huge nets, usually with little bycatch.

The exceptions are purse-seiners that put out fish aggregation devices (FADs), typically logs or wooden frames with beacons attached. Fish in the open ocean tend to gather around such floating objects. Tuna boats that use FADs catch fifty times more fish, among them manta rays and juvenile tuna, than conventional purse-seiners. The eastern Pacific and Indian Ocean tuna fisheries rely on FADs – another reason to think twice about eating canned tuna.

In general, however, purse-seining, especially for anchovies, sardines, herring and other small schooling fish, is considered one of the best industrial fishing techniques.

Pots and Traps

Submerged cages containing bait, attached to buoys by lines, can range in size from the small wooden traps I saw lobsterman Lorne Harnish using in St Margarets Bay (which hold two dozen lobsters), to the giant metal 'pots' used in the Bering Sea (which can hold hundreds of king crabs). Intelligently designed traps have doors that allow juveniles to escape. Traps can have a fairly high level of bycatch, and cause habitat damage when they are bounced around by storms or dragged across the sea floor.

THE NOT-SO-GOOD

Midwater Trawls

Trawls, cone-shaped nets that can be towed behind industrial boats for hours, are among the worst forms of fishing gear in terms of bycatch and damage to the environment. Of all trawl gear, the *least* bad is the midwater or pelagic trawl (used, for example, in the Alaska pollock fishery), which occasionally touches but does not rake the ocean floor.

Longlines

Industrial fishing boats set out baited, hooked longlines, and let them 'soak' for up to twenty hours; the lines in question can be sixty miles long and carry up to thirty-thousand hooks. In spite of improvements, such as streaming ribbons that discourage seabirds from taking the bait, irresponsibly set longlines still strip the high seas of hundreds of species of birds and amphibians, among them leatherback turtles, which get tangled in the lines and drown. Pelagic longlines, set near the surface, are the gear most responsible for devastating shark populations world-wide. In contrast, bottom longlines (which are weighted to rest near the sea floor) are usually much shorter and have a lower impact on sharks and little effect on birds and mammals.

Gill Nets

Mediterranean fisherman Christophe Holtz used a gill net when he was fishing for *rascasse* to supply the bouillabaisse pots of Marseilles. These are vertical curtains of translucent netting suspended with weighted leadlines at a variety of depths, typically set one day and retrieved the next; fish trying to pass through the nylon mesh get caught by the gills. As I saw in the Mediterranean, gill nets can entangle just about any-thing, so rates of bycatch tend to be high. It is estimated that at any one time, there are 5,400 miles of gill nets in constant contact with the floor of the North Atlantic.

Dredges

Captain Wade Murphy demonstrated a small dredge for me in the Chesapeake: a metal-framed mesh bag with a toothed lower edge that raked the bay bottom behind his sail-powered skipjack. Industrial vessels hauling larger dredges, which comb the sea bottom for shellfish, have damaged fragile habitat for fish – probably permanently – in many oceans. Thanks to dredging by the industrial scallop fishery, some parts of the North Atlantic coast are now muddy-bottomed wastelands.

THE REALLY UGLY

Drift Nets, Ghost Nets

Drift nets, those 'walls of death', set loose in the Pacific by the Japanese squid fishermen in the 1980s, could be 55 miles long, and entangled huge numbers of sharks, salmon, sea birds and tuna. Banned in international waters by the United Nations in 1992, drift nets are still out there; both the US and Europe allow smaller drift nets in coastal waters. Ghost nets are a scourge in every ocean, fouling propellers and continuing to kill long after they have been lost or forgotten.

Dynamite and Cyanide

Prime tools of coral reef destruction. Fishermen stun reef fish with explosives or poison, making them easier to retrieve for sale to the live-fish restaurant trade. The coral is blown to rubble or dies a few weeks after being exposed to cyanide. The groupers, wrasse, parrotfish and other tropical fish sold live in Asian restaurants are often captured this way.

Bottom-Trawls

Bottom-trawling, known as dragging in Atlantic Canada, involves towing a net across the sea floor. When it is done in shallow waters with a long history of trawling, over sand, gravel, or mud, it is arguably an acceptable technique: the real damage may have been done generations ago. Almost all trawls have high levels of bycatch and discards.

High-seas bottom-trawling, in contrast, is the fishing industry's weapon of mass destruction. Thanks to new technology, vessels can now

guide nets with multitonne doors over every kind of sea floor environment, quite possibly extirpating species that scientists have not yet had
a chance to describe. The species hauled up, among them 150-year-old
orange roughy and thousand-year-old coral, tend to be long-lived and
slow to regenerate.

High-seas bottom-trawlers destroy 580 square miles of seabed each
day. Nations now bottom-trawling on the high seas include Iceland,
Russia, Japan, New Zealand, Spain, Portugal, Denmark and Norway. In
order to protect their inshore trawl fleets, Canada, China and South
Korea all opposed a 2006 United Nations moratorium on high-seas
trawling.

THE LIST

Ethical seafood guides and websites typically divide the fish in markets
and on menus into best choices, good alternatives and species to avoid.
After a decade of fish-eating, and a year and a half of visiting markets
and reading menus worldwide, I have come to my own conclusions
about what is sustainable. The following list, though compiled with reference to major seafood-choice guides, is a personal one, with
commonly available species divvied up according to whether, and how
often, I eat them. The italicized words at the end of each entry summa-
rize the issues associated with a species; and the figure in parentheses is
its average trophic level – its rank on the food chain, between one and
five – based on its diet. With a few exceptions, the higher the level, the
more likely a species is to be overfished, and the greater its risk of containing contaminants.

NO, NEVER

Bluefin tuna. Often called *toro* in Japanese restaurants. Severely
overfished, and listed as critically endangered by the World Conservation Union IUCN. 'Farmed' bluefin are actually juvenile tuna taken
from the wild before they can reproduce, and fattened with smaller fish.
Mercury. (4.4)

Chilean sea bass. Also known as the Patagonian toothfish, this long-lived deep-sea fish is subject to extensive pirate fishing. Only one fishery has been certified by the Marine Stewardship Council; unless you know that your Chilean sea bass comes from the South Georgia winter longline fishery in the Antarctic – and you are unlikely to – avoid it. *Longlined, bottom-trawled. Mercury. Pirate vessels.* (4.0)

Cod, Atlantic. Most cod stocks in the western Atlantic have collapsed, and show no sign of recovery. In European waters, most cod stocks are overfished, and extensive pirate fishing is occurring in the Barents Sea. Encourage your retailer to sell line-caught (as opposed to trawled) cod. An alternative is expensive organic, farmed cod, currently being raised by companies in Scandinavia and Scotland. *Fished by pirate vessels. Bottom-trawled.* (4.3)

Grouper. These long-lived reef predators, of which there are eighty-five known species, are especially vulnerable to overfishing, and toxins tend to accumulate in their flesh *Longlined. Mercury.* (3.6)

Halibut, Atlantic. Atlantic halibut, a deep-water flatfish that can weigh up to seven hundred pounds, has been fished to the brink by trawls, and is actually considered endangered by the IUCN. An alternative is organically farmed halibut from Scotland and Norway. *Mercury. Bottom-trawled.* (4.5)

Marlin. Stocks are low in the Atlantic, and are not predicted to recover at the current rate of exploitation. *Longlined. Mercury.* (4.5)

Monkfish. Also known as anglerfish. Heavily overfished, with bottom-destroying trawls, off the US coast. Though overfished in Spanish and Portuguese waters, monkfish stocks in British and Scandinavian waters are in somewhat better shape. Some fishermen in Cornwall use gill nets, but most monkfish is still caught with sea floor-destroying trawls. *Bottom-trawled.* (4.5)

Orange roughy. These deep-sea fish, which can live to 150 years, are being heavily overfished by high-seas bottom-trawlers, which destroy fragile, slow-to-recover seamounts. They occasionally show up on the menus of white-tablecloth restaurants in Europe. Listed as threatened by the Australian government in 2006. Other deep-water fish to avoid but still sold in Britain: alfonsino, argentine, black scabbardfish, greater forkbeard, ling, rat or rabbit fish, redfish, roundnose grenadier, tusk. *Mercury. Deep-water. Bottom-trawled.* (4.3)

Shark, dogfish, skate. Sharks are undergoing catastrophic population crashes worldwide to supply the Asian shark fin soup market. Shark meat is also sold in Western supermarkets, and the similar dogfish, also heavily overfished, is sold as rock salmon in Britain. Such fish produce few young, and large coastal species are slow-growing and late to mature. Overfished skates are also caught with bottom-trawls. *Mercury. Longlined. Bottom-trawled.* (Porbeagle shark, 4.5)

DEPENDS, SOMETIMES

Abalone. Much of the abalone now sold in the world is illegally fished by poachers. Only buy this rare shellfish if you know it is farmed, as some of it now is in the Channel Islands, Ireland, California and France. *Illegally fished.* (2.0)

Alaska or walleye pollock. Caught with mid-water trawls in the Bering Sea, pollock in US waters is certified by the MSC. However, in 2008 government surveys revealed that populations of this fish, which is sold as imitation crab meat and goes into fast-food fish sandwiches and many kinds of fish fingers, had declined by 50 per cent in a single year. This is an extremely bad sign: overfishing may be driving one of the world's leading food fisheries to collapse – which means that the future of even the Filet-O-Fish is far from certain. (3.2)

Anchovy. Low in mercury, high in omega-3s. Available canned, salted, pickled in vinegar and fermented in Asian sauces. Though flavourful and good for you, anchovy numbers in the North Atlantic are now at an all-time low. Until the fishery in the Bay of Biscay is reopened, and stocks in the Mediterranean have recovered, avoid. *Overfished.* (3.1)

Clams. Farmed clams, like oysters, are a great choice, as are most clams sold in restaurants. The clams that end up in cans, however, are often caught with hydraulic dredges that permanently damage the sea floor. Avoid clams smaller than 2 inches across. *Dredged.* (2.0)

Cod, Pacific. An excellent alternative to Atlantic cod. Though there is some bycatch with trawl-caught Pacific cod, much is caught with bottom longlines, which have little bycatch. *Trawled.* (4.0)

Crab. Thanks to the disappearance of their predators, crabs are doing quite well in most places. Brown crabs from the south Devon coast, which are caught in traps, are an excellent choice. (Blue crab, 2.6)

Flounder. Mostly taken as bycatch in trawl nets, stocks of this flatfish are in decent shape. Avoid immature fish, which tend to be less than 10 inches long. *Bottom-trawled.* (3.2)

Haddock. Stocks in most areas are healthy, and haddock is a decent alternative to cod in chip shops. Much haddock, unfortunately, is still caught with trawls, with high bycatch levels of cod. Marks & Spencer is currently working with trawlermen to reduce discards in the haddock fishery. Always ask for longline-caught haddock. *Trawled.* (4.1)

Lobster. Sweet-fleshed Atlantic lobster from North American waters is generally a good choice. Spiny or rock lobster from Central America is overfished with substandard gear that kills and cripples divers. Many lobster stocks in European waters are depleted; insist on trap-caught. *Overfished. Social impact.* (2.6)

Mullet. Both red mullet, famous for its delicate flavour, and grey mullet, a streamlined herbivore, spawn in the English Channel, but little is known for certain about their abundance. Avoid immature fish (greys less than 14 inches; reds less than 9 inches). (2.1)

Octopus. Fast-growing, fecund octopi are taken as bycatch in trawl nets. They are not thought to be overfished, but avoid baby octopus, which haven't had a chance to breed. *Trawled.* (4.1)

Prawns. Be very careful about eating imported prawns (in the seafood business, the terms 'prawns' and 'shrimp' are used interchangeably). If they are farmed, they are often treated with chemicals, and intensive shrimp ponds are polluting some of the world's poorest countries. If they are wild-caught with trawls, bycatch levels can be enormous. Mexico, which farms some prawns in closed-containment systems in the desert, is one of the more responsible producers. In general, large 'tiger' or 'white' prawns should be avoided. Among wild-caught prawns, northern shrimp, pink shrimp and spot prawn from the North Atlantic are good choices; populations are booming and bycatch has been significantly reduced. *Social and environmental impact. Bycatch. Antibiotics and other contaminants.* (2.6)

Saithe or coley. Saithe, which when smoked tastes a bit like lox, is an excellent alternative to cod or haddock. Still abundant in most of the Atlantic, but favour longline-caught saithe to trawled when it is available. *Trawled.* (4.4)

Salmon. Industrially farmed salmon (the market name is generally Atlantic salmon) is spreading sea-lice to wild stocks, contaminating coastal environments, and consuming stocks of wild fish in the form of feed. Its flesh can be very high in persistent organic pollutants. Favour sustainably fished wild Alaska salmon, often available in cans, particularly sockeye, coho and pink. At a pinch, organically farmed salmon is an acceptable occasional alternative to industrially farmed. *Antibiotics, PCBs, dioxins. Environmental impact.* (Sockeye, 3.7)

Scallops. Though Atlantic scallops (giant scallops) are not overfished, most are dredged, which damages the sea floor. British retailers are starting to sell dive-caught scallops, and some are now being sustainably farmed in European waters. *Dredged.* (2.0)

Scampi. Also known as Dublin Bay prawn, Norway lobster, langoustine or nephrops. Doing quite well in the absence of big predator fish, but insist on trap-caught, rather than trawled, scampi. *Trawled.* (2.6)

Snapper. Avoid overfished northern red snapper, currently listed as vulnerable by the World Conservation Union. The trap-caught red snapper fishery in Australia, however, is well managed. *Longlined. Mercury.* (Yellowtail snapper, 4.0)

Sole, Atlantic. Plaice, sole and other flatfish, which are fished on the Atlantic sea floor using trawls, are all in rough shape. Flatfish from the Pacific (including Dover and English sole) are not overfished. Stocks of Dover sole, also known as common sole, in the North Sea are considered healthy. *PCBs. Trawled.* (3.1)

Swordfish. Avoid imported swordfish, which tends to be caught with ill-regulated longlines; favour swordfish from North American waters. There is still a handline fishery for swordfish off the east coast of Florida, and a sustainable harpoon fishery for swordfish in Nova Scotia. One in five Canadian swordfish are caught by this method. Swordfish has very high levels of mercury. *Longlined. Mercury.* (4.5)

Tilapia. Native to the Nile, this bland-fleshed fish is fed vegetable protein, so farming it does not diminish the world's stock of animal protein. However, tilapia raised in Asia is treated with antibiotics, pesticides and carbon monoxide. Since males grow to market weight faster (females are ground into fishmeal), many tilapia are treated with a hormone called methyl testosterone to induce a sex change. Some supermarkets, including Waitrose, are now selling tilapia raised in the same ponds as organic prawns from Ecuador. In general, favour tilapia from the Americas rather than Asia. *Antibiotics and other contaminants.* (2.0)

Tuna. There are many kinds of tuna on the market, and almost all of them pose problems. The tuna that ends up in cans is often caught using longlines or FADs (see p. 362) that have high levels of bycatch. Much canned tuna is albacore, which is high in mercury. Canned skipjack is a better choice: skipjack are abundant and have less mercury. Bluefin tuna (see above) are endangered. Bigeye and yellowfin tuna populations are in decline, and most of them are caught with longlines. If you can be certain your bigeye or yellowfin is caught by a troller or hook and line, eat it in good conscience. Until the tinned tuna industry starts identifying the species they are selling, though, be very wary. *Bycatch. Mercury.* (Albacore, 4.3)

Turbot. Avoid this flatfish if it comes from the North Sea, where it is overfished. Favour farmed turbot, which tends to be raised in land-based closed-containment systems, particularly those sold under the French Label Rouge, which are raised at lower stocking densities. *Trawled.* (4.0)

ABSOLUTELY, ALWAYS

Halibut, Pacific. Stocks are currently at a 30-year high, and the bottom longline fishery in Alaska is MSC-certified. An excellent alternative to overfished Atlantic halibut. (4.1)

Herring. *Aka* kippers, rollmops, solomon gundy. Now mostly fished with midwater trawls, Atlantic herring stocks are in good shape. High in omega-3s, low in toxins. In 2006, North Sea herring was certified by the MSC as sustainably fished. (3.2)

Jellyfish. Eat 'em when you can find 'em; you'll be doing the oceans a favour. Featured in Asian cuisines in the form of often delicious salads and appetizers. (2.0)

Mackerel. Fast-maturing and prolific spawners, these tasty oily fleshed fish are becoming more popular with chefs. Favour Spanish mackerel from the Atlantic over the Gulf of Mexico, which tends to contain mercury. The MSC has certified Cornwall's handline fishery. (3.7)

Oysters, mussels. All but 5 per cent of the world's oysters are farmed (the rest are tonged or dredged). Mussels and oysters clean the oceans and reduce the size of dead zones, and are farmed without chemicals. (2.0)

Sablefish. Also sold as black cod (not to be mistaken for illegally fished 'black cod' of the Atlantic), this buttery fleshed Pacific fish is sustainably fished with bottom longlines and some stocks have been certified by the MSC. Some sablefish is now farmed. (3.8)

Sardines. Abundant, plankton-eating schooling fish, sardines are sustainably fished and full of omega-3s. Canned or grilled, they make excellent eating; aka sprats, brisling, pilchard. (2.6)

Squid. Squid, caught with trawls and hook and line, are not overfished, though their abundance can change with ocean conditions. For now, don't worry too much about ordering calamari. (3.4)

Trout. Some brown and sea trout stocks are overfished. Favour organically farmed rainbow trout. Like salmon, trout it is a carnivorous fish, but since it tends to be raised in inland ponds, there is little environmental impact. (4.4)

Whiting, Blue. Jump at any chance you get to eat the fish that are now wastefully ground into fishmeal. They include blue whiting, capelin, anchoveta and sand-eel. All tend to be low in contaminants, and are excellent battered and fried. (Blue whiting, 4.0)

Sources

Below is a chapter-by-chapter list of major books, articles and websites referred to in the text, or consulted during research. *IntraFish* and *SeaFood Business*, respectively the European and American trade publications of the seafood industry, were the source of countless articles, only some of which are included below. All website URLs listed are current as of January 2008.

INTRODUCTION

Braudel, Fernand. *The Structures of Everyday Life: Civilization and Capitalism*, vol. 1. Berkeley: University of California Press, 1992.

Douglas, Kate. 'Taking the Plunge.' *New Scientist*, 25 November 2000, 2828. An article on early man's aquatic origins and the role of omega-3 acids in hominid brain development.

Duncan, David Ewing. 'Pollution Within.' *National Geographic*, October 2006. An article on mercury and other environmental toxins.

Ellis, Richard. *Aquagenesis: The Origin and Evolution of Life in the Sea.* New York: Viking, 2001.

—— *The Empty Ocean.* Washington, DC: Shearwater, 2003.

'FAO: Booming Fish Trade Now Worth $71 Billion.' *IntraFish*, June 2006.

Gesch, B. 'Influence of Supplementary Vitamins, Minerals and Essential Fatty Acids on the Antisocial Behaviour of Young Adult Prisoners.' *The British Journal of Psychiatry* 181 (2002), 22–8.

Hayden, Thomas. 'Trashing the Oceans.' *U.S. News & World Report*, 4 November 2002.

Hibbeln, Joseph R. 'Fish Consumption and Major Depression.' *Lancet* 351 (1998), 1213.

Hites, Ronald A., et al. 'Global Assessment of Organic Contaminants in Farmed Salmon.' *Science* 303 (2004), 226–9.

'Import Alert: Government Fails Consumers, Falls Short on Seafood Inspections.' *Food & Water Watch*, 2006; www.foodandwaterwatch. org/press/publications.

Kolbert, Elizabeth. 'The Darkening Sea: Carbon Emissions and the Ocean.' *New Yorker*, 20 November 2006.

Mergler, Donna, et al. 'Methylmercury Exposure and Health Effects in Humans: A Worldwide Concern.' *Ambio* [Royal Swedish Academy of Sciences] 36 (2007), 3–11.

Moore, Charles. 'Trashed: Across the Pacific Ocean, Plastics, Plastics, Everywhere.' *Natural History* 112 (2003).

Myers, Ransom. 'Rapid Worldwide Depletion of Predatory Fish Communities.' *Nature* 423 (2003), 280–3.

'The Omega Point: Diet and the Unborn Child.' *Economist*, 21 January 2006.

Rahmstorf, Stefan. 'The Future Oceans – Warming Up, Rising High, Turning Sour.' Potsdam Institute for Research into Climatic Effects, 2006.

Spotts, Peter. 'Climate Change Brews Ocean Trouble.' *Christian Science Monitor*, 8 March 2007, 13.

Squires, Sally. 'The Omega Principle.' *Washington Post*, 19 August 2003.

Woodard, Colin. *Ocean's End: Travels through Endangered Seas.* New York: Basic, 2000.

Worm, Boris, et al. 'Impacts of Biodiversity Loss on Ocean Ecosystem Services.' *Science* 314 (2006), 787–90. Paper projecting collapse of fisheries by 2048.

1: THE RISE OF THE GOBLIN

Broad, William J. *The Universe Below: Discovering the Secrets of the Deep Sea.* New York: Simon & Schuster, 1998.

Chuenpagdee, Ratana et al. 'Shifting Gears: Assessing Collateral Impacts of Fishing Methods in U.S. Waters.' *Frontiers in Ecology* 1 (2003), 517–24. Paper ranking the impact of various types of fishing gear.

Clover, Charles. 'Dealing with the Big Fish.' In *The End of the Line.* New York: New Press, 2006, 183–97.

DiGiacomo, Frank. 'To Live and Dine in N.Y.' *New York Observer*, 26 March 2001, 15. Portrait of chef Jean-Louis Palladin.

Goad, Meredith. 'Rod Mitchell and His Browne of Renown.' *Portland Press Herald* [Maine], 29 March 2006.

Graddy, Kathryn. 'Markets: The Fulton Fish Market.' *Journal of Economic Perspectives* 20 (2006), 221–36.

Greenlaw, Linda. *The Hungry Ocean.* New York: Hyperion, 1997.

Hamilton-Paterson, James. 'Troubled Waters.' *Guardian*, 28 March 2002, 4. An in-depth article on high-seas trawling.

Hedlund, Steven. 'Swindling on the Rise.' *SeaFood Business*, June 2005.

Hesser, Amanda. 'A Cod's Swift Journey from Sea to Plate.' *New York Times*, 4 March 1998. Article about Rod Mitchell's Browne Trading in Portland, Maine.

'High Seas Bottom Trawl Red Herrings: Debunking Claims of Sustainability.' Marine Conservation Biology Institute, 2005; www.mcbi.org/ publications/publications.htm.

Knecht, G. Bruce. *Hooked: Pirates, Poaching and the Perfect Fish.* New York: Rodale, 2006. Exposé on the pirate fishery for Chilean sea bass.

—— 'Restaurants: The Raw Truth.' *Wall Street Journal*, 25 March 2006,

Koslow, Tony. *The Silent Deep: The Discovery, Ecology, and Conservation of the Deep Sea.* Chicago: University of Chicago Press, 2007.

Matsuhisa, Nobuyuki. *Nobu: The Cookbook.* New York: Kodansha, 2001.

'Monkfish.' *SeaFood Business*, November 2003.

'Monkfish Assessment Summary for 2007.' *Northeast Fisheries*

Science Center Reference Document 07–13; www.nefsc.noaa.gov/nefsc/publications.

Pasternack, David and Ed Levine. *The Young Man & the Sea: Recipes & Crispy Fish Tales from Esca.* New York: Artisan, 2007.

Playfair, Susan R. *Vanishing Species: Saving the Fish, Sacrificing the Fisherman.* University Press of New England, 2005.

Singer, Mark. 'Gone Fishing: The Chef Who Catches Your Dinner.' *New Yorker,* 5 September 2005. A profile of Esca's David Pasternack.

Stevens, Melissa M. 'Goosefish/Monkfish.' *Seafood Watch Seafood Report.* Updated 6 June 2007; www.montereybayaquarium.org.

Tourondel, Laurent. *Go Fish: Fresh Ideas for American Seafood.* Hoboken, NJ: Wiley, 2004.

Waddell, Lynn. 'That Grouper on the Menu? Turns Out It Was a Fish Tale.' *New York Times,* 27 May 2007.

Weber, Michael L. *From Abundance to Scarcity: A History of U.S. Marine Fisheries Policy.* Washington, DC: Island, 2006.

2: IN THE KINGDOM OF THE OYSTERS

Brooks, William K. *The Oyster.* Baltimore: Johns Hopkins University Press, 1996.

Clark, Eleanor. *The Oysters of Locmariaquer.* Chicago: University of Chicago Press, 1964.

Crawford, Gary D. *Tilghman's Island: An Exploration.* Tilghman Island: Crawfords Nautical Books, 1992.

de la Casinière, Nicolas. *L'Huître.* Geneva: Aubanel, 2005.

Ernst, Howard R. *Chesapeake Bay Blues: Science, Politics and the Struggle to Save the Bay.* Lanham, Md: Rowman & Littlefield, 2003.

Fincham, Michael W. 'The Frenzy over Pfiesteria.' *Chesapeake Quarterly* 6, no. 1 (2007).

—— 'Invasion of the Chesapeake Bay.' *Chesapeake Quarterly* 5, no. 2 (2006). Article on how ships brought oyster parasites to the Chesapeake.

—— 'Saving Oysters . . . and Oystermen.' *Chesapeake Quarterly* 5, no. 1 (2006). Article on last skipjacks in the Chesapeake.

Fisher, M. F. K. *Consider the Oyster.* New York: North Point Press, 1988.

Franklin, H. Bruce. *The Most Important Fish in the Sea: Menhaden and America*. Washington, DC: Island, 2007.

Horton, Tom and William M. Eichbaum. *Turning the Tide: Saving the Chesapeake Bay*. Washington, DC: Island, 1991.

Kurlansky, Mark. *The Big Oyster: History on the Half Shell*. New York: Ballantine, 2006.

Lotze, Heike K., et al. 'Depletion, Degradation, and Recovery Potential of Estuaries and Coastal Seas.' *Science* 312 (2006), 1806–9.

Luckenbach, Mark. *An Introduction to Culturing Oysters in Virginia*. Williamsburg: Virginia Institute of Marine Science, 1999; www.vims.edu/oystergarden/CulturingOysters.

—— *Oyster Reef Habitat Restoration*. Williamsburg: VIMS Press, 1999.

'Microalgues toxiques,' *Cultures marines* 196 (2006), 4–7.

Neveu, Denise. *Les Huîtres: L'ostréiculteur et l'écailler*. Seyssinet: Libris, 2001.

Newell, Roger I. E. 'Ecological Changes in the Chesapeake Bay: Are They the Result of Overharvesting the American Oyster?' Chesapeake Research Consortium Publication 129 (March 1988).

Perrier, Jean-Louis. 'La Bélon du Bélon.' *Le Monde*, 9 February 1991.

Roberts, Callum. 'Slow Death of an Estuary: Chesapeake Bay.' In id., *The Unnatural History of the Sea*. Washington, DC: Island, 2007.

Schrope, Mark. 'The Dead Zones: When the Ocean's Inhabitants Try to Escape, You Know There's a Problem.' *New Scientist*, 9 December 2006, 38–42.

Warner, William W. *Beautiful Swimmers: Watermen, Crabs and the Chesapeake Bay*. New York: Little, Brown & Co., 1977.

3: PANIC AT THE CHIPPY

Excellent resources on illegal, unregulated and unreported fishing can be found online, among them www.illegal-fishing.info and blacklist.greenpeace.org; the latter contains images of many of the world's known pirate vessels.

Burkeman, Oliver. 'My Plaice or Yours?' *Guardian*, 17 May 2001. Article on regional variations in fish-and-chip shop slang.

Cherry, Drew. 'WWF Sues EU over Cod Quotas.' *IntraFish*, 20 March 2007.

Davidson, Alan. *North Atlantic Seafood: A Comprehensive Guide with Recipes.* Berkeley, Calif.: Ten Speed Press, 2003.

Frank, Kenneth T., et al. 'Trophic Cascades in a Formerly Cod-Dominated Ecosystem.' *Science* 308 (2005), 1621.

Frank, Peter. *Yorkshire Fisherfolk: A Social History of the Yorkshire Inshore Fishing Community.* Trowbridge: Cromwell Press, 2002.

Hardin, Garrett. 'The Tragedy of the Commons.' *Science* 162 (1968), 1243–8.

Kalentchenko, Mikhail. 'Analysis of Illegal Fishery for Cod in the Barents Sea,' *WWF-Russia and WWF Barents Sea Program*, April 2005; www.illegal-fishing.info.

Kurlansky, Mark. *Cod: A Biography of the Fish That Changed the World.* Toronto: Vintage, 1998.

Leigh, David. 'Marine Threat: Cod Sold in Hundreds of Chippies Linked to Russian Black Market.' *Guardian*, 20 February 2006, 15.

'Net Closed on Whitby Trawler Men.' *BBC News*, 1 December 2005; news.bbc.co.uk.

O'Hanlon, Redmond. *Trawler: A Journey Through the North Atlantic.* London: Penguin, 2004.

Pauly, Daniel and Jay Maclean. *In a Perfect Ocean: The State of Fisheries and Ecosystems in the North Atlantic Ocean.* Washington, DC: Island, 2003.

Roberts, Callum. 'The First Trawling Revolution.' In id., *The Unnatural History of the Sea.* Washington, DC: Island, 2007.

Smith, Lewis. 'How the Fish on Your Plate Makes You an Accessory to Crime at Sea.' *The Times* [London], 21 June 2006.

Walton, John K. *Fish & Chips & the British Working Class, 1870–1940.* Leicester: Leicester University Press, 1992. Essential book on the birth of the chip-shop trade.

4: SMALL POND

The ongoing spread of the invasive species *Caulerpa taxifolia* and *Caulerpa racemosa* is being mapped at www.caulerpa.org. The global database www.issg.org offers a list of the world's hundred worst invasive species.

Boudouresque, Charles F. 'Nature Conservation, Marine Protected Areas, Sustainable Development and the Flow of Invasive Species to the Mediterranean Sea.' *Science Reports of Port-Cros National Park, France* 21 (2005), 29–54.

Burdick, Alan. *Out of Eden: An Odyssey of Ecological Invasion.* New York: Farrar, Straus & Giroux, 2005.

Clark, R. B. *Marine Pollution.* Oxford: Oxford University Press, 2001.

Davidson, Alan. *Mediterranean Seafood: A Comprehensive Guide with Recipes.* Berkeley, Calif.: Ten Speed Press, 2002.

Dupuy, Jacques. 'Le Poisson dans la cuisine populaire marseillaise.' *Revue Marseille* 202 (2003), 120–5.

Dupuy, Jacques and Jo Harmelin. *Le Peuple de la mer: Pêcheurs et poissons dans le pays de Marseille.* Marseilles: Ed. Jeanne Laffitte, 2000.

Echinard, Pierre. 'Une bonne bouillabaisse.' *Revue Marseille* 202 (2003), 116–19.

Fisher, M. F. K. 'A Considerable Town.' *Two Towns in Provence.* New York: Vintage, 1983.

Galgani, F. 'Distribution and Abundance of Debris on the Continental Shelf of the North-Western Mediterranean Sea.' *Marine Pollution Bulletin* 30 (1995), 713–17.

Hansson, Hans G. 'Ctenophores of the Baltic and Adjacent Seas – The Invader *Mnemiopsis* is Here!' *Aquatic Invasions* 1 (2006), 295–8.

Liebling, A. J. 'The Soul of Bouillabaisse.' *New Yorker,* 27 October 1962, 189–202.

Lleonart, Jordi. 'Fish Stock Assessments in the Mediterranean: State of the Art.' *Scientia Marina* 67 (2002), 37–49.

Meinesz, Alexandre. *Killer Algae: The True Tale of Biological Invasion.* Chicago: University of Chicago Press, 1999.

Ruitton, Sandrine. 'First Assessment of the *Caulerpa racemosa* Invasion along the French Mediterranean Coast.' *Marine Pollution Bulletin* 50 (2005), 1061–8.

Schwabe, Calvin W. *Unmentionable Cuisine.* University Press of Virginia, 1979.

Streftaris, Nikos. 'Globalisation in Marine Ecosystems: The Story of

Non-Indigenous Marine Species across European Seas.' *Oceanography and Marine Biology: An Annual Review* 43 (2005), 419–53.

Theroux, Paul. *The Pillars of Hercules: A Grand Tour of the Mediterranean.* New York: Fawcett, 1995.

5: 'FISH SHE IS VERY SMALL'

Essential information on catches of sardines and other Atlantic species is available at www.ices.dk/fish/statlant.asp, the website of the International Council for the Exploration of the Sea.

Alder, Jackie and Daniel Pauly. 'On the Multiple Uses of Forage Fish: From Ecosystems to Markets.' Fisheries Centre Research Reports [University of British Columbia] 14 (2006).

Anginot, Philippe. *La Sardine: de la mer à la boite.* Seyssinet: Libris, 2002.

Bakun, Andrew. *Patterns in the Ocean: Ocean Processes and Marine Population Dynamics.* La Jolla: University of California Sea Grant, 1996.

Borges, M. F. 'Sardine Regime Shifts off Portugal: A Time Series Analysis of Catches and Wind Conditions.' *Scientia Marina* 67 (2002), 215–44.

Chavez, Francisco P. 'From Anchovies to Sardines and Back – Multi-decadal Change in the Pacific Ocean.' *Geophysical Research Abstracts* 5 (2003).

'Codex Standard for Canned Sardines and Sardine-Type Products,' Codex Stan 94; www.codexalimentarius.net/download/standards/108/CXS_094e.pdf.

Cury, Philippe, et al. 'The Functioning of Marine Ecosystems.' In *Responsible Fisheries in the Marine Ecosystem.* Wallingford: CAB International, 2003. A good introduction to the mechanisms of coastal upwelling.

'Fishery Statistics: Data 1990–2005.' European Commission, 2006; epp.eurostat.ec.europa.eu.

Franklin, H. Bruce. *The Most Important Fish in the Sea: Menhaden and America.* Washington, DC: Island, 2007.

McGee, Harold. *On Food and Cooking: The Science and Lore of the Kitchen.* New York: Scribner, 2004.

Molyneaux, Paul. *Swimming in Circles: Aquaculture and the End of Wild Oceans.* New York: Avalon, 2007.

Steinbeck, John. *Cannery Row.* New York: Penguin, 1994.

Sumaila, U. R., Y. Liu and P. Tyedmers. 'Small Versus Large-Scale Fishing Operations in the North Atlantic.' *Fisheries Centre Research Reports* (University of British Columbia) 9 (2001), 28–35.

Wyatt, Tim and Carmela Porteiro. 'Iberian Sardine Fisheries: Trends and Crises.' In *Large Marine Ecosystems of the North Atlantic: Changing States and Sustainability.* Amsterdam: Elsevier, 2002.

6: WAVE OF MUTILATION

'After the Tsunami: Human Rights of Vulnerable Populations.' Berkeley, Calif.: University of California Press, 2005.

Anand, S. 'The Big Churn.' *Outlook Magazine,* 30 December 2004.

'Aquaculture: Changing the Face of the Waters.' *World Bank Report* (36622); siteresources.worldbank.org.

'Cultured Prawns.' *Time,* 29 March 1963.

'Darden Goes for Aquaculture Certification, but US Shrimper Does Not Go for Darden.' *Quick Frozen Foods International,* April 2006.

Duran, G. M., et al. 'Ready-to-Eat Shrimp as an International Vehicle of Antibiotic-resistant Bacteria.' *Journal of Food Protection* 68 (2005), 2395.

'Easy Riches through "Gravid" Smuggling.' *Statesman* [India], 21 August 2006.

'FDA's Imported Seafood Safety Program Shows Some Progress, but Further Improvements Are Needed.' United States General Accounting Office, GAO-04-246 (2004).

Goss, Jasper. 'Fields of Inequality.' Thesis on shrimp farming, submitted to Griffith University, Brisbane, Australia, 2002.

Holmström, Katrin, et al. 'Antibiotic Use in Shrimp Farming and Implications for Environmental Impacts and Human Health.' *International Journal of Food Science and Technology* 38 (2003), 259.

'In the Matter of Certain Frozen or Canned Warmwater Shrimp.' U.S. International Trade Commission, Investigation No. 731-TA-1063-1068 (2004).

Kolappan, B. 'Kottilpadu, a Fishing Hamlet in Colachel, Is Deserted Now.' *Indian Express*, 3 January 2005.

Krishnakumar, R. 'An Encounter at Kanyakumari.' *Frontline*, 28 January 2005.

'Mangroves of India: State-of-the-Art Report.' Environmental Information System Centre, Ministry of Environment & Forests, New Delhi (2002).

Molyneaux, Paul. *Swimming in Circles: Aquaculture and the End of Wild Oceans*. New York: Avalon, 2007.

Naylor, R., et al. 'Effect of Aquaculture on World Fish Supplies.' *Nature* 405 (2000), 1017–24.

'A New Way to Feed the World.' *Economist*, 9 August 2003.

Nishchith, V. D. 'Role and Status of Women Employed in Seafood Processing in India.' Manila: Proceedings of International Symposium on Women in Asian Fisheries, 2001.

Oswin, S. D. 'Biodiversity of the Muthupet Mangroves.' *Seshaiyana* 6 (1998), 9–11.

'Patience Pays Off for Thai Family Business.' *South China Morning Post*, 20 September 2005.

Petit, Charles W. 'Denizens of the Deep.' *U.S. News & World Report*, 16 August 2004.

Reville, Cara, et al. 'White Spot Syndrome Virus in Frozen Shrimp Sold at Massachusetts Supermarkets.' *Journal of Shellfish Research* 24 (2005), 285–90.

Roberts, Callum. 'The Legacy of Whaling.' In id., *The Unnatural History of the Sea*. Washington, DC: Island, 2007.

Shanahan, Mike, et. al. *Smash and Grab: Conflict, Corruption, & Human Rights Abuses in the Shrimp Farming Industry*. London: Environmental Justice Foundation, 2003. www.ejfoundation.org.

Shiva, Vandana. *Stolen Harvest: The Hijacking of the Global Food Supply*. Cambridge, Mass.: South End Press, 2000.

'Suspicious Shrimp: The Health Risks of Industrialized Shrimp Production.' Food and Water Watch, 2006. www.foodandwaterwatch. org/fish/pubs/suspicious-shrimp.

Vandergeest, P. 'Certification and Communities: Alternatives for Regulating the Environmental and Social Impacts of Shrimp Farming.' *World Development* 35 (2007), 1152–71.

Vidal, John. 'How the Mangrove Shield Was Lost.' *Guardian*, 6 January 2005.

7: BUDDHA JUMP OVER THE WALL

Trophic numbers of fish species were taken from fishbase.org and seaaroundus.org.

Baum, Julia K. 'Collapse and Conservation of Shark Populations in the Northwest Atlantic.' *Science* 299 (2003), 389–92.

'China's Seafood Market.' In *Mapping Global Fisheries and Seafood Sectors*. Los Altos, Calif.: David and Lucile Packard Foundation, 2007.

Clarke, Shelley C. 'Global Estimates of Shark Catches Using Trade Records from Commercial Markets.' *Ecology Letters* 9 (2006), 1115–26.

Davidson, Alan. *A Kipper with My Tea: Selected Food Essays*. London: Macmillan, 1990.

Environmental Justice Foundation. *Pirates & Profiteers: How Pirate Fishing Fleets Are Robbing People and Oceans*. London: EJF, 2005.

Flannery, Tim. *The Weather Makers*. New York: HarperCollins, 2007.

Hopkins, Jerry. *Extreme Cuisine: The Weird and Wonderful Foods That People Eat*. Singapore: Periplus, 2004.

Jakes, Susan. 'China's Water Woes.' *Time* [Asia Edition], 9 October 2006.

'Japan Must Fight Giant Jellyfish Invasion.' *Daily Yomiuri* [Tokyo], 25 June 2006.

Lichfield, John. 'Saving the World's Rarest Shellfish.' *Independent* [London], 12 December 2005.

Mann, Charles C. 'The Rise of Big Water.' *Vanity Fair*, May 2007. An article on water pollution and the privatization of water resources in China.

Murray, G. and I. G. *The Greening of China*. Beijing: China Intercontinental Press, 2004.

Musick, John A. *The Shark Chronicles: A Scientist Tracks the Consummate Predator*. New York: Henry Holt, 2002.

Myers, Ransom A., et al. 'Cascading Effects of the Loss of Apex Predatory Sharks from a Coastal Ocean.' *Science* 315 (2007), 1846–50.

Pearce, Fred. 'A Greyer Shade of Green.' *New Scientist*, 21 June 2003. Good background on cyanide fishing in Asian seas.

Safina, Carl. *Song for the Blue Ocean.* New York: Henry Holt, 1997.

Shapiro, Judith. *Mao's War against Nature: Politics and the Environment in Revolutionary China.* Cambridge: Cambridge University Press, 2001.

Spaeth, Anthony. 'China's Toxic Shock.' *Time*, 27 November 2005.

Vallely, Paul. 'Invasion of the Jellyfish.' *Independent* [London], 12 August 2006.

Watson, R., et al. *The Marine Fisheries of China: Development and Reported Catches.* UBC Fisheries Centre Research Reports 9 (2001).

Wright, James. 'China Tips the Scales.' *SeaFood Business*, June 2006.

8: SORRY, CHARLIE

Bestor, Theodore C. *Tsukiji: The Fish Market at the Center of the World.* Berkeley and Los Angeles: University of California Press, 2004.

'A Bloody War – Whaling.' *Economist*, 3 January 2004.

Bourdain, Anthony. *The Nasty Bits.* New York: Bloomsbury, 2006.

Bowring, Richard. *The Cambridge Encyclopedia of Japan.* Cambridge: Cambridge University Press, 1993.

Corson, Trevor. *The Zen of Fish: The Story of Sushi from Samurai to Supermarket.* New York: HarperCollins, 2007.

Fackler, Martin. 'Waiter, There's Deer in My Sushi.' *New York Times*, 25 June 2007.

Glavin, Terry. 'Drifting into the Maelstrom.' In *Waiting for the Macaws and Other Stories from the Age of Extinctions.* Toronto: Viking, 2006. Excellent chapter on whaling.

'Global Whaling Debate Set to Turn Very Nasty.' *Japan Times*, 30 May 2006.

Hashimoto, Mitsuo. *Tsukiji Uogashi Sandaime.* Tokyo: Big Comics, 2007. Manga about fish dealers at Tsukiji Market.

Hemingway, Ernest. 'Tuna Fishing in Spain.' *Toronto Star Weekly*, 18 February 1922.

Hosking, Richard. *A Dictionary of Japanese Food.* Hong Kong: Periplus, 1995.

Issenberg, Sasha. *The Sushi Economy: Globalization and the Making of a Modern Delicacy.* New York: Gotham, 2007.

'Japan Targets Sanctions at Kim Jong-il's Stomach.' *Chosun Ilbo*, 8 November 2006.

'The Japanese Seafood Market.' In *Mapping Global Fisheries and Seafood Sectors*. Los Altos, Calif.: David and Lucile Packard Foundation, 2007.

Kerr, Alex. *Dogs and Demons: The Fall of Modern Japan*. London: Penguin, 2001.

McCurry, Justin. 'The Shadow of Slaughter Hangs over Whales.' *Observer*, 11 June 2006.

Nakamura, David. 'The Deadly Blowfish: Last Meal in Tokyo?' *Washington Post*, 30 July 2006.

Nakamura, Naoto. 'To Be a Good Fish Dealer in Japan.' 1995. homepage3.nifty.com/tokyoworks/English/FishDealer/Contents.html. Diverting life story of one of my guides to Tsukiji Market.

Naomichi, Ishige. 'Another Perspective on Japanese Cultural History.' *Nipponia* 36 (2006). Article on whale- and fish-eating in Japanese history.

Onishi, Norimitsu. 'Farming Bluefin Tuna, through Thick Stocks and Thin.' *New York Times*, 26 September 2006.

Parsons, E. C. M. 'It's Not Just Poor Science – Japan's "Scientific" Whaling May Be a Human Health Risk Too.' *Marine Pollution Bulletin* 52 (2005), 1118–20.

Popham, Peter. 'The World Sushi Trade: An Appetite for Disaster.' *Independent* [London], 27 May 2005.

Reid, T. R. 'The Great Tokyo Fish Market.' *National Geographic*, November 1995.

Renton, Alex. 'One In Ten Fish is Eaten in Japan.' *Observer Food Monthly*, 10 April 2005.

—— 'How Sushi Ate the World.' *Observer*, 26 February 2006.

Richie, Donald. *A Taste of Japan*. Markham: Fitzhenry & Whiteside, 1985.

Safina, Carl. *Song for the Blue Ocean*. New York: Henry Holt, 1997.

Steingarten, Jeffrey. 'Toro, Toro, Toro.' In *It Must've Been Something I Ate*. New York: Vintage, 2002.

Storelli, M. M. 'Accumulation of Mercury, Cadmium, Lead and Arsenic in Swordfish and Bluefin Tuna from the Mediterranean Sea.' *Marine Pollution Bulletin* 50 (2005), 993–1018.

Tanamura, Tyoo. *Rotary Sushi Around the World*. Tokyo: Sekaibunkasha, 2000.

Tosches, Nick. 'If You Knew Sushi.' *Vanity Fair*, June 2007. Article on Tsukiji Market and sushi in America.

'Tuna Blues: Why Isn't Anyone Listening to Dr. Barbara Block?' *Salt Water Sportsman*, 20 February 2006.

'Who Took All the Fish?' *New Scientist*, 15 May 2004. Article on competition between humans and marine mammals for fish.

Whynott, Douglas. *Giant Bluefin*. New York: North Point Press, 1996.

9: AN ECONOMY OF SCALES

Much background on salmon farms in British Columbia was taken from the extensive testimony given to the Special Committee on Sustainable Aquaculture, available online at www.leg.bc.ca/cmt/38thparl/session-1/aquaculture/index.htm.

Bureau, Dominique P. 'Rendered Products in Fish Aquaculture Feeds.' In D. Meeker, ed., *Essential Rendering*. National Renderers Association, 2006.

Cabello, Felipe C. 'Salmon Aquaculture and Transmission of the Fish Tapeworm.' *Emerging Infectious Diseases* 13 (2007), 169–71.

Cox, Sarah K. 'Diminishing Returns: An Investigation into the Five Multinational Corporations That Control B.C.'s Salmon Farming Industry.' Raincoast, 2004.

Curtis, Clifton. 'Tiny, Innumerable, Threatened.' *International Herald Tribune*, 15 September 2006. Article on harvesting of krill in the Antarctic.

Dean, Rebecca J., et al. 'Copper, Zinc and Cadmium in Marine Cage Fish Farm Sediments: An Extensive Survey.' *Environmental Pollution* 145 (2007), 84–95.

Fishman, Charles. *The Wal-Mart Effect*. New York: Penguin, 2006.

Glavin, Terry. *The Last Great Sea: A Voyage through the Human and Natural History of the North Pacific Ocean*. Vancouver: Greystone, 2003.

Hites, Ronald A., et al. 'Global Assessment of Organic Contaminants in Farmed Salmon.' *Science* 303 (2004), 226–9.

Huang, X., et al. 'Consumption Advisories for Salmon Based on Risk of Cancer and Noncancer Health Effects.' *Environmental Research* 101 (2006), 263–74.

Krkosek, Martin, et al. 'Epizootics of Wild Fish Induced by Farm Fish.' *Proceedings of the National Academy of Sciences of the USA* 103 (2006), 15506–10.

Lockwood, George. 'The Evolution of Aquaculture.' *Aquaculture Magazine*, September 2006.

Molyneaux, Paul. 'Betting the Farm? Ocean Aquaculture Won't be Exempt from the Law of Diminishing Returns, Skeptics Say.' *National Fisherman*, December 2005.

—— *Swimming in Circles: Aquaculture and the End of Wild Oceans*. New York: Avalon, 2007.

Montaigne, Fen. 'Everybody Loves Atlantic Salmon: Here's the Catch ...' *National Geographic*, July 2003.

Montgomery, David R. *King of Fish: The Thousand-Year Run of Salmon*. Cambridge, Mass.: Westview, 2004.

Morton, Alexandra, et al. *A Stain Upon the Sea: West Coast Salmon Farming*. Madeira Park, BC: Harbour, 2004.

Morton, Alexandra and Billy Proctor. *Heart of the Raincoast: A Life Story*. Victoria, BC: TouchWood, 2001.

Morton, Alexandra and John Volpe. 'A Description of Escaped Farm Atlantic Salmon *Salmo salar* Captures.' *Alaska Fishery Research Bulletin* 9 (2002), 102–10.

Naylor, R., et al. 'Fugitive Salmon: Assessing the Risks of Escaped Fish from Net-Pen Aquaculture.' *Bioscience* 55 (2005), 427–37.

Nestle, Marion. *Safe Food: Bacteria, Biotechnology, and Bioterrorism*. Berkeley and Los Angeles: University of California Press, 2004.

—— 'The Fish Counter.' In *What to Eat*. New York: Farrar, Straus & Giroux, 2006.

Robson, Peter A. *Salmon Farming: The Whole Story*. Surrey, Canada: Heritage House, 2006.

'The Salmon Scam: "Wild" Often Isn't.' *Consumer Reports*, August 2006.

Volpe, John. '"Salmon Sovereignty" and the Dilemma of Intensive Atlantic Salmon Aquaculture Development in British Columbia.' In C. C. Parrish, ed., *Resetting the Kitchen Table*. New York: Nova Science, 2007.

Whiteley, Don. '"Green Monster" Adds Sci-Fi Touch to Fight.' *Vancouver Sun*, 6 July 2005.

Wright, James. 'Merge Ahead.' *SeaFood Business*, September 2006.

10: FAST FISH, SLOW FISH; CONCLUSION

Carey, R. A. *Against the Tide: The Fate of the New England Fisherman.*
New York: Mariner, 2000.

Chuenpagdee, R. and D. Pauly. 'Slow Fish: Creating New Metaphors for
Sustainability.' In *FAO Fisheries Report* No. 782 (2005).

Clark, C. W., G. Munro and U. R. Sumaila. 'Subsidies, Buybacks and
Sustainable Fisheries.' *Journal of Environmental Economics and Management* 50 (2005), 47–58.

Clover, Charles. 'Don't Feed the Fish.' In *The End of the Line.* New York:
New Press, 2006.

Gudgeon, Chris. *Consider the Fish: Fishing for Canada from Campbell
River to Petty Harbour.* Toronto: Penguin, 1998.

Harrington, J. M., et al. 'Wasted Fisheries Resources: Discarded By-catch
in the USA.' *Fish and Fisheries* 6 (2005), 350–61.

Jacquet, J. L. and D. Pauly. 'The Rise of Seafood Awareness Campaigns
in an Era of Collapsing Fisheries.' *Marine Policy* 31 (2006), 308–13.

Millman, Lawrence. *Last Places: A Journey in the North.* New York:
Mariner, 1990.

Muir, Allan T. 'The National Sea Products Story.' *Canadian Fisherman*
(1963).

Shackell, N. L. and Martin Willison. *Marine Protected Areas and Sustainable Fisheries.* Wolfville, NS: SMPAA, 1995.

Warne, Kennedy. 'Blue Haven.' *National Geographic,* April 2007. Article
on marine reserves in New Zealand.

Weber, Michael L. *From Abundance to Scarcity: A History of U.S. Marine
Fisheries Policy.* Washington, DC: Island, 2006.

Worm, Boris, et al. 'Global Patterns of Predator Diversity in the Open
Oceans.' *Science* 309 (2005), 1365–9.

— 'Impacts of Biodiversity Loss on Ocean Ecosystem Services.' *Science*
314 (2006), 787–90. Paper projecting collapse of fisheries by 2048.

Further Reading

Baldwin, Carole C. and Julie H. Mounts. *One Fish, Two Fish, Crawfish,
Bluefish: The Smithsonian Sustainable Seafood Cookbook.* Washington,
DC: Smithsonian, 2003.

Carson, Rachel. *The Sea Around Us*. New York: Signet, 1961.

Chuenpagdee, Ratana, et al. 'Shifting Gears: Assessing Collateral Impacts of Fishing Methods in US Waters.' *Frontiers in Ecology* 1 (2003), 517–24. Paper ranking the impact of various types of fishing gear.

Clover, Charles. *The End of the Line*. New York: New Press, 2006.

Corson, Trevor. *The Secret Life of Lobsters: How Fishermen and Scientists are Unraveling the Mysteries of Our Favorite Crustacean*. New York: HarperCollins, 2005.

Davidson, Alan. *Seafood of Southeast Asia: A Comprehensive Guide with Recipes*. Berkeley, Calif.: Ten Speed Press, 2004. Like all of Davidson's seafood guides, essential.

McPhee, John. *The Founding Fish*. New York: Farrar, Straus & Giroux, 2003. The story of American shad.

Pauly, Daniel and Jay Maclean. *In a Perfect Ocean: The State of Fisheries and Ecosystems in the North Atlantic Ocean*. Washington DC: Island, 2003.

Roberts, Callum. *The Unnatural History of the Sea*. Washington, DC: Island, 2007. An instant classic that shows just how far the oceanic baselines have shifted.

Warner, William W. *Distant Water: The Fate of the North Atlantic Fisherman*. New York: Little, Brown & Co., 1983.

Wells, Martin. *Civilization and the Limpet*. Reading, Mass.: Perseus, 1998. Fascinating book by a physiologist on why sea creatures look and act like they do.

ACKNOWLEDGEMENTS

Dead Seas began on the deck of a fishing boat stranded in the Rocky Mountains. I'd like to thank the captain of that vessel, Thomas Hayden of Saskatoon, who shared with me what he had seen on the seas, then encouraged me to set off in my own direction.

My learning curve on this book was steep. Boris Worm and Heike Lotze, Martin Willison, Daniel Pauly and the team at the University of British Columbia Fisheries Centre gave me a crash course in some of the major issues facing the oceans. Special thanks go to Mary Turnipseed in New York and Emmett Duffy in Virginia for their expert commentary.

Many other people were generous with both their time and knowledge. Among them were Sergi Tudela and Bénoît Guérin of the WWF; Harekrishna Debnath, Vandana Shiva, Nimmy Paul, R. Kumar and the team at SNEHA in India; Laura Harnish of Hubbards; Richard Hosking in Japan; Tim Wyatt in Vigo; Steve Romaine and Wilfram Swartz in British Columbia; Billy Proctor in the Broughton Archipelago; Donald M. Anderson of Woods Hole; Carl Safina of the Blue Ocean Institute; and Erich Hoyt of the Whale and Dolphin Conservation Society. Zat Liu and Crystyl Mo generously introduced me to Shanghainese dining. Yumi Terashima and Warren Thayer provided sterling interpreting services in Tokyo; special thanks to Katsundo Kaneko for being a gracious host at the Pufferfish Memorial Service. Robert Izdepski of Sub Ocean Safety provided passionate commentary on the plight of spiny-lobster divers in Central America. And to Lyn Rae and Hillary Butler, *gratias vobis ago.*

I am grateful for the graciousness of those who made the long months of travel a pleasure: Di Bligh in London, Toffler Neimuth in Shanghai, Theo Lamb in Tsawwassen, Alexandra Limiati and Guillaume

Blanchaud in Paris, and Jennifer Menard in Tokyo. *Mille mercis* to Scott Chernoff, for his insight into Japanese culture, astute commentary, and timely headlines. Special thanks, as always, to Paul Grescoe for his unfailing support, dozen close readings and a thousand well-placed dashes.

The encouragement, support and expert advice of my editors – Colin Dickerman and Kathy Belden in New York, Jim Gifford in Toronto and Lorraine Baxter in London – made *Dead Seas* a reality, as did the sharp eyes of Janet Biehl and Greg Villepique. Kudos and gratitude to my agent, Michelle Tessler, for her ceaseless energy (not to mention her courage in facing a plate of Grand Central Oyster Bar shellfish).

And big thanks to all the fishermen who were patient enough to answer all the questions from an importunate deckhand.

I couldn't have written this book without the help of Audrey Grescoe, aka the spotted retriever, whose professionalism, alacrity and intelligence in researching and summarizing extremely complex issues constantly astonished me. She was dogged when necessary and brilliant in all the right places. Arf, arf, indeed.

Finally, I thank Erin Churchill, who spent far too many hours transcribing, and wittily annotating, interviews for this errant sea wizard. Her patience and encouragement sustained and strengthened me every day. Without her love and faith, *Dead Seas* would never have been written.

Visit **www.panmacmillan.com** to read more about all our books and to buy them. You will also find features, author interviews and news of any author events, and you can sign up for e-newsletters so that you're always first to hear about our new releases.